iOS Programming
THE BIG NERD RANCH GUIDE

Christian Keur & Aaron Hillegass

Big Nerd
Ranch

iOS Programming: The Big Nerd Ranch Guide

by Christian Keur and Aaron Hillegass

Copyright © 2016 Big Nerd Ranch, LLC

Big Nerd Ranch, LLC
200 Arizona Ave NE
Atlanta, GA 30307
(770) 817-6373
http://www.bignerdranch.com/
book-comments@bignerdranch.com

The 10-gallon hat with propeller logo is a trademark of Big Nerd Ranch, LLC.

Exclusive worldwide distribution of the English edition of this book by

Pearson Technology Group
800 East 96th Street
Indianapolis, IN 46240 USA
http://www.informit.com

ISBN-10 0134682335
ISBN-13 978-0134682334

Sixth edition, first printing, December 2016

Acknowledgments

While our names appear on the cover, many people helped make this book a reality. We would like to take this chance to thank them.

- First and foremost we would like to thank Joe Conway for his work on the earlier editions of this book. He authored the first three editions and contributed greatly to the fourth edition as well. Many of the words in this book are still his, and for that, we are very grateful.

- Juan Pablo Claude wrote some of the content and contributed his expertise and opinions to make this book even better. His work is greatly appreciated.

- A couple other people went above and beyond with their help on this book. They are Mikey Ward and Chris Morris.

- The other instructors who teach the iOS Bootcamp fed us a never-ending stream of suggestions and corrections. They are Ben Scheirman, Bolot Kerimbaev, Brian Hardy, Chris Morris, JJ Manton, John Gallagher, Jonathan Blocksom, Joseph Dixon, Juan Pablo Claude, Mark Dalrymple, Matt Bezark, Matt Mathias, Mike Zornek, Mikey Ward, Pouria Almassi, Robert Edwards, Rod Strougo, Scott Ritchie, Step Christopher, Thomas Ward, TJ Usiyan, Tom Harrington, and Zachary Waldowski. These instructors were often aided by their students in finding book errata, so many thanks are due to all the students who attend the iOS Bootcamp.

- Thanks to all of the employees at Big Nerd Ranch who helped review the book, provided suggestions, and found errata.

- Our tireless editor, Elizabeth Holaday, took our distracted mumblings and made them into readable prose.

- Anna Bentley and Simone Payment jumped in to provide copyediting and proofing.

- Ellie Volckhausen designed the cover. (The photo is of the bottom bracket of a bicycle frame.)

- Chris Loper at IntelligentEnglish.com designed and produced the print and ebook versions of the book.

- The amazing team at Pearson Technology Group patiently guided us through the business end of book publishing.

The final and most important thanks goes to our students, whose questions inspired us to write this book and whose frustrations inspired us to make it clear and comprehensible.

Table of Contents

Introduction

As an aspiring iOS developer, you face three major tasks:

- *You must learn the Swift language.* Swift is the recommended development language for iOS. The first two chapters of this book are designed to give you a working knowledge of Swift.

- *You must master the big ideas.* These include things like delegation, archiving, and the proper use of view controllers. The big ideas take a few days to understand. When you reach the halfway point of this book, you will understand these big ideas.

- *You must master the frameworks.* The eventual goal is to know how to use every method of every class in every framework in iOS. This is a project for a lifetime: There are hundreds of classes and thousands of methods available in iOS, and Apple adds more classes and methods with every release of iOS. In this book, you will be introduced to each of the subsystems that make up the iOS SDK, but you will not study each one deeply. Instead, our goal is to get you to the point where you can search and understand Apple's reference documentation.

We have used this material many times at our iOS bootcamps at Big Nerd Ranch. It is well tested and has helped thousands of people become iOS developers. We sincerely hope that it proves useful to you.

Prerequisites

This book assumes that you are already motivated to learn to write iOS apps. We will not spend any time convincing you that the iPhone, iPad, and iPod touch are compelling pieces of technology.

We also assume that you have some experience programming and know something about object-oriented programming. If this is not true, you should probably start with *Swift Programming: The Big Nerd Ranch Guide*.

What Has Changed in the Sixth Edition?

All of the code in this book has been updated for Swift 3.0, which was a major update to the Swift language. Throughout the book, you will see how to use Swift's capabilities and features to write better iOS applications. We have come to love Swift at Big Nerd Ranch and believe you will, too.

Other additions include new chapters on debugging and accessibility and improved coverage of Core Data. We have also updated various chapters to use the technologies and APIs introduced in iOS 10.

This edition assumes that the reader is using Xcode 8.1 or later and running applications on an iOS 10 or later device.

Besides these obvious changes, we made thousands of tiny improvements that were inspired by questions from our readers and our students. Every chapter of this book is just a little better than the corresponding chapter from the fifth edition.

Our Teaching Philosophy

This book will teach you the essential concepts of iOS programming. At the same time, you will type in a lot of code and build a bunch of applications. By the end of the book, you will have knowledge *and* experience. However, all the knowledge should not (and, in this book, will not) come first. That is the traditional way of learning we have all come to know and hate. Instead, we take a learn-while-doing approach. Development concepts and actual coding go together.

Here is what we have learned over the years of teaching iOS programming:

- We have learned what ideas people must grasp to get started programming, and we focus on that subset.

- We have learned that people learn best when these concepts are introduced *as they are needed*.

- We have learned that programming knowledge and experience grow best when they grow together.

- We have learned that "going through the motions" is much more important than it sounds. Many times we will ask you to start typing in code before you understand it. We realize that you may feel like a trained monkey typing in a bunch of code that you do not fully grasp. But the best way to learn coding is to find and fix your typos. Far from being a drag, this basic debugging is where you really learn the ins and outs of the code. That is why we encourage you to type in the code yourself. You could just download it, but copying and pasting is not programming. We want better for you and your skills.

What does this mean for you, the reader? To learn this way takes some trust – and we appreciate yours. It also takes patience. As we lead you through these chapters, we will try to keep you comfortable and tell you what is happening. However, there will be times when you will have to take our word for it. (If you think this will bug you, keep reading – we have some ideas that might help.) Do not get discouraged if you run across a concept that you do not understand right away. Remember that we are intentionally *not* providing all the knowledge you will ever need all at once. If a concept seems unclear, we will likely discuss it in more detail later when it becomes necessary. And some things that are not clear at the beginning will suddenly make sense when you implement them the first (or the twelfth) time.

People learn differently. It is possible that you will love how we hand out concepts on an as-needed basis. It is also possible that you will find it frustrating. In case of the latter, here are some options:

- Take a deep breath and wait it out. We will get there, and so will you.

- Check the index. We will let it slide if you look ahead and read through a more advanced discussion that occurs later in the book.

- Check the online Apple documentation. This is an essential developer tool, and you will want plenty of practice using it. Consult it early and often.

- If Swift or object-oriented programming concepts are giving you a hard time (or if you think they will), you might consider backing up and reading our *Swift Programming: The Big Nerd Ranch Guide*.

How to Use This Book

This book is based on the class we teach at Big Nerd Ranch. As such, it was designed to be consumed in a certain manner.

Set yourself a reasonable goal, like, "I will do one chapter every day." When you sit down to attack a chapter, find a quiet place where you will not be interrupted for at least an hour. Shut down your email, your Twitter client, and your chat program. This is not a time for multitasking; you will need to concentrate.

Do the actual programming. You can read through a chapter first, if you like. But the real learning comes when you sit down and code as you go. You will not really understand the idea until you have written a program that uses it and, perhaps more importantly, debugged that program.

A couple of the exercises require supporting files. For example, in the first chapter you will need an icon for your Quiz application, and we have one for you. You can download the resources and solutions to the exercises from www.bignerdranch.com/solutions/iOSProgramming6ed.zip.

There are two types of learning. When you learn about the Peloponnesian War, you are simply adding details to a scaffolding of ideas that you already understand. This is what we will call "Easy Learning." Yes, learning about the Peloponnesian War can take a long time, but you are seldom flummoxed by it. Learning iOS programming, on the other hand, is "Hard Learning," and you may find yourself quite baffled at times, especially in the first few days. In writing this book, we have tried to create an experience that will ease you over the bumps in the learning curve. Here are two things you can do to make the journey easier:

- Find someone who already knows how to write iOS applications and will answer your questions. In particular, getting your application onto a device the first time is usually very frustrating if you are doing it without the help of an experienced developer.

- Get enough sleep. Sleepy people do not remember what they have learned.

How This Book Is Organized

In this book, each chapter addresses one or more ideas of iOS development through discussion and hands-on practice. For more coding practice, most chapters include challenge exercises. We encourage you to take on at least some of these. They are excellent for firming up your grasp of the concepts introduced in the chapter and for making you a more confident iOS programmer. Finally, most chapters conclude with one or two For the More Curious sections that explain certain consequences of the concepts that were introduced earlier.

Chapter 1 introduces you to iOS programming as you build and deploy a tiny application called Quiz. You will get your feet wet with Xcode and the iOS simulator along with all the steps for creating projects and files. The chapter includes a discussion of Model-View-Controller and how it relates to iOS development.

Chapter 2 provides an overview of Swift, including basic syntax, types, optionals, initialization, and how Swift is able to interact with the existing iOS frameworks. You will also get experience working in a playground, Xcode's prototyping tool.

In Chapter 3, you will focus on the iOS user interface as you learn about views and the view hierarchy and create an application called WorldTrotter.

Chapter 4 introduces delegation, an important iOS design pattern. You will also add a text field to WorldTrotter.

In Chapter 5, you will expand WorldTrotter and learn about using view controllers for managing user interfaces. You will get practice working with views and view controllers as well as navigating between screens using a tab bar.

In Chapter 6, you will learn how to manage views and view controllers in code. You will add a segmented control to WorldTrotter that will let you switch between various map types.

Chapter 7 introduces the concepts and techniques of internationalization and localization. You will learn about **Locale**, strings tables, and **Bundle** as you localize parts of WorldTrotter.

In Chapter 8, you will learn about and add different types of animations to the Quiz project that you created in Chapter 1.

Chapter 9 will walk you through some of the tools at your disposal for debugging – finding and fixing issues in your application.

Chapter 10 introduces the largest application in the book – Homepwner. ("Homepwner" is not a typo; you can find the definition of "pwn" at www.wiktionary.org.) This application keeps a record of your items in case of fire or other catastrophe. Homepwner will take eight chapters to complete.

In Chapter 10 – Chapter 12, you will work with tables. You will learn about table views, their view controllers, and their data sources. You will learn how to display data in a table, how to allow the user to edit the table, and how to improve the interface.

Chapter 13 introduces stack views, which will help you create complex interfaces easily. You will use a stack view to add a new screen to Homepwner that displays an item's details.

Chapter 14 builds on the navigation experience gained in Chapter 5. You will use **UINavigationController** to give Homepwner a drill-down interface and a navigation bar.

Chapter 15 introduces the camera. You will take pictures and display and store images in Homepwner.

In Chapter 16, you will add persistence to Homepwner, using archiving to save and load the application data.

In Chapter 17, you will learn about size classes, and you will use these to update Homepwner's interface to scale well across various screen sizes.

In Chapter 18 and Chapter 19, you will create a drawing application named TouchTracker to learn about touch events. You will see how to add multitouch capability and how to use **UIGestureRecognizer** to respond to particular gestures. You will also get experience with the first responder and responder chain concepts and more practice using structures and dictionaries.

Chapter 20 introduces web services as you create the Photorama application. This application fetches and parses JSON data from a server using **URLSession** and **JSONSerialization**.

In Chapter 21, you will learn about collection views as you build an interface for Photorama using **UICollectionView** and **UICollectionViewCell**.

In Chapter 22 and Chapter 23, you will add persistence to Photorama using Core Data. You will store and load images and associated data using an **NSManagedObjectContext**.

Chapter 24 will walk you through making your applications accessible to more people by adding VoiceOver information.

Style Choices

This book contains a lot of code. We have attempted to make that code and the designs behind it exemplary. We have done our best to follow the idioms of the community, but at times we have wandered from what you might see in Apple's sample code or code you might find in other books. In particular, you should know up front that we nearly always start a project with the simplest template project: the single view application. When your app works, you will know it is because of your efforts – not because of behavior built into the template.

Typographical Conventions

To make this book easier to read, certain items appear in certain fonts. Classes, types, methods, and functions appear in a bold, fixed-width font. Classes and types start with capital letters, and methods and functions start with lowercase letters. For example, "In the **loadView()** method of the **RexViewController** class, create a constant of type **String**."

Variables, constants, and filenames appear in a fixed-width font but are not bold. So you will see, "In ViewController.swift, add a variable named fido and initialize it to "Rufus"."

Application names, menu choices, and button names appear in a sans serif font. For example, "Open Xcode and select New Project... from the File menu. Select Single View Application and then click Next."

All code blocks are in a fixed-width font. Code that you need to type in is bold; code that you need to delete is struck through. For example, in the following code, you would delete the line import Foundation and type in the two lines beginning **@IBOutlet**. The other lines are already in the code and are included to let you know where to add the new lines.

```
import Foundation
import UIKit

class ViewController: UIViewController {

    @IBOutlet var questionLabel: UILabel!
    @IBOutlet var answerLabel: UILabel!

}
```

Necessary Hardware and Software

To build the applications in this book, you must have Xcode 8.1, which requires a Mac running macOS El Capitan version 10.11.4 or later. Xcode, Apple's Integrated Development Environment, is available on the App Store. Xcode includes the iOS SDK, the iOS simulator, and other development tools.

You should join the Apple Developer Program, which costs $99/year, because:

- Downloading the latest developer tools is free for members.

- You cannot put an app in the store until you are a member.

If you are going to take the time to work through this entire book, membership in the Apple Developer Program is worth the cost. Go to developer.apple.com/programs/ios/ to join.

What about iOS devices? Most of the applications you will develop in the first half of the book are for iPhone, but you will be able to run them on an iPad. On the iPad screen, iPhone applications appear in an iPhone-sized window. Not a compelling use of iPad, but that is OK when you are starting with iOS. In the early chapters, you will be focused on learning the fundamentals of the iOS SDK, and these are the same across iOS devices. Later in the book, you will see how to make applications run natively on both iOS device families.

Excited yet? Good. Let's get started.

1

A Simple iOS Application

In this chapter, you are going to write an iOS application named Quiz. This application will show a question and then reveal the answer when the user taps a button. Tapping another button will show the user a new question (Figure 1.1).

Figure 1.1 Your first application: Quiz

When you are writing an iOS application, you must answer two basic questions:

- How do I get my objects created and configured properly? (Example: "I want a button here that says Next Question.")

- How do I make my app respond to user interaction? (Example: "When the user taps the button, I want this piece of code to be executed.")

Most of this book is dedicated to answering these questions.

As you go through this first chapter, you will probably not understand everything that you are doing, and you may feel ridiculous just going through the motions. But going through the motions is enough for now. Mimicry is a powerful form of learning; it is how you learned to speak, and it is how you will start iOS programming. As you become more capable, you will experiment and challenge yourself to do creative things on the platform. For now, go ahead and do what we show you. The details will be explained in later chapters.

Creating an Xcode Project

Open Xcode and, from the File menu, select New → Project.... (If Xcode opens to a welcome screen, select Create a new Xcode project.)

A new workspace window will appear and a sheet will slide down from its toolbar. At the top, find the iOS section and then the Application area (Figure 1.2). You are offered several application templates to choose from. Select Single View Application.

Figure 1.2 Creating a project

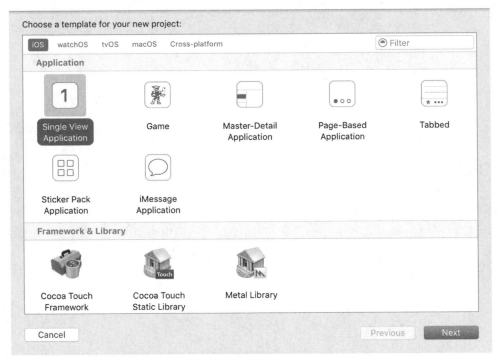

This book was created for Xcode 8.1. The names of these templates may change with new Xcode releases. If you do not see a Single View Application template, use the simplest-sounding template. You can also visit the Big Nerd Ranch forum for this book at forums.bignerdranch.com for help working with newer versions of Xcode.

Click Next and, in the next sheet, enter Quiz for the Product Name (Figure 1.3). The organization name and identifier are required to continue. You can use Big Nerd Ranch or any organization name you would like. For the organization identifier, you can use com.bignerdranch or com.*yourcompanynamehere*.

From the Language pop-up menu, choose Swift, and from the Devices pop-up menu, choose Universal. Make sure that the Use Core Data checkbox is unchecked.

Figure 1.3 Configuring a new project

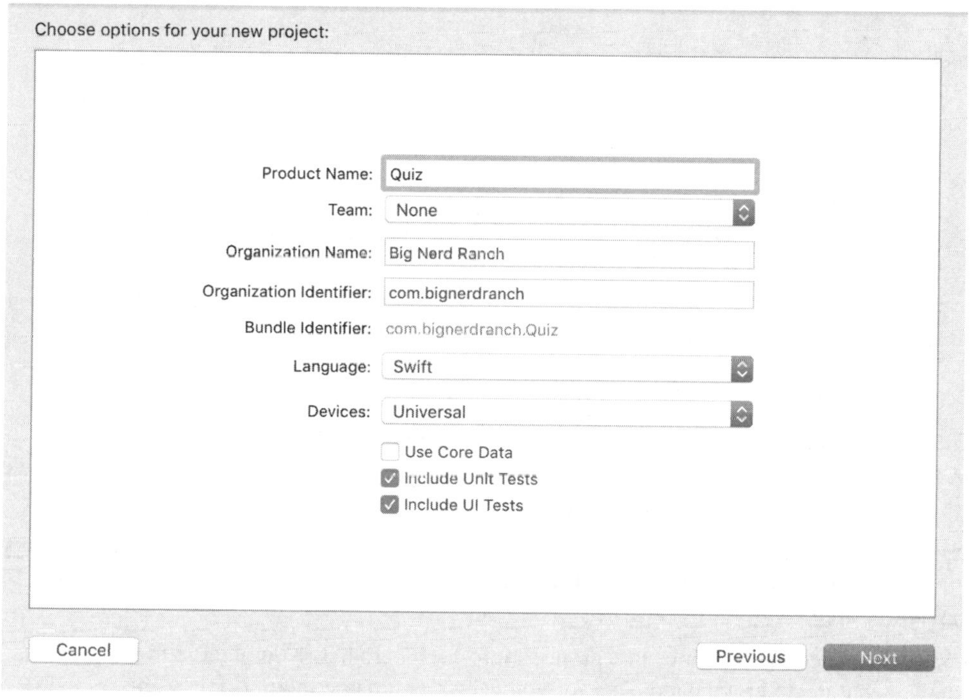

Click Next and, in the final sheet, save the project in the directory where you plan to store the exercises in this book. Click Create to create the Quiz project.

Your new project opens in the Xcode workspace window (Figure 1.4).

Figure 1.4 Xcode workspace window

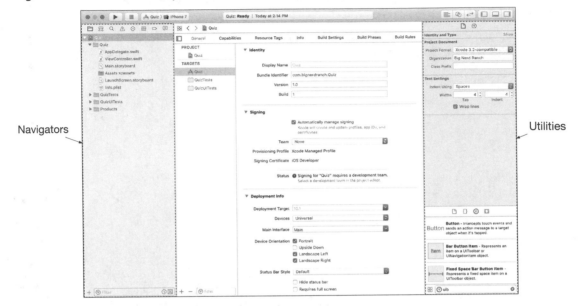

Navigators

Utilities

The lefthand side of the workspace window is the *navigator area*. This area displays different *navigators* – tools that show you different parts of your project. You can open a navigator by selecting one of the icons in the *navigator selector*, which is the bar just above the navigator area.

The navigator currently open is the *project navigator*. The project navigator shows you the files that make up a project (Figure 1.5). You can select one of these files to open it in the *editor area* to the right of the navigator area.

The files in the project navigator can be grouped into folders to help you organize your project. A few groups have been created by the template for you. You can rename them, if you want, or add new ones. The groups are purely for the organization of files and do not correlate to the filesystem in any way.

Figure 1.5 Quiz application's files in the project navigator

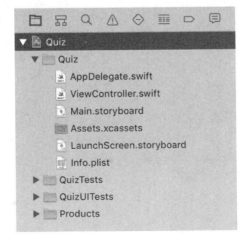

Model-View-Controller

Before you begin your application, let's discuss a key concept in application architecture: *Model-View-Controller*, or MVC. MVC is a design pattern used in iOS development. In MVC, every instance belongs to either the *model layer*, the *view layer*, or the *controller layer*. (*Layer* here simply refers to one or more objects that together fulfill a role.)

- The *model layer* holds data and knows nothing about the user interface, or UI. In Quiz, the model will consist of two ordered lists of strings: one for questions and another for answers.

  Usually, instances in the model layer represent real things in the world of the user. For example, when you write an app for an insurance company, your model will almost certainly contain a custom type called **InsurancePolicy**.

- The *view layer* contains objects that are visible to the user. Examples of *view objects*, or *views*, are buttons, text fields, and sliders. View objects make up an application's UI. In Quiz, the labels showing the question and answer and the buttons beneath them are view objects.

- The *controller layer* is where the application is managed. *Controller objects*, or *controllers*, are the managers of an application. Controllers configure the views that the user sees and make sure that the view and model objects stay synchronized.

  In general, controllers typically handle "And then?" questions. For example, when the user selects an item from a list, the controller determines what the user sees next.

Figure 1.6 shows the flow of control in an application in response to user input, such as the user tapping a button.

Figure 1.6 MVC pattern

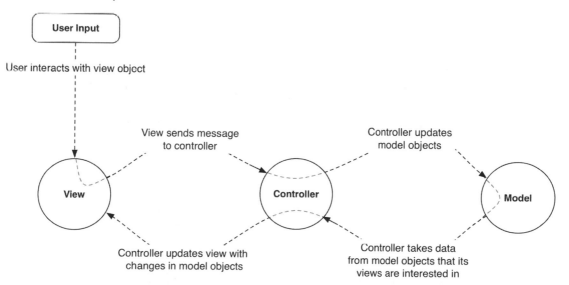

Notice that models and views do not talk to each other directly; controllers sit squarely in the middle of everything, receiving messages and dispatching instructions.

Designing Quiz

You are going to write the Quiz application using the MVC pattern. Here is a breakdown of the instances you will be creating and working with:

- The model layer will consist of two instances of **[String]**.

- The view layer will consist of two instances of **UILabel** and two instances of **UIButton**.

- The controller layer will consist of an instance of **ViewController**.

These instances and their relationships are laid out in the diagram for Quiz shown in Figure 1.7.

Figure 1.7 Object diagram for Quiz

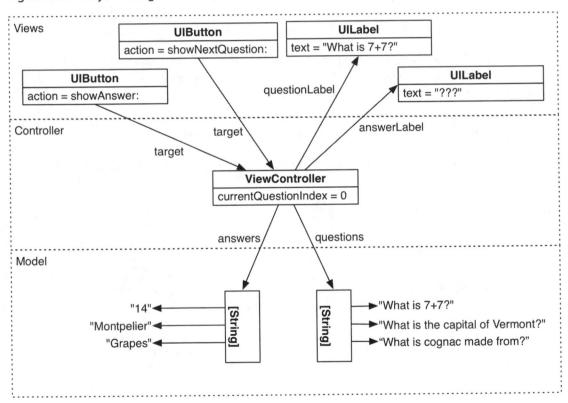

Figure 1.7 is the big picture of how the finished Quiz application will work. For example, when the Next Question button is tapped, it will trigger a *method* in **ViewController**. A method is a lot like a function – a list of instructions to be executed. This method will retrieve a new question from the array of questions and ask the top label to display that question.

It is OK if this diagram does not make sense yet – it will by the end of the chapter. Refer back to it as you build the app to see how it is taking shape.

You are going to build Quiz in steps, starting with the visual interface for the application.

Interface Builder

You are using the Single View Application template because it is the simplest template that Xcode offers. Still, this template has a significant amount of magic in that some critical components have already been set up for you. For now, you will just use these components, without attempting to gain a deep understanding of how they work. The rest of the book will be concerned with those details.

In the project navigator, click once on the Main.storyboard file. Xcode will open its graphic-style editor called Interface Builder.

Interface Builder divides the editor area into two sections: the *document outline*, on the lefthand side, and the *canvas*, on the right.

This is shown in Figure 1.8. If what you see in your editor area does not match the figure, you may have to click on the Show Document Outline button. (If you have additional areas showing, do not worry about them.) You may also have to click on the disclosure triangles in the document outline to reveal content.

Figure 1.8 Interface Builder showing Main.storyboard

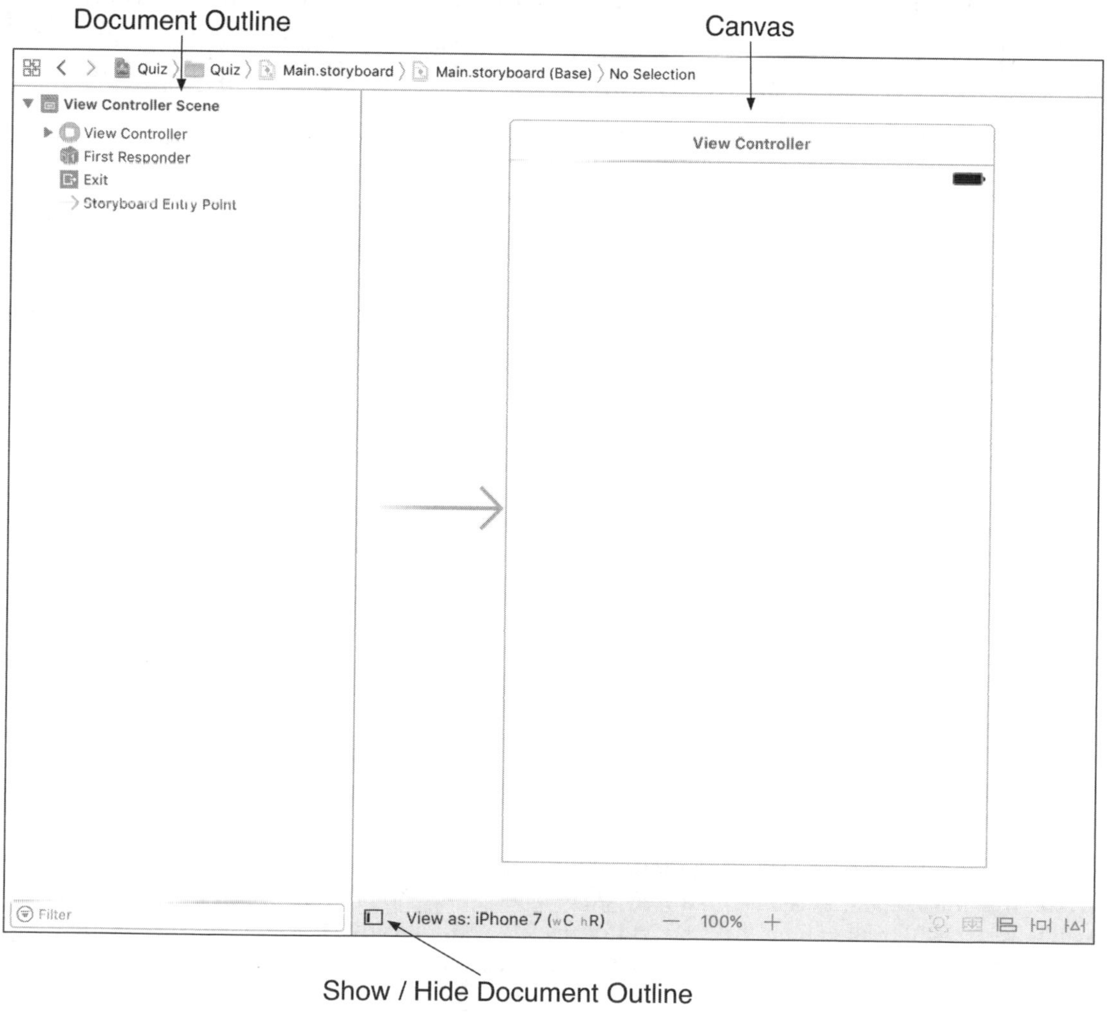

The rectangle that you see in the Interface Builder canvas is called a *scene* and represents the only "screen" or view your application has at this time (remember that you used the single view application template to create this project).

In the next section, you will learn how to create a UI for your application using Interface Builder. Interface Builder lets you drag objects from a library onto the canvas to create instances and also lets you establish connections between those objects and your code. These connections can result in code being called by a user interaction.

A crucial feature of Interface Builder is that it is not a graphical representation of code contained in other files. Interface Builder is an object editor that can create instances of objects and manipulate their properties. When you are done editing an interface, it does not generate code that corresponds to the work you have done. A .storyboard file is an archive of object instances to be loaded into memory when necessary.

Building the Interface

Let's get started on your interface. You have selected Main.storyboard to reveal its single scene in the canvas (Figure 1.9).

Figure 1.9 The scene in Main.storyboard

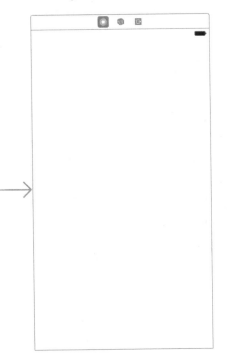

To start, make sure your scene is sized for iPhone 7. At the bottom of the canvas, find the View as button. It will likely say something like View as: iPhone 7 (wC hR). (The wC hR will not make sense right now; we will explain it in Chapter 17.) If it says iPhone 7 already, then you are all set. If not, click on the View as button and select the fourth device from the left, which corresponds to iPhone 7 (Figure 1.10).

Figure 1.10 Viewing the scene for iPhone 7

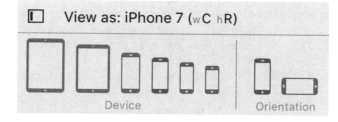

It is time to add your view objects to that blank slate.

Creating view objects

Make sure that the utility area within Xcode's window is visible. You may need to click on the rightmost button of the ☐ ☐ ☐ control in the top-right corner of the window. The utility area is to the right of the editor area and has two sections: the *inspector* and the *library*. The top section is the inspector, which displays settings for a file or object that is selected in the editor area. The bottom section is the library, which lists items that you can add to a file or project.

At the top of each section in the utility area is a selector for different inspectors and libraries (Figure 1.11).

Figure 1.11 Xcode utility area

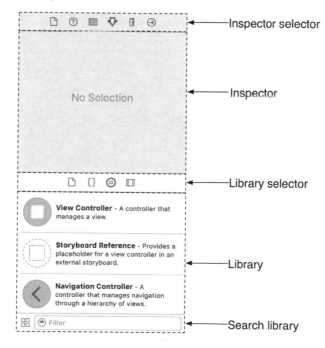

Your application interface requires four view objects: two buttons to accept user input and two text labels to display information. To add them, first make sure you can see the object library, as shown in Figure 1.11, by selecting the ⊚ tab from the library selector.

The object library contains the objects that you can add to a storyboard file to compose your interface. Find the Label object by either scrolling down through the list or by using the search bar at the bottom of the library. Select this object in the library and drag it onto the view object on the canvas. Drag the label around the canvas and notice the dashed blue lines that appear when the label is near the center of the canvas (Figure 1.12). These guidelines will help you lay out your interface.

Figure 1.12 Adding a label to the canvas

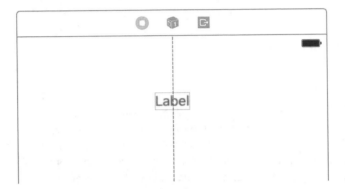

Using the guidelines, position the label in the horizontal center of the view and near the top, as shown in Figure 1.12. Eventually, this label will display questions to the user. Drag a second label onto the view and position it in the horizontal center, closer to the middle. This label will display answers.

Next, find Button in the object library and drag two buttons onto the view. Position one below each label.

You have now added four view objects to the **ViewController**'s UI. Notice that they also appear in the document outline. Your interface should look like Figure 1.13.

Figure 1.13 Building the Quiz interface

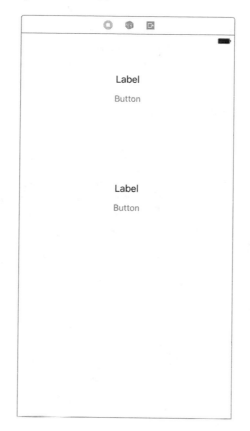

Configuring view objects

Now that you have created the view objects, you can configure their attributes. Some attributes of a view, like size, position, and text, can be changed directly on the canvas. For example, you can resize an object by selecting it in the canvas or the document outline and then dragging its corners and edges in the canvas.

Begin by renaming the labels and buttons. Double-click on each label and replace the text with ???. Then double-click the upper button and change its name to Next Question. Rename the lower button to Show Answer. The results are shown in Figure 1.14.

Figure 1.14 Renaming the labels and buttons

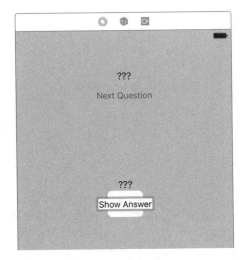

You may have noticed that because you have changed the text in the labels and buttons, and therefore their widths, they are no longer neatly centered in the scene. Click on each of them and drag to center them again, as shown in Figure 1.15.

Figure 1.15 Centering the labels and buttons

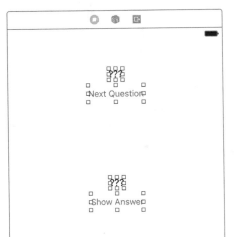

Running on the simulator

To test your UI, you are going to run Quiz on Xcode's iOS simulator.

To prepare Quiz to run on the simulator, find the current scheme pop-up menu on the Xcode toolbar (Figure 1.16).

Figure 1.16 iPhone 7 scheme selected

Current scheme pop-up menu

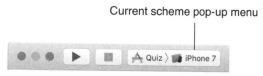

If it says something generic like iPhone 7, then the project is set to run on the simulator and you are good to go. If it says something like Christian's iPhone, then click and choose iPhone 7 from the pop-up menu. The iPhone 7 scheme will be your simulator default throughout this book.

Click the triangular play button in the toolbar. This will build (compile) and then run the application. You will be doing this often enough that you may want to learn and use the keyboard shortcut Command-R.

After the simulator launches you will see that the interface has all the views you added, neatly centered as you configured them in Interface Builder.

Now go back to the current scheme pop-up menu and select iPhone 7 Plus as your simulator of choice. Run the application again and you will notice that while the views you added are still present, they are not centered as they were on iPhone 7. This is because the labels and buttons currently have a fixed position on a screen, and they do not remain centered on the main view. To correct this problem, you will use a technology called *Auto Layout*.

A brief introduction to Auto Layout

As of now, your interface looks nice in the Interface Builder canvas. But iOS devices come in ever more screen sizes, and applications are expected to support all screen sizes and orientations – and perhaps more than one device type. You need to guarantee that the layout of view objects will be correct regardless of the screen size or orientation of the device running the application. The tool for this task is Auto Layout.

Auto Layout works by specifying position and size *constraints* for each view object in a scene. These constraints can be relative to neighboring views or to *container* views. A container view is just a view object that, as the name suggests, contains another view. For example, take a look at the document outline for Main.storyboard (Figure 1.17).

Figure 1.17 Document layout with a container view

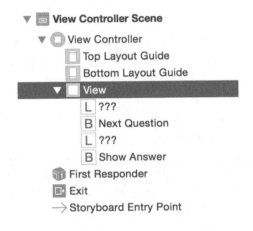

You can see in the document outline that the labels and buttons you added are indented with respect to a View object. This view object is the container of the labels and buttons, and the objects can be positioned and sized relative to this view.

To begin specifying Auto Layout constraints, select the top label by clicking on it either on the canvas or in the document outline. At the bottom of the canvas, notice the Auto Layout menus, shown in Figure 1.18.

Figure 1.18 The Auto Layout menus

With the top label still selected, click on the 🏳 icon to reveal the Align menu shown in Figure 1.19.

Figure 1.19 Centering the top label in the container

Within the Align menu, check the Horizontally in Container checkbox to center the label in the container. Then click the Add 1 Constraint button. This constraint guarantees that on any size screen, in any orientation, the label will be centered horizontally.

Now you need to add more constraints to center the lower label and the buttons with respect to the top label and to lock the spacing between them. Select the four views by Command-clicking on them one after another and then click on the ⊢◻⊣ icon to open the *Add New Constraints menu* shown in Figure 1.20.

Figure 1.20 Adding constraints to center and fix the spacing between views

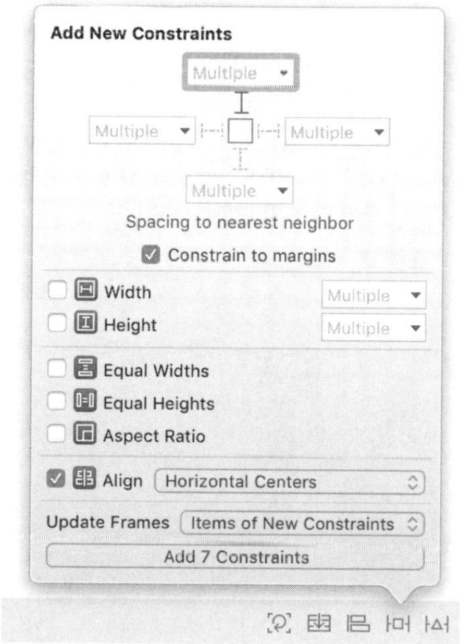

Click on the red vertical dashed segment near the top of the menu. When you click on the segment, it will become solid red (shown in Figure 1.20), indicating that the distance of each view is pinned to its nearest top neighbor. Also, check the Align box and then select Horizontal Centers from the pop-up menu. For Update Frames, make sure that you have Items of New Constraints selected. Finally, click on the Add 7 Constraints button at the bottom of the menu.

If you made any mistakes while adding constraints, you may see red or orange constraints and frames on the canvas instead of the correct blue lines. If that is the case, you will want to clear the existing constraints and go through the steps above again. To clear constraints, first select the background (container) view. Then click the ⊢△⊣ icon to open the Resolve Auto Layout Issues menu. Select Clear Constraints under the All Views in View Controller section (Figure 1.21). This will clear away any constraints that you have added and give you a fresh start on adding the constraints back in.

Figure 1.21 Clearing constraints

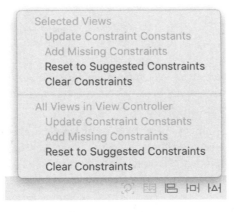

Auto Layout can be a difficult tool to master, and that is why you are starting to use it in the first chapter of this book. By starting early, you will have more chances to use it and get used to its complexity. Also, dealing with problems before things get too complicated will help you debug layout issues with confidence.

To confirm that your interface behaves correctly, build and run the application on the iPhone 7 Plus simulator. After confirming that the interface looks correct, build and run the application on the iPhone 7 simulator. The labels and buttons should be centered on both.

Making connections

A *connection* lets one object know where another object is in memory so that the two objects can communicate. There are two kinds of connections that you can make in Interface Builder: outlets and actions. An *outlet* is a reference to an object. An *action* is a method that gets triggered by a button or some other view that the user can interact with, like a slider or a picker.

Let's start by creating outlets that reference the instances of **UILabel**. Time to leave Interface Builder and write some code.

Declaring outlets

In the project navigator, find and select the file named ViewController.swift. The editor area will change from Interface Builder to Xcode's code editor.

In ViewController.swift, start by deleting any code that the template added between class ViewController: UIViewController { and the final brace, so that the file looks like this:

```
import UIKit

class ViewController: UIViewController {

}
```

(For simplicity, we will not show the line import UIKit again for this file.)

Next, add the following code that declares two properties. (Throughout this book, new code for you to add will be shown in bold. Code for you to delete will be struck through.) Do not worry about understanding the code or properties right now; just get it in.

```
class ViewController: UIViewController {
    @IBOutlet var questionLabel: UILabel!
    @IBOutlet var answerLabel: UILabel!
}
```

This code gives every instance of **ViewController** an outlet named questionLabel and an outlet named answerLabel. The view controller can use each outlet to reference a particular **UILabel** object (i.e., one of the labels in your view). The @IBOutlet keyword tells Xcode that you will connect these outlets to label objects using Interface Builder.

Setting outlets

In the project navigator, select `Main.storyboard` to reopen Interface Builder.

You want the `questionLabel` outlet to point to the instance of **UILabel** at the top of the UI.

In the document outline, find the View Controller Scene section and the View Controller object within it. In your case, the View Controller stands in for an instance of **ViewController**, which is the object responsible for managing the interface defined in `Main.storyboard`.

Control-drag (or right-click and drag) from the View Controller in the document outline to the top label in the scene. When the label is highlighted, release the mouse and keyboard; a black panel will appear. Select questionLabel to set the outlet, as shown in Figure 1.22.

Figure 1.22 Setting `questionLabel`

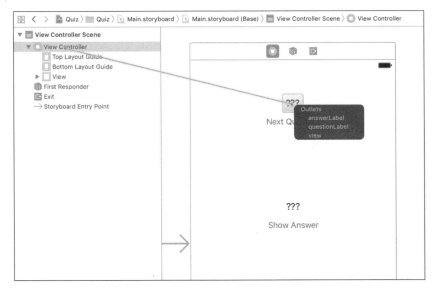

(If you do not see `questionLabel` in the connections panel, double-check your `ViewController.swift` file for typos.)

Now, when the storyboard file is loaded, the **ViewController**'s questionLabel outlet will automatically reference the instance of **UILabel** at the top of the screen, which will allow the **ViewController** to tell the label what question to display.

Set the `answerLabel` outlet the same way: Control-drag from the ViewController to the bottom **UILabel** and select `answerLabel` (Figure 1.23).

Figure 1.23 Setting answerLabel

Notice that you drag *from* the object with the outlet that you want to set *to* the object that you want that outlet to point to.

Your outlets are all set. The next connections you need to make involve the two buttons.

Defining action methods

When a **UIButton** is tapped, it calls a method on another object. That object is called the *target*. The method that is triggered is called the *action*. This action is the name of the method that contains the code to be executed in response to the button being tapped.

In your application, the target for both buttons will be the instance of **ViewController**. Each button will have its own action. Let's start by defining the two action methods: **showNextQuestion(_:)** and **showAnswer(_:)**.

Reopen ViewController.swift and add the two action methods after the outlets.

```
class ViewController: UIViewController {
    @IBOutlet var questionLabel: UILabel!
    @IBOutlet var answerLabel: UILabel!

    @IBAction func showNextQuestion(_ sender: UIButton) {

    }

    @IBAction func showAnswer(_ sender: UIButton) {

    }
}
```

You will flesh out these methods after you make the target and action connections. The @IBAction keyword tells Xcode that you will be making these connections in Interface Builder.

Setting targets and actions

Switch back to Main.storyboard. Let's start with the Next Question button. You want its target to be ViewController and its action to be showNextQuestion(_:).

To set an object's target, you Control-drag *from* the object *to* its target. When you release the mouse, the target is set, and a pop-up menu appears that lets you select an action.

Select the Next Question button in the canvas and Control-drag to the View Controller in the document outline. When the View Controller is highlighted, release the mouse button and choose showNextQuestion: under Sent Events in the pop-up menu, as shown in Figure 1.24.

Figure 1.24 Setting Next Question target/action

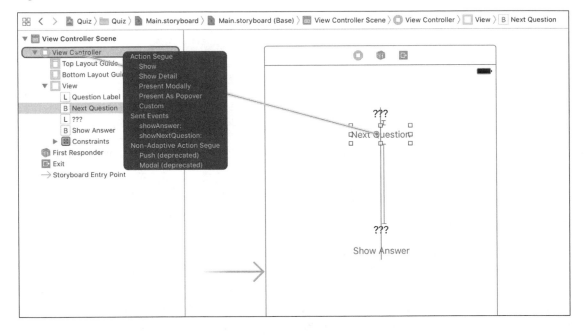

Now for the Show Answer button. Select the button and Control-drag from the button to the View Controller. Choose showAnswer: from the pop-up menu.

Summary of connections

There are now five connections between the **ViewController** and the view objects. You have set the properties answerLabel and questionLabel to reference the label objects – two connections. The **ViewController** is the target for both buttons – two more. The project's template made one additional connection: The view property of **ViewController** is connected to the View object that represents the background of the application. That makes five.

You can check these connections in the *connections inspector*. Select the View Controller in the document outline. Then, in the utilities area, click the ⊖ tab to reveal the connections inspector (Figure 1.25).

Figure 1.25 Checking connections in the connections inspector

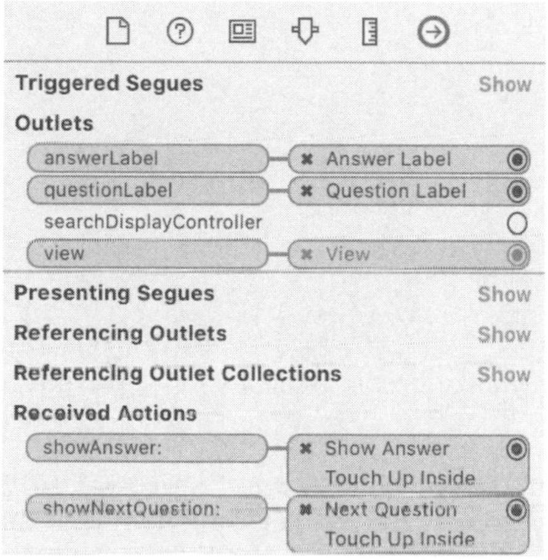

Your storyboard file is complete. The view objects have been created and configured and all the necessary connections have been made to the controller object. Let's move on to creating and connecting your model objects.

Creating the Model Layer

View objects make up the UI, so developers typically create, configure, and connect view objects using Interface Builder. The parts of the model layer, on the other hand, are typically set up in code.

In the project navigator, select `ViewController.swift`. Add the following code that declares two arrays of strings and an integer.

```
class ViewController: UIViewController {
    @IBOutlet var questionLabel: UILabel!
    @IBOutlet var answerLabel: UILabel!

    let questions: [String] = [
        "What is 7+7?",
        "What is the capital of Vermont?",
        "What is cognac made from?"
    ]
    let answers: [String] = [
        "14",
        "Montpelier",
        "Grapes"
    ]
    var currentQuestionIndex: Int = 0
    ...
}
```

The arrays are ordered lists containing questions and answers. The integer will keep track of what question the user is on.

Notice that the arrays are declared using the `let` keyword, whereas the integer is declared using the `var` keyword. A *constant* is denoted with the `let` keyword; its value cannot change. The `questions` and `answers` arrays are constants. The questions and answers in this quiz will not change and, in fact, cannot be changed from their initial values.

A *variable*, on the other hand, is denoted by the `var` keyword; its value is allowed to change. You made the `currentQuestionIndex` property a variable because its value must be able to change as the user cycles through the questions and answers.

Implementing action methods

Now that you have questions and answers, you can finish implementing the action methods. In ViewController.swift, update **showNextQuestion(_:)** and **showAnswer(_:)**.

```
...
@IBAction func showNextQuestion(_ sender: UIButton) {
    currentQuestionIndex += 1
    if currentQuestionIndex == questions.count {
        currentQuestionIndex = 0
    }

    let question: String = questions[currentQuestionIndex]
    questionLabel.text = question
    answerLabel.text = "???"
}

@IBAction func showAnswer(_ sender: UIButton) {
    let answer: String = answers[currentQuestionIndex]
    answerLabel.text = answer
}
...
```

Loading the first question

Just after the application is launched, you will want to load the first question from the array and use it to replace the '???' placeholder in the questionLabel label. A good way to do this is by *overriding* the **viewDidLoad()** method of **ViewController**. ("Override" means that you are providing a custom implementation for a method.) Add the method to ViewController.swift.

```
class ViewController: UIViewController {
    ...
    override func viewDidLoad() {
        super.viewDidLoad()
        questionLabel.text = questions[currentQuestionIndex]
    }
}
```

All the code for your application is now complete!

Building the Finished Application

Build and run the application on the iPhone 7 simulator, as you did earlier.

If building turns up any errors, you can view them in the *issue navigator* by selecting the ⚠ tab in the navigator area (Figure 1.26).

Figure 1.26 Issue navigator with example errors and warnings

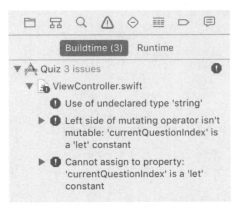

Click on any error or warning in the issue navigator to be taken to the file and the line of code where the issue occurred. Find and fix any problems (i.e., code typos!) by comparing your code with the code in this chapter. Then try running the application again. Repeat this process until your application compiles.

After your application has compiled, it will launch in the iOS simulator. Play around with the Quiz application. You should be able to tap the Next Question button and see a new question in the top label; tapping Show Answer should show the right answer. If your application is not working as expected, double-check your connections in Main.storyboard.

You have built a working iOS app! Take a moment to bask in the glory.

OK, enough basking. Your app works, but it needs some spit and polish.

Application Icons

While running Quiz, select Hardware → Home from the simulator's menu. You will see that Quiz's icon is a boring, default tile. Let's give Quiz a better icon.

An *application icon* is a simple image that represents the application on the iOS Home screen. Different devices require different-sized icons, some of which are shown in Table 1.1.

Table 1.1 Application icon sizes by device

Device	Application icon sizes
5.5-inch iPhone	180x180 pixels (@3x)
4.7-inch and 4.0-inch iPhone	120x120 pixels (@2x)
7.9-inch and 9.7-inch iPad	152x152 pixels (@2x)
12.9-inch iPad	167x167 pixels (@2x)

We have prepared an icon image file (size 120x120) for the Quiz application. You can download this icon (along with resources for other chapters) from www.bignerdranch.com/solutions/ iOSProgramming6ed.zip. Unzip iOSProgramming6ed.zip and find the Quiz-120.png file in the 0-Resources/Project App Icons directory of the unzipped folder.

You are going to add this icon to your application bundle as a *resource*. In general, there are two kinds of files in an application: code and resources. Code (like ViewController.swift) is used to create the application itself. Resources are things like images and sounds that are used by the application at runtime.

In the project navigator, find `Assets.xcassets`. Select this file to open it and then select AppIcon from the resource list on the lefthand side (Figure 1.27).

Figure 1.27 Showing the Asset Catalog

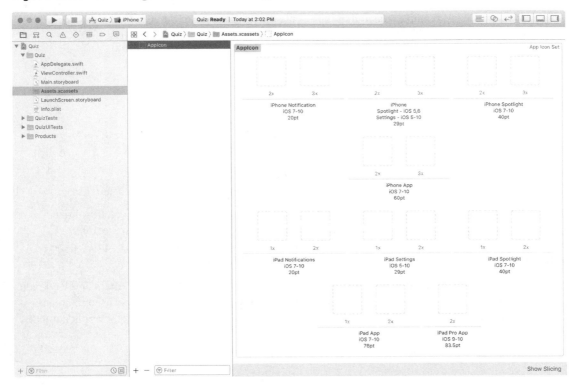

This panel is the *Asset Catalog*, where you can manage all of the images that your application will need.

Drag the `Quiz-120.png` file from Finder onto the 2x slot of the iPhone App section (Figure 1.28). This will copy the file into your project's directory on the filesystem and add a reference to that file in the Asset Catalog. (You can Control-click on a file in the Asset Catalog and select the option to Show in Finder to confirm this.)

Figure 1.28 Adding the app icon to the Asset Catalog

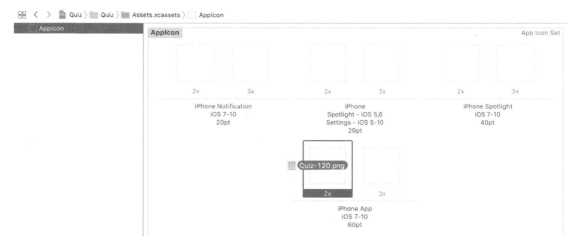

Build and run the application again. Switch to the simulator's Home screen either by clicking Hardware → Home, as you did before, or by using the keyboard shortcut Command-Shift-H. You should see the new icon.

(If you do not see the icon, delete the application and then build and run again to redeploy it. To do this, the easiest option is to reset the simulator by clicking Simulator → Reset Content and Settings.... This will remove all applications and reset the simulator to its default settings. You should see the app icon the next time you run the application.)

Launch Screen

Another item you should set for the project is the *launch image*, which appears while an application is loading. The launch image has a specific role in iOS: It conveys to the user that the application is indeed launching and depicts the UI that the user will interact with once the application loads. Therefore, a good launch image is a content-less screenshot of the application. For example, the Clock application's launch image shows the four tabs along the bottom, all in the unselected state. Once the application loads, the correct tab is selected and the content becomes visible. (Keep in mind that the launch image is replaced after the application has launched; it does not become the background image of the application.)

An easy way to accomplish this is to allow Xcode to generate the possible launch screen images for you using a *launch screen file*.

Open the project settings by clicking on the top-level Quiz in the project navigator. Under App Icons and Launch Images, choose Main.storyboard from the Launch Screen File dropdown (Figure 1.29). Launch images will now be generated from `Main.storyboard`.

Figure 1.29 Setting the launch screen file

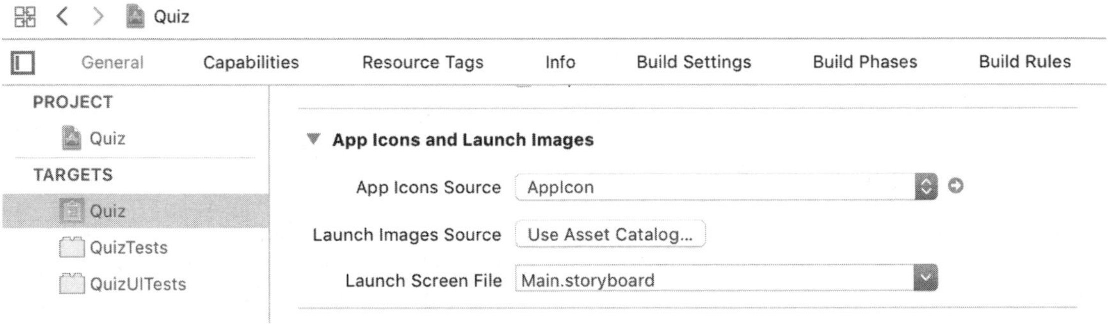

It is difficult to see the results of this change, because the launch image is typically shown for only a short time. However, it is a good practice to set the launch image even though its role is so brief.

Congratulations! You have written your first application and even added some details to make it polished. You will return to Quiz later in the book. The next chapter covers some basics of Swift to prepare you for more coding.

2

The Swift Language

Swift is a new language that Apple introduced in 2014. It replaces Objective-C as the recommended development language for iOS and Mac. In this chapter, you are going to focus on the basics of Swift. You will not learn everything, but you will learn enough to get started. Then, as you continue through the book, you will learn more Swift while you learn iOS development.

Swift maintains the expressiveness of Objective-C while introducing a syntax that is safer, succinct, and readable. It emphasizes type safety and adds advanced features such as optionals, generics, and sophisticated structures and enumerations. Most importantly, Swift allows the use of these new features while relying on the same tested, elegant iOS frameworks that developers have built upon for years.

If you know Objective-C, then the challenge is recasting what you know. It may seem awkward at first, but we have come to love Swift at Big Nerd Ranch and believe you will, too.

If you do not think you will be comfortable picking up Swift at the same time as iOS development, you may want to start with *Swift Programming: The Big Nerd Ranch Guide* or Apple's Swift tutorials, which you can find at `developer.apple.com/swift`. But if you have some programming experience and are willing to learn "on the job," you can start your Swift education here and now.

Types in Swift

Swift types can be arranged into three basic groups: *structures*, *classes*, and *enumerations* (Figure 2.1). All three can have:

- *properties* – values associated with a type

- *initializers* – code that initializes an instance of a type

- *instance methods* – functions specific to a type that can be called on an instance of that type

- *class* or *static methods* – functions specific to a type that can be called on the type itself

Figure 2.1 Swift building blocks

Structures	Enumerations	Classes
```struct MyStruct { // properties // initializers // methods }```	```enum MyEnum { // properties // initializers // methods }```	```class MyClass: SuperClass { // properties // initializers // methods }```

Swift's structures (or "structs") and enumerations (or "enums") are significantly more powerful than in most languages. In addition to supporting properties, initializers, and methods, they can also conform to protocols and can be extended.

Swift's implementation of typically "primitive" types such as numbers and Boolean values may surprise you: They are all structures. In fact, all of these Swift types are structures:

Numbers:	`Int`, `Float`, `Double`
Boolean:	`Bool`
Text:	`String`, `Character`
Collections:	`Array<Element>`, `Dictionary<Key:Hashable,Value>`, `Set<Element:Hashable>`

This means that standard types have properties, initializers, and methods of their own. They can also conform to protocols and be extended.

Finally, a key feature of Swift is *optionals*. An optional allows you to store either a value of a particular type or no value at all. You will learn more about optionals and their role in Swift later in this chapter.

Using Standard Types

In this section, you are going to experiment with standard types in an Xcode *playground*. A playground lets you write code and see the results without the overhead of manually running an application and checking the output.

In Xcode, select File → New → Playground.... You can accept the default name for this file; you will only be here briefly. Make sure the platform is iOS (Figure 2.2).

Figure 2.2 Configuring a playground

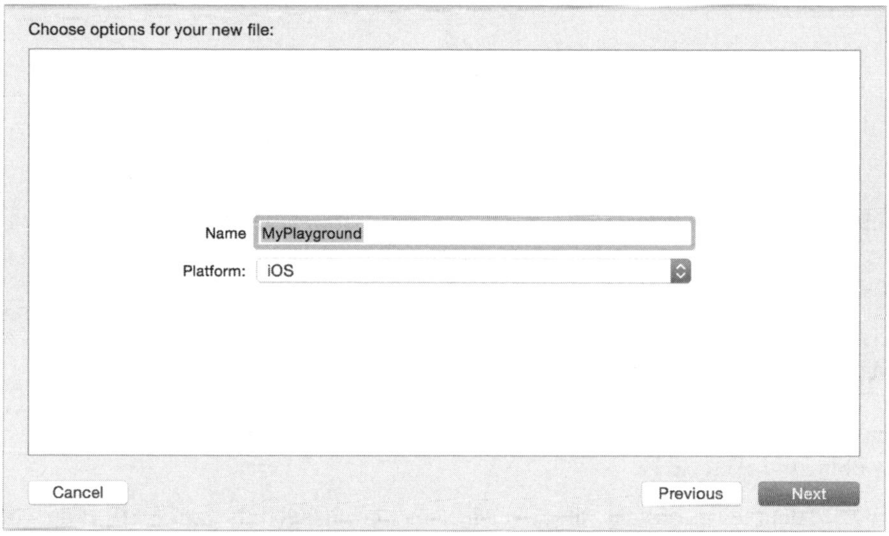

Click Next and save this file in a convenient place.

When the file opens, notice that the playground is divided into two sections (Figure 2.3). The larger white area to the left is the editor where you write code. The gray column on the right is the *sidebar*. The playground compiles and executes your code after every line and shows the results in the sidebar.

Figure 2.3 A playground

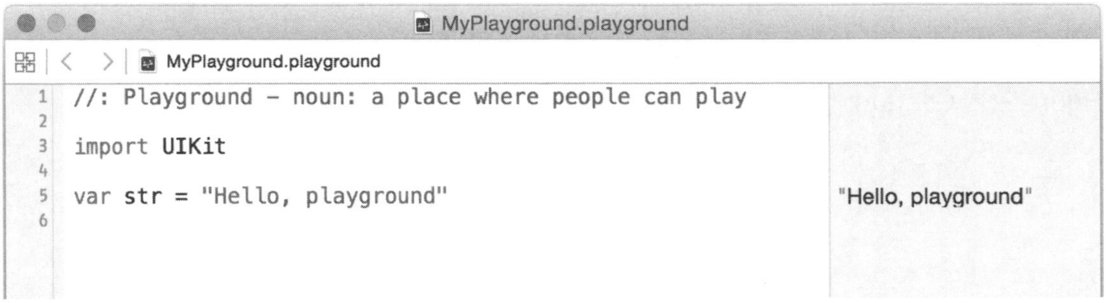

In the example code, the var keyword denotes a variable, so the value of str can be changed from its initial value. Type in the code below to change the value of str, and you will see the results appear in the sidebar to the right.

```
var str = "Hello, playground"          "Hello, playground"
str = "Hello, Swift"                    "Hello, Swift"
```

(Notice that we are showing sidebar results to the right of the code for the benefit of readers who are not actively doing the exercise.)

The let keyword denotes a constant value, which cannot be changed. In your Swift code, you should use let unless you expect the value will need to change. Add a constant to the mix:

```
var str = "Hello, playground"          "Hello, playground"
str = "Hello, Swift"                    "Hello, Swift"
let constStr = str                      "Hello, Swift"
```

Because constStr is a constant, attempting to change its value will cause an error.

```
var str = "Hello, playground"          "Hello, playground"
str = "Hello, Swift"                    "Hello, Swift"
let constStr = str                      "Hello, Swift"
constStr = "Hello, world"
```

An error appears, indicated by the red symbol to the left of the offending line. Click the symbol to get more information about the error. In this case, the error reads Cannot assign to value: 'constStr' is a 'let' constant.

An error in the playground code will prevent you from seeing any further results in the sidebar, so you usually want to address it right away. Remove the line that attempts to change the value of constStr.

```
var str = "Hello, playground"          "Hello, playground"
str = "Hello, Swift"                    "Hello, Swift"
let constStr = str                      "Hello, Swift"
constStr = "Hello, world"
```

Inferring types

At this point, you may have noticed that neither the `constStr` constant nor the `str` variable has a specified type. This does not mean they are untyped! Instead, the compiler infers their types from the initial values. This is called *type inference*.

You can find out what type was inferred using Xcode's Quick Help. Option-click on `constStr` in the playground to see the Quick Help information for this constant, shown in Figure 2.4.

Figure 2.4 `constStr` is of type **String**

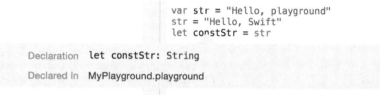

Option-clicking to reveal Quick Help will work for any symbol.

Specifying types

If your constant or variable has an initial value, you can rely on type inference. If a constant or variable does not have an initial value or if you want to ensure that it is a certain type, you can specify the type in the declaration.

Add more variables with specified types:

```
var str = "Hello, playground"            "Hello, playground"
str = "Hello, Swift"                     "Hello, Swift"
let constStr = str                       "Hello, Swift"

var nextYear: Int
var bodyTemp: Float
var hasPet: Bool
```

Note that the sidebar does not report any results because these variables do not yet have values.

Let's go over these new types and how they are used.

Number and Boolean types

The most common type for integers is **Int**. There are additional integer types based on word size and signedness, but Apple recommends using **Int** unless you really have a reason to use something else.

For floating-point numbers, Swift provides three types with different levels of precision: **Float** for 32-bit numbers, **Double** for 64-bit numbers, and **Float80** for 80-bit numbers.

A Boolean value is expressed in Swift using the type **Bool**. A **Bool**'s value is either `true` or `false`.

Collection types

The Swift standard library offers three collections: *arrays*, *dictionaries*, and *sets*.

An array is an ordered collection of elements. The array type is written as **Array<T>**, where T is the type of element that the array will contain. Arrays can contain elements of any type: a standard type, a structure, or a class.

Add a variable for an array of integers:

```
var hasPet: Bool
var arrayOfInts: Array<Int>
```

Arrays are strongly typed. Once you declare an array as containing elements of, say, **Int**, you cannot add a **String** to it.

There is a shorthand syntax for declaring arrays: You can simply use square brackets around the type that the array will contain. Update the declaration of arrayOfInts to use the shorthand:

```
var hasPet: Bool
var arrayOfInts: Array<Int>
var arrayOfInts: [Int]
```

A dictionary is an unordered collection of key-value pairs. The values can be of any type, including structures and classes. The keys can be of any type as well, but they must be unique. Specifically, the keys must be *hashable*, which allows the dictionary to guarantee that the keys are unique and to access the value for a given key more efficiently. Basic Swift types such as **Int**, **Float**, **Character**, and **String** are all hashable.

Like Swift arrays, Swift dictionaries are strongly typed and can only contain keys and values of the declared type. For example, you might have a dictionary that stores capital cities by country. The keys for this dictionary would be the country names, and the values would be the city names. Both keys and values would be strings, and you would not be able to add a key or value of any other type.

Add a variable for such a dictionary:

```
var arrayOfInts: [Int]
var dictionaryOfCapitalsByCountry: Dictionary<String,String>
```

There is a shorthand syntax for declaring dictionaries, too. Update dictionaryOfCapitalsByCountry to use the shorthand:

```
var arrayOfInts: [Int]
var dictionaryOfCapitalsByCountry: Dictionary<String,String>
var dictionaryOfCapitalsByCountry: [String:String]
```

A set is similar to an array in that it contains a number of elements of a certain type. However, sets are unordered, and the members must be unique as well as hashable. The unorderedness of sets makes them faster when you simply need to determine whether something is a member of a set. Add a variable for a set:

```
var winningLotteryNumbers: Set<Int>
```

Unlike arrays and dictionaries, sets do not have a shorthand syntax.

Literals and subscripting

Standard types can be assigned literal values, or *literals*. For example, `str` is assigned the value of a string literal. A string literal is formed with double quotes. Contrast the literal value assigned to `str` with the nonliteral value assigned to `constStr`:

```
var str = "Hello, playground"              "Hello, playground"
str = "Hello, Swift"                        "Hello, Swift"
let constStr = str                          "Hello, Swift"
```

Add two number literals to your playground:

```
let number = 42                             42
let fmStation = 91.1                        91.1
```

Arrays and dictionaries can be assigned literal values as well. The syntax for creating literal arrays and dictionaries resembles the shorthand syntax for specifying these types.

```
let countingUp = ["one", "two"]                    ["one", "two"]
let nameByParkingSpace = [13: "Alice", 27: "Bob"]  [13: "Alice", 27: "Bob"]
```

Swift also provides *subscripting* as shorthand for accessing arrays. To retrieve an element in an array, you provide the element's index in square brackets after the array name.

```
let countingUp = ["one", "two"]            ["one", "two"]
let secondElement = countingUp[1]          "two"
...
```

Notice that index 1 retrieves the second element; an array's index always starts at 0.

When subscripting an array, be sure that you are using a valid index. Attempting to access an out-of-bounds index results in a *trap*. A trap is a runtime error that stops the program before it gets into an unknown state.

Subscripting also works with dictionaries – more on that later in this chapter.

Initializers

So far, you have initialized your constants and variables using literal values. In doing so, you created *instances* of a specific type. An instance is a particular embodiment of a type. Historically, this term has been only used with classes, but in Swift it is used to describe structures and enumerations, too. For example, the constant secondElement holds an instance of **String**.

Another way of creating instances is by using an *initializer* on the type. Initializers are responsible for preparing the contents of a new instance of a type. When an initializer is finished, the instance is ready for action. To create a new instance using an initializer, you use the type name followed by a pair of parentheses and, if required, arguments. This signature – the combination of type and arguments – corresponds to a specific initializer.

Some standard types have initializers that return empty literals when no arguments are supplied. Add an empty string, an empty array, and an empty set to your playground.

```
let emptyString = String()                    ""
let emptyArrayOfInts = [Int]()                 0 elements
let emptySetOfFloats = Set<Float>()            0 elements
```

Other types have default values:

```
let defaultNumber = Int()                      0
let defaultBool = Bool()                        false
```

Types can have multiple initializers. For example, **String** has an initializer that accepts an **Int** and creates a string based on that value.

```
let number = 42                                42
let meaningOfLife = String(number)             "42"
```

To create a set, you can use the **Set** initializer that accepts an array literal:

```
let availableRooms = Set([205, 411, 412])      {412, 205, 411}
```

Float has several initializers. The parameter-less initializer returns an instance of **Float** with the default value. There is also an initializer that accepts a floating-point literal.

```
let defaultFloat = Float()                      0.0
let floatFromLiteral = Float(3.14)              3.14
```

If you use type inference for a floating-point literal, the type defaults to **Double**. Create the following constant with a floating-point literal:

```
let easyPi = 3.14                              3.14
```

Use the **Float** initializer that accepts a **Double** to create a **Float** from this **Double**:

```
let easyPi = 3.14                              3.14
let floatFromDouble = Float(easyPi)            3.14
```

You can achieve the same result by specifying the type in the declaration.

```
let easyPi = 3.14                              3.14
let floatFromDouble = Float(easyPi)            3.14
let floatingPi: Float = 3.14                   3.14
```

Properties

A *property* is a value associated with an instance of a type. For example, **String** has the property isEmpty, which is a **Bool** that tells you whether the string is empty. **Array<T>** has the property count, which is the number of elements in the array as an **Int**. Access these properties in your playground:

```
let countingUp = ["one", "two"]          ["one", "two"]
let secondElement = countingUp[1]        "two"
countingUp.count                         2
...
let emptyString = String()
emptyString.isEmpty                      true
```

Instance methods

An *instance method* is a function that is specific to a particular type and can be called on an instance of that type. Try out the **append(_:)** instance method from **Array<T>**. You will first need to change your **countingUp** array from a constant to a variable.

```
let countingUp = ["one", "two"]
var countingUp = ["one", "two"]          ["one", "two"]
let secondElement = countingUp[1]        "two"
countingUp.count
countingUp.append("three")               ["one", "two", "three"]
```

The **append(_:)** method accepts an element of the array's type and adds it to the end of the array. We will discuss methods, including naming, in Chapter 3.

Optionals

Swift types can be *optional*, which is indicated by appending ? to a type name.

```
var anOptionalFloat: Float?
var anOptionalArrayOfStrings: [String]?
var anOptionalArrayOfOptionalStrings: [String?]?
```

An optional lets you express the possibility that a variable may not store a value at all. The value of an optional will either be an instance of the specified type or nil.

Throughout this book, you will have many chances to use optionals. What follows is an example to get you familiar with the syntax so that you can focus on the use of the optionals later.

Imagine a group of instrument readings:

```
var reading1: Float
var reading2: Float
var reading3: Float
```

Sometimes, an instrument might malfunction and not report a reading. You do not want this malfunction showing up as, say, 0.0. You want it to be something completely different that tells you to check your instrument or take some other action.

You can do this by declaring the readings as optionals. Add these declarations to your playground.

```
var reading1: Float?                                      nil
var reading2: Float?                                      nil
var reading3: Float?                                      nil
```

As an optional float, each reading can contain either a **Float** or nil. If not given an initial value, then the value defaults to nil.

You can assign values to an optional just like any other variable. Assign floating-point literals to the readings:

```
reading1 = 9.8                                           9.8
reading2 = 9.2                                           9.2
reading3 = 9.7                                           9.7
```

However, you cannot use these optional floats like non-optional floats – even if they have been assigned **Float** values. Before you can read the value of an optional variable, you must address the possibility of its value being nil. This is called *unwrapping* the optional.

You are going to try out two ways of unwrapping an optional variable: optional binding and forced unwrapping. You will implement forced unwrapping first. This is not because it is the better option – in fact, it is the less safe one. But implementing forced unwrapping first will let you see the dangers and understand why optional binding is typically better.

To forcibly unwrap an optional, you append a ! to its name. First, try averaging the readings as if they were non-optional variables:

```
reading1 = 9.8                                           9.8
reading2 = 9.2                                           9.2
reading3 = 9.7                                           9.7
let avgReading = (reading1 + reading2 + reading3) / 3
```

This results in an error because optionals require unwrapping. Forcibly unwrap the readings to fix the error:

```
let avgReading = (reading1 + reading2 + reading3) / 3
let avgReading = (reading1! + reading2! + reading3!) / 3        9.566667
```

Everything looks fine, and you see the correct average in the sidebar. But a danger lurks in your code. When you forcibly unwrap an optional, you tell the compiler that you are sure that the optional will not be nil and can be treated as if it were a normal **Float**. But what if you are wrong? To find out, comment out the assignment of reading3, which will return it to its default value, nil.

```
reading1 = 9.8                                                 9.8
reading2 = 9.2                                                 9.2
reading3 = 9.7
// reading3 = 9.7
```

You now have an error. Xcode may have opened its *debug area* at the bottom of the playground with information about the error. If it did not, select View → Debug Area → Show Debug Area. The error reads:

```
fatal error: unexpectedly found nil while unwrapping an Optional value
```

If you forcibly unwrap an optional and that optional turns out to be nil, it will cause a trap, stopping your application.

A safer way to unwrap an optional is *optional binding*. Optional binding works within a conditional if-let statement: You assign the optional to a temporary constant of the corresponding non-optional type. If your optional has a value, then the assignment is valid and you proceed using the non-optional constant. If the optional is nil, then you can handle that case with an else clause.

Change your code to use an if-let statement that tests for valid values in all three readings.

```
let avgReading = (reading1! + reading2! + reading3!) / 3
if let r1 = reading1,
    let r2 = reading2,
    let r3 = reading3 {
        let avgReading = (r1 + r2 + r3) / 3
} else {
    let errorString = "Instrument reported a reading that was nil."
}
```

reading3 is currently nil, so its assignment to r3 fails, and the sidebar shows the error string.

To see the other case in action, restore the line that assigns a value to reading3. Now that all three readings have values, all three assignments are valid, and the sidebar updates to show the average of the three readings.

Subscripting dictionaries

Recall that subscripting an array beyond its bounds causes a trap. Dictionaries are different. The result of subscripting a dictionary is an optional:

```
let nameByParkingSpace = [13: "Alice", 27: "Bob"]          [13: "Alice", 27: "Bob"]
let space13Assignee: String? = nameByParkingSpace[13]      "Alice"
let space42Assignee: String? = nameByParkingSpace[42]      nil
```

If the key is not in the dictionary, the result will be `nil`. As with other optionals, it is common to use if-let when subscripting a dictionary:

```
let space13Assignee: String? = nameByParkingSpace[13]
if let space13Assignee = nameByParkingSpace[13] {
    print("Key 13 is assigned in the dictionary!")
}
```

Loops and String Interpolation

Swift has all the control flow statements that you may be familiar with from other languages: if-else, while, for, for-in, repeat-while, and switch. Even if they are familiar, however, there may be some differences from what you are accustomed to. The key difference between these statements in Swift and in C-like languages is that while enclosing parentheses are not necessary on these statements' expressions, Swift *does* require braces on clauses. Additionally, the expressions for if and while-like statements must evaluate to a **Bool**.

Swift does not have the traditional C-style for loop that you might be accustomed to. Instead, you can accomplish the same thing a little more cleanly using Swift's **Range** type and the for-in statement:

```
let range = 0..<countingUp.count
for i in range {
    let string = countingUp[i]
    // Use 'string'
}
```

The most direct route would be to enumerate the items in the array themselves:

```
for string in countingUp {
    // Use 'string'
}
```

What if you wanted the index of each item in the array? Swift's **enumerated()** function returns a sequence of integers and values from its argument:

```
for (i, string) in countingUp.enumerated() {
    // (0, "one"), (1, "two")
}
```

What are those parentheses, you ask? The **enumerated()** function returns a sequence of *tuples*. A tuple is an ordered grouping of values similar to an array, except each member may have a distinct type. In this example the tuple is of type **(Int, String)**. We will not spend much time on tuples in this book; they are not used in iOS APIs because Objective-C does not support them. However, they can be useful in your Swift code.

Another application of tuples is in enumerating the contents of a dictionary:

```
let nameByParkingSpace = [13: "Alice", 27: "Bob"]

for (space, name) in nameByParkingSpace {
    let permit = "Space \(space): \(name)"
}
```

Did you notice that curious markup in the string literal? That is Swift's *string interpolation*. Expressions enclosed between \(and) are evaluated and inserted into the string at runtime. In this example you are using local variables, but any valid Swift expression, such as a method call, can be used.

To see the values of the `permit` variable for each iteration of the loop, first click on the circular Show Result indicator at the far right end of the results sidebar for the line `let permit = "Space \(space): \(name)"`. You will see the current value of `permit` under the code. Control-click on the result and select Value History (Figure 2.5). This can be very useful for visualizing what is happening in your playground code's loops.

Figure 2.5 Using the Value History to see the results of string interpolation

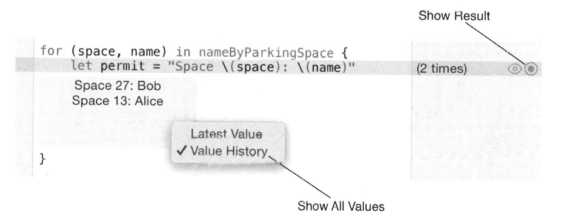

41

Enumerations and the Switch Statement

An enumeration is a type with a discrete set of values. Define an enum describing pies:

```swift
enum PieType {
    case apple
    case cherry
    case pecan
}

let favoritePie = PieType.apple
```

Swift has a powerful switch statement that, among other things, is great for matching on enum values:

```swift
let name: String
switch favoritePie {
case .apple:
    name = "Apple"
case .cherry:
    name = "Cherry"
case .pecan:
    name = "Pecan"
}
```

The cases for a switch statement must be exhaustive: Each possible value of the switch expression must be accounted for, whether explicitly or via a `default:` case. Unlike in C, Swift switch cases do not fall through – only the code for the case that is matched is executed. (If you need the fall-through behavior of C, you can explicitly request it using the `fallthrough` keyword.)

Switch statements can match on many types, even ranges:

```swift
let macOSVersion: Int = ...
switch macOSVersion {
case 0...8:
    print("A big cat")
case 9:
    print("Mavericks")
case 10:
    print("Yosemite")
case 11:
    print("El Capitan")
case 12:
    print("Sierra")
default:
    print("Greetings, people of the future! What's new in 10.\(macOSVersion)?")
}
```

For more on the switch statement and its pattern matching capabilities, see the *Control Flow* section in Apple's *The Swift Programming Language* guide. (More on that in just a moment.)

Enumerations and raw values

Swift enums can have raw values associated with their cases:

```
enum PieType: Int {
    case apple = 0
    case cherry
    case pecan
}
```

With the type specified, you can ask an instance of **PieType** for its rawValue and then initialize the enum type with that value. This returns an optional, since the raw value may not correspond with an actual case of the enum, so it is a great candidate for optional binding.

```
let pieRawValue = PieType.pecan.rawValue
// pieRawValue is an Int with a value of 2

if let pieType = PieType(rawValue: pieRawValue) {
    // Got a valid 'pieType'!
}
```

The raw value for an enum is often an **Int**, but it can be any integer or floating-point number type as well as the **String** and **Character** types.

When the raw value is an integer type, the values automatically increment if no explicit value is given. For **PieType**, only the **apple** case is given an explicit value. The values for **cherry** and **pecan** are automatically assigned a rawValue of 1 and 2, respectively.

There is more to enumerations. Each case of an enumeration can have associated values. You will learn more about associated values in Chapter 20.

Exploring Apple's Swift Documentation

To explore Apple's documentation on Swift, start at `developer.apple.com/swift`. Here are two particular resources to look for. We suggest bookmarking them and visiting them when you want to review a particular concept or dig a little deeper.

The Swift Programming Language This guide describes many features of Swift. It starts with the basics and includes example code and lots of detail. It also contains the language reference and formal grammar of Swift.

Swift Standard Library Reference The standard library reference lays out the details of Swift types, protocols, and global (or *free*) functions.

Your homework is to browse through the *Types* section of the *Swift Standard Library Reference* and the sections of *The Swift Programming Language* guide on *The Basics*, *Strings and Characters*, and *Collection Types*. Solidify what you learned in this chapter and become familiar with the information these resources offer. If you know where to find the details when you need them, then you will feel less pressure to memorize them – letting you focus on iOS development instead.

3

Views and the View Hierarchy

Over the next five chapters, you are going to build an application named WorldTrotter. When it is complete, this app will convert values between degrees Fahrenheit and degrees Celsius. In this chapter, you will learn about views and the view hierarchy through creating WorldTrotter's UI. At the end of this chapter, your app will look like Figure 3.1.

Figure 3.1 WorldTrotter

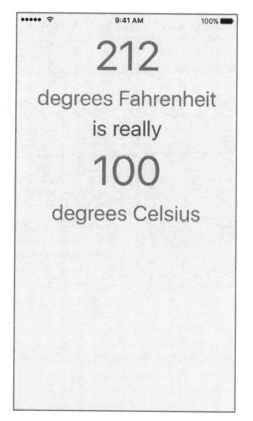

Let's start with a little bit of the theory behind views and the view hierarchy.

View Basics

Recall from Chapter 1 that views are objects that are visible to the user, like buttons, text fields, and sliders. View objects make up an application's UI. A view:

- is an instance of **UIView** or one of its subclasses

- knows how to draw itself

- can handle events, like touches

- exists within a hierarchy of views whose root is the application's window

Let's look at the *view hierarchy* in greater detail.

The View Hierarchy

Every application has a single instance of **UIWindow** that serves as the container for all the views in the application. **UIWindow** is a subclass of **UIView**, so the window is itself a view. The window is created when the application launches. Once the window is created, other views can be added to it.

When a view is added to the window, it is said to be a *subview* of the window. Views that are subviews of the window can also have subviews, and the result is a hierarchy of view objects with the window at its root (Figure 3.2).

Figure 3.2 An example view hierarchy and the interface that it creates

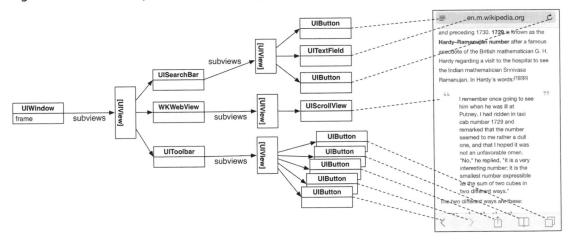

Once the view hierarchy is created, it will be drawn to the screen. This process can be broken into two steps:

- Each view in the hierarchy, including the window, draws itself. It renders itself to its *layer*, which you can think of as a bitmap image. (The layer is an instance of **CALayer**.)

- The layers of all the views are composited together on the screen.

Figure 3.3 depicts another example view hierarchy and the two drawing steps.

Figure 3.3 Views render themselves and then are composited together

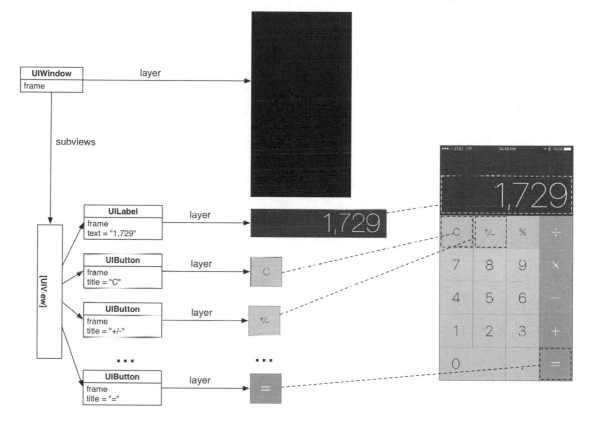

For WorldTrotter, you are going to create an interface composed of different views. There will be four instances of **UILabel** and one instance of **UITextField** that will allow the user to enter a temperature in Fahrenheit. Let's get started.

Creating a New Project

In Xcode, select File → New → Project... (or use the keyboard shortcut Command-Shift-N). Under the iOS section at the top, choose the Single View Application template under Application and click Next.

Enter WorldTrotter for the product name. Make sure that Swift is selected from the Language dropdown and that Universal is selected from the Devices dropdown. Also make sure the Use Core Data box is unchecked (Figure 3.4). Click Next and then Create on the following screen.

Figure 3.4 Configuring WorldTrotter

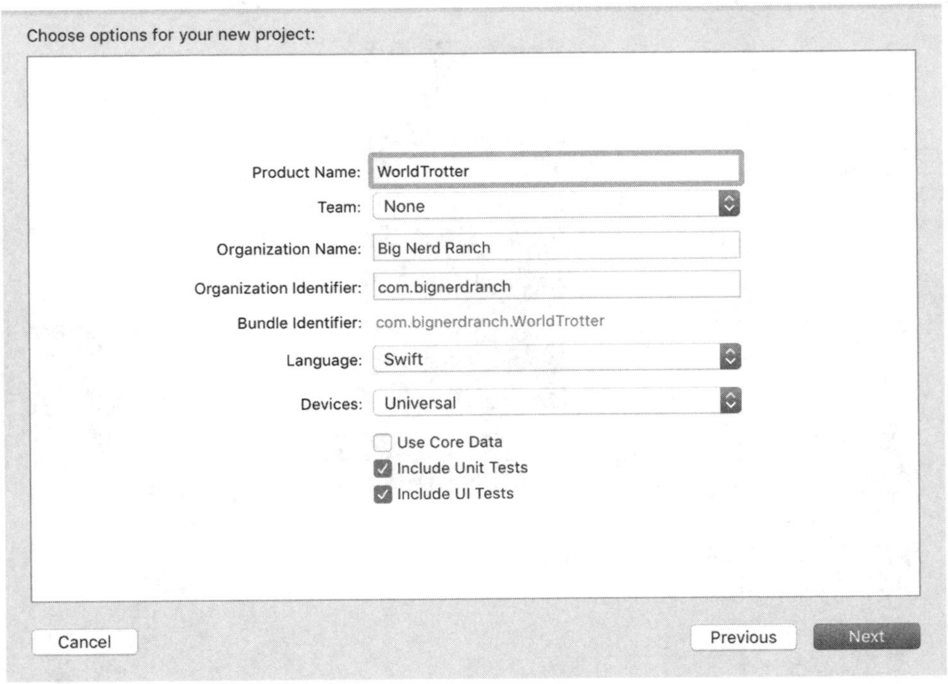

Views and Frames

When you initialize a view programmatically, you use its **init(frame:)** designated initializer. This method takes one argument, a **CGRect**, that will become the view's frame, a property on **UIView**.

```
var frame: CGRect
```

A view's frame specifies the view's size and its position relative to its superview. Because a view's size is always specified by its frame, a view is always a rectangle.

A **CGRect** contains the members origin and size. The origin is a structure of type **CGPoint** and contains two **CGFloat** properties: x and y. The size is a structure of type **CGSize** and has two **CGFloat** properties: width and height (Figure 3.5).

Figure 3.5 **CGRect**

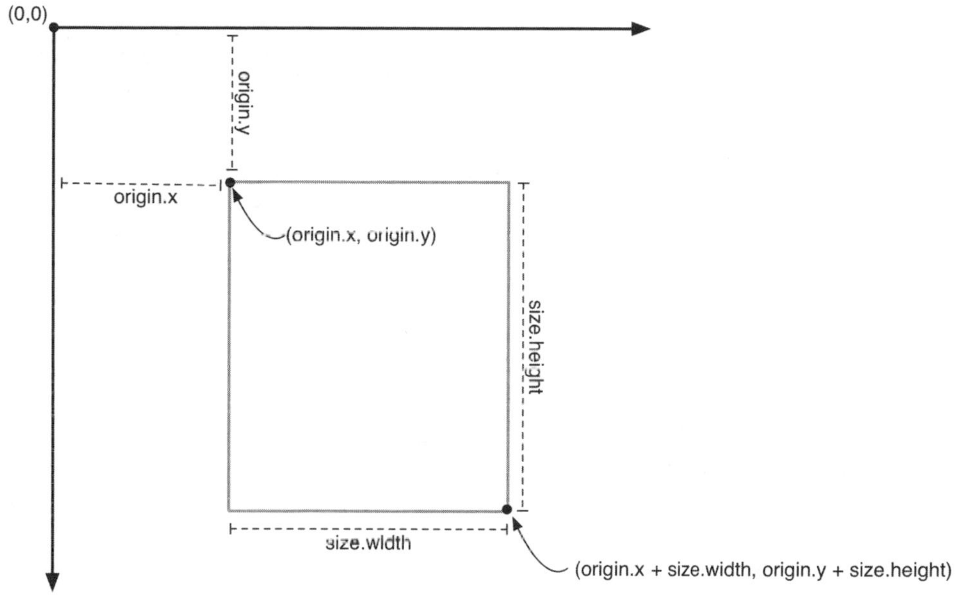

When the application is launched, the view for the initial view controller is added to the root-level window. This view controller is represented by the **ViewController** class defined in ViewController.swift. We will discuss what a view controller is in Chapter 5, but for now, it is sufficient to know that a view controller has a view and that the view associated with the main view controller for the application is added as a subview of the window.

Before you create the views for WorldTrotter, you are going to add some practice views programmatically to explore views and their properties and see how the interfaces for applications are created.

Open ViewController.swift and delete any methods that the template created. Your file should look like this:

```
import UIKit

class ViewController: UIViewController {

}
```

(UIKit, which you also saw in Chapter 1, is a *framework*. A framework is a collection of related classes and resources. The UIKit framework defines many of the UI elements that your users see, as well as other iOS-specific classes. You will be using a few different frameworks as you go through this book.)

Right after the view controller's view is loaded into memory, its **viewDidLoad()** method is called. This method gives you an opportunity to customize the view hierarchy, so it is a great place to add your practice views.

In ViewController.swift, override **viewDidLoad()**. Create a **CGRect** that will be the frame of a **UIView**. Next, create an instance of **UIView** and set its backgroundColor property to blue. Finally, add the **UIView** as a subview of the view controller's view to make it part of the view hierarchy. (Much of this will not look familiar. That is fine. We will explain more after you enter the code.)

```
class ViewController: UIViewController {

    override func viewDidLoad() {
        super.viewDidLoad()

        let firstFrame = CGRect(x: 160, y: 240, width: 100, height: 150)
        let firstView = UIView(frame: firstFrame)
        firstView.backgroundColor = UIColor.blue
        view.addSubview(firstView)
    }

}
```

To create a **CGRect**, you use its initializer and pass in the values for origin.x, origin.y, size.width, and size.height.

To set the backgroundColor, you use the UIColor class property blue. This is a computed property that initializes an instance of **UIColor** that is configured to be blue. There are a number of **UIColor** class properties for common colors, such as green, black, and clear.

Build and run the application (Command-R). You will see a blue rectangle that is the instance of **UIView**. Because the origin of the **UIView**'s frame is (160, 240), the rectangle's top-left corner is 160 points to the right and 240 points down from the top-left corner of its superview. The view stretches 100 points to the right and 150 points down from its origin, in accordance with its frame's size (Figure 3.6).

Figure 3.6 WorldTrotter with one **UIView**

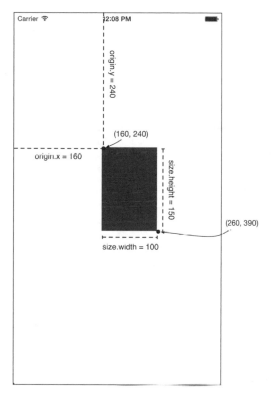

Note that these values are in points, not pixels. If the values were in pixels, then they would not be consistent across displays of different resolutions (i.e., Retina versus non-Retina). A point is a relative unit of a measure; it will be a different number of pixels depending on how many pixels are in the display. Sizes, positions, lines, and curves are always described in points to allow for differences in display resolution.

Figure 3.7 represents the view hierarchy that you have created.

Figure 3.7 Current view hierarchy

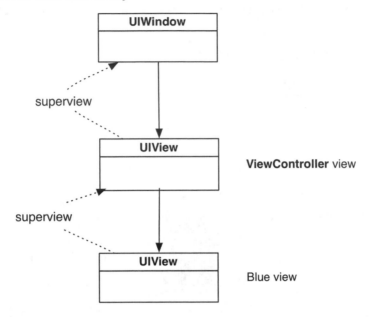

Every instance of **UIView** has a superview property. When you add a view as a subview of another view, the inverse relationship is automatically established. In this case, the **UIView**'s superview is the **UIWindow**.

Let's experiment with the view hierarchy. First, in ViewController.swift, create another instance of **UIView** with a different frame and background color.

```
override func viewDidLoad() {
    super.viewDidLoad()

    let firstFrame = CGRect(x: 160, y: 240, width: 100, height: 150)
    let firstView = UIView(frame: firstFrame)
    firstView.backgroundColor = UIColor.blue
    view.addSubview(firstView)

    let secondFrame = CGRect(x: 20, y: 30, width: 50, height: 50)
    let secondView = UIView(frame: secondFrame)
    secondView.backgroundColor = UIColor.green
    view.addSubview(secondView)
}
```

Build and run again. In addition to the blue rectangle, you will see a green square near the top-left corner of the window. Figure 3.8 shows the updated view hierarchy.

Figure 3.8 Updated view hierarchy with two subviews as siblings

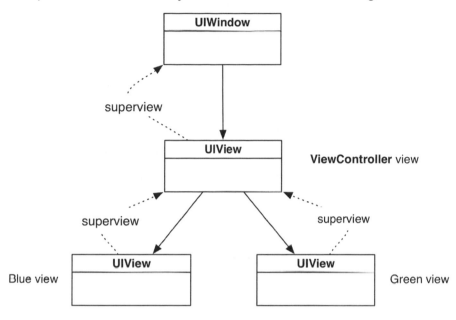

Now you are going to adjust the view hierarchy so that one instance of **UIView** is a subview of the other **UIView** instead of the view controller's view. In ViewController.swift, add secondView as a subview of firstView.

```
...
let secondView = UIView(frame: secondFrame)
secondView.backgroundColor = UIColor.green
view.addSubview(secondView)
firstView.addSubview(secondView)
```

Your view hierarchy is now four levels deep, as shown in Figure 3.9.

Figure 3.9 One **UIView** as a subview of the other

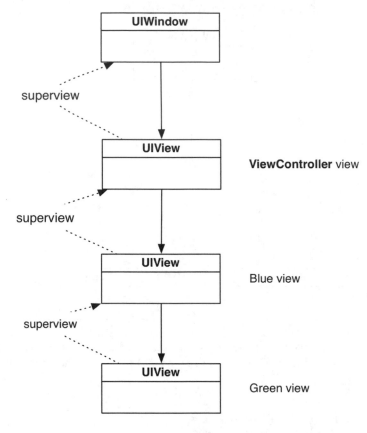

Build and run the application. Notice that secondView's position on the screen has changed (Figure 3.10). A view's frame is relative to its superview, so the top-left corner of secondView is now inset (20, 30) points from the top-left corner of firstView.

Figure 3.10 WorldTrotter with new hierarchy

(If the green instance of **UIView** looks smaller than it did previously, that is just an optical illusion. Its size has not changed.)

Now that you have seen the basics of views and the view hierarchy, you can start working on the interface for WorldTrotter. Instead of building up the interface programmatically, you will use Interface Builder to visually lay out the interface, as you did in Chapter 1.

In ViewController.swift, start by removing your practice code.

```
override func viewDidLoad() {
    super.viewDidLoad()

    let firstFrame = CGRect(x: 160, y: 240, width: 100, height: 150)
    let firstView = UIView(frame: firstFrame)
    firstView.backgroundColor = UIColor.blue
    view.addSubview(firstView)

    let secondFrame = CGRect(x: 20, y: 30, width: 50, height: 50)
    let secondView = UIView(frame: secondFrame)
    secondView.backgroundColor = UIColor.green
    firstView.addSubview(secondView)
}
```

Now let's add some views to the interface and set their frames.

Open `Main.storyboard`. At the bottom of the canvas, make sure the View as button is configured to display an iPhone 7 device.

From the object library, drag five instances of **UILabel** onto the canvas. Set their text to match Figure 3.11. As shown, space them out vertically on the top half of the interface and center them horizontally.

Figure 3.11 Adding labels to the interface

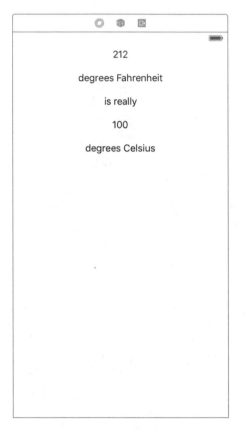

Select the top label so you can see its frame in Interface Builder. Open its *size inspector* – the fifth tab in the utilities area. (The keyboard shortcuts for the utilities tabs are Command-Option plus the tab number. The size inspector is the fifth tab, so its keyboard shortcut is Command-Option-5.)

Under the View section, find Frame Rectangle. (If you do not see it, you might need to select it from the Show pop-up menu.) The values shown are the view's frame, and they dictate the position of the view onscreen (Figure 3.12).

Figure 3.12 View frame values

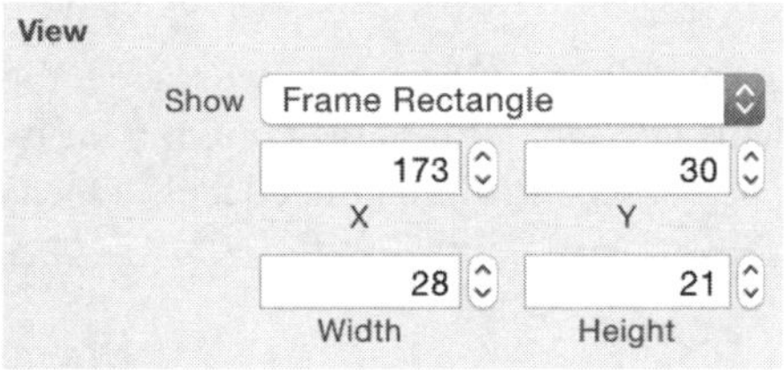

Build and run the application on the iPhone 7 simulator. The interface on the simulator will look identical to the interface that you laid out in Interface Builder.

Customizing the labels

Let's make the interface look a little bit better by customizing the view properties.

In Main.storyboard, select the background view. Open the attributes inspector and give the app a new background color: Find and click the Background dropdown and click Other.... Select the second tab (the Color Sliders tab) and choose RGB Sliders from the dropdown. In the box near the bottom, enter a Hex Color # of F5F4F1 (Figure 3.13). This will give the background a warm gray color.

Figure 3.13 Changing the background color

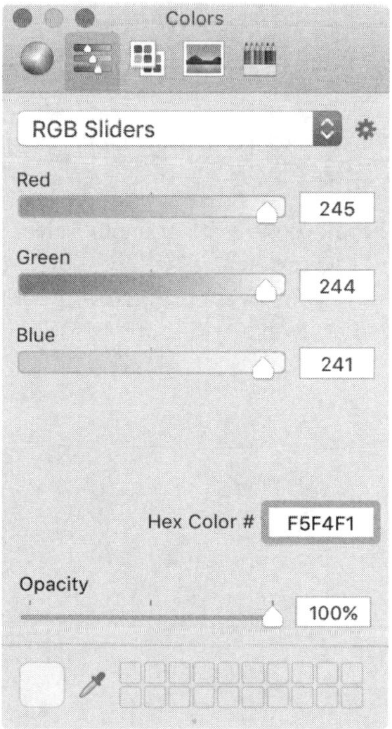

You can customize attributes common to selected views simultaneously. You will use this to give many of the labels a larger font size as well as a burnt orange text color.

Select the top two and bottom two labels by Command-clicking them in the document outline. Make sure the attributes inspector is open and update the text color: Under the Label section, find Color and open the pop-up menu. Select the Color Sliders tab again and enter a Hex Color # of E15829.

Now let's update the font. Select the 212 and 100 labels. Under the Label section in the attributes inspector, find Font and click on the text icon next to the current font. In the popover that appears, make the Size 70 (Figure 3.14). Select the remaining three labels. Open their Font pop-up and make the Size 36.

Figure 3.14 Customizing the labels' font

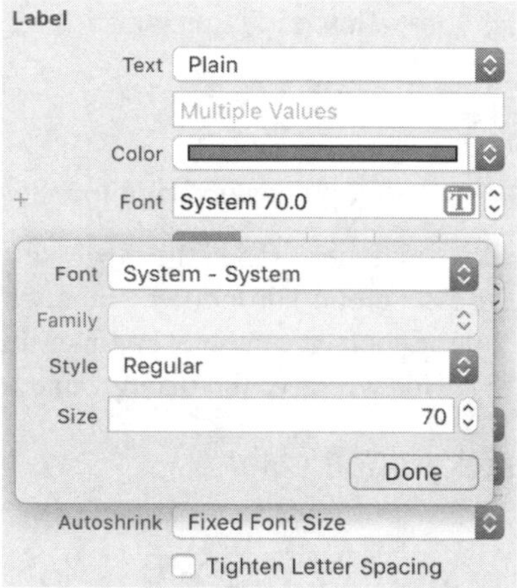

Now that the font size is larger, the text no longer fits within the bounds of the label. You could resize the labels manually, but there is an easier way.

Select the top label on the canvas. From Xcode's Editor menu, select Size to Fit Content (Command-=). This will resize the label to exactly fit its text contents. Repeat the process for the other four labels. (You can select all four labels to resize them all at once.) Now move the labels so that they are again nicely aligned vertically and centered horizontally (Figure 3.15).

Figure 3.15 Updating the label frames

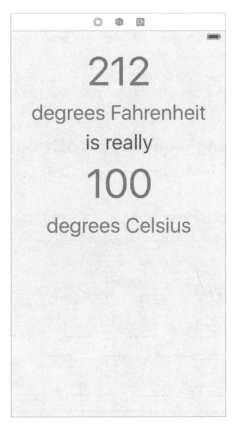

Build and run the application on the iPhone 7 simulator. Now build and run the application on the iPhone 7 Plus simulator. Notice that the labels are no longer centered – instead, they appear shifted slightly to the left.

You have just seen two of the major problems with absolute frames. First, when the contents change (like when you changed the font size), the frames do not automatically update. Second, the view does not look equally good on different sizes of screens.

In general, you should not use absolute frames for your views. Instead, you should use Auto Layout to flexibly compute the frames for you based on constraints that you specify for each view. For example, what you really want for WorldTrotter is for the labels to remain the same distance from the top of the screen and to remain horizontally centered within their superview. They should also update if the font or text of the labels change. This is what you will accomplish in the next section.

The Auto Layout System

Before you can fix the labels to have them lay out flexibly, you need to learn a little theory about the Auto Layout system. As you saw in Chapter 1, absolute coordinates make your layout fragile because they assume that you know the size of the screen ahead of time.

Using Auto Layout, you can describe the layout of your views in a relative way that enables their frames to be determined at runtime so that the frames' definitions can take into account the screen size of the device that the application is running on.

The alignment rectangle and layout attributes

The Auto Layout system is based on the *alignment rectangle*. This rectangle is defined by several *layout attributes* (Figure 3.16).

Figure 3.16 Layout attributes defining an alignment rectangle of a view

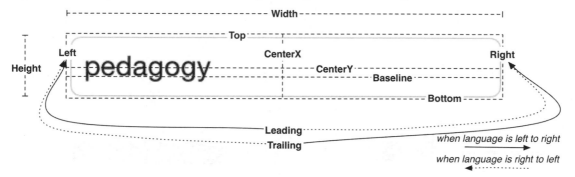

Width/Height	These values determine the alignment rectangle's size.
Top/Bottom Left/Right	These values determine the spacing between the given edge of the alignment rectangle and the alignment rectangle of another view in the hierarchy.
CenterX CenterY	These values determine the center point of the alignment rectangle.
FirstBaseline LastBaseline	These values are the same as the bottom attribute for most, but not all, views. For example, **UITextField** defines its baselines as the bottom of the text it displays rather than the bottom of the alignment rectangle. This keeps "descenders" (the parts of letters like "g" and "p" that descend below the baseline) from being obscured by a view right below the text field. For multiline text labels and text views, the first and last baseline refer to the first and last line of text. In all other situations, the first and last baseline are the same.
Leading Trailing	These values are language-specific attributes. If the device is set to a language that reads left to right (e.g., English), then the leading attribute is the same as the left attribute and the trailing attribute is the same as the right attribute. If the language reads right to left (e.g., Arabic), then the leading attribute is on the right and the trailing attribute is on the left. Interface Builder automatically prefers leading and trailing over left and right, and, in general, you should as well.

By default, every view has an alignment rectangle, and every view hierarchy uses Auto Layout.

The alignment rectangle is very similar to the frame. In fact, these two rectangles are often the same. Whereas the frame encompasses the entire view, the alignment rectangle only encompasses the content that you wish to use for alignment purposes. Figure 3.17 shows an example where the frame and the alignment rectangle are different.

Figure 3.17 Frame vs alignment rectangle

Frame   Alignment rectangle

You cannot define a view's alignment rectangle directly. You do not have enough information (like screen size) to do that. Instead, you provide a set of *constraints*. Taken together, these constraints enable the system to determine the layout attributes, and thus the alignment rectangle, for each view in the view hierarchy.

Constraints

A *constraint* defines a specific relationship in a view hierarchy that can be used to determine a layout attribute for one or more views. For example, you might add a constraint like, "The vertical space between these two views should always be 8 points," or, "These views must always have the same width." A constraint can also be used to give a view a fixed size, like, "This view's height should always be 44 points."

You do not need a constraint for every layout attribute. Some values may come directly from a constraint; others will be computed by the values of related layout attributes. For example, if a view's constraints set its left edge and its width, then the right edge is already determined (left edge + width = right edge, always). As a general rule of thumb, you need at least two constraints per dimension (horizontal and vertical).

If, after all of the constraints have been considered, there is still an ambiguous or missing value for a layout attribute, then there will be errors and warnings from Auto Layout and your interface will not look as you expect on all devices. Debugging these problems is important, and you will get some practice later in this chapter.

How do you come up with constraints? Let's see how, using the labels that you have laid out on the canvas.

First, describe what you want the view to look like independent of screen size. For example, you might say that you want the top label to be:

- 8 points from the top of the screen
- centered horizontally in its superview
- as wide and as tall as its text

To turn this description into constraints in Interface Builder, it will help to understand how to find a view's *nearest neighbor*. The nearest neighbor is the closest sibling view in the specified direction (Figure 3.18).

Figure 3.18 Nearest neighbor

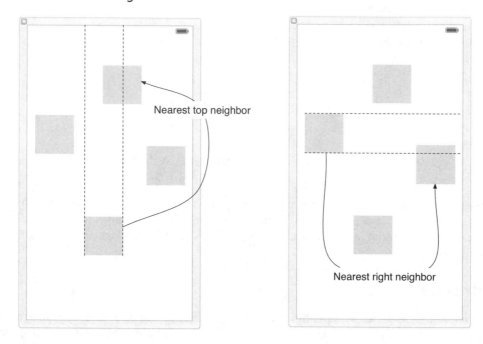

If a view does not have any siblings in the specified direction, then the nearest neighbor is its superview, also known as its container.

Now you can spell out the constraints for the label:

1. The label's top edge should be 8 points away from its nearest neighbor (which is its container – the view of the **ViewController**).

2. The label's center should be the same as its superview's center.

3. The label's width should be equal to the width of its text rendered at its font size.

4. The label's height should be equal to the height of its text rendered at its font size.

If you consider the first and fourth constraints, you can see that there is no need to explicitly constrain the label's bottom edge. It will be determined from the constraints on the label's top edge and the label's height. Similarly, the second and third constraints together determine the label's right and left edges.

Now that you have a plan for the top label, you can add these constraints. Constraints can be added using Interface Builder or in code. Apple recommends that you add constraints using Interface Builder whenever possible, and that is what you will do here. However, if your views are created and configured programmatically, then you can add constraints in code. In Chapter 6, you will practice that approach.

Adding constraints in Interface Builder

Let's get started constraining that top label.

Select the top label on the canvas. In the bottom-right corner of the canvas, find the Auto Layout constraint menus (Figure 3.19).

Figure 3.19 Auto Layout constraint menus

Auto Layout constraint menus

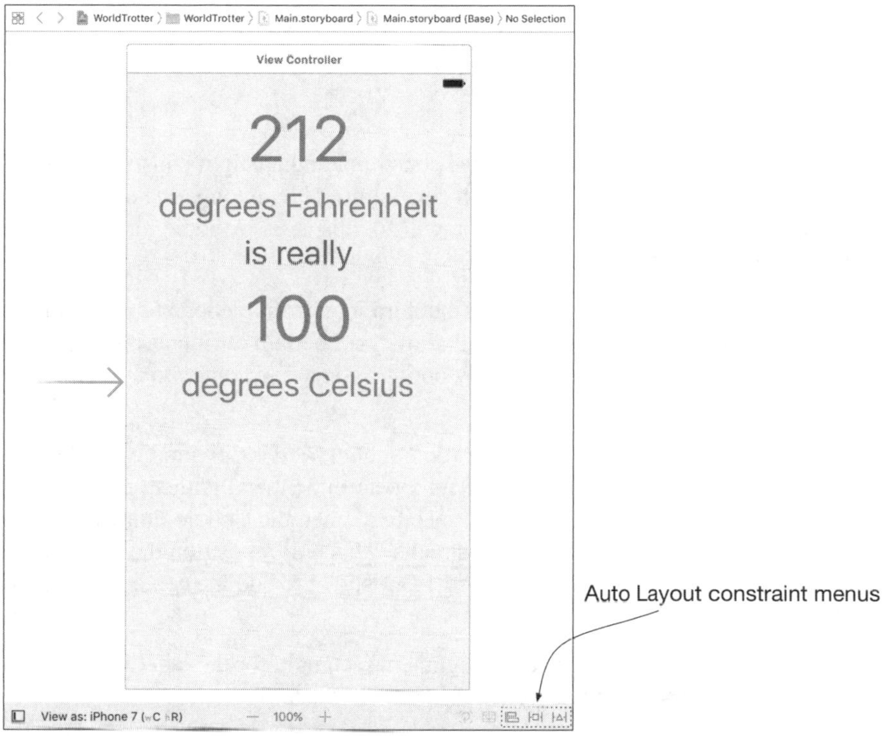

Click the ⊢□⊣ icon (the fourth from the left) to reveal the Add New Constraints menu. This menu shows you the current size and position of the label.

At the top of the Add New Constraints menu are four values that describe the label's current spacing from its nearest neighbor on the canvas. For this label, you are only interested in the top value.

To turn this value into a constraint, click the top red strut separating the value from the square in the middle. The strut will become a solid red line.

In the middle of the menu, find the label's Width and Height. The values next to Width and Height indicate the current canvas values. To constrain the label's width and height to the current canvas values, check the boxes next to Width and Height. The button at the bottom of the menu reads Add 3 Constraints. Click this button.

At this point, you have not specified enough constraints to fully determine the alignment rectangle. The red outline around the label indicates that its alignment rectangle is incompletely defined, and Interface Builder will help you determine what the problem is.

In the top-right corner of Interface Builder, notice the yellow warning sign (Figure 3.20). Click on this icon to reveal the issue: `Horizontal position is ambiguous for "212".`

Figure 3.20 Horizontal ambiguity

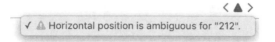

You have added two vertical constraints (a top edge constraint and a height constraint), but you have only added one horizontal constraint (a width constraint). Having only one constraint makes the horizontal position of the label ambiguous. You will fix this issue by adding a center alignment constraint between the label and its superview.

With the top label still selected, click the 🖿 icon (the third icon from the left) to reveal the Align menu. If you have multiple views selected, this menu will allow you to align attributes among the views. Because you have only selected one label, the only options you are given are to align the view within its container.

In the Align menu, check Horizontally in Container (do not click Add 1 Constraint yet). Once you add this constraint, there will be enough constraints to fully determine the alignment rectangle. To ensure that the frame of the label matches the constraints specified, open the Update Frames pop-up menu from the Align menu and select Items of New Constraints. This will reposition the label to match the constraints that have been added. Now click on Add 1 Constraint to add the centering constraint and reposition the label.

The label's constraints are all blue now that the alignment rectangle for the label is fully specified. Additionally, the warning at the top-right corner of Interface Builder is now gone.

Build and run the application on the iPhone 7 simulator and the iPhone 7 Plus simulator. The top label will remain centered in both simulators.

Intrinsic content size

Although the top label's position is flexible, its size is not. This is because you have added explicit width and height constraints to the label. If the text or font were to change, you would be in the same position you were in earlier. The size of the frame is absolute, so the frame would not hug to the content.

This is where the *intrinsic content size* of a view comes into play. You can think of the intrinsic content size as the size that a view "wants" to be. For labels, this size is the size of the text rendered at the given font. For images, this is the size of the image itself.

A view's intrinsic content size acts as implicit width and height constraints. If you do not specify constraints that explicitly determine the width, the view will be its intrinsic width. The same goes for the height.

With this knowledge, let the top label have a flexible size by removing the explicit width and height constraints.

In Main.storyboard, select the width constraint on the label. You can do this by clicking on the constraint on the canvas. Alternatively, in the document outline, you can click on the disclosure triangle next to the 212 label, then disclose the list of constraints for the label (Figure 3.21).

Figure 3.21 Selecting the width constraint

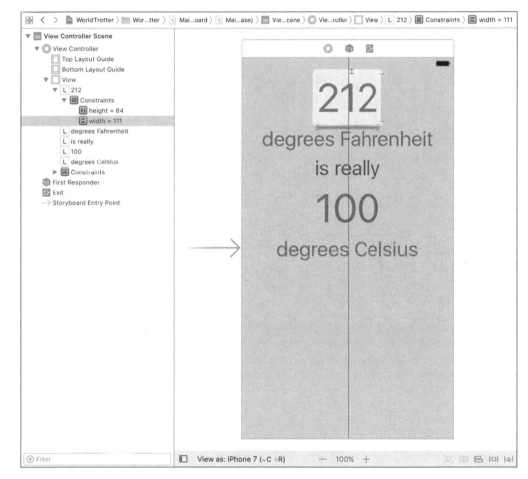

Once you have selected the width constraint, press the Delete key. Do the same for the height constraint.

Notice that the constraints for the label are still blue. Because the width and height are being inferred from the label's intrinsic content size, there are still enough constraints to determine the label's alignment rectangle.

Misplaced views

As you have seen, blue constraints indicate that the alignment rectangle for a view is fully specified. Orange constraints often indicate a *misplaced view*. This means that the frame for the view in Interface Builder is different than the frame that Auto Layout has computed.

A misplaced view is very easy to fix. That is good, because it is also a very common issue that you will encounter when working with Auto Layout.

Give your top label a misplaced view so that you can see how to resolve this issue. Resize the top label on the canvas using the resize controls and look for the yellow warning in the top-right corner of the canvas. Click on this warning icon to reveal the problem: Frame for "212" will be different at run time (Figure 3.22).

Figure 3.22 Misplaced view warning

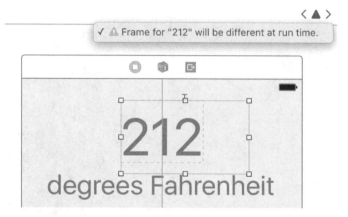

As the warning says, the frame at runtime will not be the same as the frame specified on the canvas. If you look closely, you will see an orange dotted line that indicates what the runtime frame will be.

Build and run the application. Notice that the label is still centered despite the new frame that you gave it in Interface Builder. This might seem great – you get the result that you want, after all. But the disconnect between what you have specified in Interface Builder and the constraints computed by Auto Layout will cause problems down the line as you continue to build your views. Let's fix the misplaced view.

Back in the storyboard, select the top label on the canvas. Click the ⊙ icon (the left-most icon) to update the frame of the label to match the frame that the constraints will compute.

You will get very used to updating the frames of views as you work with Auto Layout. One word of caution: If you try to update the frames for a view that does not have enough constraints, you will almost certainly get unexpected results. If that happens, undo the change and inspect the constraints to see what is missing.

At this point, the top label is in good shape. It has enough constraints to determine its alignment rectangle, and the view is laying out the way you want.

Becoming proficient with Auto Layout takes a lot of experience, so in the next section you are going to remove the constraints from the top label and then add constraints to all of the labels.

Adding more constraints

Let's flesh out the constraints for the rest of the views. Before you do that, you will remove the existing constraints from the top label.

Select the top label on the canvas. Open the Resolve Auto Layout Issues menu and select Clear Constraints from the Selected Views section (Figure 3.23).

Figure 3.23 Clearing constraints

You are going to add the constraints to all of the views in two steps. First you will center the top label horizontally within the superview. Then you will add constraints that pin the top of each label to its nearest neighbor while aligning the centers of all of the labels.

Select the top label. Open the Align menu and choose Horizontally in Container with a constant of 0. Make sure that Update Frames has None selected; remember that you do not want to update the frame of a view that does not have enough constraints, and this one constraint will certainly not provide enough information to compute the alignment rectangle. Go ahead and Add 1 Constraint.

Now select all five labels on the canvas. It can be very convenient to add constraints to multiple views simultaneously. Open the Add New Constraints menu and make the following choices:

1. Select the top strut and make sure it has a constant of 8.

2. From the Align menu, choose Horizontal Centers.

3. From the Update Frames menu, choose Items of New Constraints.

Your menu should match Figure 3.24. Once it does, click Add 9 Constraints. This will add the constraints to the views and update their frames to reflect the Auto Layout changes.

Figure 3.24 Adding more constraints with the Add New Constraints menu

Build and run the application on the iPhone 7 simulator. The views will be centered within the interface. Now build and run the application on the iPhone 7 Plus simulator. Unlike earlier in the chapter, all of the labels remain centered on the larger interface.

Auto Layout is a crucial technology for every iOS developer. It helps you create flexible layouts that work across a range of devices and interface sizes. It also takes a lot of practice to master. You will get a lot of experience using Auto Layout as you work through this book.

Bronze Challenge: More Auto Layout Practice

Remove all of the constraints from the **ViewController** interface and then add them back in. Try to do this without consulting the book.

4

Text Input and Delegation

WorldTrotter looks good, but so far it does not do anything. In this chapter, you are going to add an instance of **UITextField** to WorldTrotter. The text field will allow the user to type in a temperature in Fahrenheit that will then be converted to Celsius and displayed on the interface (Figure 4.1).

Figure 4.1 WorldTrotter with a **UITextField**

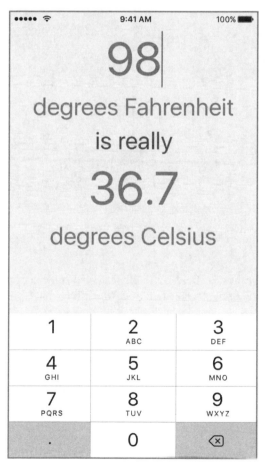

Text Editing

The first thing you are going to do is add a **UITextField** to the interface and set up the constraints for that text field. This text field will replace the top label in the interface that currently has the text "212."

Open Main.storyboard. Select the top label and press the Delete key to remove this subview. The constraints for all of the other labels will turn red because they were all directly or indirectly anchored to that top label (Figure 4.2). That is OK; you will fix them shortly.

Figure 4.2 Ambiguous frames for the labels

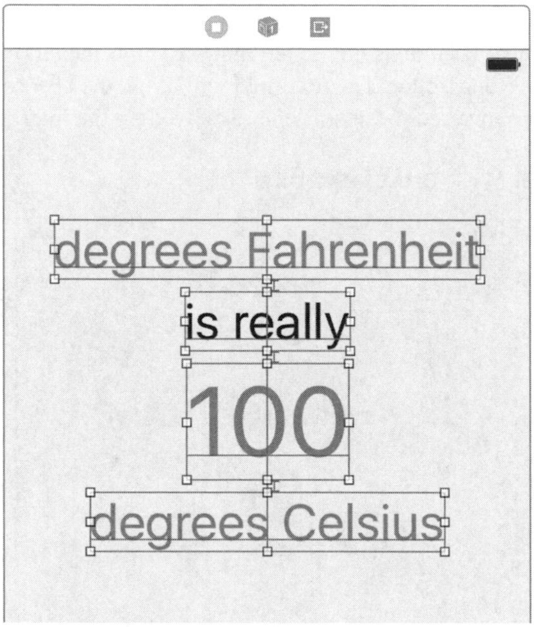

Open the object library and drag a Text Field to the top of the canvas where the label you deleted was previously placed.

Now set up the constraints for this text field. With the text field selected, open the Align menu and align the view Horizontally in Container with a constant of 0. Make sure that Update Frames is set to None and then Add 1 Constraint.

Now open the Add New Constraints menu. Give the text field a top edge constraint of 8 points, a bottom edge constraint of 8 points, and a width of 250 (Figure 4.3). Add these three constraints.

Figure 4.3 Text field Add New Constraints menu

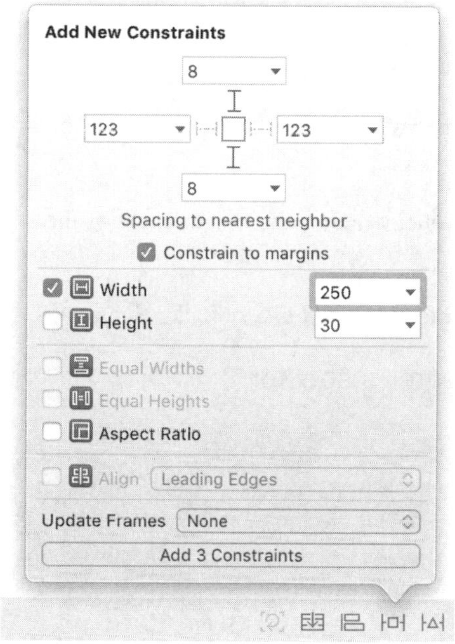

Finally, select the text field and the label right below it. Open the Align menu, select Horizontal Centers with a constant of 0, Update Frames for All Frames in Container, and finally Add 1 Constraint (Figure 4.4).

Figure 4.4 Aligning the text field

Next, customize some of the text field properties. Open the attributes inspector for the text field and make the following changes:

- Set the text color (from the Color menu) to burnt orange.

- Set the font size to System 70.

- Set the Alignment to centered.

- Set the placeholder text to be **value**. This is the text that will be displayed when the user has not entered any text.

- Set the Border Style to be none, which is the first element of the segmented control with the dotted lines.

The attributes inspector for your text field should look like Figure 4.5.

Figure 4.5 Text field attributes inspector

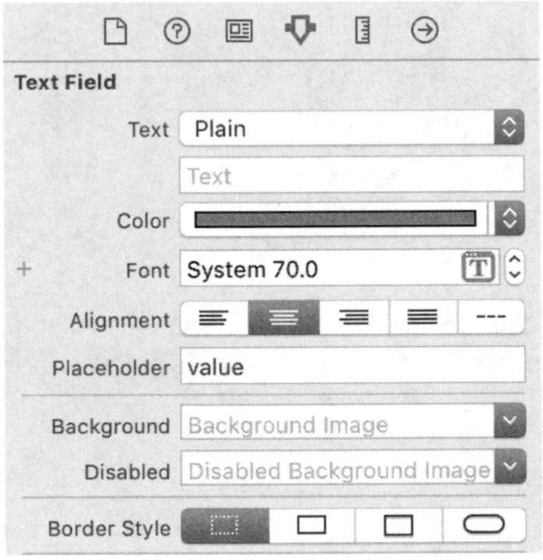

Because the text field's font changed, the views on the canvas now are misplaced. Select the gray background view, open the Resolve Auto Layout Issues menu, and select Update Frames from the All Views in View Controller section. The text field and labels will be repositioned to match their constraints (Figure 4.6).

Figure 4.6 Updated frames

Build and run the application. Tap on the text field and enter some text. If you do not see the keyboard, click the simulator's Hardware menu and select Keyboard → Toggle Software Keyboard or use the keyboard shortcut Command-K. By default, the simulator treats your computer's keyboard as a Bluetooth keyboard connected to the simulator. This is not usually what you want. Instead, you want the simulator to mimic an iOS device running without any accessories attached by using the onscreen keyboard.

Keyboard attributes

When a text field is tapped, the keyboard automatically slides up onto the screen. (You will see why this happens later in this chapter.) The keyboard's appearance is determined by a set of the **UITextField**'s properties called the **UITextInputTraits**. One of these properties is the type of keyboard that is displayed. For this application, you want to use the decimal pad.

In the attributes inspector for the text field, find the attribute named Keyboard Type and choose Decimal Pad. In the same section, you can see some of the other text input traits that you can customize for the keyboard. Change both Correction and Spell Checking to No (Figure 4.7).

Figure 4.7 Keyboard text input traits

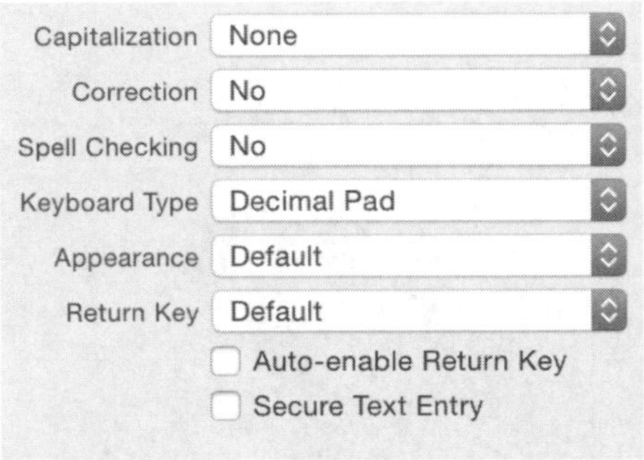

Build and run the application. Tapping on the text field will now reveal the decimal pad.

Responding to text field changes

The next step of the project will be to update the Celsius label when text is typed into the text field. You are going to need to write some code to do this. Specifically, this code will go into the view controller subclass associated with this interface.

Currently, that corresponds with the **ViewController** class defined in ViewController.swift. However, **ViewController** is not a very descriptive name for a view controller that manages the conversion between Fahrenheit and Celsius. Having descriptive type names allows you to more easily maintain your projects as they grow larger. You are going to delete this file and replace it with a more descriptive class.

In the project navigator, find ViewController.swift and delete it. Then create a new file by selecting File → New → File... (or press Command-N). With iOS selected at the top, choose Swift File under the Source label and click Next.

On the next pane, name this file ConversionViewController. Save the file in the WorldTrotter group within the WorldTrotter project and make sure that the WorldTrotter target is checked, as shown in Figure 4.8. Click Create, and Xcode will open ConversionViewController.swift in the editor.

Figure 4.8 Saving a Swift file

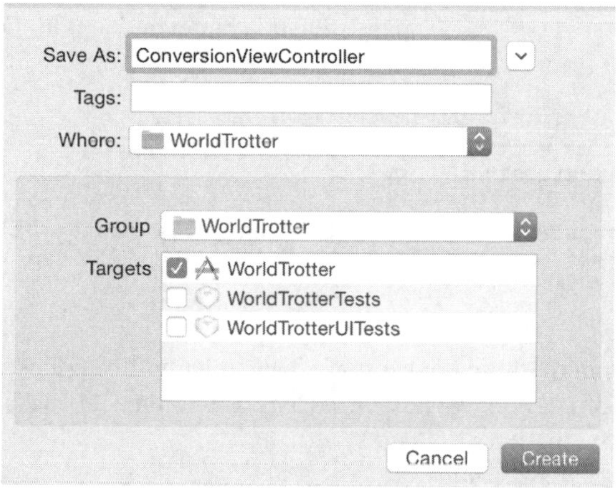

In ConversionViewController.swift, import UIKit and define a new view controller named **ConversionViewController**.

```
import Foundation
import UIKit

class ConversionViewController: UIViewController {

}
```

Now you need to associate the interface you created in Main.storyboard with this new view controller.

Open Main.storyboard and select the View Controller, either in the document outline or by clicking the yellow circle above the interface.

Open the identity inspector, which is the third tab in the utilities view (Command-Option-3). At the top, find the Custom Class section and change the Class to ConversionViewController (Figure 4.9). (You will learn what all of this is doing in Chapter 5.)

Figure 4.9 Changing the custom class

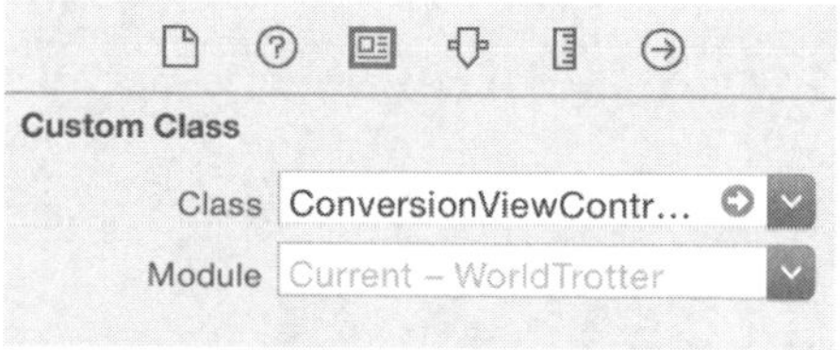

You saw in Chapter 1 that a button can send events to a controller when the button is tapped. Text fields are another control (both **UIButton** and **UITextField** are subclasses of **UIControl**) and can send an event when the text changes.

To get this all working, you will need to create an outlet to the Celsius text label and create an action for the text field to call when the text changes.

Open ConversionViewController.swift and define this outlet and action. For now, the label will be updated with whatever text the user types into the text field.

```
class ConversionViewController: UIViewController {

    @IBOutlet var celsiusLabel: UILabel!

    @IBAction func fahrenheitFieldEditingChanged(_ textField: UITextField) {
        celsiusLabel.text = textField.text
    }
}
```

Open Main.storyboard to make these connections. The outlet will be connected just as you did in Chapter 1. Control-drag from the Conversion View Controller to the Celsius label (the one that currently says "100") and connect it to the celsiusLabel.

Connecting the action will be a little different because you want the action to be triggered when the editing changes.

Select the text field on the canvas and open its connections inspector from the utility pane (the right-most tab, or Command-Option-6). The connections inspector allows you to make connections and see what connections have already been made.

You are going to have changes to the text field trigger the action you defined in **ConversionViewController**. In the connections inspector, locate the Sent Events section and the Editing Changed event. Click and drag from the circle to the right of Editing Changed to the Conversion View Controller and click the fahrenheitFieldEditingChanged: action in the pop-up menu (Figure 4.10).

Figure 4.10 Connecting the editing changed event

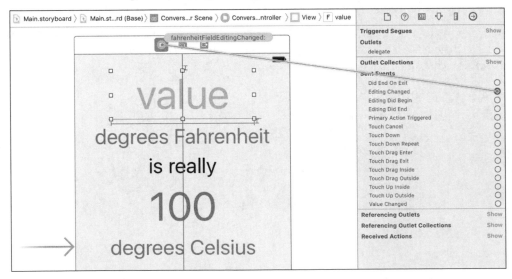

Build and run the application. Tap the text field and type some numbers. The Celsius label will mimic the text that is typed in. Now delete the text in the text field and notice how the label seems to go away. A label with no text has an intrinsic content width and height of 0, so the labels below it move up. Let's fix this issue.

In ConversionViewController.swift, update **fahrenheitFieldEditingChanged(_:)** to display "???" if the text field is empty.

```
@IBAction func fahrenheitFieldEditingChanged(_ textField: UITextField) {
    celsiusLabel.text = textField.text

    if let text = textField.text, !text.isEmpty {
        celsiusLabel.text = text
    } else {
        celsiusLabel.text = "???"
    }
}
```

If the text field has text and that text is not empty, it will be set on the celsiusLabel. If either of those conditions are not true, then the celsiusLabel will be given the string "???".

Build and run the application. Add some text, delete it, and confirm that the celsiusLabel is populated with "???" when the text field is empty.

Dismissing the keyboard

Currently, there is no way to dismiss the keyboard. Let's add that functionality. One common way of doing this is by detecting when the user taps the Return key and using that action to dismiss the keyboard; you will use this approach in Chapter 14. Because the decimal pad does not have a Return key, you will allow the user to tap on the background view to trigger the dismissal.

When the text field is tapped, the method **becomeFirstResponder()** is called on it. This is the method that, among other things, causes the keyboard to appear. To dismiss the keyboard, you call the method **resignFirstResponder()** on the text field. You will learn more about these methods in Chapter 14.

For WorldTrotter, you will need an outlet to the text field and a method that is triggered when the background view is tapped. This method will call **resignFirstResponder()** on the text field outlet. Let's take care of the code first.

Open ConversionViewController.swift and declare an outlet near the top to reference the text field.

```
@IBOutlet var celsiusLabel: UILabel!
@IBOutlet var textField: UITextField!
```

Now implement an action method that will dismiss the keyboard when called.

(In the code above, we included existing code so that you could position the new code correctly. In the code below, we do not provide that context because the position of the new code is not important so long as it is within the curly braces for the type being implemented – in this case, the **ConversionViewController** class. When a code block includes all new code, we suggest that you put it at the end of the type's implementation, just inside the final closing brace. In Chapter 15, you will see how to easily navigate within an implementation file when your files get longer and more complex.)

```
@IBAction func dismissKeyboard(_ sender: UITapGestureRecognizer) {
    textField.resignFirstResponder()
}
```

Two things are still needed: The textField outlet needs to be connected in the storyboard file, and you need a way of triggering the **dismissKeyboard(_:)** method you added.

To take care of the first item, open Main.storyboard and select the Conversion View Controller. Control-drag from the Conversion View Controller to the text field on the canvas and connect it to the textField outlet.

Now you need a way of triggering the method you implemented. You will use a *gesture recognizer* to accomplish this.

A gesture recognizer is a subclass of **UIGestureRecognizer** that detects a specific touch sequence and calls an action on its target when that sequence is detected. There are gesture recognizers that detect taps, swipes, long presses, and more. In this chapter, you will use a **UITapGestureRecognizer** to detect when the user taps the background view. You will learn more about gesture recognizers in Chapter 19.

In Main.storyboard, find Tap Gesture Recognizer in the object library. Drag this object onto the background view for the Conversion View Controller. You will see a reference to this gesture recognizer in the scene dock, the row of icons above the canvas.

Control-drag from the gesture recognizer in the scene dock to the Conversion View Controller and connect it to the dismissKeyboard: method (Figure 4.11).

Figure 4.11 Connecting the gesture recognizer action

Implementing the Temperature Conversion

With the basics of the interface wired up, let's implement the conversion from Fahrenheit to Celsius. You are going to store the current Fahrenheit value and compute the Celsius value whenever the text field changes.

In ConversionViewController.swift, add a property for the Fahrenheit value. This will be an optional measurement for temperature (a **Measurement<UnitTemperature>?**).

```
@IBOutlet var celsiusLabel: UILabel!
var fahrenheitValue: Measurement<UnitTemperature>?
```

The reason this property is optional is because the user might not have typed in a number, similar to the empty string issue you fixed earlier.

Now add a computed property for the Celsius value. This value will be computed based on the Fahrenheit value.

```
var fahrenheitValue: Measurement<UnitTemperature>?

var celsiusValue: Measurement<UnitTemperature>? {
    if let fahrenheitValue = fahrenheitValue {
        return fahrenheitValue.converted(to: .celsius)
    } else {
        return nil
    }
}
```

First you check to see whether there is a Fahrenheit value. If there is, you convert this value to the equivalent value in Celsius. If there is no Fahrenheit value, then you cannot compute a Celsius value and so you return nil.

Any time the Fahrenheit value changes, the Celsius label needs to be updated. Take care of that next.

Add a method to **ConversionViewController** that updates the celsiusLabel.

```
func updateCelsiusLabel() {
    if let celsiusValue = celsiusValue {
        celsiusLabel.text = "\(celsiusValue.value)"
    } else {
        celsiusLabel.text = "???"
    }
}
```

You want this method to be called whenever the Fahrenheit value changes. To do this, you will use a *property observer*, which is a chunk of code that gets called whenever a property's value changes.

A property observer is declared using curly braces immediately after the property declaration. Inside the braces, you declare your observer using either willSet or didSet, depending on whether you want to be notified immediately before or immediately after the property value changes, respectively.

Add a property observer to fahrenheitValue that gets called after the property value changes.

```
var fahrenheitValue: Measurement<UnitTemperature>? {
    didSet {
        updateCelsiusLabel()
    }
}
```

(One small note: Property observers are not triggered when the property value is changed from within an initializer.)

With that logic in place, you can now update the Fahrenheit value when the text field changes (which, in turn, will trigger an update of the Celsius label).

In **fahrenheitFieldEditingChanged(_:)**, delete your earlier nonconverting implementation and instead update the Fahrenheit value.

```
@IBAction func fahrenheitFieldEditingChanged(_ textField: UITextField) {

    if let text = textField.text, !text.isEmpty {
        celsiusLabel.text = text
    } else {
        celsiusLabel.text = "???"
    }

    if let text = textField.text, let value = Double(text) {
        fahrenheitValue = Measurement(value: value, unit: .fahrenheit)
    } else {
        fahrenheitValue = nil
    }
}
```

First you check whether the text field has some text. If so, you check to see whether that text can be represented by a **Double**. For example, "3.14" can be represented by a **Double**, but both "three" and "1.2.3" cannot. If both of those checks pass, then the Fahrenheit value is set to a **Measurement** initialized with that **Double** value. If either of those checks fails, then the Fahrenheit value is set to nil.

Build and run the application. The conversion between Fahrenheit and Celsius works great – so long as you enter a valid number. (It also shows more digits than you probably want it to, which you will address in a moment.)

It would be nice if the celsiusLabel was updated when the application first launched instead of still showing the value "100".

Override **viewDidLoad()** to set the initial value, similar to what you did in Chapter 1.

```
override func viewDidLoad() {
    super.viewDidLoad()

    updateCelsiusLabel()
}
```

In the remainder of this chapter, you will update WorldTrotter to address two issues: You will format the Celsius value to show a precision up to one fractional digit, and you will not allow the user to type in more than one decimal separator.

There are a couple of other issues with your app, but you will focus on these two for now. One of the other issues will be presented as a challenge at the end of this chapter. Let's start with updating the precision of the Celsius value.

Number formatters

You use a *number formatter* to customize the display of a number. There are other formatters for formatting dates, energy, mass, length, measurements, and more.

Create a constant number formatter in `ConversionViewController.swift`.

```
let numberFormatter: NumberFormatter = {
    let nf = NumberFormatter()
    nf.numberStyle = .decimal
    nf.minimumFractionDigits = 0
    nf.maximumFractionDigits = 1
    return nf
}()
```

Here you are using a closure to instantiate the number formatter. You are creating a **NumberFormatter** with the .decimal style and configuring it to display no more than one fractional digit. You will learn more about this new syntax for declaring properties in Chapter 16.

Now modify **updateCelsiusLabel()** to use this formatter.

```
func updateCelsiusLabel() {
    if let celsiusValue = celsiusValue {
        celsiusLabel.text = "\(celsiusValue.value)"
        celsiusLabel.text =
            numberFormatter.string(from: NSNumber(value: celsiusValue.value))
    } else {
        celsiusLabel.text = "???"
    }
}
```

Build and run the application. Play around with Fahrenheit values to see the formatter at work. You should never see more than one fractional digit on the Celsius label.

In the next section, you will update the application to accept a maximum of one decimal separator in the text field. To do this, you will use a common iOS design pattern called *delegation*.

Delegation

Delegation is an object-oriented approach to *callbacks*. A callback is a function that is supplied in advance of an event and is called every time the event occurs. Some objects need to make a callback for more than one event. For instance, the text field needs to "callback" when the user enters text as well as when the user presses the Return key.

However, there is no built-in way for two (or more) callback functions to coordinate and share information. This is the problem addressed by delegation – you supply a single *delegate* to receive all of the event-related callbacks for a particular object. This delegate object can then store, manipulate, act on, and relay the information from the callbacks as it sees fit.

When the user types into a text field, that text field will ask its delegate if it wants to accept the changes that the user has made. For WorldTrotter, you want to deny that change if the user attempts to enter a second decimal separator. The delegate for the text field will be the instance of **ConversionViewController**.

Conforming to a protocol

The first step is enabling instances of the **ConversionViewController** class to perform the role of **UITextField** delegate by declaring that **ConversionViewController** conforms to the **UITextFieldDelegate** *protocol*. For every delegate role, there is a corresponding protocol that declares the methods that an object can call on its delegate.

The **UITextFieldDelegate** protocol looks like this:

```
protocol UITextFieldDelegate: NSObjectProtocol {
    optional func textFieldShouldBeginEditing(_ textField: UITextField) -> Bool
    optional func textFieldDidBeginEditing(_ textField: UITextField)
    optional func textFieldShouldEndEditing(_ textField: UITextField) -> Bool
    optional func textFieldDidEndEditing(_ textField: UITextField)
    optional func textField(_ textField: UITextField,
                            shouldChangeCharactersIn range: NSRange,
                            replacementString string: String) -> Bool
    optional func textFieldShouldClear(_ textField: UITextField) -> Bool
    optional func textFieldShouldReturn(_ textField: UITextField) -> Bool
}
```

This protocol, like all protocols, is declared with `protocol` followed by its name, **UITextFieldDelegate**. The **NSObjectProtocol** after the colon refers to the **NSObject** protocol and tells you that **UITextFieldDelegate** inherits all of the methods in the **NSObject** protocol. The methods specific to **UITextFieldDelegate** are declared next.

You cannot create instances of a protocol; it is simply a list of methods and properties. Instead, implementation is left to each type that conforms to the protocol.

In a class's declaration, the protocols that the class conforms to are in a comma-delimited list following the superclass (if there is one). In ConversionViewController.swift, declare that **ConversionViewController** conforms to the **UITextFieldDelegate** protocol.

```
class ConversionViewController: UIViewController, UITextFieldDelegate {
```

Protocols used for delegation are called *delegate protocols*, and the naming convention for a delegate protocol is the name of the delegating class plus the word **Delegate**. Not all protocols are delegate protocols, however, and you will see an example of a different kind of protocol in Chapter 16. The protocols we have mentioned so far are part of the iOS SDK, but you can also write your own protocols.

Using a delegate

Now that you have declared **ConversionViewController** as conforming to the **UITextFieldDelegate** protocol, you can set the delegate property of the text field.

Open Main.storyboard and Control-drag from the text field to the Conversion View Controller. Choose delegate from the popover to connect the delegate property of the text field to the **ConversionViewController**.

Next, you are going to implement the **UITextFieldDelegate** method that you are interested in – **textField(_:shouldChangeCharactersIn:replacementString:)**. Because the text field calls this method on its delegate, you must implement it in ConversionViewController.swift.

In ConversionViewController.swift, implement **textField(_:shouldChangeCharactersIn:replacementString:)** to print the text field's current text as well as the replacement string. For now, just return true from this method.

```
func textField(_ textField: UITextField,
              shouldChangeCharactersIn range: NSRange,
              replacementString string: String) -> Bool {

    print("Current text: \(textField.text)")
    print("Replacement text: \(string)")

    return true
}
```

Notice that Xcode was able to autocomplete this method because **ConversionViewController** conforms to **UITextFieldDelegate**. It is a good idea to declare a protocol before implementing methods from the protocol so that Xcode can offer this support.

Build and run the application. Enter several digits in the text field and watch Xcode's console (Figure 4.12). It prints out the current text of the text field as well as the replacement string.

Figure 4.12 Printing to the console

Consider this "current text" and "replacement text" information in light of your goal of preventing multiple decimal separators. Logically, if the existing string has a decimal separator and the replacement string has a decimal separator, the change should be rejected.

In ConversionViewController.swift, update **textField(_:shouldChangeCharactersIn:replacementString:)** to use this logic.

```
func textField(_ textField: UITextField,
              shouldChangeCharactersIn range: NSRange,
              replacementString string: String) -> Bool {

    print("Current text: \(textField.text)")
    print("Replacement text: \(string)")

    return true

    let existingTextHasDecimalSeparator = textField.text?.range(of: ".")
    let replacementTextHasDecimalSeparator = string.range(of: ".")

    if existingTextHasDecimalSeparator != nil,
        replacementTextHasDecimalSeparator != nil {
        return false
    } else {
        return true
    }
}
```

Build and run the application. Attempt to enter multiple decimal separators; the application will reject the second decimal separator that you enter.

More on protocols

In the **UITextFieldDelegate** protocol, there are two kinds of methods: methods that handle information updates and methods that handle requests for input. For example, the text field's delegate implements the **textFieldDidBeginEditing(_:)** method if it wants to know when the user taps on the text field.

On the other hand, **textField(_:shouldChangeCharactersIn:replacementString:)** is a request for input. A text field calls this method on its delegate to ask whether the replacement string should be accepted or rejected. The method returns a **Bool**, which is the delegate's answer.

Methods declared in a protocol can be required or optional. By default, protocol methods are required, meaning that a class conforming to the protocol must have an implementation of those methods. If a protocol has optional methods, these are preceded by the directive optional. Looking back at the **UITextFieldDelegate** protocol, you can see that all of its methods are optional. This is typically true of delegate protocols.

Bronze Challenge: Disallow Alphabetic Characters

Currently, the user can enter alphabetic characters either by using a Bluetooth keyboard or by pasting copied text into the text field. Fix this issue. Hint: You will want to use the **NSCharacterSet** class.

BIG NERD RANCH
CODING BOOTCAMPS

Big Nerd Ranch bootcamps cover a lot of ground in just days. With our retreat-style training, we'll subject you to the most intensive app development course you can imagine, and when you finish, you'll be part of an elite corps: the few, the proud, the nerds.

Our distraction-free training gives you the opportunity to master new skills in an intensive environment—no meetings, no phone calls, just learning.

 Big Nerd Ranch's training was unlike any other class I've had. I learned skills that make me exceptionally more valuable, giving me a leg up on the competition. Since my first Big Nerd Ranch class, I've written software used in The White House, held positions at AT&T and Disney—and ultimately landed at Apple.

—Josh Paul, Alumnus

We offer classes in iOS, Android, Front-End Web, Back-End Web, macOS and Design. Use code **BNRGUIDE100** for $100 off a bootcamp of your choice.

www.bignerdranch.com

5

View Controllers

A view controller is an instance of a subclass of **UIViewController**. A view controller manages a view hierarchy. It is responsible for creating view objects that make up the hierarchy and for handling events associated with the view objects in its hierarchy.

So far, WorldTrotter has a single view controller, **ConversionViewController**. In this chapter, you will update it to use multiple view controllers. The user will be able to switch between two view hierarchies – one for viewing the **ConversionViewController** and another for displaying a map (Figure 5.1).

Figure 5.1 The two faces of WorldTrotter

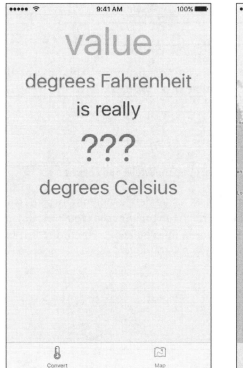 

The View of a View Controller

As subclasses of **UIViewController**, all view controllers inherit an important property:

```
var view: UIView!
```

This property points to a **UIView** instance that is the root of the view controller's view hierarchy. When the view of a view controller is added as a subview of the window, the view controller's entire view hierarchy is added, as shown in Figure 5.2.

Figure 5.2 Object diagram for WorldTrotter

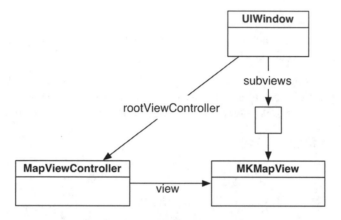

A view controller's view is not created until it needs to appear on the screen. This optimization is called *lazy loading*, and it can conserve memory and improve performance.

There are two ways that a view controller can create its view hierarchy:

- in Interface Builder, by using an interface file such as a storyboard

- programmatically, by overriding the **UIViewController** method **loadView()**

You saw the first approach in Chapter 3. First, you created a sample view hierarchy programmatically, then you switched to Interface Builder to create the interface for **ConversionViewController** using a storyboard file. You will continue to use Interface Builder in this chapter as you further explore view controllers. In Chapter 6, you will get experience creating programmatic views using **loadView()**.

Setting the Initial View Controller

Although a storyboard can have many view controllers, each storyboard file has exactly one *initial view controller*. The initial view controller acts as an entry point into the storyboard. You are going to add and configure another view controller to the canvas and set it to be the initial view controller for the storyboard.

Open Main.storyboard. From the object library, drag a View Controller onto the canvas (Figure 5.3). (To make space on the canvas, you can zoom out by Control-clicking on the background, using the zoom controls at the bottom of the canvas, or using pinch gestures on your trackpad.)

Figure 5.3 Adding a view controller to the canvas

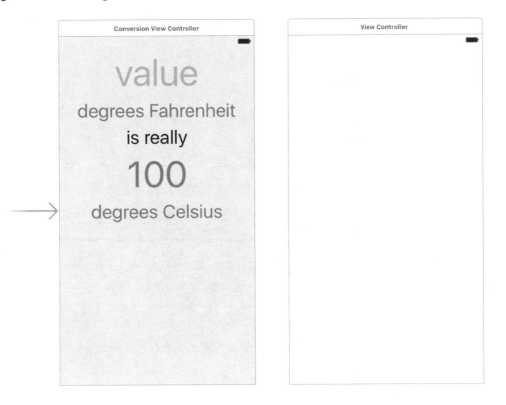

You want this view controller to display an **MKMapView** – a class designed to display a map – instead of the existing white **UIView**.

Select the view of the View Controller – not the View Controller itself! – and press Delete to remove this view from the canvas. Then drag a Map Kit View from the object library onto the view controller to set it as the **view** for this view controller (Figure 5.4).

Figure 5.4 Adding a map view to the canvas

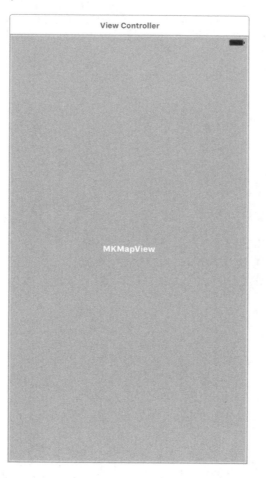

Now select the View Controller and open its attributes inspector. Under the View Controller section, check the box next to Is Initial View Controller (Figure 5.5). Did you notice that the gray arrow on the canvas that was pointing at the Conversion View Controller is now pointing to the View Controller? The arrow, as you have probably surmised, indicates the initial view controller. Another way to assign the initial view controller is to drag that arrow from one view controller to another on the canvas.

Figure 5.5 Setting the initial view controller

View Controller

Title

☑ Is Initial View Controller

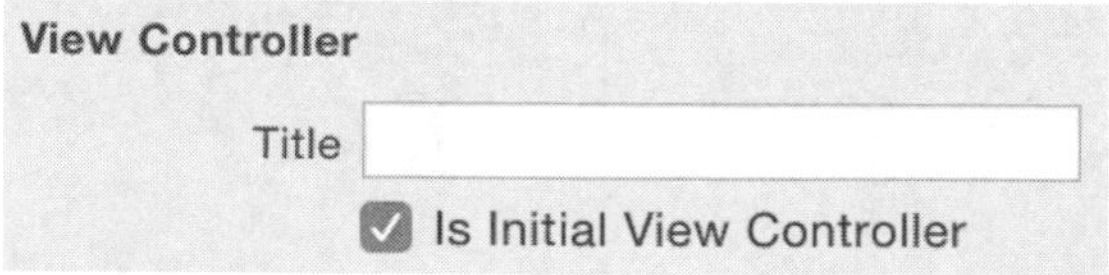

There is a quirk that would cause problems if you were to build and run the app right now. (Try it, if you like.) **MKMapView** is in a *framework* that is not currently being loaded into the application. A framework is a shared library of code that includes associated resources such as interface files and images. You briefly learned about frameworks in Chapter 3, and you have been using a couple of frameworks already: UIKit and Foundation are both frameworks.

So far, you have been including frameworks in your app by using the import keyword, like so:

```
import UIKit
```

Now you need to import the MapKit framework so that the **MKMapView** will load. However, if you import the MapKit framework using the import keyword without including any code that uses that framework, the compiler will optimize it out – even though you are using a map view in your storyboard.

Instead, you need to manually link the MapKit framework to the app.

With the project navigator open, click on the WorldTrotter project at the top of the list to open the project settings. Find and open the General tab in the settings. Scroll down to the bottom and find the section labeled Linked Frameworks and Libraries. Click on the + at the bottom and search for MapKit.framework. Select this framework and click Add (Figure 5.6).

Figure 5.6 Adding the MapKit framework

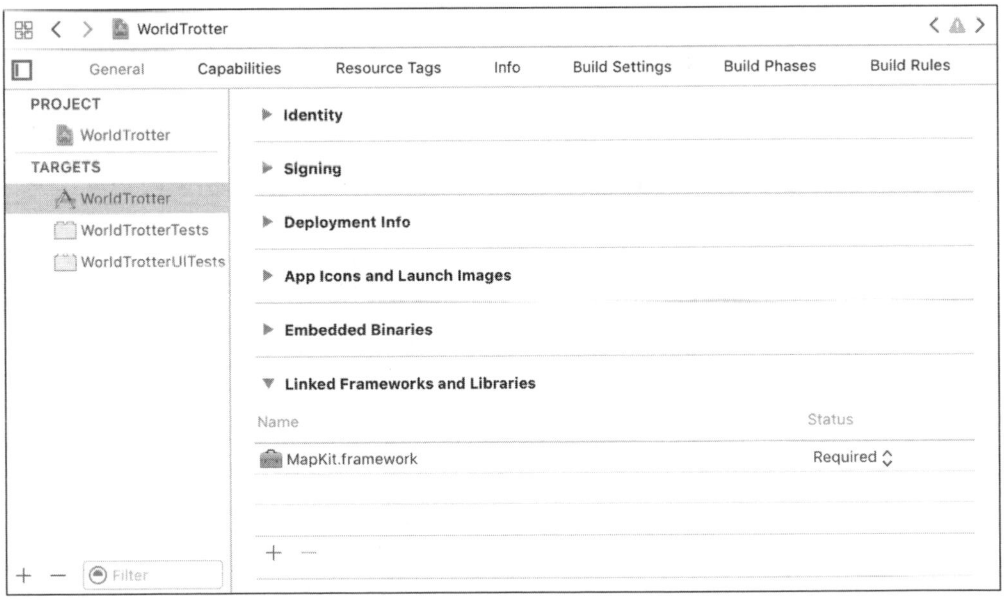

Now you can build and run the application. Because you have changed the initial view controller, the map shows up instead of the view of the **ConversionViewController**.

As mentioned above, there can only be one initial view controller associated with a given storyboard. You saw this earlier when you set the View Controller to be the initial view controller. At that point, the Conversion View Controller was no longer the initial view controller for this storyboard. Let's take a look at how this requirement works with the root level **UIWindow** to add the initial view controller's view to the window hierarchy.

UIWindow has a rootViewController property. When a view controller is set as the window's rootViewController, that view controller's view gets added to the window's view hierarchy. When this property is set, any existing subviews on the window are removed and view controller's view gets added to the window with the appropriate Auto Layout constraints.

Each application has one *main interface*, a reference to a storyboard. When the application launches, the initial view controller for the main interface gets set as the rootViewController of the window.

The main interface for an application is set in the project settings. Still in the General tab of the project settings, find the Deployment Info section. Here you will see the Main Interface setting (Figure 5.7). This is set to Main, which corresponds to Main.storyboard.

Figure 5.7 An application's main interface

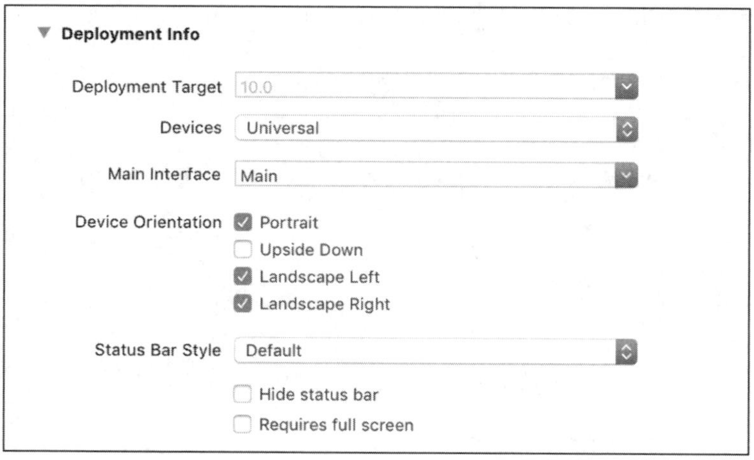

UITabBarController

View controllers become more interesting when the user has a way to switch between them. Throughout this book, you will learn a number of ways to present view controllers. In this chapter, you will create a **UITabBarController** that will allow the user to swap between the **ConversionViewController** and the **UIViewController** displaying the map.

UITabBarController keeps an array of view controllers. It also maintains a tab bar at the bottom of the screen with a tab for each view controller in its array. Tapping on a tab results in the presentation of the view of the view controller associated with that tab.

Open Main.storyboard and select the View Controller. From the Editor menu, choose Embed In → Tab Bar Controller. This will add the View Controller to the view controllers array of the Tab Bar Controller. You can see this represented by the Relationship arrow pointing from the Tab Bar Controller to the View Controller (Figure 5.8). Additionally, Interface Builder knows to make the Tab Bar Controller the initial view controller for the storyboard.

Figure 5.8 Tab bar controller with one view controller

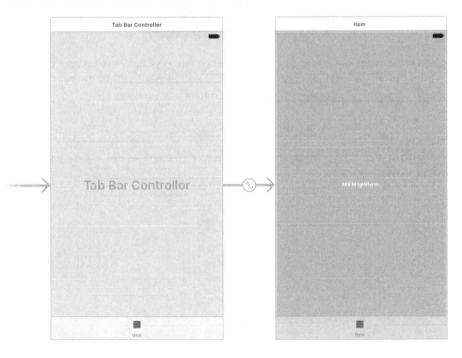

A tab bar controller is not very useful with just one view controller. Add the Conversion View Controller to the Tab Bar Controller's view controllers array.

Control-drag from the Tab Bar Controller to the Conversion View Controller. From the Relationship Segue section, choose view controllers (Figure 5.9).

Figure 5.9 Adding a view controller to the tab bar controller

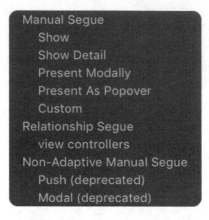

Build and run the application. Tap on the two tabs at the bottom to switch between the two view controllers. At the moment, the tabs just say Item, which is not very helpful. In the next section, you will update the tab bar items to make the tabs more descriptive and obvious.

UITabBarController is itself a subclass of **UIViewController**. A **UITabBarController**'s view is a **UIView** with two subviews: the tab bar and the view of the selected view controller (Figure 5.10).

Figure 5.10 **UITabBarController** diagram

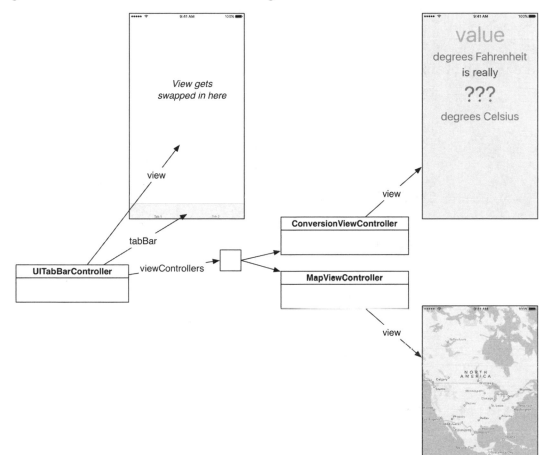

Tab bar items

Each tab on the tab bar can display a title and an image, and each view controller maintains a
tabBarItem property for this purpose. When a view controller is contained by a **UITabBarController**,
its tab bar item appears in the tab bar. Figure 5.11 shows an example of this relationship in iPhone's
Phone application.

Figure 5.11 **UITabBarItem** example

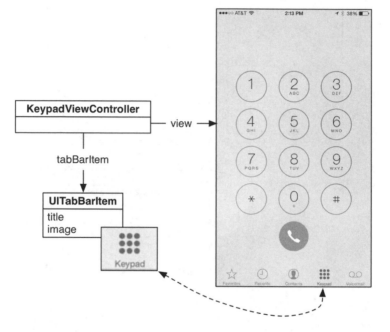

First, you need to add a few files to your project that will be the images for the tab bar items. In the
project navigator, open the Asset Catalog by opening Assets.xcassets.

An *asset* is a set of files from which a single file will be selected at runtime based on the user's device
configuration (more on that at the end of this chapter). You are going to add a ConvertIcon asset and a
MapIcon asset, each with images at three different resolutions.

In the 0 - Resources directory of the file that you downloaded earlier (www.bignerdranch.com/
solutions/iOSProgramming6ed.zip), find ConvertIcon.png, ConvertIcon@2x.png,
ConvertIcon@3x.png, MapIcon.png, MapIcon@2x.png, and MapIcon@3x.png. Drag these files into the
images set list on the left side of the Asset Catalog (Figure 5.12).

Figure 5.12 Adding images to the Asset Catalog

[Asset Catalog screenshot showing WorldTrotter > WorldTrotter > Assets.xcassets > ConvertIcon with AppIcon, ConvertIcon, and MapIcon items. ConvertIcon Image Set shows thermometer icons at 1x, 2x, 3x (Universal). MapIcon Image Set shows map icons at 1x, 2x, 3x (Universal). Bottom has Filter and Show Slicing.]

The tab bar item properties can be set either programmatically or in a storyboard. Because your data is static, the storyboard will be the best place to set the tab bar item properties.

In Main.storyboard, locate the View Controller (it is now labeled Item). Notice that a tab bar with the tab bar item in it was added to the interface because the view controller will be presented within a tab bar controller. This is very useful when laying out your interface.

Select this tab bar item and open its attributes inspector. Under the Bar Item section, change the Title to "Map" and choose MapIcon from the Image menu. You can also change the text of the tab bar item by double-clicking on the text on the canvas. The tab bar will be updated to reflect these values (Figure 5.13).

Figure 5.13 View Controller's tab bar item

Now find the Conversion View Controller and select its tab bar item. Set the Title to be "Convert" and the Image to be ConvertIcon.

Let's also change the first tab to be the Convert View Controller. The order of the tabs is determined by the order of the view controllers within the tab bar controller's viewControllers array. You can change the order in a storyboard by dragging the tabs at the bottom of the Tab Bar Controller.

Find the Tab Bar Controller on the canvas. Drag the Convert tab to be in the first position.

Build and run the application. Not only are the tab bar items at the bottom more descriptive, but the **ConvertViewController** is now the first view controller that is displayed (Figure 5.14).

Figure 5.14 Tab bar items with labels and icons

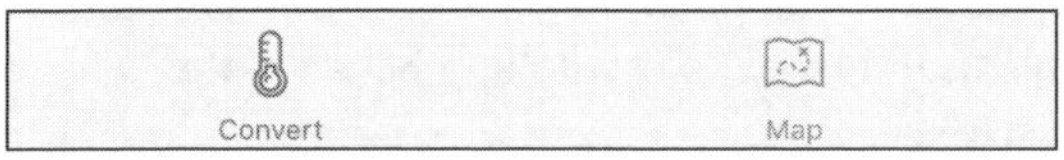

[Tab bar showing two items: Convert (thermometer icon) and Map (map icon).]

Loaded and Appearing Views

Now that you have two view controllers, the lazy loading of views mentioned earlier becomes more important. When the application launches, the tab bar controller defaults to loading the view of the first view controller in its array, which is the **ConvertViewController**. The **MapViewController**'s view is not needed and will only be needed when (or if) the user taps the tab to see it.

You can test this behavior for yourself. When a view controller finishes loading its view, **viewDidLoad()** is called, and you can override this method to make it print a message to the console, allowing you to see that it was called.

You are going to add code to both view controllers. However, there is no code currently associated with the view controller displaying the map because everything has been configured using the storyboard. Now that you want to add code to that view controller, you are going to create a view controller subclass and associate it with that interface.

Create a new Swift file (Command-N) and name it MapViewController. Open MapViewController.swift and define a **UIViewController** subclass named **MapViewController**.

```
import Foundation
import UIKit

class MapViewController: UIViewController {

}
```

Now open Main.storyboard and select the map's view controller. Open its identity inspector and change the Class to MapViewController.

Now that you have associated the **MapViewController** class with the view controller on the canvas, you can add code to both **ConversionViewController** and **MapViewController** to print to the console when their **viewDidLoad()** method is called.

In ConversionViewController.swift, update **viewDidLoad()** to print a statement to the console.

```
override func viewDidLoad() {
    super.viewDidLoad()

    print("ConversionViewController loaded its view.")

    updateCelsiusLabel()
}
```

In MapViewController.swift, override the same method.

```
override func viewDidLoad() {
    super.viewDidLoad()

    print("MapViewController loaded its view.")
}
```

Build and run the application. The console reports that **ConversionViewController** loaded its view right away. Tap **MapViewController**'s tab, and the console will report that its view is now loaded. At this point, both views have been loaded, so switching between the tabs now will no longer trigger **viewDidLoad()**. (Try it and see.)

Accessing subviews

Often, you will want to do some extra initialization or configuration of subviews defined in Interface Builder before they appear to the user. So where can you access a subview? There are two main options, depending on what you need to do. The first option is the **viewDidLoad()** method that you overrode to spot lazy loading. This method is called after the view controller's interface file is loaded, at which point all of the view controller's outlets will reference the appropriate objects. The second option is another **UIViewController** method, **viewWillAppear(_:)**. This method is called just before a view controller's view is added to the window.

Which should you choose? Override **viewDidLoad()** if the configuration only needs to be done once during the run of the app. Override **viewWillAppear(_:)** if you need the configuration to be done each time the view controller's view appears onscreen.

Interacting with View Controllers and Their Views

Let's look at some methods that are called during the lifecycle of a view controller and its view. Some of these methods you have already seen, and some are new.

- **init(coder:)** is the initializer for **UIViewController** instances created from a storyboard.

  When a view controller instance is created from a storyboard, its **init(coder:)** gets called once. You will learn more about this method in Chapter 16.

- **init(nibName:bundle:)** is the designated initializer for **UIViewController**.

  When a view controller instance is created without the use of a storyboard, its **init(nibName:bundle:)** gets called once. Note that in some apps, you may end up creating several instances of the same view controller class. This method will get called once on each view controller as it is created.

- **loadView()** is overridden to create a view controller's view programmatically.

- **viewDidLoad()** is overridden to configure views created by loading an interface file. This method gets called after the view of a view controller is created.

- **viewWillAppear(_:)** is overridden to configure views created by loading an interface file.

  This method and **viewDidAppear(_:)** get called every time your view controller is moved onscreen. **viewWillDisappear(_:)** and **viewDidDisappear(_:)** get called every time your view controller is moved offscreen.

Silver Challenge: Dark Mode

Whenever the **ConversionViewController** is viewed, update its background color based on the time of day. In the evening, the background should be a dark color. Otherwise, the background should be a light color. You will need to override **viewWillAppear(_:)** to accomplish this. (If that is not enough excitement in your life, you can change the background color each time the view controller is viewed.)

For the More Curious: Retina Display

With the release of iPhone 4, Apple introduced the Retina display for iPhone and iPod touch. The Retina display has much higher resolution compared to earlier devices. Let's look at what you should do to make graphics look their best on both displays.

For vector graphics, you do not need to do anything; your code will render as crisply as the device allows. However, if you draw using Core Graphics functions, these graphics will appear differently on different devices. In Core Graphics (also called Quartz), lines, curves, text, etc. are described in terms of points. On a non-Retina display, a point is 1x1 pixel. On most Retina displays, a point is 2x2 pixels (Figure 5.15). The exceptions are the 5.5-inch iPhones, which have a higher-resolution Retina display where a point is 3x3 pixels.

Figure 5.15 Rendering to different resolutions

 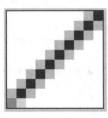 

As described to   As rendered to   As rendered to
Core Graphics   a non-Retina display a 2x Retina display
(vector graphics)   (1 point = 1x1 pixel) (1 point = 2x2 pixels)

Given these differences, bitmap images (like JPEG or PNG files) will be unattractive if the image is not tailored to the device's screen type. Say your application includes a small image of 25x25 pixels. If this image is displayed on a 2x Retina display, then the image must be stretched to cover an area of 50x50 pixels. At this point, the system does a type of averaging called *anti-aliasing* to keep the image from looking jagged. The result is an image that is not jagged – but it is fuzzy (Figure 5.16).

Figure 5.16 Fuzziness from stretching an image

You could use a larger file instead, but the averaging would then cause problems in the other direction when the image is shrunk for a non-Retina display. The only solution is to bundle two image files with your application: one at a pixel resolution equal to the number of points on the screen for non-Retina displays and one twice that size in pixels for Retina displays.

Fortunately, you do not have to write any extra code to handle which image gets loaded on which device. All you have to do is associate the different resolution images in the Asset Catalog with a single asset. Then, when you use **UIImage**'s **init(named:)** initializer to load the image, this method looks in the bundle and gets the appropriate file for the particular device.

6

Programmatic Views

In this chapter, you will update WorldTrotter to create the view for **MapViewController** programmatically (Figure 6.1). In doing so, you will learn more about view controllers and how to set up constraints and controls (such as **UIButton**s) programmatically.

Figure 6.1 WorldTrotter with programmatic views

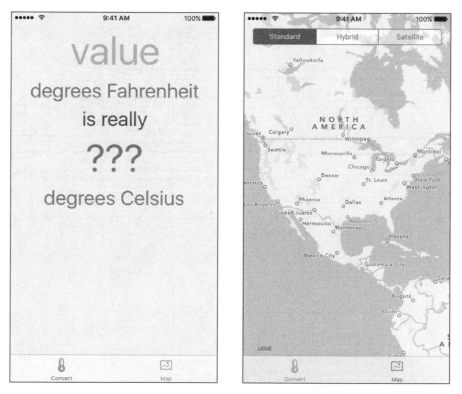

Currently, the view for **MapViewController** is defined in the storyboard. The first step, then, is to remove this view from the storyboard so you can instead create it programmatically.

In Main.storyboard, select the map view associated with **Map View Controller** and press Delete (Figure 6.2).

Figure 6.2 Deleting the view

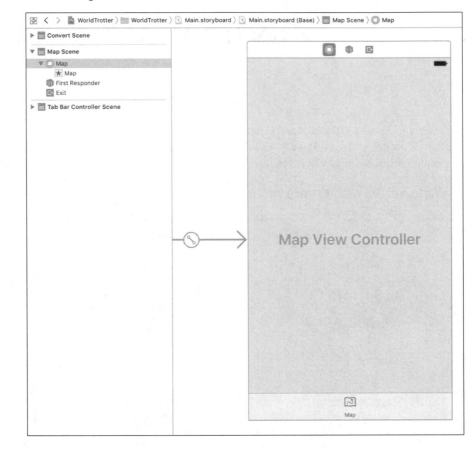

Creating a View Programmatically

You learned in Chapter 5 that you create a view controller's view programmatically by overriding the **UIViewController** method **loadView()**.

Open MapViewController.swift and override **loadView()** to create an instance of **MKMapView** and set it as the view of the view controller. You will need a reference to the map view later on, so create a property for it as well.

```
import UIKit
import MapKit

class MapViewController: UIViewController {

    var mapView: MKMapView!

    override func loadView() {
        // Create a map view
        mapView = MKMapView()

        // Set it as *the* view of this view controller
        view = mapView
    }

    override func viewDidLoad() {
        super.viewDidLoad()

        print("MapViewController loaded its view.")
    }

}
```

When a view controller is created, its view property is nil. If a view controller is asked for its view and its view is nil, then the **loadView()** method is called.

Build and run the application. Although the application looks the same, the map view is being created programmatically instead of through Interface Builder.

Programmatic Constraints

In Chapter 3, you learned about Auto Layout constraints and how to add them using Interface Builder. In this section, you will learn how to add constraints to an interface programmatically.

Apple recommends that you create and constrain your views in Interface Builder whenever possible. However, if your views are created in code, then you will need to constrain them programmatically. The interface for **MapViewController** is created programmatically, so it is a great candidate for programmatic constraints.

To learn about programmatic constraints, you are going to add a **UISegmentedControl** to **MapViewController**'s interface. A segmented control allows the user to choose between a discrete set of options, and you will use one to allow the user to switch between map types: standard, hybrid, and satellite.

In MapViewController.swift, update **loadView()** to add a segmented control to the interface.

```
override func loadView() {
    // Create a map view
    mapView = MKMapView()

    // Set it as *the* view of this view controller
    view = mapView

    let segmentedControl
            = UISegmentedControl(items: ["Standard", "Hybrid", "Satellite"])
    segmentedControl.backgroundColor
            = UIColor.white.withAlphaComponent(0.5)
    segmentedControl.selectedSegmentIndex = 0

    segmentedControl.translatesAutoresizingMaskIntoConstraints = false
    view.addSubview(segmentedControl)
}
```

(Note that due to page size restrictions we are showing some of these declarations split across two lines. You should enter each declaration on a single line.)

The line of code regarding translating constraints has to do with an older system for scaling interfaces – *autoresizing masks*. Before Auto Layout was introduced, iOS applications used autoresizing masks to allow views to scale for different-sized screens at runtime.

Every view has an autoresizing mask. By default, iOS creates constraints that match the autoresizing mask and adds them to the view. These translated constraints will often conflict with explicit constraints in the layout and cause an unsatisfiable constraints problem. The fix is to turn off this default translation by setting the property translatesAutoresizingMaskIntoConstraints to false. (There is more about Auto Layout and autoresizing masks at the end of this chapter.)

Anchors

When you work with Auto Layout programmatically, you will use *anchors* to create your constraints. Anchors are properties on the view that correspond to attributes that you might want to constrain to an anchor on another view. For example, you might constrain the leading anchor of one view to the leading anchor of another view. This would have the effect of the two views' leading edges being aligned.

Let's create some constraints to do the following.

- The top anchor of the segmented control should be equal to the top anchor of its superview.

- The leading anchor of the segmented control should be equal to the leading anchor of its superview.

- The trailing anchor of the segmented control should be equal to the trailing anchor of its superview.

In `MapViewController.swift`, create these constraints in **loadView()**.

```
let segmentedControl
        = UISegmentedControl(items: ["Standard", "Hybrid", "Satellite"])
segmentedControl.backgroundColor
        = UIColor.white.withAlphaComponent(0.5)
segmentedControl.selectedSegmentIndex = 0

segmentedControl.translatesAutoresizingMaskIntoConstraints = false
view.addSubview(segmentedControl)

let topConstraint
        = segmentedControl.topAnchor.constraint(equalTo: view.topAnchor)
let leadingConstraint
        = segmentedControl.leadingAnchor.constraint(equalTo: view.leadingAnchor)
let trailingConstraint
        = segmentedControl.trailingAnchor.constraint(equalTo: view.trailingAnchor)
```

Xcode will alert you to a problem with each line you have entered. You will fix them in a moment.

Anchors have a method **constraint(equalTo:)** that will create a constraint between the two anchors. There are a few other constraint creation methods on **NSLayoutAnchor**, including one that accepts a constant as an argument:

```
func constraint(equalTo anchor: NSLayoutAnchor<AnchorType>,
                constant c: CGFloat) -> NSLayoutConstraint
```

Activating constraints

You now have three **NSLayoutConstraint** instances. However, these constraints will have no effect on the layout until you explicitly activate them by setting their isActive properties to true. This will resolve Xcode's complaint.

In MapViewController.swift, activate the constraints at the end of **loadView()**.

```
let topConstraint =
    segmentedControl.topAnchor.constraint(equalTo: view.topAnchor)
let leadingConstraint =
    segmentedControl.leadingAnchor.constraint(equalTo: view.leadingAnchor)
let trailingConstraint =
    segmentedControl.trailingAnchor.constraint(equalTo: view.trailingAnchor)

topConstraint.isActive = true
leadingConstraint.isActive = true
trailingConstraint.isActive = true
```

Constraints need to be added to the most recent *common ancestor* for the views associated with the constraint. Figure 6.3 shows a view hierarchy along with the common ancestor for two views.

Figure 6.3 Common ancestor

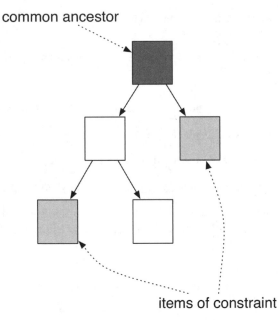

If a constraint is related to just one view (such as when adding a width or height constraint to a view), then that view is considered the common ancestor.

By setting the active property on a constraint to true, the constraint will work its way up the hierarchy for the items to find the common ancestor to add the constraint to. It will then call the method **addConstraint(_:)** on the appropriate view. Setting the active property is preferable to calling **addConstraint(_:)** or **removeConstraint(_:)** yourself.

Build and run the application and switch to the `MapViewController`. The segmented control is now pinned to the top, leading, and trailing edges of its superview (Figure 6.4).

Figure 6.4 Segmented control added to the screen

Although the constraints are doing the right thing, the interface does not look good. The segmented control is underlapping the status bar, and it would look better if the segmented control was inset from the leading and trailing edges of the screen. Let's tackle the status bar issue first.

Layout guides

View controllers expose two layout guides to assist with layout content: the `topLayoutGuide` and the `bottomLayoutGuide`. The layout guides indicate the extent to which the view controller's view contents will be visible. Using `topLayoutGuide` will allow your content to not underlap the status bar or navigation bar at the top of the screen. (You will learn about navigation bars in Chapter 14.) Using the `bottomLayoutGuide` will allow your content to not underlap the tab bar at the bottom of the screen.

The layout guides expose three anchors that you can use to add constraints: `topAnchor`, `bottomAnchor`, and `heightAnchor`. Because you want the segmented control to be under the status bar, you will constrain the bottom anchor of the top layout guide to the top anchor of the segmented control.

In `MapViewController.swift`, update the segmented control's constraints in **loadView()**. Make the segmented control be 8 points below the top layout guide.

```
let topConstraint =
    segmentedControl.topAnchor.constraint(equalTo: view.topAnchor)
let topConstraint =
    segmentedControl.topAnchor.constraint(equalTo: topLayoutGuide.bottomAnchor,
                                          constant: 8)
let leadingConstraint =
    segmentedControl.leadingAnchor.constraint(equalTo: view.leadingAnchor)
let trailingConstraint =
    segmentedControl.trailingAnchor.constraint(equalTo: view.trailingAnchor)

topConstraint.isActive = true
leadingConstraint.isActive = true
trailingConstraint.isActive = true
```

Build and run the application. The segmented control now appears below the status bar. By using the layout guides instead of a hardcoded constant, the views will adapt based on the context they appear in.

Now let's update the segmented control so that it is inset from the leading and trailing edges of its superview.

Margins

Although you could inset the segmented control using a constant on the constraint, it is much better to use the *margins* of the view controller's view.

Every view has a `layoutMargins` property that denotes the default spacing to use when laying out content. This property is an instance of **UIEdgeInsets**, which you can think of as a type of frame. When adding constraints, you will use the `layoutMarginsGuide`, which exposes anchors that are tied to the edges of the `layoutMargins`.

The primary advantage of using the margins is that the margins can change depending on the device type (iPad or iPhone) as well as the size of the device. Using the margins will give you content that looks good on any device.

Update the segmented control's leading and trailing constraints in **loadView()** to use the margins.

```
let topConstraint =
    segmentedControl.topAnchor.constraint(equalTo: topLayoutGuide.bottomAnchor,
                                          constant: 8)
let leadingConstraint =
    segmentedControl.leadingAnchor.constraint(equalTo: view.leadingAnchor)
let trailingConstraint =
    segmentedControl.trailingAnchor.constraint(equalTo: view.trailingAnchor)

let margins = view.layoutMarginsGuide
let leadingConstraint =
    segmentedControl.leadingAnchor.constraint(equalTo: margins.leadingAnchor)
let trailingConstraint =
    segmentedControl.trailingAnchor.constraint(equalTo: margins.trailingAnchor)

topConstraint.isActive = true
leadingConstraint.isActive = true
trailingConstraint.isActive = true
```

Build and run the application again. The segmented control is now inset from the view's margins (Figure 6.5).

Figure 6.5 Segmented control with updated constraints

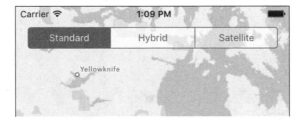

Explicit constraints

It is helpful to understand how these methods that you have used create constraints. **NSLayoutConstraint** has the following initializer:

```
convenience init(item view1: Any,
                 attribute attr1: NSLayoutAttribute,
                 relatedBy relation: NSLayoutRelation,
                 toItem view2: Any?,
                 attribute attr2: NSLayoutAttribute,
                 multiplier: CGFloat,
                 constant c: CGFloat)
```

This initializer creates a single constraint using two layout attributes of two view objects. The multiplier is the key to creating a constraint based on a ratio. The constant is a fixed number of points, similar to what you used in your spacing constraints.

The layout attributes are defined as constants in the **NSLayoutConstraint** class:

- NSLayoutAttribute.left
- NSLayoutAttribute.leading
- NSLayoutAttribute.top
- NSLayoutAttribute.width
- NSLayoutAttribute.centerX
- NSLayoutAttribute.firstBaseline

- NSLayoutAttribute.right
- NSLayoutAttribute.trailing
- NSLayoutAttribute.bottom
- NSLayoutAttribute.height
- NSLayoutAttribute.centerY
- NSLayoutAttribute.lastBaseline

There are additional attributes that handle the margins associated with a view, such as NSLayoutAttribute.leadingMargin.

Let's consider a hypothetical constraint. Say you wanted the width of the image view to be 1.5 times its height. You could make that happen with the following code. (Do not type this hypothetical constraint in your code! It will conflict with others you already have.)

```
let aspectConstraint = NSLayoutConstraint(item: imageView,
                                          attribute: .width,
                                          relatedBy: .equal,
                                          toItem: imageView,
                                          attribute: .height,
                                          multiplier: 1.5,
                                          constant: 0.0)
```

To understand how this initializer works, think of this constraint as the equation shown in Figure 6.6.

Figure 6.6 **NSLayoutConstraint** equation

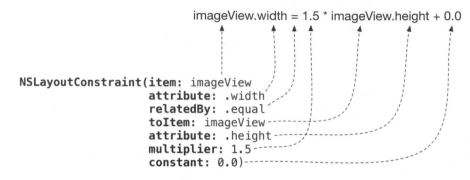

You relate a layout attribute of one view to the layout attribute of another view using a multiplier and a constant to define a single constraint.

Programmatic Controls

Now let's update the segmented control to change the map type when the user taps on a segment.

A **UISegmentedControl** is a subclass of **UIControl**. You worked with another **UIControl** subclass in Chapter 1, the **UIButton** class. Controls are responsible for calling methods on their target in response to some event.

Control events are of type **UIControlEvents**. Here are a few of the common control events that you will use:

UIControlEvents.touchDown	A touch down on the control.
UIControlEvents.touchUpInside	A touch down followed by a touch up while still within the bounds of the control.
UIControlEvents.valueChanged	A touch that causes the value of the control to change.
UIControlEvents.editingChanged	A touch that causes an editing change for a **UITextField**.

You used **.touchUpInside** for the **UIButton** in Chapter 1 (it is the default event when you Control-drag to connect actions in Interface Builder), and you saw the **.editingChanged** event in Chapter 4. For the segmented control, you will use the **.valueChanged** event.

In `MapViewController.swift`, update **loadView()** to add a target-action pair to the segmented control and associate it with the **.valueChanged** event.

```
override func loadView() {
    // Create a map view
    mapView = MKMapView()

    // Set it as *the* view of this view controller
    view = mapView

    let segmentedControl
            = UISegmentedControl(items: ["Standard", "Satellite", "Hybrid"])
    segmentedControl.backgroundColor
            = UIColor.white.withAlphaComponent(0.5)
    segmentedControl.selectedSegmentIndex = 0

    segmentedControl.addTarget(self,
                          action: #selector(MapViewController.mapTypeChanged(_:)),
                          for: .valueChanged)
    ...
```

Next, implement the action method in **MapViewController** that the event will trigger. This method will check which segment was selected and update the map accordingly.

```
func mapTypeChanged(_ segControl: UISegmentedControl) {
    switch segControl.selectedSegmentIndex {
    case 0:
        mapView.mapType = .standard
    case 1:
        mapView.mapType = .hybrid
    case 2:
        mapView.mapType = .satellite
    default:
        break
    }
}
```

Build and run the application. Change the selected segment and the map will update.

Bronze Challenge: Another Tab

Create a new view controller and add it to the tab bar controller. This view controller should display a **WKWebView**, which is a class used to display web content. The web view should display www.bignerdranch.com for you to book your next vacation.

Silver Challenge: User's Location

Add a button to the **MapViewController** that displays and zooms in on the user's current location. You will need to use delegation to accomplish this. Refer to the documentation for **MKMapViewDelegate**.

Gold Challenge: Dropping Pins

Map views can display pins, which are instances of **MKPinAnnotationView**. Add three pins to the map view: one where you were born, one where you are now, and one at an interesting location you have visited in the past. Add a button to the interface that allows the map to display the location of a pin. Subsequent taps should simply cycle through the list of pins.

For the More Curious: NSAutoresizingMaskLayoutConstraint

As we mentioned earlier, before Auto Layout iOS applications used another system for managing layout: autoresizing masks. Each view had an autoresizing mask that constrained its relationship with its superview, but this mask could not affect relationships between sibling views.

By default, views create and add constraints based on their autoresizing masks. However, these translated constraints often conflict with the explicit constraints in your layout, which results in an unsatisfiable constraints problem.

To see this happen, comment out the line in **loadView()** that turns off the translation of autoresizing masks.

```
// segmentedControl.translatesAutoresizingMaskIntoConstraints = false
view.addSubview(segmentedControl)
```

Now the segmented control has a resizing mask that will be translated into a constraint. Build and run the application and navigate to the map interface. You will not like what you see. The console will report the problem and its solution.

```
Unable to simultaneously satisfy constraints.
Probably at least one of the constraints in the following list is one you don't
want. Try this: (1) look at each constraint and try to figure out which you don't
expect; (2) find the code that added the unwanted constraint or constraints and
fix it. (Note: If you're seeing NSAutoresizingMaskLayoutConstraints that you don't
understand, refer to the documentation for the UIView property
translatesAutoresizingMaskIntoConstraints)
(
    "<NSAutoresizingMaskLayoutConstraint:0x7fb6b8e0ad00
      h=--& v=--& H:[UISegmentedControl:0x7fb6b9897390(212)]>",
    "<NSLayoutConstraint:0x7fb6b9975350 UISegmentedControl:0x7fb6b9897390.leading
      == UILayoutGuide:0x7fb6b9972640'UIViewLayoutMarginsGuide'.leading>",
    "<NSLayoutConstraint:0x7fb6b9975460 UISegmentedControl:0x7fb6b9897390.trailing
      == UILayoutGuide:0x7fb6b9972640'UIViewLayoutMarginsGuide'.trailing>",
    "<NSLayoutConstraint:0x7fb6b8e0b370 'UIView-Encapsulated-Layout-Width'
      H:[MKMapView:0x7fb6b8d237c0(0)]>",
    "<NSLayoutConstraint:0x7fb6b9972020 'UIView-leftMargin-guide-constraint'
      H:|-(0)-[UILayoutGuide:0x7fb6b9972640'UIViewLayoutMarginsGuide'](LTR)
      (Names: '|':MKMapView:0x7fb6b8d237c0 )>",
    "<NSLayoutConstraint:0x7fb6b9974f50 'UIView-rightMargin-guide-constraint'
      H:[UILayoutGuide:0x7fb6b9972640'UIViewLayoutMarginsGuide']-(0)-|(LTR)
      (Names: '|':MKMapView:0x7fb6b8d237c0 )>"
)

Will attempt to recover by breaking constraint
<NSLayoutConstraint:0x7fb6b9975460 UISegmentedControl:0x7fb6b9897390.trailing
  == UILayoutGuide:0x7fb6b9972640'UIViewLayoutMarginsGuide'.trailing>

Make a symbolic breakpoint at UIViewAlertForUnsatisfiableConstraints to catch
this in the debugger.
The methods in the UIConstraintBasedLayoutDebugging category on UIView listed
in <UIKit/UIView.h> may also be helpful.
```

Let's go over this output. Auto Layout is reporting that it is Unable to simultaneously satisfy constraints. This happens when a view hierarchy has constraints that conflict.

Then, the console spits out some handy tips and a list of all constraints that are involved, with their descriptions. Let's look at the format of one of these constraints more closely.

```
<NSLayoutConstraint:0x7fb6b9975350 UISegmentedControl:0x7fb6b9897390.leading
  == UILayoutGuide:0x7fb6b9972640'UIViewLayoutMarginsGuide'.leading>
```

This description indicates that the constraint located at memory address 0x7fb6b9975350 is setting the leading edge of the **UISegmentedControl** (at 0x7fb6b9897390) equal to the leading edge of the margin of the **UILayoutGuide** (at 0x7fb6b9972640).

Five of these constraints are instances of **NSLayoutConstraint**. One, however, is an instance of **NSAutoresizingMaskLayoutConstraint**. This constraint is the product of the translation of the image view's autoresizing mask.

Finally, Auto Layout tells you how it is going to solve the problem by listing the conflicting constraint that it will ignore. Unfortunately, it chooses poorly and ignores one of your explicit instances of **NSLayoutConstraint** instead of the **NSAutoresizingMaskLayoutConstraint**. This is why your interface looks like it does.

The note before the constraints are listed is very helpful: The **NSAutoresizingMaskLayoutConstraint** needs to be removed. Better yet, you can prevent this constraint from being added in the first place by explicitly disabling translation in **loadView()**:

```
// segmentedControl.translatesAutoresizingMaskIntoConstraints = false
view.addSubview(segmentedControl)
```

7

Localization

The appeal of iOS is global – iOS users live in many countries and speak many languages. You can ensure that your application is ready for a global audience through the processes of *internationalization* and *localization*.

Internationalization is making sure your native cultural information (like language, currency, date format, number format, etc.) is not hardcoded into your application. Localization is the process of providing the appropriate data in your application based on the user's Language and Region Format settings. You can find these settings in the iOS Settings application (Figure 7.1). Select the General row and then the Language & Region row.

Figure 7.1 Language and region settings

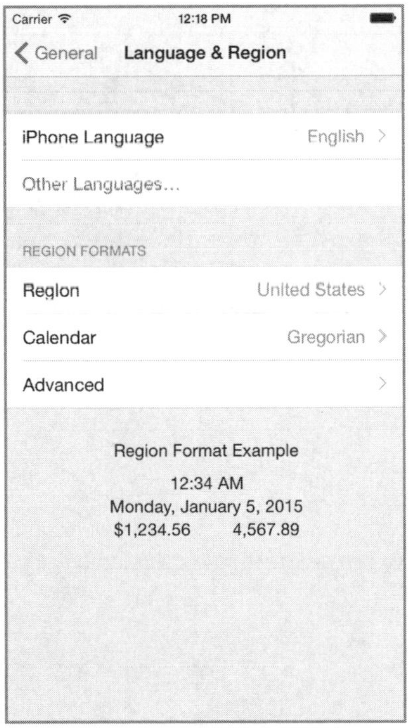

Here, users can set their region, like United States or United Kingdom. (Why does Apple use "region" instead of "country"? Some countries have more than one region with different settings. Scroll through the options in Region to see for yourself.)

Apple makes internationalization and localization relatively simple. An application that takes advantage of the localization APIs does not even need to be recompiled to be distributed in other languages or regions. (By the way, because "internationalization" and "localization" are long words, you will sometimes see them abbreviated as i18n and L10n, respectively.)

In this chapter, you will first internationalize the WorldTrotter application and then localize it into Spanish (Figure 7.2).

Figure 7.2 Localized WorldTrotter

Internationalization

In this first section, you will use the **NumberFormatter** and **NSNumber** classes to internationalize the **ConversionViewController**.

Formatters

In Chapter 4, you used an instance of **NumberFormatter** to set the text of the Celsius label in **ConversionViewController**. **NumberFormatter** has a **locale** property, which is set to the device's current locale. Whenever you use a **NumberFormatter** to create a number, it checks its **locale** property and sets the format accordingly. So the text of the Celsius label has been internationalized from the start.

Locale knows how different regions display symbols, dates, and decimals and whether they use the metric system. An instance of **Locale** represents one region's settings for these variables. When you access the current property on **Locale**, the instance of **Locale** that represents the user's region setting is returned. Once you have that instance of **Locale**, you can ask it questions, like, "Does this region use the metric system?" or, "What is the currency symbol for this region?"

```
let currentLocale = Locale.current
let isMetric = currentLocale.usesMetricSystem
let currencySymbol = currentLocale.currencySymbol
```

Even though the Celsius label is already internationalized, there is still a problem with it. Change the system region to Spain to see. Select the active scheme pop-up and select Edit Scheme... (Figure 7.3).

Figure 7.3 Edit scheme

Make sure that Run is selected on the lefthand side and then select the Options tab at the top. In the Application Region pop-up, select Europe and then Spain (Figure 7.4). Finally, Close the active scheme window.

Figure 7.4 Selecting a different region

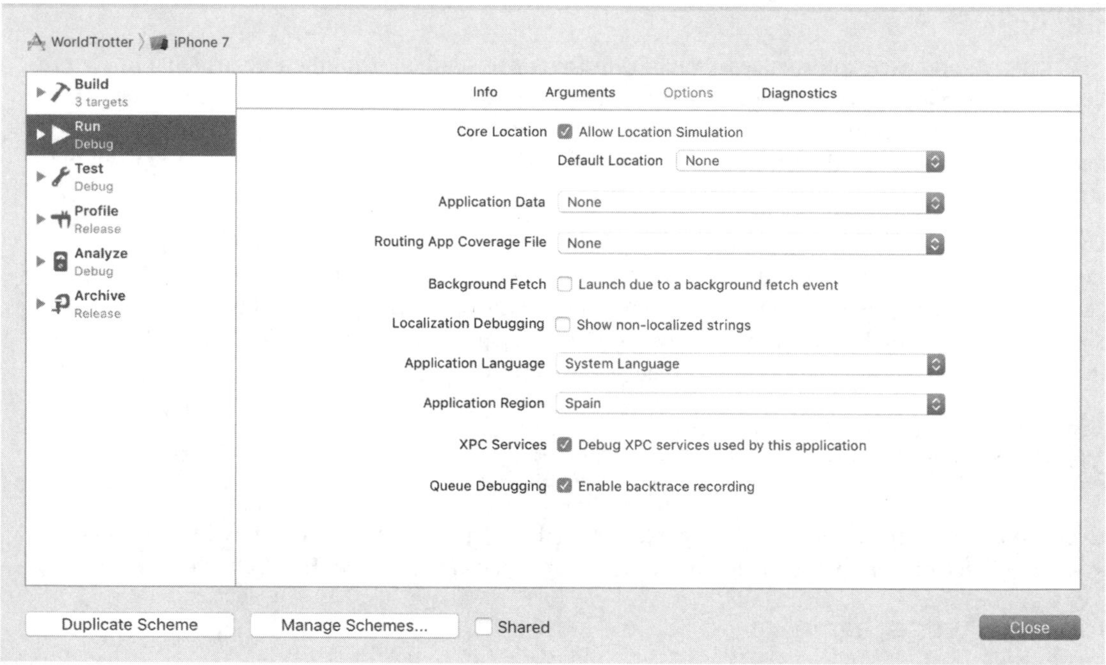

Build and run the application. On the `ConversionViewController`, tap the text field and make sure the software keyboard is visible. You may already notice one difference: In Spain, the decimal separator is a comma instead of a period (and the thousands separator is a period instead of a comma), so the number written 123,456.789 in the United States would be written 123.456,789 in Spain.

Attempt to type in multiple decimal separators (the comma) and notice that the application happily allows it. Whoops! Your code for disallowing multiple decimal separators checks for a period instead of using a locale-specific decimal separator. Let's fix that.

Open ConversionViewController.swift and update
textField(_:shouldChangeCharactersIn:replacementString:) to use the locale-specific decimal
separator.

```
func textField(_ textField: UITextField,
               shouldChangeCharactersIn range: NSRange,
               replacementString string: String) -> Bool {

    let existingTextHasDecimalSeparator = textField.text?.range(of: ".")
    let replacementTextHasDecimalSeparator = string.range(of: ".")

    let currentLocale = Locale.current
    let decimalSeparator = currentLocale.decimalSeparator ?? "."

    let existingTextHasDecimalSeparator
            = textField.text?.range(of: decimalSeparator)
    let replacementTextHasDecimalSeparator = string.range(of: decimalSeparator)

    if existingTextHasDecimalSeparator != nil,
        replacementTextHasDecimalSeparator != nil {
        return false
    } else {
        return true
    }
}
```

Build and run the application. The application no longer allows you to type in multiple decimal
separators, and it does this in a way that is independent of the user's region choice.

But there is still a problem. If you type in a number with a decimal separator that is not a period, the
conversion to Celsius is not happening – the Celsius label displays "???". What is going on here? In
fahrenheitFieldEditingChanged(_:), you are using an initializer for the **Double** type that takes in a
string as its argument. This initializer does not know how to handle a string that uses something other
than a period for its decimal separator.

Let's fix this code using the **NumberFormatter** class. In ConversionViewController.swift, update
fahrenheitFieldEditingChanged(_:) to convert the text field's string into a number in a locale-
independent way.

```
@IBAction func fahrenheitFieldEditingChanged(_ textField: UITextField) {
    if let text = textField.text, let value = Double(text) {
        fahrenheitValue = Measurement(value: value, unit: .fahrenheit)
    if let text = textField.text, let number = numberFormatter.number(from: text) {
        fahrenheitValue = Measurement(value: number.doubleValue, unit: .fahrenheit)
    } else {
        fahrenheitValue = nil
    }
}
```

Here you are using the number formatter's instance method **number(from:)** to convert the string into
a number. Because the number formatter is aware of the locale, it is able to convert the string into a
number. If the string contains a valid number, the method returns an instance of **NSNumber**. **NSNumber** is
a class that can represent a variety of number types, including **Int**, **Float**, **Double**, and more. You can
ask an instance of **NSNumber** for its value represented as one of those values. You are doing that here to
get the doubleValue of the number.

Build and run the application. Now that you are converting the string in a locale-independent way, the text field's value is properly converted to its Celsius value (Figure 7.5).

Figure 7.5 Conversion with a comma separator

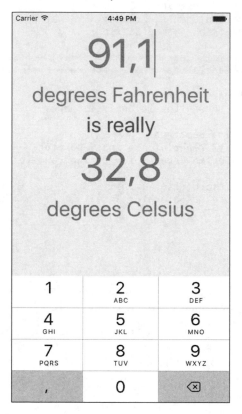

Base internationalization

When internationalizing, you ask the instance of **Locale** questions. But the **Locale** only has a few region-specific variables. This is where localization – creating application-specific substitutions for different region and language settings – comes into play. Localization usually involves either generating multiple copies of resources (like images, sounds, and interface files) for different regions and languages or creating and accessing *strings tables* (which you will see later in the chapter) to translate text into different languages.

Before you go through the process of localizing resources, you must understand how an iOS application handles localized resources.

When you build a target in Xcode, an application bundle is created. All of the resources that you added to the target in Xcode are copied into this bundle along with the executable itself. This bundle is represented at runtime by an instance of **Bundle** known as the *main bundle*. Many classes work with the **Bundle** to load resources.

Localizing a resource puts another copy of the resource in the application bundle. These resources are organized into language-specific directories, known as lproj directories. Each one of these directories is the name of the localization suffixed with lproj. For example, the American English localization is en_US, where en is the English language code and US is the United States of America region code, so the directory for American English resources is en_US.lproj. (The region can be omitted if you do not need to make regional distinctions in your resource files.) These language and region codes are standard on all platforms, not just iOS.

When a bundle is asked for the path of a resource file, it first looks at the root level of the bundle for a file of that name. If it does not find one, it looks at the locale and language settings of the device, finds the appropriate lproj directory, and looks for the file there. Thus, just by localizing resource files, your application will automatically load the correct file.

One option for localizing resource files is to create separate storyboard files and manually edit each string in each file. However, this approach does not scale well if you are planning multiple localizations. What happens when you add a new label or button to your localized storyboard? You have to add this view to the storyboard for every language. Not fun.

To simplify the process of localizing interface files, Xcode has a feature called *base internationalization*. Base internationalization creates the Base.lproj directory, which contains the main interface files. Localizing individual interface files can then be done by creating just the Localizable.strings files. It is still possible to create the full interface files, in case localization cannot be done by changing strings alone. However, with the help of Auto Layout, string replacement is sufficient for most localization needs. In the next section, you will use Auto Layout to prepare your layout for localization.

Preparing for localization

Open Main.storyboard and show the assistant editor either by clicking View → Assistant Editor → Show Assistant Editor or with the keyboard shortcut Option-Command-Return. From the jump bar dropdown, select Preview (Figure 7.6). The *preview assistant* allows you to easily see how your interface will look across screen sizes and orientations as well as between different localized languages.

Figure 7.6 Opening the preview assistant

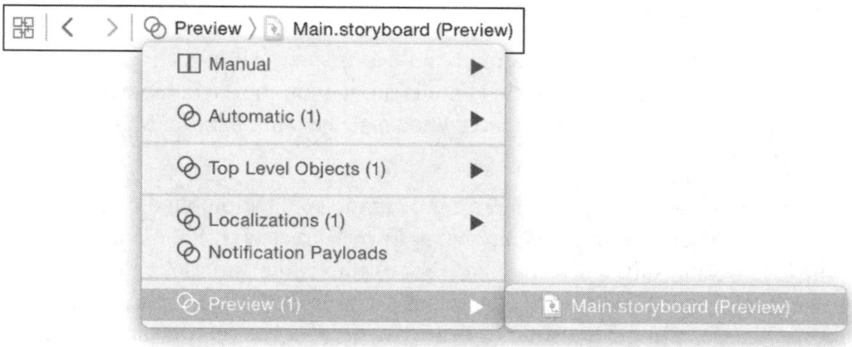

In the storyboard, select the Conversion View Controller to see its preview (Figure 7.7).

Figure 7.7 Preview assistant

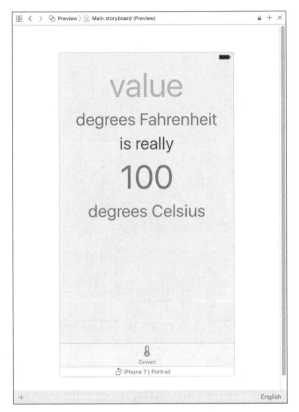

Notice the controls in the lower corners of the preview assistant. The + button on the left side allows you to add additional screen sizes to the preview canvas. This allows you to easily see how changes to your interface propagate across screen sizes and orientations simultaneously. The button on the right side allows you to select a language to preview this interface in.

(If your preview is for a configuration other than iPhone 7, use the + button to add this configuration. Then click on whatever preview opened by default and press the Delete key to remove it.)

You have not localized the application into another language yet, but Xcode supplies a *pseudolanguage* for you to use. Pseudolanguages help you internationalize your applications before receiving translations for all of your strings and assets. The built-in pseudolanguage, **Double-Length Pseudolanguage**, mimics languages that are more verbose by repeating whatever text string is in the text element. So, for example, "is really" becomes "is really is really."

Select the Language pop-up that says English and choose Double-Length Pseudolanguage. The labels all have their text doubled (Figure 7.8).

Figure 7.8 Doubled text strings

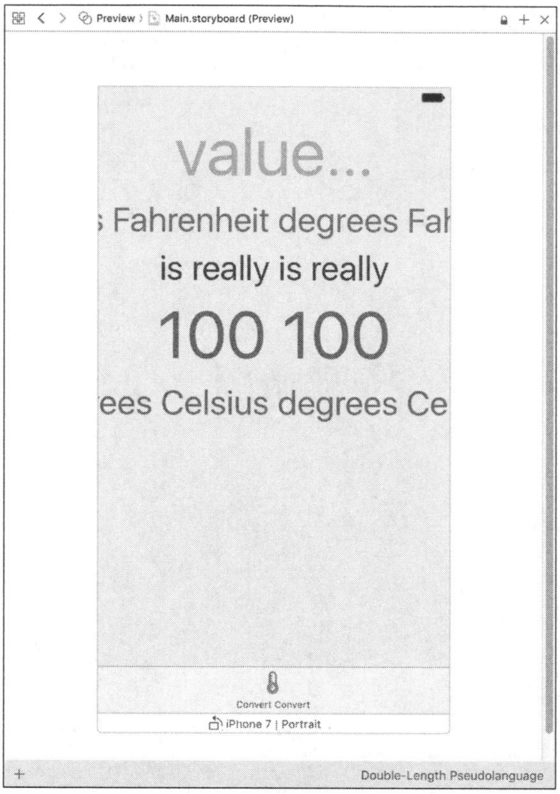

The double-length pseudolanguage reveals a problem immediately: The labels go off both the left and right edges of the screen, and you are unable to read the entire strings. The fix is to constrain all of the labels so that their leading and trailing edges stay within the margins of their superview. Then you will need to change the line count for the labels to 0, which tells the labels that their text should wrap to multiple lines if needed. You are going to start by fixing one label, then repeat the steps for the rest of the labels.

In the canvas, select the degrees Fahrenheit label. You are going to add constraints to this label in a new way. Control-drag from the label to the left side of the superview. When you do, a context-sensitive pop-up will appear giving you the constraints that make sense for this direction (Figure 7.9). Select Leading Space to Container Margin from the list.

Figure 7.9 Creating constraints by Control-dragging

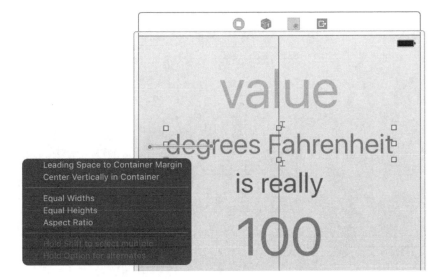

The direction that you drag influences which possible constraints are displayed. A horizontal drag will show horizontal constraints, and a vertical drag will show vertical constraints. A diagonal drag will show both horizontal and vertical constraints, which is useful for setting up many constraints simultaneously.

Now Control-drag from the degrees Fahrenheit label to the right side of the superview and select Trailing Space to Container Margin.

On their own, these constraints are not very good. They maintain the existing fixed distance between the leading and trailing edges of the label, as you can see in the preview assistant (Figure 7.10).

Figure 7.10 Preview assistant with new constraints

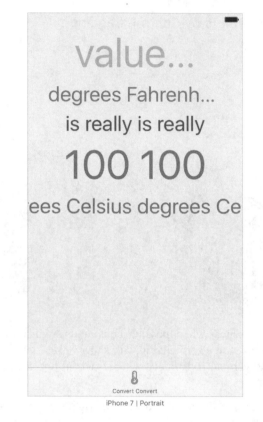

What you really want is for the distance between the label and the margins to be greater than or equal to 0. You can do this with *inequality constraints*.

Select the leading constraint by clicking on the I bar to the left of the label. Open its attributes inspector and change the Relation to Greater Than or Equal and the Constant to 0 (Figure 7.11).

Figure 7.11 Inequality constraint

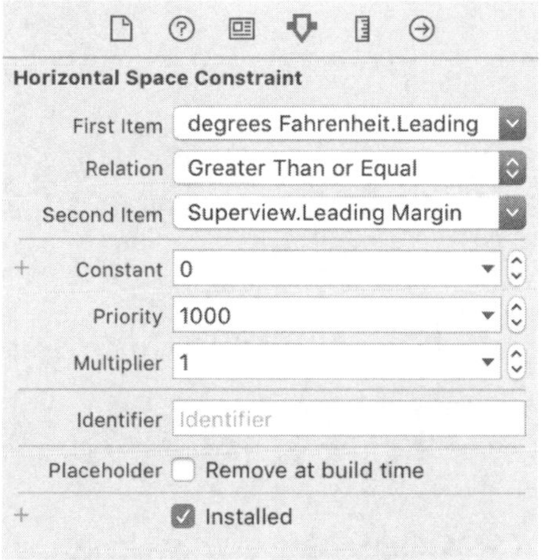

Do the same for the trailing constraint. Take a look at the preview assistant; the interface is looking better, but the label is still being truncated.

Select the label and open its attributes inspector. Change the Lines count to 0. Now take a look at the preview assistant; the label is no longer being truncated and instead the text flows to a second line. Because the other labels are each related to the label above them, they have automatically been moved down.

Repeat the steps above for the other labels. You will need to:

- Add a leading and trailing constraint to each label.

- Set the constraints' relation to Greater Than or Equal and the constant to 0. (A shortcut for editing a constraint is to double-click on it.)

- Change the label's line count to 0.

When you are done, the preview assistant with the double-length pseudolanguage will look like Figure 7.12.

Figure 7.12 Preview assistant with final constraints

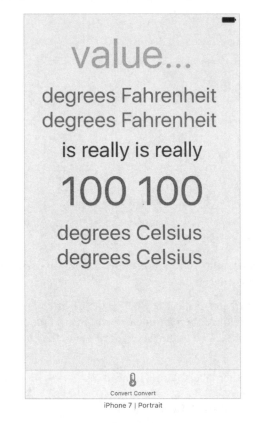

At this point, you are done with the preview assistant. You can close the assistant editor with the x in the top-right corner.

Localization

WorldTrotter is now internationalized – its interface is able to adapt to various languages and regions. Now it is time to localize the app – that is, to update the strings and resources in the application for a new language. In this section, you are going to localize the interface of WorldTrotter: the Main.storyboard file. You will create English and Spanish localizations, which will create two lproj directories in addition to the base one.

Start by localizing a storyboard file. Select Main.storyboard in the project navigator.

Open the *file inspector* by clicking the ▯ tab in the inspector selector or by using the keyboard shortcut Option-Command-1. Find the section in this inspector named Localization. Check the English box and make sure that the dropdown says Localizable Strings (Figure 7.13). This will create a strings table that you will use later to localize the application.

Figure 7.13 Localizing into English

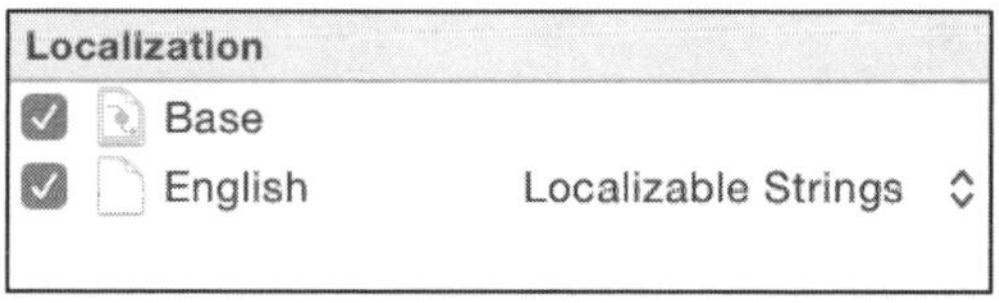

Next, in the project navigator, select the WorldTrotter project at the top. Then select WorldTrotter under the Project section in the side list, and make sure the Info tab is open. (If you cannot see the side list, you can open it using the Show projects and targets list button in the upper-left corner (Figure 7.14).)

Figure 7.14 Showing the project settings

Show/Hide projects and targets list

PROJECT

WorldTrotter

TARGETS

WorldTrotter

WorldTrotterTests

WorldTrotterUITests

Click the + button under Localizations and select Spanish (es). In the dialog, you can uncheck the LaunchScreen.storyboard file; keep the Main.storyboard file checked. Make sure that the reference language is Base and the file type is Localizable Strings. Click Finish. This creates an es.lproj folder and generates the Main.strings file in it that contains all the strings from the base interface file. The Localizations configuration should look like Figure 7.15.

Figure 7.15 Localizations

⊞ ‹ › 📄 WorldTrotter				
▣		Info	Build Settings	

PROJECT
- 📄 WorldTrotter

TARGETS
- 🅐 WorldTrotter
- 📁 WorldTrotterTests
- 📁 WorldTrotterUITests

▼ **Deployment Target**

iOS Deployment Target `10.0` ▾

▼ **Configurations**

Name		Based on Configuration File
▶ Debug		No Configurations Set
▶ Release		No Configurations Set

+ −

Use `Release` ▾ for command-line builds

▼ **Localizations**

Language	Resources
English — Development Language	2 Files Localized
Spanish	1 File Localized

+ −

☑ Use Base Internationalization

+ − ⊙ Filter

Look in the project navigator. Click the disclosure button next to Main.storyboard (Figure 7.16). Xcode moved the Main.storyboard file to the Base.lproj directory and created the Main.strings file in the es.lproj directory.

Figure 7.16 Localized storyboard in the project navigator

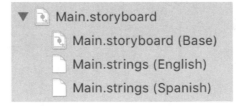

134

Click on the Spanish version of Main.strings. When this file opens, the text is not in Spanish. You have to translate localized files yourself; Xcode is not *that* smart.

Edit this file according to the following text. The numbers and order may be different in your file, but you can use the text and title fields in the comments to match up the translations.

```
/* Class = "UITabBarItem"; title = "Map"; ObjectID = "6xh-o5-yRt"; */
"6xh-o5-yRt.title" = "Map" "Mapa";

/* Class = "UILabel"; text = "degrees Celsius"; ObjectID = "7la-u7-mx6"; */
"7la-u7-mx6.text" = "degrees Celsius" "grados Celsius";

/* Class = "UILabel"; text = "degrees Fahrenheit"; ObjectID = "Dic-rs-P0S"; */
"Dic-rs-P0S.text" = "degrees Fahrenheit" "grados Fahrenheit";

/* Class = "UILabel"; text = "100"; ObjectID = "Eso-Wf-EyH"; */
"Eso-Wf-EyH.text" = "100";

/* Class = "UITextField"; placeholder = "value"; ObjectID = "On4-jV-YlY"; */
"On4-jV-YlY.placeholder" = "value" "valor";

/* Class = "UILabel"; text = "is really"; ObjectID = "wtF-xR-gbZ"; */
"wtF-xR-gbZ.text" = "is really" "es realmente";

/* Class = "UITabBarItem"; title = "Convert"; ObjectID = "zLY-50-CeX"; */
"zLY-50-CeX.title" = "Convert" "Convertir";
```

Now that you have finished localizing this storyboard file, let's test it out. First, there is a little Xcode glitch to be aware of: Sometimes Xcode ignores a resource file's changes when you build an application. To ensure that your application is being built from scratch, first delete it from your device or simulator. (Press and hold its icon in the launcher. When it starts to wiggle, tap the delete badge.) Relaunch Xcode. (Yes, exit and start it again.) Then, choose Clean from the Product menu. Finally, to be absolutely sure, press and hold the Option key while opening the Product menu and choose Clean Build Folder.... This will force the application to be entirely recompiled, rebundled, and reinstalled.

Open the active scheme pop-up and select Edit Scheme. Make sure Run is selected on the lefthand side and open the Options tab. Open the Application Language pop-up and select Spanish. Finally, confirm that Spain is still selected from the Application Region pop-up. Close the window.

Build and run the application. Make sure you are viewing the **ConversionViewController**, and you will see the interface in Spanish. Because you set the constraints on the labels to accommodate different lengths of text, they resize themselves appropriately (Figure 7.17).

Figure 7.17 Spanish **ConversionViewController**

NSLocalizedString and strings tables

In many places in your applications, you create **String** instances dynamically or display string literals to the user. To display translated versions of these strings, you must create a strings table. A strings table is a file containing a list of key-value pairs for all of the strings that your application uses and their associated translations. It is a resource file that you add to your application, but you do not need to do a lot of work to get data from it.

You might use a string in your code like this:

```
let greeting = "Hello!"
```

To internationalize the string in your code, you replace literal strings with the function **NSLocalizedString(_:comment:)**.

```
let greeting = NSLocalizedString("Hello!", comment: "The greeting for the user")
```

This function takes two arguments: a key and a comment that describes the string's use. The key is the lookup value in a strings table. At runtime, **NSLocalizedString(_:comment:)** will look through the strings tables bundled with your application for a table that matches the user's language settings. Then, in that table, the function gets the translated string that matches the key.

Now you are going to internationalize the strings that the **MapViewController** displays in its segmented control. In MapViewController.swift, locate the **loadView()** method and update the initializer for the segmented control to use localized strings.

```
override func loadView() {
    // Create a map view
    mapView = MKMapView()

    // Set it as *the* view of this view controller
    view = mapView

    let segmentedControl
          = UISegmentedControl(items: ["Standard", "Satellite", "Hybrid"])

    let standardString = NSLocalizedString("Standard", comment: "Standard map view")
    let satelliteString
          = NSLocalizedString("Satellite", comment: "Satellite map view")
    let hybridString = NSLocalizedString("Hybrid", comment: "Hybrid map view")
    let segmentedControl
          = UISegmentedControl(items: [standardString, satelliteString, hybridString])
```

Once you have files that have been internationalized with the **NSLocalizedString(_:comment:)** function, you can generate strings tables with a command-line application.

Open the Terminal app. This is a Unix terminal; it is used to run command-line tools. You want to navigate to the location of MapViewController.swift. If you have never used the Terminal app before, here is a handy trick. In Terminal, type the following:

```
cd
```

followed by a space. (Do not press Return yet.)

Next, open Finder and locate MapViewController.swift and the folder that contains it. Drag the icon of that folder onto the Terminal window. Terminal will fill out the path for you. It will look something like this:

```
cd /Users/cbkeur/iOSDevelopment/WorldTrotter/WorldTrotter/
```

Press Return. The current working directory of Terminal is now this directory.

Use the terminal command ls to print out the contents of the working directory and confirm that MapViewController.swift is in that list.

To generate the strings table, enter the following into Terminal and press Return:

```
genstrings MapViewController.swift
```

The resulting file, Localizable.strings, contains the strings from **MapViewController**. Drag this new file from Finder into the project navigator (or use the File → Add Files to "WorldTrotter"... menu item). When the application is compiled, this resource will be copied into the main bundle.

Open `Localizable.strings`. The file should look something like this:

```
/* Hybrid map view */
"Hybrid" = "Hybrid";

/* Satellite map view */
"Satellite" = "Satellite";

/* Standard map view */
"Standard" = "Standard";
```

Notice that the comment above your string is the second argument you supplied to the **NSLocalizedString** function. Even though the function does not require the comment argument, including it will make your localizing life easier.

Now that you have created `Localizable.strings`, you need to localize it in Xcode. Open its file inspector and click the Localize... button in the utility area. Make sure Base is selected from the pop-up and click Localize. Add the Spanish and English localization by checking the box next to each language.

In the project navigator, click on the disclosure triangle that now appears next to `Localizable.strings`. Open the Spanish version. The string on the lefthand side is the *key* that is passed to the **NSLocalizedString(_:comment:)** function, and the string on the righthand side is what is returned. Change the text on the righthand side to the Spanish translations shown below. (To type an accented character, such as "é," press and hold the appropriate character on your keyboard and then press the appropriate number from the pop-up.)

```
/* Hybrid map view */
"Hybrid" = "Hybrid" "Híbrido";

/* Satellite map view */
"Satellite" = "Satellite" "Satélite";

/* Standard map view */
"Standard" = "Standard" "Estándar";
```

Build and run the application again. Now all those strings, including the titles in the segmented control, will appear in Spanish (Figure 7.18). If they do not, you might need to delete the application, clean your project, and rebuild. (Or check your scheme language setting.)

Figure 7.18 Spanish **MapViewController**

Internationalization and localization are very important for your app to reach the largest audience. Additionally, as you saw early in this chapter, your app might not work for some users if you have not properly internationalized it. You will internationalize (but not localize) your projects in the rest of this book.

Over the past five chapters, you have built a rather impressive application that allows the user to convert between Celsius and Fahrenheit as well as display a map in a few different ways. Not only does this application scale well on all iPhone screen sizes, but it is also localized into another language. Congratulations!

Bronze Challenge: Another Localization

Practice makes perfect. Localize WorldTrotter for another language. Use a translation website if you need help with the language.

For the More Curious: Bundle's Role in Internationalization

The real work of taking advantage of localizations is done for you by the class **Bundle**. A bundle represents a location on the filesystem that groups the compiled code and resources together. The "main bundle" is another name for the application bundle, which contains all of the resources and the executable for the application. You will learn more about the application bundle in Chapter 16.

When an application is built, all of the lproj directories are copied into the main bundle. Figure 7.19 shows the main bundle for WorldTrotter (with some additional images added to the project).

Figure 7.19 Application bundle

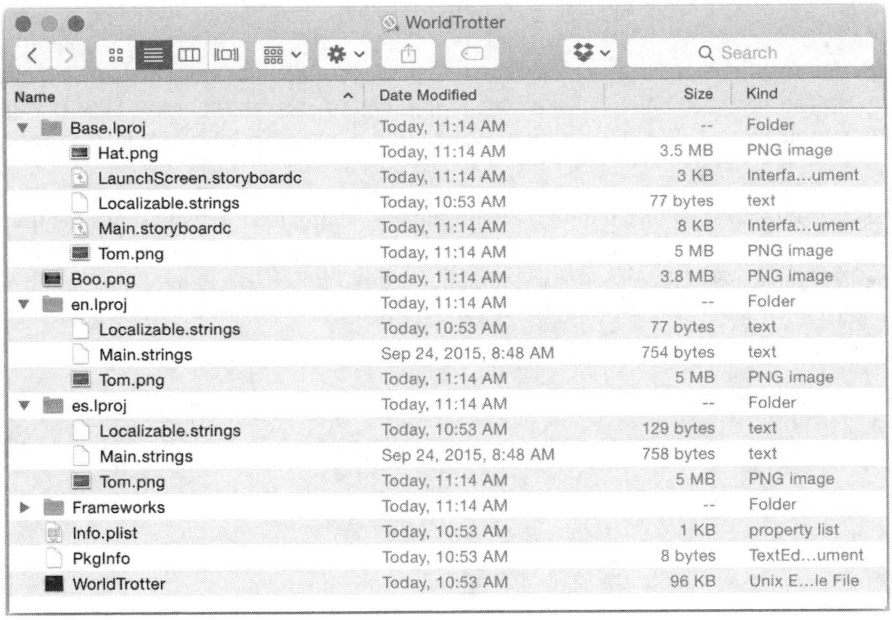

Bundle knows how to search through localization directories for every type of resource using the instance method **url(forResource:withExtension:)**. When you want a path to a resource bundled with your application, you call this method on the main bundle. Here is an example using the resource file Boo.png:

```
let path = Bundle.main.url(forResource:"Boo", withExtension: "png")
```

When attempting to locate the resource, the bundle first checks to see whether the resource exists at the top level of the application bundle. If so, it returns the full URL to that file. If not, the bundle gets the device's language and region settings and looks in the appropriate lproj directories to construct the

URL. If it still does not find it, it looks within the Base.lproj directory. Finally, if no file is found, it returns nil.

In the application bundle shown in Figure 7.19, if the user's language is set to Spanish, **Bundle** will find Boo.png at the top level, Tom.png in es.lproj, and Hat.png in Base.lproj.

When you add a new localization to your project, Xcode does not automatically remove the resources from the top-level directory. This is why you must delete and clean an application when you localize a file – otherwise, the previous unlocalized file will still be in the root level of the application bundle. Even though there are lproj folders in the application bundle, the bundle finds the top-level file first and returns its URL.

For the More Curious: Importing and Exporting as XLIFF

The industry-standard format for localization data is the XLIFF data type, which stands for XML Localisation Interchange File Format (and XML stands for Extensible Markup Language). When working with translators, you will often send them an XLIFF file containing the data in the application to localize, and they will give you back a localized XLIFF file for you to import.

Xcode natively supports importing and exporting localization data in XLIFF. The exporting process will take care of finding and exporting the localized strings within the project, which you previously did manually using the genstrings tool.

To export the localizable strings in XLIFF, select the project (WorldTrotter) in the project navigator. Then select the Editor menu, and then Export For Localization.... On the next screen, you can choose whether to export existing translations (which is probably a good idea so the translator does not do redundant work) and which languages you would like exported (Figure 7.20).

Figure 7.20 Exporting localization data as XLIFF

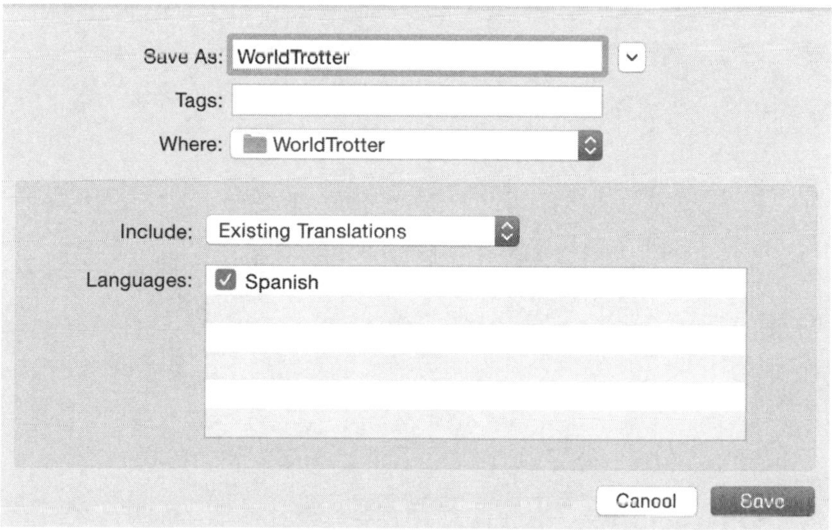

To import localizations, select the project (WorldTrotter) in the project navigator. Then select Editor → Import Localizations.... After choosing a file, you will be able to confirm the updates before you import.

8

Controlling Animations

The word "animation" is derived from a Latin word that means "the act of bringing to life." In your applications, animations can smoothly bring interface elements onscreen or into focus, they can draw the user's attention to an actionable item, and they can give clear indications of how your app is responding to the user's actions. In this chapter, you will return to your Quiz app and use a variety of animation techniques to bring it to life.

Before updating Quiz, though, let's take a look at what can be animated by looking at the documentation. To open the documentation, open Xcode's Help menu and select Documentation and API Reference. This will open the documentation in a new window.

With the documentation open, use the search bar at the top to search for "UIView." Under API Reference in the search results, click UIView to open the class reference, then scroll down to the section titled *Animations*. The documentation gives some animation recommendations (which we will follow in this book) and lists the properties on **UIView** that can be animated (Figure 8.1).

Figure 8.1 **UIView** animation documentation

UIView

Animations

Changes to several view properties can be animated—that is, changing the property creates an animation that conveys the change to the user over a short period of time. The `UIView` class does most of the work of performing the actual animations but you must still indicate which property changes you want to be animated. There are two different ways to initiate animations:

- In iOS 4 and later, use the block-based animation methods. (Recommended)
- Use the begin/commit animation methods.

The block-based animation methods (such as `animate(withDuration:animations:)`) greatly simplify the creation of animations. With one method call, you specify the animations to be performed and the options for the animation. However, block-based animations are available only in iOS 4 and later. If your application runs on earlier versions of iOS, you must use the `beginAnimations(_:context:)` and `commitAnimations()` class methods to mark the beginning and ending of your animations.

The following properties of the `UIView` class are animatable:

- `frame`
- `bounds`
- `center`
- `transform`
- `alpha`

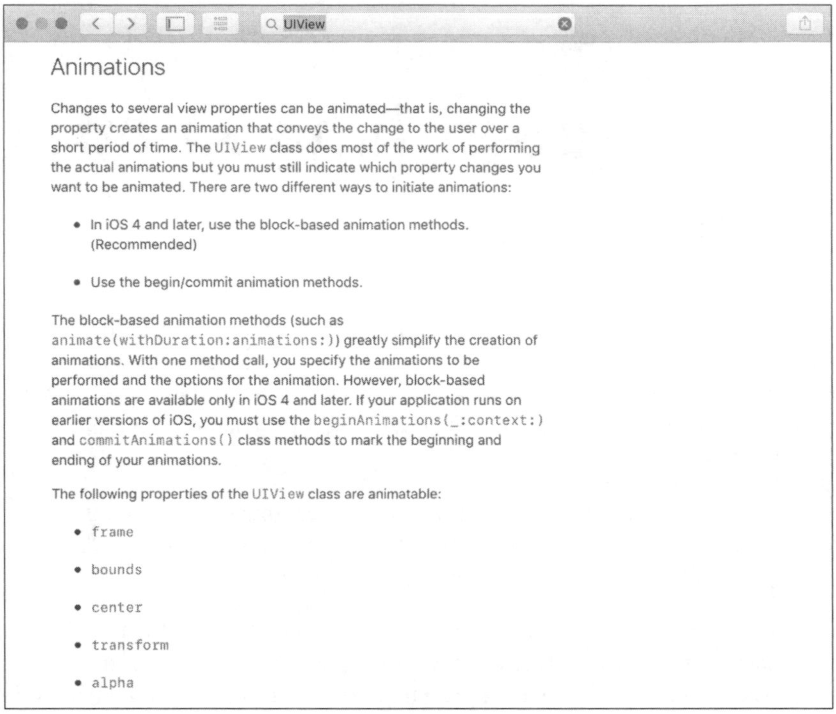

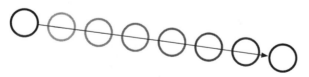

Basic Animations

The documentation is always a good starting point for learning about any iOS technology. With that little bit of information under your belt, let's go ahead and add some animations to Quiz. The first type of animation you are going to use is the *basic animation*. A basic animation animates between a start value and an end value (Figure 8.2).

Figure 8.2 Basic animation

The first animation you are going to add will animate the `alpha` value (the degree of transparency) of the question label associated with **`ViewController`**. When the user advances to the next question, you will use an animation to fade in the label. There are class methods on **`UIView`** that will allow you to accomplish this. The simplest **`UIView`** animation method is:

```
class func animate(withDuration duration: TimeInterval, animations: () -> Void)
```

This class method takes two arguments: a `duration` of type **`TimeInterval`** (which is an alias for a **`Double`**) and an `animations` variable that is a closure.

Closures

A *closure* is a discrete bundle of functionality that can be passed around your code. Closures are a lot like functions and methods. In fact, functions and methods are just special cases of closures.

Closures have a lightweight syntax that allows them to be easily passed in as arguments to functions and methods. A closure can even be the return type of a function or method. In this section, you will use a closure to specify the animations that you want to occur.

The signature of a closure is a comma-separated list of arguments within parentheses followed by a return arrow and the return type:

```
(arguments) -> return type
```

Notice that this syntax is similar to the syntax for functions:

```
func functionName(arguments) -> return type
```

Now take a look again at the closure signature that the animations argument expects:

```
class func animate(withDuration duration: TimeInterval, animations: () -> Void)
```

This closure takes in no arguments and does not return anything. (You will also see this return type expressed as (), which means the same thing as Void.)

The closure signature is pretty straightforward and familiar, but how do you declare a closure in code? Closure syntax takes the following form:

```
{ (arguments) -> return type in
    // code
}
```

You write a closure expression inside braces ({}). The closure's arguments are listed inside parentheses immediately after the opening brace. A closure's return type comes after the parameters and uses the regular syntax. The keyword in is used to separate the closure's arguments and return type from the statements inside of its body.

Open Quiz.xcodeproj. In ViewController.swift, add a new method to handle the animations and declare a closure constant that takes in no arguments and does not return anything.

```
func animateLabelTransitions() {

    let animationClosure = { () -> Void in

    }
}
```

Now you have a constant that references a chunk of functionality. Currently, however, this closure does not actually *do* anything. Add functionality to the closure that sets the alpha of the questionLabel to 1. Then, pass this closure as an argument to **animate(withDuration:animations:)**.

```
func animateLabelTransitions() {

    let animationClosure = { () -> Void in
        self.questionLabel.alpha = 1
    }

    // Animate the alpha
    UIView.animate(withDuration: 0.5, animations: animationClosure)
}
```

The questionLabel already has an alpha of 1 when it comes onscreen, so you will not see anything animate if you build and run. To address this, override **viewWillAppear(_:)** to reset the questionLabel's alpha to 0 each time the **ViewController**'s view comes onscreen.

```
override func viewWillAppear(_ animated: Bool) {
    super.viewWillAppear(animated)

    // Set the label's initial alpha
    questionLabel.alpha = 0
}
```

The code above works great, but you can make it more concise. Update the code.

```
func animateLabelTransitions() {

    let animationClosure = { () -> Void in
        self.questionLabel.alpha = 1
    }

    // Animate the alpha
    UIView.animate(withDuration: 0.5, animations: animationClosure)
    UIView.animate(withDuration: 0.5, animations: {
        self.questionLabel.alpha = 1
    })
}
```

You have made two changes: First, you are passing in the closure *anonymously* (i.e., passing it directly into the method instead of assigning it to a variable or constant). Second, you have removed the type information because the closure can infer this from the context.

Now call the **animateLabelTransitions()** method whenever the user taps the Next Question button.

```
@IBAction func showNextQuestion(_ sender: UIButton) {
    currentQuestionIndex += 1
    if currentQuestionIndex == questions.count {
        currentQuestionIndex = 0
    }

    let question: String = questions[currentQuestionIndex]
    questionLabel.text = question
    answerLabel.text = "???"

    animateLabelTransitions()
}
```

Build and run the application. When you tap on the Next Question button, the label will fade into view. Animations provide a less jarring user experience than having views just pop into existence.

Another Label

The animation works great the first time the Next Question button is pressed, but there is no visible animation on subsequent button presses because the label already has an alpha value of 1. In this section, you are going to add another label to the interface. When the Next Question button is pressed, the existing label will fade out while the new label (with the text of the next question) will fade in.

At the top of `ViewController.swift`, replace your declaration of a single label with two labels.

```
@IBOutlet var questionLabel: UILabel!
@IBOutlet var currentQuestionLabel: UILabel!
@IBOutlet var nextQuestionLabel: UILabel!
@IBOutlet var answerLabel: UILabel!
```

Xcode flags four places where you need to replace `questionLabel` with one of your new labels. Update **viewDidLoad()** to use `currentQuestionLabel`. Update **viewWillAppear(_:)** and **showNextQuestion(_:)** to use `nextQuestionLabel`.

```
func viewDidLoad() {
    super.viewDidLoad()
    questionLabel.text = questions[currentQuestionIndex]
    currentQuestionLabel.text = questions[currentQuestionIndex]
}

override func viewWillAppear(_ animated: Bool) {
    super.viewWillAppear(animated)

    // Set the label's initial alpha
    questionLabel.alpha = 0
    nextQuestionLabel.alpha = 0
}

@IBAction func showNextQuestion(_ sender: UIButton) {
    currentQuestionIndex += 1
    if currentQuestionIndex == questions.count {
        currentQuestionIndex = 0
    }

    let question: String = questions[currentQuestionIndex]
    questionLabel.text = question
    nextQuestionLabel.text = question
    answerLabel.text = "???"

    animateLabelTransitions()
}
```

Now update **animateLabelTransitions()** to animate the alpha of the two labels. You will fade out the `currentQuestionLabel` and fade in the `nextQuestionLabel` simultaneously.

```
func animateLabelTransitions() {

    // Animate the alpha
    UIView.animate(withDuration: 0.5, animations: {
        self.questionLabel.alpha = 1
        self.currentQuestionLabel.alpha = 0
        self.nextQuestionLabel.alpha = 1
    })
}
```

Open Main.storyboard. Now that the code has been updated for these two labels, you need to make the connections. Control-click on the View Controller to see a list of connections. Notice that the existing questionLabel is still present with a yellow warning sign next to it (Figure 8.3). Click on the x to remove this connection.

Figure 8.3 Missing connection

Connect the currentQuestionLabel outlet to the existing question label by dragging from the circle next to currentQuestionLabel to the label on the canvas.

Now drag a new Label onto the interface and position it next to the existing question label. Connect the nextQuestionLabel to this new label.

You want this label to be in the same position as the existing question label. As you have likely guessed, the best way to achieve this is through constraints. Control-drag from the nextQuestionLabel to the currentQuestionLabel and select Top. Then Control-drag upward from the nextQuestionLabel to its superview and select Center Horizontally in Container.

At this point, nextQuestionLabel is misplaced. Select the label, open the Resolve Auto Layout Issues menu, and select Update Frames. The labels will now be on top of one another.

Build and run the application. Tap the Next Question button and you will see a graceful fade for both of the labels.

If you tap it again, however, no fade occurs because the nextQuestionLabel already has an alpha of 1. To fix this, you will swap the references to the two labels. When the animation completes, the currentQuestionLabel needs to be set to the onscreen label, and the nextQuestionLabel needs to be set to the offscreen label. You will use a *completion handler* on the animation to accomplish this.

Animation Completion

The method **animate(withDuration:animations:)** returns immediately. That is, it starts the animation, but it does not wait for the animation to complete. What if you want to know when an animation completes? For instance, you might want to chain animations together or update another object when the animation completes. To know when the animation finishes, pass a closure for the completion argument. You will use this opportunity to swap the two label references.

In ViewController.swift, update **animateLabelTransitions()** to use the **UIView** animation method that has the most parameters, including one that takes in a completion closure.

```
func animateLabelTransitions() {

    // Animate the alpha
    UIView.animate(withDuration: 0.5, animations: {
        self.currentQuestionLabel.alpha = 0
        self.nextQuestionLabel.alpha = 1
    })
    UIView.animate(withDuration: 0.5,
        delay: 0,
        options: [],
        animations: {
            self.currentQuestionLabel.alpha = 0
            self.nextQuestionLabel.alpha = 1
        },
        completion: { _ in
            swap(&self.currentQuestionLabel,
                &self.nextQuestionLabel)
    })
}
```

The delay indicates how long the system should wait before triggering the animation. We will talk about the options later in this chapter. For now, you are passing in an empty array.

In the completion closure, you need to tell the system that what used to be the currentQuestionLabel is now the nextQuestionLabel and that what used to be the nextQuestionLabel is now the currentQuestionLabel. To accomplish this, you use the **swap(_:_:)** function, which accepts two references and swaps them.

Build and run the application. Now you are able to transition between all of the questions.

Animating Constraints

In this section, you are going to extend your animation to have the nextQuestionLabel property fly in from the left side of the screen and the currentQuestionLabel fly out to the right side of the screen when the user presses the Next Question button. In doing so, you will learn how to animate constraints.

First, you need a reference to the constraints that need to be modified. So far, all of your @IBOutlets have been to view objects. But outlets are not limited to views – in fact, any object in your interface file can have an outlet, including constraints.

At the top of `ViewController.swift`, declare two outlets for the two labels' centering constraints.

```
@IBOutlet var currentQuestionLabel: UILabel!
@IBOutlet var currentQuestionLabelCenterXConstraint: NSLayoutConstraint!
@IBOutlet var nextQuestionLabel: UILabel!
@IBOutlet var nextQuestionLabelCenterXConstraint: NSLayoutConstraint!
@IBOutlet var answerLabel: UILabel!
```

Now open `Main.storyboard`. You want to connect these two outlets to their respective constraints. The easiest way to accomplish this is using the document outline. Click the disclosure triangle next to Constraints in the document outline and locate Current Question Label CenterX Constraint. Control-drag from the View Controller to that constraint (Figure 8.4) and select the correct outlet. Do the same for Next Question Label CenterX Constraint.

Figure 8.4 Connecting a constraint outlet

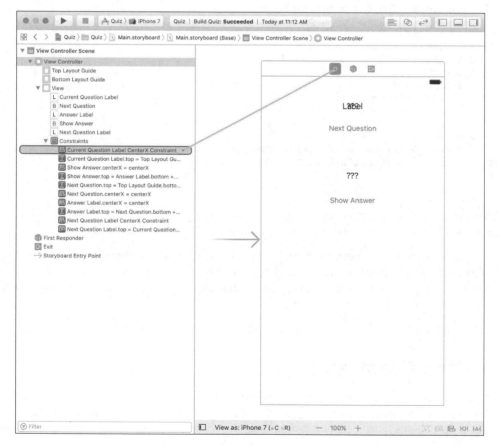

Currently, the Next Question button and the answer subviews have their center X constrained to the center X of the `currentQuestionLabel`. When you implement the animation for this label to slide offscreen, the other subviews will go with it. This is not what you want.

Select the constraint that centers the X value of the Next Question button to the `currentQuestionLabel` and delete it. Then Control-drag upward from the Next Question button to its superview and select Center Horizontally in Container.

Next, you want the two question labels to be one screen width apart. The center of nextQuestionLabel will be half of the screen width to the left of the view. The center of the currentQuestionLabel will be at its current position, centered in the screen.

When the animation is triggered, both labels will move a full screen width to the right, placing the nextQuestionLabel at the center of the screen and the currentQuestionLabel half a screen width to the right of the screen (Figure 8.5).

Figure 8.5 Sliding the labels

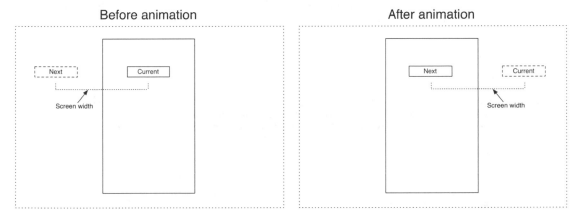

To accomplish this, when the view of **ViewController** is loaded, you need to move the nextQuestionLabel to its offscreen position.

In ViewController.swift, add a new method and call it from **viewDidLoad()**.

```
func viewDidLoad() {
    super.viewDidLoad()
    currentQuestionLabel.text = questions[currentQuestionIndex]

    updateOffScreenLabel()
}

func updateOffScreenLabel() {
    let screenWidth = view.frame.width
    nextQuestionLabelCenterXConstraint.constant = -screenWidth
}
```

Now you want to animate the labels to go from left to right. Animating constraints is a bit different than animating other properties. If you modify the constant of a constraint within an animation block, no animation will occur. Why? After a constraint is modified, the system needs to recalculate the frames for all of the related views in the hierarchy to accommodate this change. It would be expensive for any constraint change to trigger this automatically. (Imagine if you updated quite a few constraints – you would not want it to recalculate the frames after each change.) So you must ask the system to recalculate the frames when you are done. To do this, you call the method **layoutIfNeeded()** on a view. This will force the view to lay out its subviews based on the latest constraints.

In ViewController.swift, update **animateLabelTransitions()** to change the constraint constants and then force the layout of the views.

```
func animateLabelTransitions() {

    // Animate the alpha
    // and the center X constraints
    let screenWidth = view.frame.width
    self.nextQuestionLabelCenterXConstraint.constant = 0
    self.currentQuestionLabelCenterXConstraint.constant += screenWidth

    UIView.animate(withDuration: 0.5,
        delay: 0,
        options: [],
        animations: {
            self.currentQuestionLabel.alpha = 0
            self.nextQuestionLabel.alpha = 1

            self.view.layoutIfNeeded()
        },
        completion: { _ in
            swap(&self.currentQuestionLabel,
                &self.nextQuestionLabel)
    })
}
```

Finally, in the completion handler, you need to swap the two constraint outlets and reset the nextQuestionLabel to be on the left side of the screen.

```
func animateLabelTransitions() {

    // Animate the alpha
    // and the center X constraints
    let screenWidth = view.frame.width
    self.nextQuestionLabelCenterXConstraint.constant = 0
    self.currentQuestionLabelCenterXConstraint.constant += screenWidth

    UIView.animate(withDuration: 0.5,
        delay: 0,
        options: [],
        animations: {
            self.currentQuestionLabel.alpha = 0
            self.nextQuestionLabel.alpha = 1

            self.view.layoutIfNeeded()
        },
        completion: { _ in
            swap(&self.currentQuestionLabel,
                &self.nextQuestionLabel)
            swap(&self.currentQuestionLabelCenterXConstraint,
                &self.nextQuestionLabelCenterXConstraint)

            self.updateOffScreenLabel()
    })
}
```

Build and run the application. The animation works almost perfectly. The labels slide on and off the screen, and the alpha value animates appropriately as well.

There is one small problem to fix, but it can be a bit difficult to see. To see it more easily, turn on Slow Animations from the Debug menu in the simulator (Command-T). The width of all of the labels gets animated (to see this on the answerLabel, you need to click the Show Answer button). This is because the intrinsic content size changes when the text changes. The fix is to force the view to lay out its subviews before the animation begins. This will update the frames of all three labels to accommodate the next text before the alpha and sliding animations start.

Update **animateLabelTransitions()** to force the view to lay out its subviews before the animation begins.

```
func animateLabelTransitions() {

    // Force any outstanding layout changes to occur
    view.layoutIfNeeded()

    // Animate the alpha
    // and the center X constraints
    let screenWidth = view.frame.width
    self.nextQuestionLabelCenterXConstraint.constant = 0
    self.currentQuestionLabelCenterXConstraint.constant += screenWidth

    UIView.animate(withDuration: 0.5,
        delay: 0,
        options: [],
        animations: {
            self.currentQuestionLabel.alpha = 0
            self.nextQuestionLabel.alpha = 1

            self.view.layoutIfNeeded()
        },
        completion: { _ in
            swap(&self.currentQuestionLabel,
                &self.nextQuestionLabel)
            swap(&self.currentQuestionLabelCenterXConstraint,
                &self.nextQuestionLabelCenterXConstraint)

            self.updateOffScreenLabel()
    })
}
```

Build and run the application and cycle through some questions and answers. The minor animation issue is now resolved.

Timing Functions

The acceleration of the animation is controlled by its timing function. By default, animations use an ease-in/ease-out timing function. To use a driving analogy, this would mean the driver accelerates smoothly from rest to a constant speed and then gradually slows down at the end, coming to rest.

Other timing functions include linear (a constant speed from beginning to end), ease-in (accelerating to a constant speed and then ending abruptly), and ease-out (beginning at full speed and then slowing down at the end).

In ViewController.swift, update the animation in animateLabelTransitions() to use a linear timing function.

```
UIView.animate(withDuration: 0.5,
    delay: 0,
    options: [.curveLinear],
    animations: {
        self.currentQuestionLabel.alpha = 0
        self.nextQuestionLabel.alpha = 1

        self.view.layoutIfNeeded()
    },
    completion: { _ in
        swap(&self.currentQuestionLabel,
            &self.nextQuestionLabel)
        swap(&self.currentQuestionLabelCenterXConstraint,
            &self.nextQuestionLabelCenterXConstraint)

        self.updateOffScreenLabel()
})
```

Now, as opposed to using the default ease-in/ease-out animation curve, the animation will have a linear animation curve. Build and run the application. The difference is subtle, but it is noticeable if you watch for it.

The options parameter takes in a **UIViewAnimationOptions** argument. Why is this argument in square brackets? There are many options for an animation in addition to the timing function. Because of this, you need a way of specifying more than one option – an array. **UIViewAnimationOptions** conforms to the **OptionSet** protocol, which allows you to group multiple values using an array.

Here are some of the possible animation options that you can pass into the options parameter.

Animation curve options

Control the acceleration of the animation. Possible values are:
- UIViewAnimationOptions.curveEaseInOut
- UIViewAnimationOptions.curveEaseIn
- UIViewAnimationOptions.curveEaseOut
- UIViewAnimationOptions.curveLinear

UIViewAnimationOptions.allowUserInteraction

By default, views cannot be interacted with when animating. Specifying this option overrides the default. This can be useful for repeating animations, such as a pulsing view.

UIViewAnimationOptions.repeat

Repeats the animation indefinitely; often paired with the UIViewAnimationOptions.autoreverse option.

UIViewAnimationOptions.autoreverse

Runs the animation forward and then backward, returning the view to its initial state.

Be sure to check out the *Constants* section of the *UIView Class Reference* to see all of the possible options.

Bronze Challenge: Spring Animations

iOS has a powerful physics engine built in. An easy way to harness this power is by using a spring animation.

```
// UIView

class func animate(withDuration duration: TimeInterval,
    delay: TimeInterval,
    usingSpringWithDamping dampingRatio: CGFloat,
    initialSpringVelocity velocity: CGFloat,
    options: UIViewAnimationOptions,
    animations: () -> Void,
    completion: ((Bool) -> Void)?)
```

Use this method to have the two labels animate on and off the screen in a spring-like fashion. Refer to the **UIView** documentation to understand each of the arguments.

Silver Challenge: Layout Guides

If you rotate into landscape, the nextQuestionLabel becomes visible. Instead of hardcoding the spacing constraint's constant, use an instance of **UILayoutGuide** to space the two labels apart. This layout guide should have a width constraint equal to the **ViewController**'s view to ensure that the nextQuestionLabel remains offscreen when not animating.

9

Debugging

As you write an application, you will inevitably make mistakes. Even worse, from time to time you will have errors in your application's design. Xcode's debugger (called LLDB) is the fundamental tool that will help you find these bugs and fix them. This chapter gives you an overview of Xcode's debugger and its basic functions.

A Buggy Project

You will use a simple project to guide you through your exploration of the Xcode debugger. Open Xcode and create a new project for an iOS single view application. Name the project Buggy and make sure Language is set to Swift, Devices is set to iPhone, and Use Core Data, Include Unit Tests, and Include UI Tests are all unchecked (Figure 9.1). Click Next.

Figure 9.1 Configuring Buggy

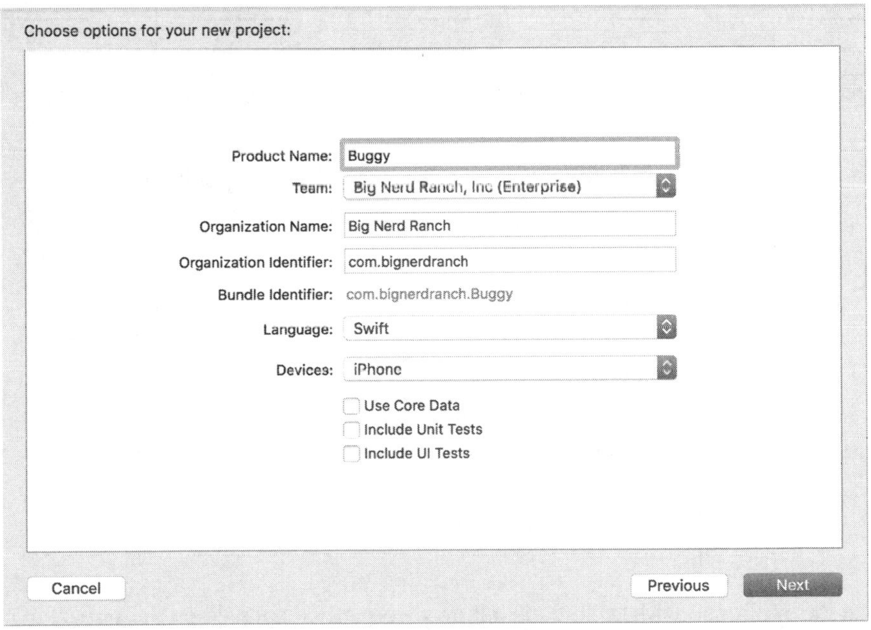

As you write this application's code, keep in mind that it is a buggy project. You may be asked to type code you know is incorrect. Do not fix it as you type it in; those errors will help you learn about debugging techniques.

To get started, open Main.storyboard and drag a **UIButton** onto the View Controller Scene. Double-click on the new button and change its title to "Tap me!" With the button still selected, open the Auto Layout Align menu. Check Horizontally in Container and click Add 1 Constraint. Next, open the Add New Constraints menu. Pin the distance to the top of the container, check the Width and Height boxes, and click Add 3 Constraints.

Your results should look something like Figure 9.2, but do not worry if your actual dimensions and spacing are a bit different.

Figure 9.2 Auto Layout constraints for the Tap me! button

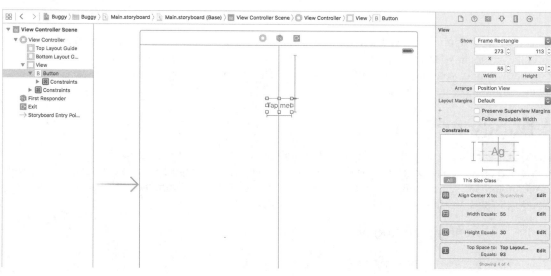

Now you need to implement a method for this button to trigger and then connect it to the button in the storyboard.

Open ViewController.swift and implement an action method for the button to trigger.

```
@IBAction func buttonTapped(_ sender: UIButton) {

}
```

Now open Main.storyboard and Control-drag from the button to the View Controller and connect it to the buttonTapped: option.

Back in ViewController.swift, add a **print()** statement to the **buttonTapped(_:)** method to confirm that the method is called in response to a button tap.

```
@IBAction func buttonTapped(_ sender: UIButton) {
    print("Called buttonTapped(_:)")
}
```

Build and run the application. Make sure the button is correctly displayed on the screen and that you can tap it. Also confirm that the Called buttonTapped(_:) message prints to the console when you tap the button.

Debugging Basics

The simplest debugging uses the console. Interpreting the information provided in the console when an application crashes or intentionally logging information to the console allows you to observe and zero in on your code's failures. Let's look at some examples of how the console can support your quest for bug-free code.

Interpreting console messages

Time to add some mayhem to the Buggy project. Suppose that after considering the UI for a while, you decide that a switch would be a better control than a button. Open `ViewController.swift` and make the following changes to the **buttonTapped(_:)** method.

```
@IBAction func buttonTapped(_ sender: UIButton) {
@IBAction func switchToggled(_ sender: UISwitch) {
    print("Called buttonTapped(_:)")
}
```

You renamed the action to reflect the change of control and you changed the type of `sender` to **UISwitch**.

Unfortunately, you forgot to update the interface in `Main.storyboard`. Build and run the application, then tap on the button. The application will crash and you will see a message logged to the console similar to the one on the next page. (We have truncated some of the information to fit on the page.)

```
2016-08-24 12:52:38.463 Buggy[1961:47078] -[Buggy.ViewController buttonTapped:]:
unrecognized selector sent to instance 0x7ff6db708870
2016-08-24 12:52:38.470 Buggy[1961:47078] *** Terminating app due to uncaught
exception 'NSInvalidArgumentException',
reason: '-[Buggy.ViewController buttonTapped:]: unrecognized selector sent to
instance 0x7ff6db708870'
*** First throw call stack:
(
    0   CoreFoundation      [...] __exceptionPreprocess + 171
    1   libobjc.A.dylib     [...] objc_exception_throw + 48
    2   CoreFoundation      [...] -[NSObject(NSObject) doesNotRecognizeSelector:] + 132
    3   CoreFoundation      [...] ___forwarding___ + 1013
    4   CoreFoundation      [...] _CF_forwarding_prep_0 + 120
    5   UIKit               [...] -[UIApplication sendAction:to:from:forEvent:] + 83
    6   UIKit               [...] -[UIControl sendAction:to:forEvent:] + 67
    7   UIKit               [...] -[UIControl _sendActionsForEvents:withEvent:] + 444
    8   UIKit               [...] -[UIControl touchesEnded:withEvent:] + 668
    9   UIKit               [...] -[UIWindow _sendTouchesForEvent:] + 2747
   10   UIKit               [...] -[UIWindow sendEvent:] + 4011
   11   UIKit               [...] -[UIApplication sendEvent:] + 371
   12   UIKit               [...] __dispatchPreprocessedEventFromEventQueue + 3248
   13   UIKit               [...] __handleEventQueue + 4879
   14   CoreFoundation      [...] __CFRUNLOOP_IS_CALLING_OUT_TO_A_SOURCE0_PERFORM_FUNCTION
   15   CoreFoundation      [...] __CFRunLoopDoSources0 + 556
   16   CoreFoundation      [...] __CFRunLoopRun + 918
   17   CoreFoundation      [...] CFRunLoopRunSpecific + 420
   18   GraphicsServices    [...] GSEventRunModal + 161
   19   UIKit               [...] UIApplicationMain + 159
   20   Buggy               [...] main + 111
   21   libdyld.dylib       [...] start + 1
)
libc++abi.dylib: terminating with uncaught exception of type NSException
```

The message in the console looks pretty scary and hard to understand, but it is not as bad as it first seems. The really useful information is at the very top. Let's start with the very first line.

```
2016-08-24 12:52:38.463 Buggy[1961:47078] -[Buggy.ViewController buttonTapped:]:
unrecognized selector sent to instance 0x7ff6db708870
```

There is a time stamp, the name of the application, and the statement unrecognized selector sent to instance 0x7ff6db708870. To make sense of this information, remember that an iOS application may be written in Swift, but it is still built on top of Cocoa Touch, which is a collection of frameworks written in Objective-C. Objective-C is a dynamic language, and when a message is sent to an instance, the Objective-C runtime finds the actual method to be called at that precise time based on its *selector*, a kind of ID.

Thus, the statement that an unrecognized selector [was] sent to instance 0x7ff6db708870 means that the application tried to call a method on an instance that did not have it.

Which instance was it? You have two pieces of information about it. First, it is a **Buggy.ViewController**. (Why not just **ViewController**? Swift namespaces include the name of the module, which in this case is the application's name.) Second, it is located at memory address 0x7ff6db708870 (your actual address will likely be different).

The expression [Buggy.ViewController buttonTapped.] is a representation of Objective-C code. A message in Objective-C is always enclosed in square brackets in the form [receiver selector]. The *receiver* is the class or instance to which the message is sent. The dash (-) before the opening square bracket indicates that the receiver is an instance of **ViewController**. (A plus sign (+) would indicate that the receiver was the class itself.)

In short, this line from the console tells you that the selector buttonTapped: was sent to an instance of Buggy.ViewController but it was not recognized.

The next line of the message adds the information that the app was terminated due to an "uncaught exception" and specifies the type of the exception as **NSInvalidArgumentException**.

The bulk of the console message is the *stack trace*, a list of all the functions or methods that were called up to the point of the application crash. Knowing which logical path the application took before crashing can help you reproduce and fix a bug. None of the calls in the stack trace had a chance to return, and they are listed with the most recent call on top. Here is the stack trace again:

```
*** First throw call stack:
(
    0   CoreFoundation      [...] __exceptionPreprocess + 171
    1   libobjc.A.dylib     [...] objc_exception_throw + 48
    2   CoreFoundation      [...] -[NSObject(NSObject) doesNotRecognizeSelector:] + 132
    3   CoreFoundation      [...] ___forwarding___ + 1013
    4   CoreFoundation      [...] _CF_forwarding_prep_0 + 120
    5   UIKit               [...] -[UIApplication sendAction:to:from:forEvent:] + 83
    6   UIKit               [...] -[UIControl sendAction:to:forEvent:] + 67
    7   UIKit               [...] -[UIControl _sendActionsForEvents:withEvent:] + 444
    8   UIKit               [...] -[UIControl touchesEnded:withEvent:] + 668
    9   UIKit               [...] -[UIWindow _sendTouchesForEvent:] + 2747
   10   UIKit               [...]  [UIWindow sendEvent:] + 4011
   11   UIKit               [...] -[UIApplication sendEvent:] + 371
   12   UIKit               [...] __dispatchPreprocessedEventFromEventQueue + 3248
   13   UIKit               [...] __handleEventQueue + 4879
   14   CoreFoundation      [...] __CFRUNLOOP_IS_CALLING_OUT_TO_A_SOURCE0_PERFORM_FUNCTION
   15   CoreFoundation      [...] __CFRunLoopDoSources0 + 556
   16   CoreFoundation      [...] __CFRunLoopRun + 918
   17   CoreFoundation      [...] CFRunLoopRunSpecific + 420
   18   GraphicsServices    [...] GSEventRunModal + 161
   19   UIKit               [...] UIApplicationMain + 159
   20   Buggy               [...] main + 111
   21   libdyld.dylib       [...] start + 1
)
```

Each row in the list includes a call number, the module name, a memory address (which we have removed to fit the rest on the page), and a symbol representing the function or method. If you scan the stack trace from the bottom up, you can get a sense that the application starts in the **main** function of Buggy at the line identified with call number 20, receives an event recognized as a touch at call number 9, and then tries to send the corresponding action to the button's target at call number 7. The selector for the action is not found (call number 2: -[NSObject(NSObject) doesNotRecognizeSelector:]), resulting in an exception being raised (call number 1: objc_exception_throw).

Although this breakdown of the console message is specific to one error type out of many possibilities, understanding the basic structure of these messages will help you make sense of the error messages you will encounter in the future. As you gain more experience, you will start associating error messages with types of problems and you will become better at debugging code.

Fixing the first bug

Reviewing ViewController.swift, you discover that you changed your action method from **buttonTapped(_:)** to **switchToggled(_:)**, which is why the selector buttonTapped: is not being recognized.

To fix the bug, you have two choices. You could update the action connected to the button on Main.storyboard to match your new action method. Or you could revert the name change on the **switchToggled(_:)** method. You decide that you do not want a switch after all, so open ViewController.swift and change your method back to its earlier implementation. (Remember what we told you: Make the changes exactly as shown, even if you see a problem.)

```
@IBAction func switchToggled(_ sender: UISwitch) {
@IBAction func buttonTapped(_ sender: UISwitch) {
    print("Called buttonTapped(_:)")
}
```

Build and run the application. It works fine … or does it? Actually, there is a problem, which you will resolve in the next section.

Caveman debugging

The current implementation of **ViewController**'s **buttonTapped(_:)** method just logs a statement to the console. This is an example of a technique that is fondly called *caveman debugging*: strategically placing print() calls in your code to verify that functions and methods are being called (and called in the proper sequence) and to log variable values to the console to keep an eye on important data.

Like the cavemen in the insurance commercials, caveman debugging is not as outmoded as the name might suggest, and modern developers continue to rely on messages logged to the console.

To explore what caveman debugging can do for you, log the state of the sender control when **buttonTapped(_:)** is called in ViewController.swift.

```
@IBAction func buttonTapped(_ sender: UISwitch) {
    print("Called buttonTapped(_:)")
    // Log the control state:
    print("Is control on? \(sender.isOn)")
}
```

In the @IBAction methods you have written throughout this book, you have been passing in an argument called sender. This argument is a reference to the *control* sending the message. A control is a subclass of **UIControl**; you have worked with a few **UIControl** subclasses so far, including **UIButton**, **UITextField**, and **UISegmentedControl**. As you can see in **buttonTapped(_:)**'s signature, the sender in this case is an instance of a **UISwitch**. The **isOn** property is a Boolean indicating whether the switch instance is in the on state or not.

Build and run the application. Try tapping the button. Oops! You have an unrecognized selector error again.

```
Called buttonTapped(_:)
2016-08-30 09:30:57.730 Buggy[9738:1177400] -[UIButton isOn]:
unrecognized selector sent to instance 0x7fcc5d104cd0
2016-08-30 09:30:57.734 Buggy[9738:1177400] *** Terminating app due to uncaught
exception 'NSInvalidArgumentException', reason: '-[UIButton isOn]: unrecognized
selector sent to instance 0x7fcc5d104cd0'
```

The console message begins with the `Called buttonTapped(_:)` line, indicating that the action was indeed called. But then the application crashes because the **isOn** selector is sent to an instance of a **UIButton**.

You can probably see the problem: `sender` is typed as a **UISwitch** in **buttonTapped(_:)**, but the action is actually attached to a **UIButton** instance in `Main.storyboard`.

To confirm this hypothesis, log the address of `sender` in `ViewController.swift`, just before you call the **isOn** property.

```
@IBAction func buttonTaped(_ sender: UISwitch) {
    print("Called buttonTapped(_:)")
    // Log sender:
    print("sender: \(sender)")
    // Log the control state:
    print("Is control on? \(sender.isOn)")
}
```

Build and run the application one more time. After tapping the button and crashing the application, check the first few lines of the console log, which will look something like this:

```
Called buttonTapped(_:)
sender: <UIButton: 0x7fcf8c508bb0; frame = (160 84; 55 30); opaque = NO;
autoresize = RM+BM; layer = <CALayer: 0x618000220ea0>>
2016-08-30 09:45:00.562 Buggy[9946:1187061] -[UIButton isOn]: unrecognized selector
sent to instance 0x7fcf8c508bb0
2016-08-30 09:45:00.567 Buggy[9946:1187061] *** Terminating app due to uncaught
exception 'NSInvalidArgumentException', reason: '-[UIButton isOn]: unrecognized
selector sent to instance 0x7fcf8c508bb0'
```

In the line after `Called buttonTapped(_:)`, you get information about the sender. As expected, it is an instance of a **UIButton** and it exists in memory at address 0x7fcf8c508bb0. Further down the log you can confirm that this is the same instance to which you are sending the **isOn** message. A button cannot respond to a **UISwitch** property, so the app crashes.

To fix this problem, correct the **buttonTapped(_:)** definition in `ViewController.swift`. While you are there, delete the extra calls to **print()**, which you will not need again.

```
@IBAction func buttonTaped(_ sender: UISwitch) {
@IBAction func buttonTaped(_ sender: UIButton) {
    print("Called buttonTapped(_:)")
    // Log sender:
    print("sender: \(sender)")
    // Log the control state:
    print("Is control on? \(sender.isOn)")
}
```

Swift has four literal expressions that can assist you in logging information to the console (Table 9.1):

Table 9.1 Literal expressions useful for debugging

Literal	Type	Value
#file	String	The name of the file where the expression appears.
#line	Int	The line number the expression appears on.
#column	Int	The column number the expression begins in.
#function	String	The name of the declaration the expression appears in.

To illustrate the use of these literal expressions, update your call to **print()** in the **buttonTapped(_:)** method in ViewController.swift.

```
@IBAction func buttonTapped(_ sender: UIButton) {
    print("Called buttonTapped(_:)")
    print("Method: \(#function) in file: \(#file) line: \(#line) called.")
}
```

Build and run the application. As you tap the button, you will see a message logged to the console that is equivalent to the one below.

```
Method: buttonTapped in file: /Users/juampa/Desktop/Buggy/Buggy/ViewController.swift
    at line: 13 was called.
```

While caveman debugging is useful, be aware that print() statements are not stripped from your code as you build your project for release.

The Xcode Debugger: LLDB

To continue your debugging experiments, you are going to add another bug to your application. Add the code below to ViewController.swift. Notice that you will be using an **NSMutableArray**, the Objective-C counterpart of Swift's **Array**, to make the bug a little harder to find.

```
@IBAction func buttonTapped(_ sender: UIButton) {
    print("Method: \(#function) in file: \(#file) line: \(#line) called.")

    badMethod()
}

func badMethod() {
    let array = NSMutableArray()

    for i in 0..<10 {
        array.insert(i, at: i)
    }

    // Go one step too far emptying the array (notice the range change):
    for _ in 0...10 {
        array.remove(at: 0)
    }
}
```

Build and run the application to confirm that a tap on the button results in the application crashing with an uncaught **NSRangeException** exception. Use your freshly acquired knowledge to study and interpret the error message as much as possible.

If you used a Swift **Array** type to create this bug, Xcode would have been able to highlight the line of code that caused the exception. Because you used an **NSMutableArray**, the code that raised the exception is deep within the Cocoa Touch framework. Frequently this is the case when debugging; problems are not so obvious and you need to do some investigative work.

Setting breakpoints

Assume that you do not know the direct cause of the crash. You just know it happens after you tap the application's button. A reasonable way to proceed would be to stop the application after the button is tapped and step through the code until you get a clue as to the problem.

Open ViewController.swift. To stop an application at a specified location in the code, you set a *breakpoint*. The simplest way to set a breakpoint is to click on the gutter to the left of the editor pane next to the line where you want execution to stop. Try it: Click to the left of the line @IBAction func buttonTapped(_ sender: UIButton) {. A blue marker indicating the new breakpoint will appear (Figure 9.3).

Figure 9.3 Setting a breakpoint

After a breakpoint is set, you can toggle it by clicking on the blue marker directly. If you click on the marker once, it will become disabled, indicated by a paler shade of blue (Figure 9.4).

Figure 9.4 Disabling a breakpoint

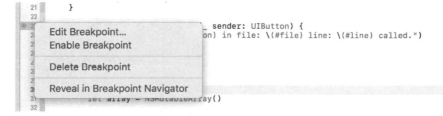

Another click re-enables the breakpoint. You can also enable, disable, delete, or edit a breakpoint by Control-clicking on the marker. A contextual menu will appear, as shown in Figure 9.5.

Figure 9.5 Modifying a breakpoint

Selecting Reveal in Breakpoint Navigator opens the breakpoint navigator in Xcode's left pane with a list of all the breakpoints in your application (Figure 9.6). You can also open the breakpoint navigator by clicking its icon in the navigator selector.

Figure 9.6 The breakpoint navigator

Stepping through code

Make sure your breakpoint on the **buttonTapped(_:)** method is set and active after all the clicking you did in the previous section. Run the application and tap on the button.

Your application hits the breakpoint and stops executing, and Xcode takes you to the line of code that would be executed next, which is highlighted in green. It also opens some new information areas (Figure 9.7).

Figure 9.7 Xcode stopped at a breakpoint

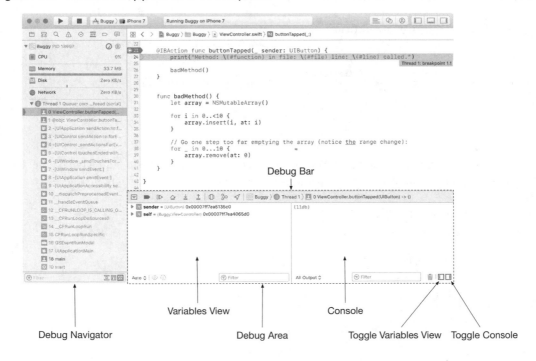

You are familiar with the console and have already seen the debug navigator. The new areas here are the variables view and the debug bar, which together with the console make up the debug area. (If you cannot see the variables view, click on the ☐ icon on the bottom-right corner of the debug area.)

The variables view can help you discover the values of variables and constants within the scope of the breakpoint. However, trying to find a particular value can require a fair amount of digging.

Initially, all you will see listed in the variables view are the sender and self arguments passed to the **buttonTapped(_:)** method. Click on the disclosure triangle for sender, and you will see that it contains a UIKit.UIControl property. Within it there is a _targetActions array that contains the button's attached target-action pairs.

Open the _targetActions array, open the first item ([0]), and then select the _target property. Tap the space bar while _target is selected, and a Quick Look window will open, showing a preview of the variable (which is an instance of **ViewController**). The Quick Look is shown in Figure 9.8.

Figure 9.8 Inspecting variables in the variables view

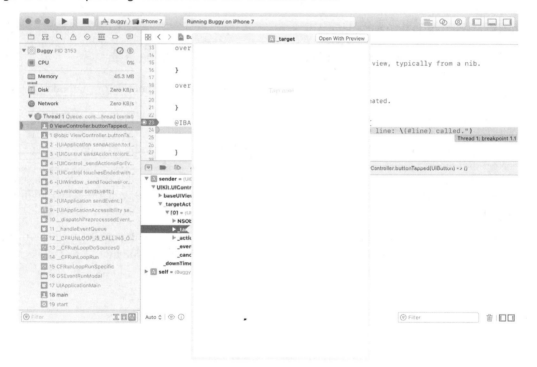

In the same section as the _target, you will see the _selector. Next to it, you will see (SEL) "buttonTapped:". The (SEL) indicates that this is a selector, and "buttonTapped:" is the name of the selector.

In this contrived example, it does not help you much to dig to find the _target and the _action; however, once you start working with larger, more complex applications, it can be especially useful to use the variables view. You do need to know what you are looking for, such as the _target and the _action – but finding the value that you are interested in can be very helpful in tracking down bugs.

Now it is time to start advancing through the code. You can do this using the buttons on the debug bar, shown in Figure 9.9.

Figure 9.9 The debug bar

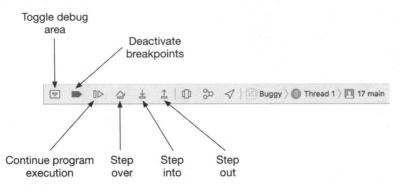

The important buttons in the debug bar are:

- Continue program execution ($\triangleright$) – resumes normal execution of the program

- Step over ($\triangleq$) – executes a single line of code without entering any function or method call

- Step into ($\downarrow$) – executes the next line of code, including entering a function or method call

- Step out ($\uparrow$) – continues execution until the current function or method is exited

Click the $\triangleq$ button until you highlight the badMethod() line (do not execute this line). Note that you do not step into the **print()** method – because it is an Apple-written method, you know there will be no problems there.

With badMethod() highlighted, click the $\downarrow$ button to step into the **badMethod()** method, and continue stepping through the code with $\downarrow$ until the application crashes. It will take you quite a few clicks, and it will look like you are going through the same lines of code over and over – in fact, you are, as the code loops over the ranges.

As you step through the code, you can pause to mouseover i and array.remove to see their values update (Figure 9.10).

Figure 9.10 Examining the value of a variable

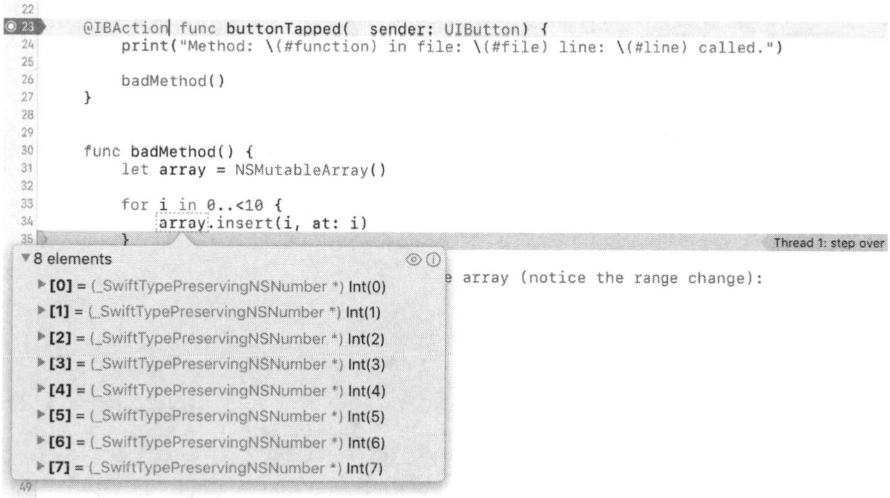

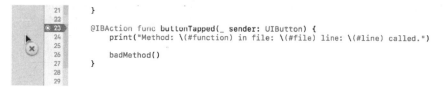

Once the application crashes, you have confirmation that the crash occurs within the **badMethod()** method. With this knowledge you can now delete or disable the breakpoint at the func buttonTapped(_ sender: UIButton) line.

To delete a breakpoint, Control-click it and select Delete Breakpoint. You can also delete a breakpoint by dragging the blue marker out of the gutter, as shown in Figure 9.11.

Figure 9.11 Dragging a marker to delete the breakpoint

Occasionally, you want to be notified when a line of code is triggered, but you do not need any additional information or for the application to pause when it hits that line. To accomplish this, you can add a sound to a breakpoint and have it automatically continue execution after being triggered.

Add a new breakpoint at the `array.insert(i, at: i)` line of the **badMethod()** method. Then Control-click on the marker and select Edit Breakpoint.... Click on the Add Action button and select Sound from the pop-up menu. Finally, check the box to Automatically continue after evaluating actions (Figure 9.12).

Figure 9.12 Enabling special actions

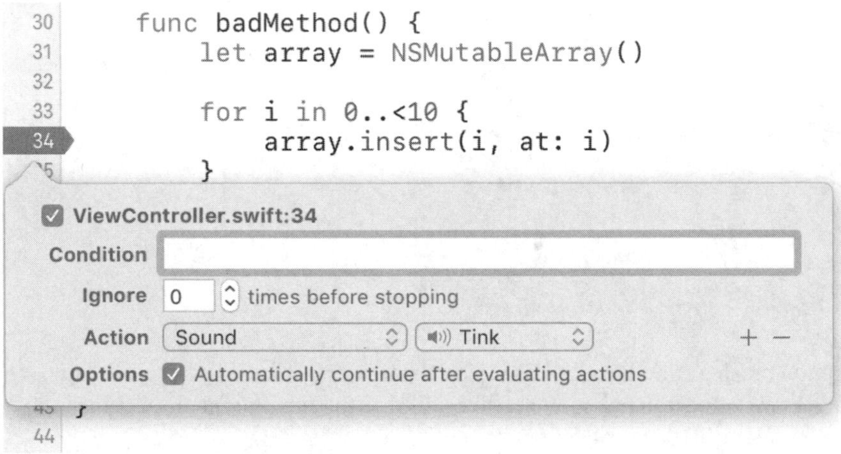

You have configured the breakpoint to make an alert sound instead of stopping execution every time it is encountered. Run the application again and tap the button. You should hear a sequence of sounds, and then the application will crash.

It seems the application is safely completing the `for` loop, but you need to be sure. Find and Control-click your breakpoint marker again, selecting Edit Breakpoint... as before. In the editor pop-up, click the + to the right of the sound action to add a new action.

From the pop-up, select Log Message. In the Text field, enter Pass number %H (%H is the *breakpoint hit count*, a reference to the number of times the breakpoint has been encountered). Finally, make sure the Log message to console radio button is selected (Figure 9.13).

Figure 9.13 Assigning multiple actions to a breakpoint

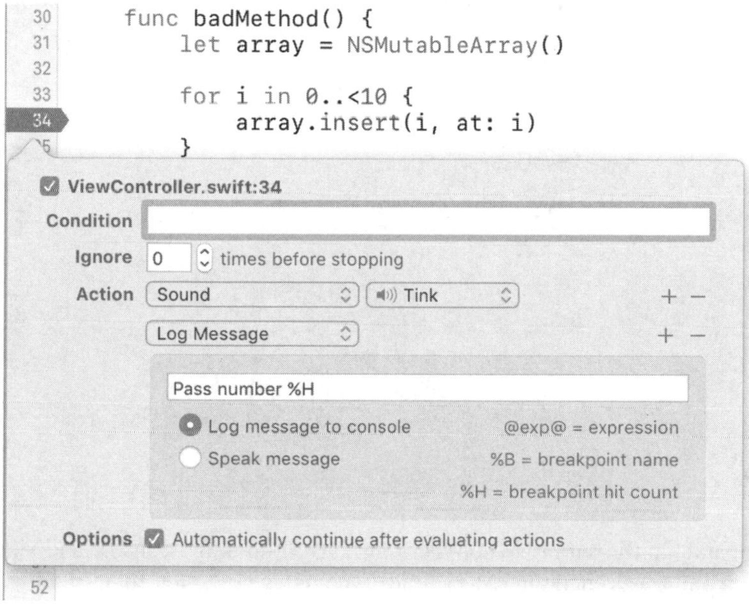

```
30    func badMethod() {
31        let array = NSMutableArray()
32
33        for i in 0..<10 {
34            array.insert(i, at: i)
 5        }
```

☑ **ViewController.swift:34**

Condition [   ]

Ignore [0] ⬍ times before stopping

Action [Sound   ⬍] [◀)) Tink   ⬍]   + −

[Log Message   ⬍]   + −

[Pass number %H   ]

● Log message to console   @exp@ = expression
○ Speak message   %B = breakpoint name
                                %H = breakpoint hit count

Options ☑ Automatically continue after evaluating actions

```
52
```

Run the application again and tap the button. You will hear the sequence of sounds again, and the application will crash as before. But this time, if you watch the console (or scroll up after the application crashes), you will see that the breakpoint was encountered 10 times. This confirms that your code is completing the loop safely.

Delete your current breakpoint and add a new one on the line `array.remove(at: 0)`. Edit the breakpoint to log the pass number and continue automatically, as before (Figure 9.14).

Figure 9.14 Adding a logging breakpoint

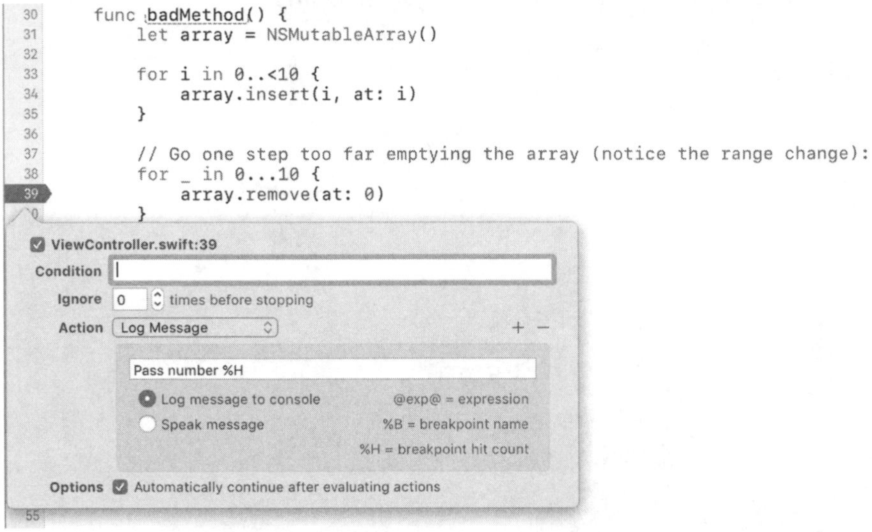

```
30    func badMethod() {
31        let array = NSMutableArray()
32
33        for i in 0..<10 {
34            array.insert(i, at: i)
35        }
36
37        // Go one step too far emptying the array (notice the range change):
38        for _ in 0...10 {
39            array.remove(at: 0)
40        }
```

```
☑ ViewController.swift:39
Condition   [|                                                      ]
Ignore   [0  ⇕] times before stopping
Action   [ Log Message          ⇕]                          +  —

         [ Pass number %H                                    ]
         ● Log message to console        @exp@ = expression
         ○ Speak message                 %B = breakpoint name
                                         %H = breakpoint hit count

Options  ☑ Automatically continue after evaluating actions
55
```

Run the application and tap the button. When it crashes, scroll up in the console and you will see that the second breakpoint was encountered 11 times. That is one time too many, and you have your smoking gun. It also explains the **NSRangeException** logged on the console as the application crashes. Carefully read the crash log on the console again and make as much sense of it as possible.

Before fixing the problem, take the time to explore a couple more debugging strategies. First, disable or delete any remaining breakpoints in the application.

In these simple examples, you have known just where to look to find the bug in your code, but in real-world development you will often have no idea where in your application a bug is hiding. It would be nice if you could tell which line of code is causing an uncaught exception resulting in a crash.

It would be nice – and with an *exception breakpoint*, you can do just that. Open the breakpoint navigator and click on the + in the lower-left corner of the window. From the contextual menu, select Exception Breakpoint.... A new exception breakpoint is created and a pop-up appears. Make sure it catches all exceptions on throw, as shown in Figure 9.15.

Figure 9.15 Adding an exception breakpoint

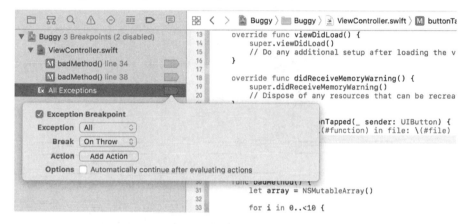

Run the application and tap the button once again. The application automatically stops and Xcode takes you to the line that directly causes the exception to be raised. Note, however, that there is no console log. That is because the application has not crashed yet. To see the crash and read the cause, click on the ▷ button on the debug bar until you see the crash.

This strategy is the one to begin with as you tackle a new bug. In fact, many programmers always keep an exception breakpoint active while developing. Why did we make you wait so long to use it? Because if you had started with an exception breakpoint, you would not have needed to learn about the other debugging strategies, and they have their uses, too. Feel free to remove this breakpoint if you would like; you will not need it again.

You are going to try one final technique: the symbolic breakpoint. These are breakpoints specified not by line number, but by the name of a function or method, referred to as a *symbol*. Symbolic breakpoints are triggered when the symbol is called – whether the symbol is in your code or in a framework for which you have no code.

Add a new symbolic breakpoint in the breakpoint navigator by clicking the + button on the lower-left corner and, from the contextual menu, selecting Symbolic Breakpoint.... In the pop-up, specify "badMethod" as the symbol, as shown in Figure 9.16. This means that every time **badMethod()** is called, the application will stop.

Figure 9.16 Adding a symbolic breakpoint

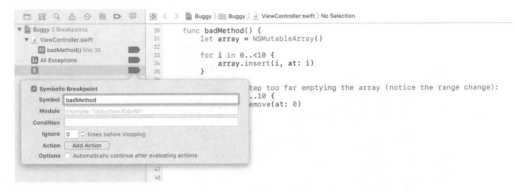

Run the application to test the breakpoint. The application should stop at **badMethod()** after you tap the Tap me! button.

In a real-world app, it is rare that you would use a symbolic breakpoint on a method that you created; you would likely add a normal breakpoint like the ones you saw earlier in this chapter. Symbolic breakpoints are most useful to stop on a method that you did not write, such as a method in one of Apple's frameworks. For example, you might want to know whenever the method **loadView()** is triggered for any view controller within the application.

Finally, fix the bug.

```
func badMethod() {
    let array = NSMutableArray()

    for i in 0..<10 {
        array.insert(i, at: i)
    }

    // Go one step too far emptying the array (notice the range change):
    for _ in 0...10 {
    for _ in 0..<10 {
        array.remove(at: 0)
    }
}
```

The LLDB console

A great feature of Xcode's LLDB debugger is that it has a command-line interface. The console area is not only used to read messages, but also can be used to type LLDB commands. The debugger command-line interface is active whenever you see the blue (lldb) prompt on the console.

Make sure your symbolic breakpoint on **badMethod()** is still active, run the application, and tap the button to break at that point. Look at the console and you will see the (lldb) prompt (Figure 9.17). Click beside the prompt, and you can type commands.

Figure 9.17 The (lldb) prompt on the console

```
Method: buttonTapped in file: /Users/juampa/Desktop/Buggy/
Buggy/ViewController.swift line: 24 called.
(lldb)
```

All Output ⌄   ⊙ Filter   🗑 | ☐☐

One of the most useful LLDB commands is print-object, abbreviated po. This command prints a nice description of any instance. Try it out by typing on the console.

```
(lldb) po self
<Buggy.ViewController: 0x7fae9852bf20>
```

The response to the command is that self is an instance of **ViewController**. Now advance one line of code with the command step; this will initialize the array constant reference. Print the reference's value with po.

```
(lldb) step
(lldb) po array
0 elements
```

The response 0 elements is not very useful, as it does not give you a lot of information. The print command, abbreviated p, can be more verbose. Try it.

```
(lldb) p array
(NSMutableArray) $R3 = 0x00007fae98517c00 "0 values" {}
```

Frequently, using the console with print or print-object to examine variables is much more convenient than Xcode's variables view pane.

Another useful LLDB command is expression, abbreviated expr. This command allows you to enter Swift code to modify variables. For example, add some data to the array, look at the contents, and continue execution.

```
(lldb) expr array.insert(1, at: 0)
(lldb) p array
(NSMutableArray) $R5 = 0x00007fae98517c00 "1 value" {
  [0] = 0xb000000000000013 Int64(1)
}
(lldb) po array
▿ 1 element
  - [0] : 1
  (lldb) continue
```

Perhaps more surprisingly, you can also change the UI with LLDB expressions. Try changing the button's tintColor to red.

```
(lldb) expr self.view.tintColor = UIColor.red
(lldb) continue
```

There are many LLDB commands. To learn more, enter the help command at the (lldb) prompt.

10

UITableView and UITableViewController

Many iOS applications show the user a list of items and allow the user to select, delete, or reorder items on the list. Whether an application displays a list of people in the user's address book or a list of best-selling items on the App Store, it is a **UITableView** doing the work.

A **UITableView** displays a single column of data with a variable number of rows. Figure 10.1 shows some examples of **UITableView**.

Figure 10.1 Examples of **UITableView**

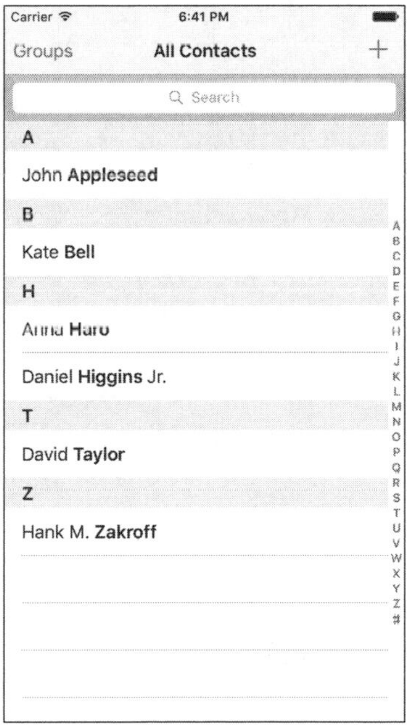

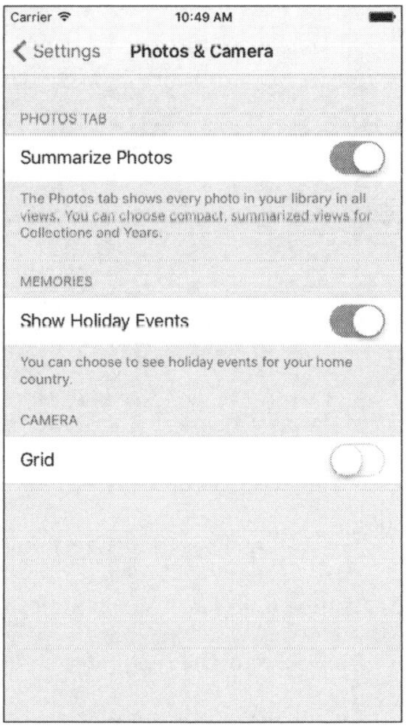

Beginning the Homepwner Application

In this chapter, you are going to start an application called Homepwner that keeps an inventory of all your possessions. In the case of a fire or other catastrophe, you will have a record for your insurance company. ("Homepwner," by the way, is not a typo. If you need a definition for the word "pwn," visit www.wiktionary.org.)

So far, your iOS projects have been small, but Homepwner will grow into a realistically complex application over the course of eight chapters. By the end of this chapter, Homepwner will present a list of **Item** instances in a **UITableView**, as shown in Figure 10.2.

Figure 10.2 Homepwner: phase 1

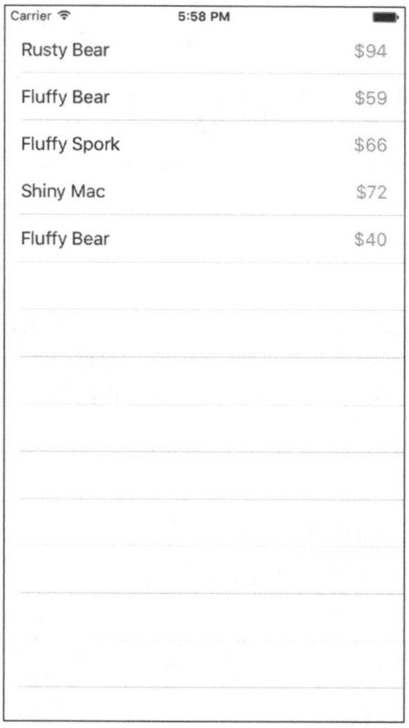

To get started, open Xcode and create a new iOS Single View Application project. Configure it as shown in Figure 10.3.

Figure 10.3 Configuring Homepwner

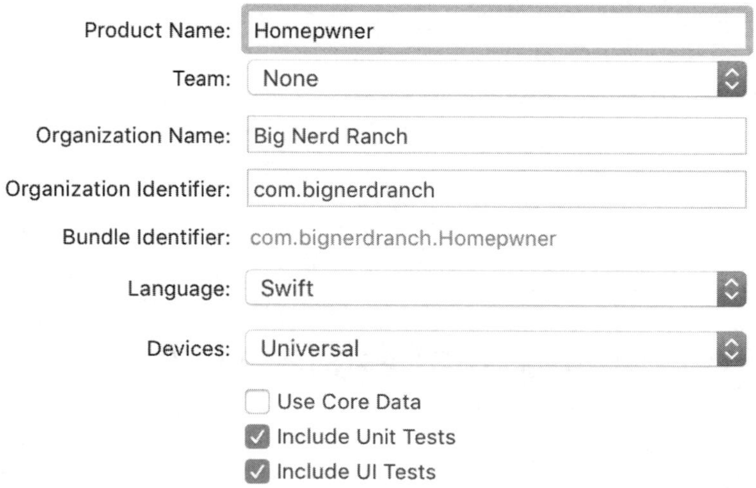

UITableViewController

A **UITableView** is a view object. Recall that in the MVC design pattern, which iOS developers do their best to follow, each class falls into exactly one of the following categories:

- *model*: holds data and knows nothing about the UI

- *view*: is visible to the user and knows nothing about the model objects

- *controller*: keeps the UI and the model objects in sync and controls the flow of the application

As a view object, a **UITableView** does not handle application logic or data. When using a **UITableView**, you must consider what else is necessary to get the table working in your application:

- A **UITableView** typically needs a view controller to handle its appearance on the screen.

- A **UITableView** needs a *data source*. A **UITableView** asks its data source for the number of rows to display, the data to be shown in those rows, and other tidbits that make a **UITableView** a useful UI. Without a data source, a table view is just an empty container. The dataSource for a **UITableView** can be any type of object as long as it conforms to the **UITableViewDataSource** protocol.

- A **UITableView** typically needs a *delegate* that can inform other objects of events involving the **UITableView**. The delegate can be any object as long as it conforms to the **UITableViewDelegate** protocol.

An instance of the class **UITableViewController** can fill all three roles: view controller, data source, and delegate.

UITableViewController is a subclass of **UIViewController** and therefore has a view. A **UITableViewController**'s view is always an instance of **UITableView**, and the **UITableViewController** handles the preparation and presentation of the **UITableView**.

When a **UITableViewController** creates its view, the dataSource and delegate properties of the **UITableView** are automatically set to point at the **UITableViewController** (Figure 10.4).

Figure 10.4 **UITableViewController-UITableView** relationship

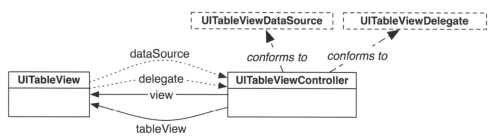

Subclassing **UITableViewController**

You are going to implement a subclass of **UITableViewController** for Homepwner. Create a new Swift file named ItemsViewController. In ItemsViewController.swift, define a **UITableViewController** subclass named **ItemsViewController**.

```
import Foundation
import UIKit

class ItemsViewController: UITableViewController {

}
```

Now open Main.storyboard. You want the initial view controller to be a table view controller. Select the existing View Controller on the canvas and press Delete. Then drag a Table View Controller from the object library onto the canvas. With the Table View Controller selected, open its identity inspector and change the class to ItemsViewController. Finally, open the attributes inspector for Items View Controller and check the box for Is Initial View Controller.

Build and run your application. You should see an empty table view, as shown in Figure 10.5. As a subclass of **UIViewController**, a **UITableViewController** inherits the view property. When this property is accessed for the first time, the **loadView()** method is called, which creates and loads a view object. A **UITableViewController**'s view is always an instance of **UITableView**, so asking for the view of a **UITableViewController** gets you a bright, shiny, and empty table view.

Figure 10.5 Empty **UITableView**

You no longer need the ViewController.swift file that the template created for you. Select this file in the project navigator and press Delete.

Creating the Item Class

Your table view needs some rows to display. Each row in the table view will display an item with information such as a name, serial number, and value in dollars.

Create a new Swift file named `Item`. In `Item.swift`, define the `Item` class and give it four properties.

```
import Foundation
import UIKit

class Item: NSObject {
    var name: String
    var valueInDollars: Int
    var serialNumber: String?
    let dateCreated: Date
}
```

`Item` inherits from `NSObject`. `NSObject` is the base class that most Objective-C classes inherit from. All of the UIKit classes that you have worked with – `UIView`, `UITextField`, and `UIViewController`, to name a few – inherit either directly or indirectly from `NSObject`. Your own classes will often need to inherit from `NSObject` when they need to interface with the runtime system.

Notice that `serialNumber` is an optional `String`, necessary because an item may not have a serial number. Also, notice that none of the properties have a default value. You will need to give them values in a designated initializer.

Custom initializers

You learned about struct initializers in Chapter 2. Initializers on structs are fairly straightforward because structs do not support inheritance. Classes, on the other hand, have some rules for initializers to support inheritance.

Classes can have two kinds of initializers: *designated initializers* and *convenience initializers*.

A designated initializer is a primary initializer for the class. Every class has at least one designated initializer. A designated initializer ensures that all properties in the class have a value. Once it ensures that, a designated initializer calls a designated initializer on its superclass (if it has one).

Implement a new designated initializer on the `Item` class that sets the initial values for all of the properties.

```
import UIKit

class Item: NSObject {
    var name: String
    var valueInDollars: Int
    var serialNumber: String?
    let dateCreated: Date

    init(name: String, serialNumber: String?, valueInDollars: Int) {
        self.name = name
        self.valueInDollars = valueInDollars
        self.serialNumber = serialNumber
        self.dateCreated = Date()

        super.init()
    }
}
```

This initializer takes in arguments for the name, serialNumber, and valueInDollars. Because the argument names and the property names are the same, you must use self to distinguish the property from the argument.

Now that you have implemented your own custom initializer, you lose the free initializer – **init()** – that classes have. The free initializer is useful when all of your class's properties have default values and you do not need to do additional work to create the new instance. The **Item** class does not satisfy this criteria, so you have declared a custom initializer for the class.

Every class must have at least one designated initializer, but convenience initializers are optional. You can think of convenience initializers as helpers. A convenience initializer always calls another initializer on the same class. Convenience initializers are indicated by the convenience keyword before the initializer name.

Add a convenience initializer to **Item** that creates a randomly generated item.

```
convenience init(random: Bool = false) {
    if random {
        let adjectives = ["Fluffy", "Rusty", "Shiny"]
        let nouns = ["Bear", "Spork", "Mac"]

        var idx = arc4random_uniform(UInt32(adjectives.count))
        let randomAdjective = adjectives[Int(idx)]

        idx = arc4random_uniform(UInt32(nouns.count))
        let randomNoun = nouns[Int(idx)]

        let randomName = "\(randomAdjective) \(randomNoun)"
        let randomValue = Int(arc4random_uniform(100))
        let randomSerialNumber =
            UUID().uuidString.components(separatedBy: "-").first!

        self.init(name: randomName,
            serialNumber: randomSerialNumber,
            valueInDollars: randomValue)
    } else {
        self.init(name: "", serialNumber: nil, valueInDollars: 0)
    }
}
```

If random is true, the instance is configured with a random name, serial number, and value. (The **arc4random_uniform** function returns a random value between 0, inclusive, and the value passed in as the argument, exclusive.) Notice that at the end of both branches of the conditional, you are calling through to the designated initializer for **Item**. Convenience initializers must call another initializer on the same type, whereas designated initializers must call a designated initializer on its superclass.

The **Item** class is ready for work. In the next section you will display an array of **Item** instances in a table view.

UITableView's Data Source

The process of providing rows to a **UITableView** in Cocoa Touch (the collection of frameworks used to build iOS apps) is different from the typical procedural programming task. In a procedural design, you tell the table view what it should display. In Cocoa Touch, the table view asks another object – its dataSource – what it should display. In this case, the **ItemsViewController** is the data source, so it needs a way to store item data.

You are going to use an array to store the **Item** instances, but with a twist. The array that holds the **Item** instances will be abstracted into another object – an **ItemStore** (Figure 10.6).

Figure 10.6 Homepwner object diagram

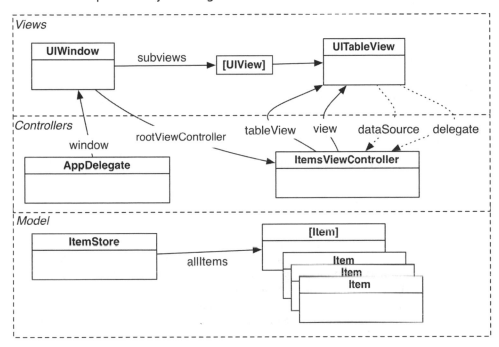

If an object wants to see all of the items, it will ask the **ItemStore** for the array that contains them. In future chapters, the store will be responsible for performing operations on the array, like reordering, adding, and removing items. It will also be responsible for saving and loading the items from disk.

Create a new Swift file named ItemStore. In ItemStore.swift, define the **ItemStore** class and declare a property to store the list of **Item**s.

```
import Foundation
import UIKit

class ItemStore {

    var allItems = [Item]()

}
```

ItemStore is a Swift *base class* – it does not inherit from any other class. Unlike the **Item** class that you defined earlier, **ItemStore** does not require any of the behavior that **NSObject** affords.

The **ItemsViewController** will call a method on **ItemStore** when it wants a new **Item** to be created. The **ItemStore** will oblige, creating the object and adding it to an array of instances of **Item**.

In ItemStore.swift, implement **createItem()** to create and return a new **Item**.

```
@discardableResult func createItem() -> Item {
    let newItem = Item(random: true)

    allItems.append(newItem)

    return newItem
}
```

The @discardableResult annotation means that a caller of this function is free to ignore the result of calling this function. Take a look at the following code listing that illustrates this effect.

```
// This is OK
let newItem = itemStore.createItem()

// This is also OK; the result is not assigned to a variable
itemStore.createItem()
```

Giving the controller access to the store

In ItemsViewController.swift, add a property for an **ItemStore**.

```
class ItemsViewController: UITableViewController {

    var itemStore: ItemStore!
}
```

Now, where should you set this property on the **ItemsViewController** instance? When the application first launches, the **AppDelegate**'s **application(_:didFinishLaunchingWithOptions:)** method is called. The **AppDelegate** is declared in AppDelegate.swift and, as the name implies, serves as the delegate for the application itself. It is responsible for handling the changes in state that the application goes through. You will learn more about the **AppDelegate** and the states that the application goes through in Chapter 16.

Open AppDelegate.swift. Access the **ItemsViewController** (which will be the rootViewController of the window) and set its itemStore property to be a new instance of **ItemStore**.

```
func application(_ application: UIApplication, didFinishLaunchingWithOptions
        launchOptions: [UIApplicationLaunchOptionsKey : Any]?) -> Bool {
    // Override point for customization after application launch.

    // Create an ItemStore
    let itemStore = ItemStore()

    // Access the ItemsViewController and set its item store
    let itemsController = window!.rootViewController as! ItemsViewController
    itemsController.itemStore = itemStore

    return true
}
```

Finally, in ItemStore.swift, implement the designated initializer to add five random items

```
init() {
    for _ in 0..<5 {
        createItem()
    }
}
```

As a quick aside, if **createItem()** was not annotated with @discardableResult, then the call to that function would have needed to look like:

```
// Call the function, but ignore the result
let _ = createItem()
```

At this point you may be wondering why itemStore was set externally on the **ItemsViewController**. Why didn't the **ItemsViewController** instance itself just create an instance of the store? The reason for this approach is based on a fairly complex topic called the *dependency inversion principle*. The essential goal of this principle is to decouple objects in an application by inverting certain dependencies between them. This results in more robust and maintainable code.

The dependency inversion principle states that:

1. High-level objects should not depend on low-level objects. Both should depend on abstractions.

2. Abstractions should not depend on details. Details should depend on abstractions.

The abstraction required by the dependency inversion principle in Homepwner is the concept of a "store." A store is a lower-level object that retrieves and saves **Item** instances through details that are only known to that class. **ItemsViewController** is a higher-level object that only knows that it will be provided with a utility object (the store) from which it can obtain a list of **Item** instances and to which it can pass new or updated **Item** instances to be stored persistently. This results in a decoupling because **ItemsViewController** is not dependent on **ItemStore**. In fact, as long as the store abstraction is respected, **ItemStore** could be replaced by another object that fetches **Item** instances differently (such as by using a web service) without any changes to **ItemsViewController**.

A common pattern used when implementing the dependency inversion principle is *dependency injection*. In its simplest form, higher-level objects do not assume which lower-level objects they need to use. Instead, those are passed to them through an initializer or property. In your implementation of **ItemsViewController**, you used injection through a property to give it a store.

Implementing data source methods

Now that there are some items in the store, you need to teach **ItemsViewController** how to turn those items into rows that its **UITableView** can display. When a **UITableView** wants to know what to display, it calls methods from the set of methods declared in the **UITableViewDataSource** protocol.

Open the documentation and search for the **UITableViewDataSource** protocol reference. Scroll down to the section titled Configuring a Table View (Figure 10.7).

Figure 10.7 **UITableViewDataSource** protocol documentation

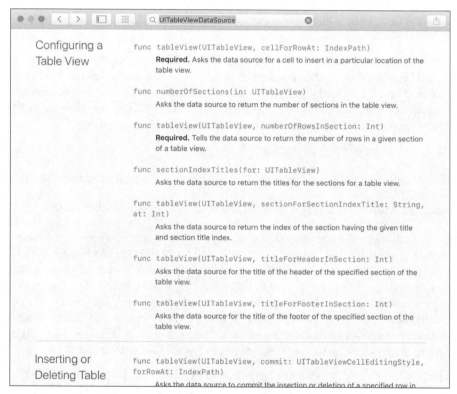

In the Configuring a Table View section, notice that two of the methods are marked **Required**. For **ItemsViewController** to conform to **UITableViewDataSource**, it must implement **tableView(_:numberOfRowsInSection:)** and **tableView(_:cellForRowAt:)**. These methods tell the table view how many rows it should display and what content to display in each row.

Whenever a **UITableView** needs to display itself, it calls a series of methods (the required methods plus any optional ones that have been implemented) on its dataSource. The required method **tableView(_:numberOfRowsInSection:)** returns an integer value for the number of rows that the **UITableView** should display. In the table view for Homepwner, there should be a row for each entry in the store.

In ItemsViewController.swift, implement **tableView(_:numberOfRowsInSection:)**.

```
override func tableView(_ tableView: UITableView,
        numberOfRowsInSection section: Int) -> Int {
    return itemStore.allItems.count
}
```

Wondering about the section that this method refers to? Table views can be broken up into sections, with each section having its own set of rows. For example, in the address book, all names beginning with "C" are grouped together in a section. By default, a table view has one section, and in this chapter you will work with only one. Once you understand how a table view works, it is not hard to use multiple sections. In fact, using sections is the first challenge at the end of this chapter.

The second required method in the **UITableViewDataSource** protocol is **tableView(_:cellForRowAt:)**. To implement this method, you need to learn about another class – **UITableViewCell**.

UITableViewCells

Each row of a table view is a view. These views are instances of **UITableViewCell**. In this section, you will create the instances of **UITableViewCell** to fill the table view.

A cell itself has one subview – its contentView (Figure 10.8). The contentView is the superview for the content of the cell. The cell may also have an accessory view.

Figure 10.8 **UITableViewCell** layout

The accessory view shows an action-oriented icon, such as a checkmark, a disclosure icon, or an information button. These icons are accessed through predefined constants for the appearance of the accessory view. The default is **UITableViewCellAccessoryType.none**, and that is what you are going to use in this chapter. You will see the accessory view again in Chapter 23. (Curious now? See the documentation for **UITableViewCell** for more details.)

The real meat of a **UITableViewCell** is the contentView, which has three subviews of its own (Figure 10.9). Two of those subviews are **UILabel** instances that are properties of **UITableViewCell** named textLabel and detailTextLabel. The third subview is a **UIImageView** called imageView. In this chapter, you will use textLabel and detailTextLabel.

Figure 10.9 **UITableViewCell** hierarchy

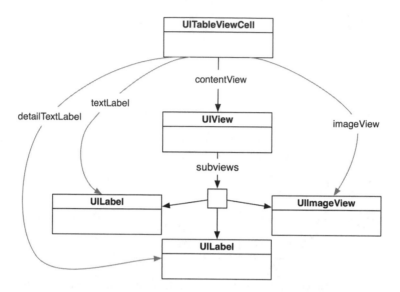

Each cell also has a **UITableViewCellStyle** that determines which subviews are used and their position within the contentView. Examples of these styles and their constants are shown in Figure 10.10.

Figure 10.10 **UITableViewCellStyle**: styles and constants

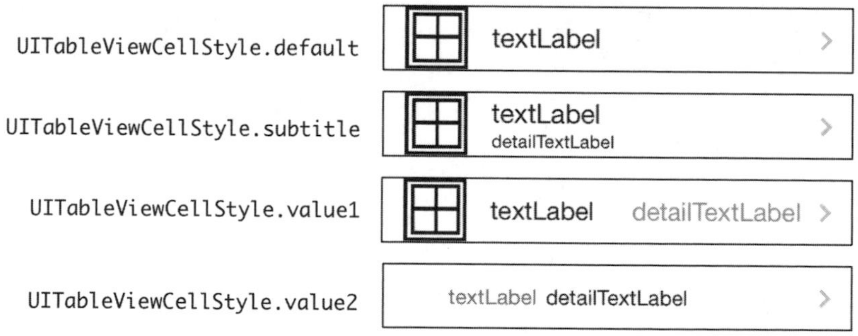

UITableViewCellStyle.default	textLabel
UITableViewCellStyle.subtitle	textLabel / detailTextLabel
UITableViewCellStyle.value1	textLabel detailTextLabel
UITableViewCellStyle.value2	textLabel detailTextLabel

Creating and retrieving UITableViewCells

For now, each cell will display the name of an **Item** as its textLabel and the valueInDollars of the **Item** as its detailTextLabel. To make this happen, you need to implement the second required method from the **UITableViewDataSource** protocol, **tableView(_:cellForRowAt:)**. This method will create a cell, set its textLabel to the name of the **Item**, set its detailTextLabel to the valueInDollars of the **Item**, and return it to the **UITableView** (Figure 10.11).

Figure 10.11 **UITableViewCell** retrieval

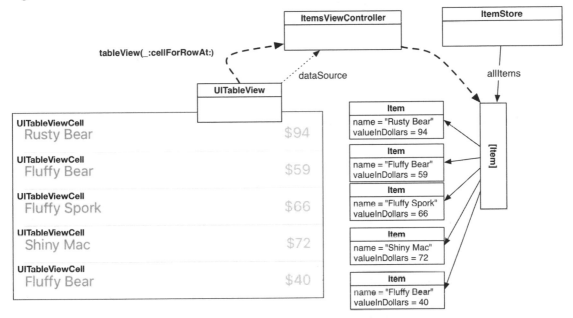

How do you decide which cell an **Item** corresponds to? One of the parameters sent to **tableView(_:cellForRowAt:)** is an **IndexPath**, which has two properties: section and row. When this method is called on a data source, the table view is asking, "Can I have a cell to display in section X, row Y?" Because there is only one section in this exercise, your implementation will only be concerned with the index path's row.

In ItemsViewController.swift, implement **tableView(_:cellForRowAt:)** so that the *n*th row displays the *n*th entry in the allItems array.

```
override func tableView(_ tableView: UITableView,
        cellForRowAt indexPath: IndexPath) -> UITableViewCell {
    // Create an instance of UITableViewCell, with default appearance
    let cell = UITableViewCell(style: .value1, reuseIdentifier: "UITableViewCell")

    // Set the text on the cell with the description of the item
    // that is at the nth index of items, where n = row this cell
    // will appear in on the tableview
    let item = itemStore.allItems[indexPath.row]

    cell.textLabel?.text = item.name
    cell.detailTextLabel?.text = "$\(item.valueInDollars)"

    return cell
}
```

Build and run the application now and you will see a **UITableView** populated with a list of random items.

Reusing UITableViewCells

iOS devices have a limited amount of memory. If you were displaying a list with thousands of entries in a **UITableView**, you would have thousands of instances of **UITableViewCell**. Most of these cells would take up memory needlessly. After all, if the user cannot see a cell onscreen, then there is no reason for that cell to have a claim on memory.

To conserve memory and improve performance, you can reuse table view cells. When the user scrolls the table, some cells move offscreen. Offscreen cells are put into a pool of cells available for reuse. Then, instead of creating a brand new cell for every request, the data source first checks the pool. If there is an unused cell, the data source configures it with new data and returns it to the table view (Figure 10.12).

Figure 10.12 Reusable instances of **UITableViewCell**

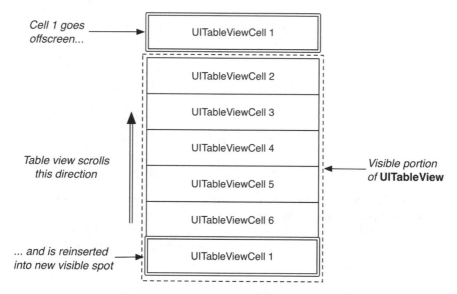

There is one problem to be aware of: Sometimes a **UITableView** has different types of cells. Occasionally, you subclass **UITableViewCell** to create a special look or behavior. However, different subclasses floating around the pool of reusable cells create the possibility of getting back a cell of the wrong type. You must be sure of the type of the cell returned so that you can be sure of what properties and methods it has.

Note that you do not care about getting any specific cell out of the pool because you are going to change the cell content anyway. What you need is a cell of a specific type. The good news is that every cell has a reuseIdentifier property of type **String**. When a data source asks the table view for a reusable cell, it passes a string and says, "I need a cell with this reuse identifier." By convention, the reuse identifier is typically the name of the cell class.

To reuse cells, you need to register either a prototype cell or a class with the table view for a specific reuse identifier. You are going to register the default **UITableViewCell** class. You tell the table view, "Hey, any time I ask for a cell with *this reuse identifier*, give me back a cell that is *this specific class*." The table view will either give you a cell from the reuse pool or instantiate a new cell if there are no cells of that type in the reuse pool.

Open Main.storyboard. Notice in the table view that there is a section for Prototype Cells (Figure 10.13).

Figure 10.13 Prototype cells

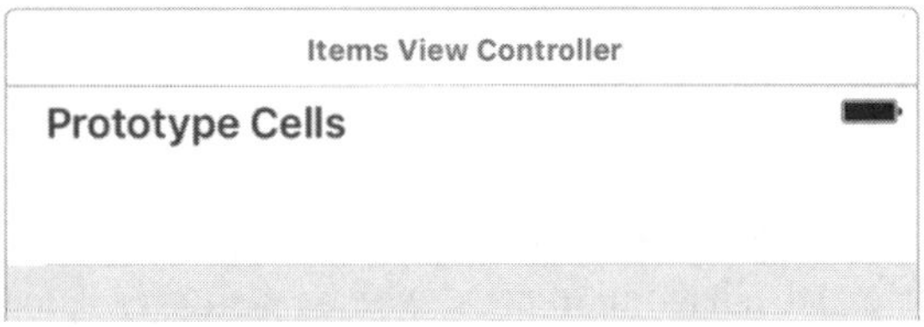

In this area, you can configure the different kinds of cells that you need for the associated table view. If you are creating custom cells, this is where you will set up the interface for the cells. **ItemsViewController** only needs one kind of cell, and using one of the built-in styles will work great for now, so you will only need to configure some attributes on the cell that is already on the canvas.

Select the prototype cell and open its attributes inspector. Change the Style to Right Detail (which corresponds to **UITableViewCellStyle.value1**) and give it an Identifier of UITableViewCell (Figure 10.14).

Figure 10.14 Table view cell attributes

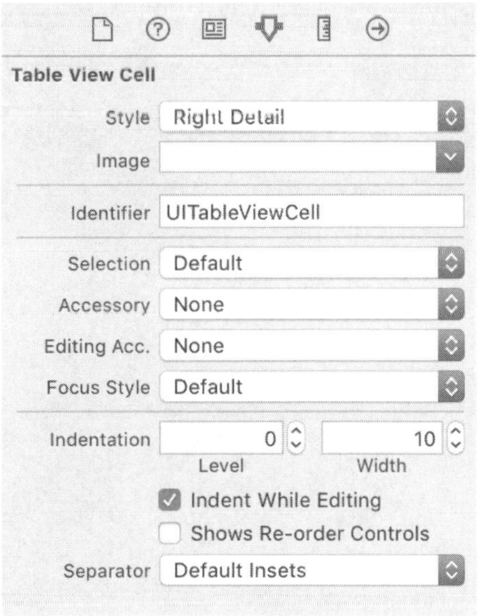

Next, in `ItemsViewController.swift`, update **`tableView(_:cellForRowAt:)`** to reuse cells.

```
override func tableView(_ tableView: UITableView,
        cellForRowAt indexPath: IndexPath) -> UITableViewCell {
    // Create an instance of UITableViewCell, with default appearance
    let cell = UITableViewCell(style: .value1, reuseIdentifier: "UITableViewCell")

    // Get a new or recycled cell
    let cell = tableView.dequeueReusableCell(withIdentifier: "UITableViewCell",
        for: indexPath)
    ...
}
```

The method **`dequeueReusableCell(withIdentifier:for:)`** will check the pool, or queue, of cells to see whether a cell with the correct reuse identifier already exists. If so, it will "dequeue" that cell. If there is not an existing cell, a new cell will be created and returned.

Build and run the application. The behavior of the application should remain the same. Reusing cells means that you only have to create a handful of cells, which puts fewer demands on memory. Your application's users (and their devices) will thank you.

Content Insets

As you have been running the application throughout this chapter, you might have noticed that the first table view cell underlaps the status bar (Figure 10.15). The interfaces for the applications you create fill up the entire window of the device. The status bar, if visible, is placed on top of the interface, so your interfaces must account for the placement of the status bar.

Figure 10.15 Table view cell underlapping status bar

To have the table view cells not underlap the status bar, you will add some padding to the top of the table view. A **UITableView** is a subclass of **UIScrollView**, from which it inherits the contentInset property. You can think of the content inset as padding for all four sides of the scroll view.

In ItemsViewController.swift, override **viewDidLoad()** to update the table view content inset.

```
override func viewDidLoad() {
    super.viewDidLoad()

    // Get the height of the status bar
    let statusBarHeight = UIApplication.shared.statusBarFrame.height

    let insets = UIEdgeInsets(top: statusBarHeight, left: 0, bottom: 0, right: 0)
    tableView.contentInset = insets
    tableView.scrollIndicatorInsets = insets
}
```

The top of the table view is given a content inset equal to the height of the status bar. This will make the content appear below the status bar when the table view is scrolled to the top. The scroll indicators will also underlap the status bar, so you give them the same insets to have them appear just below the status bar.

Notice that you access the tableView property on the **ItemsViewController** to get at the table view. This property is inherited from **UITableViewController** and returns the controller's table view. While you can get the same object by accessing the view of a **UITableViewController**, using tableView tells the compiler that the returned object will be an instance of **UITableView**. Thus, calling a method or accessing a property that is specific to **UITableView** will not generate an error.

Build and run the application. The table view cell content no longer underlaps the status bar when the table view is scrolled to the top (Figure 10.16).

Figure 10.16 Table view with adjusted content inset

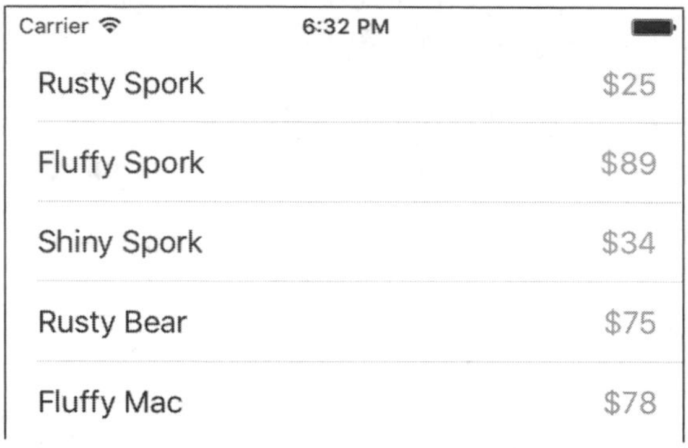

Carrier 🛜	6:32 PM	
Rusty Spork		$25
Fluffy Spork		$89
Shiny Spork		$34
Rusty Bear		$75
Fluffy Mac		$78

Bronze Challenge: Sections

Have the **UITableView** display two sections – one for items worth more than $50 and one for the rest. Before you start this challenge, copy the folder containing the project and all of its source files in Finder. Then tackle the challenge in the copied project; you will need the original to build on in the following chapters.

Silver Challenge: Constant Rows

Make it so the last row of the **UITableView** always has the text "No more items!" Make sure this row appears regardless of the number of items in the store (including 0 items).

Gold Challenge: Customizing the Table

Make each row's height 60 points, except for the last row from the silver challenge, which should remain 44 points. Then, change the font size of every row except the last to 20 points. Finally, make the background of the **UITableView** display an image. (To make this pixel-perfect, you will need an image of the correct size depending on your device. Refer to the chart in Chapter 1.)

11

Editing UITableView

In the last chapter, you created an application that displays a list of **Item** instances in a **UITableView**. The next step is allowing the user to interact with the table – to add, delete, and move rows. Figure 11.1 shows what Homepwner will look like by the end of this chapter.

Figure 11.1 Homepwner in editing mode

Editing Mode

UITableView has an editing property, and when this property is set to true, the **UITableView** enters editing mode. Once the table view is in editing mode, the rows of the table can be manipulated by the user. Depending on how the table view is configured, the user can change the order of the rows, add rows, or remove rows. (Editing mode does not allow the user to edit the *content* of a row.)

But first, the user needs a way to put the **UITableView** in editing mode. For now, you are going to include a button in the *header view* of the table. A header view appears at the top of a table and is useful for adding section-wide or table-wide titles and controls. It can be any **UIView** instance.

Note that the table view uses the word "header" in two different ways: There can be a table header and section headers. Likewise, there can be a table footer and section footers (Figure 11.2).

Figure 11.2 Headers and footers

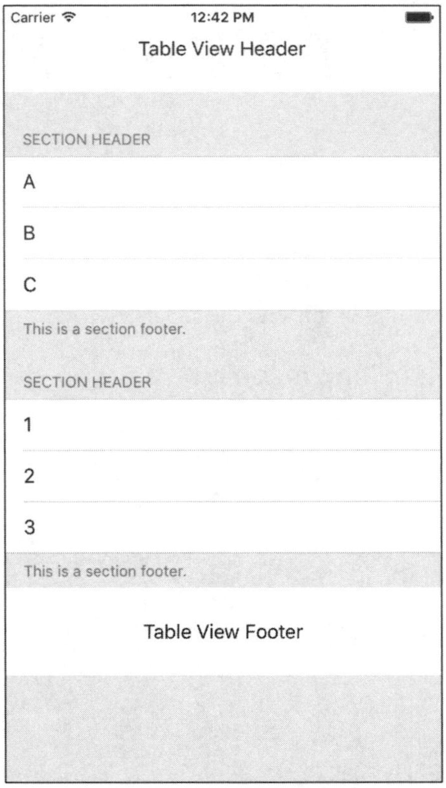

You are creating a table header view. It will have two subviews that are instances of **UIButton**: one to toggle editing mode and the other to add a new **Item** to the table. You could create this view programmatically, but in this case you will create the view and its subviews in the storyboard file.

First, let's set up the necessary code. Reopen Homepwner.xcodeproj. In ItemsViewController.swift, stub out two methods in the implementation.

```
class ItemsViewController: UITableViewController {

    var itemStore: ItemStore!

    @IBAction func addNewItem(_ sender: UIButton) {

    }

    @IBAction func toggleEditingMode(_ sender: UIButton) {

    }
```

Now open Main.storyboard. From the object library, drag a View to the very top of the table view, above the prototype cell. This will add the view as a header view for the table view. Resize the height of this view to be about 60 points. (You can use the size inspector if you want to make it exact.)

Now drag two Buttons from the object library to the header view. Change their text and position them as shown in Figure 11.3. You do not need to be exact – you will add constraints soon to position the buttons.

Figure 11.3 Adding buttons to the header view

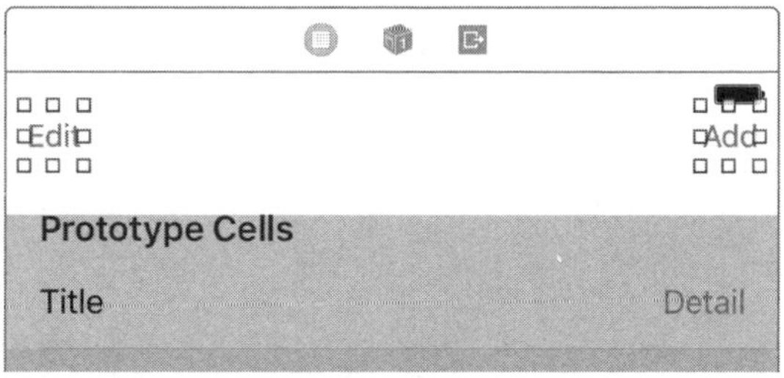

Select both of the buttons and open the Auto Layout Align menu. Select Vertically in Container with a constant of 0. Make sure Update Frames is set to None, and then click Add 2 Constraints (Figure 11.4).

Figure 11.4 Align menu constraints

Open the Add New Constraints menu and configure it as shown in Figure 11.5. Make sure the values for the leading and trailing constraints save after you have typed them; sometimes the values do not save, so it can be a bit tricky. When you have done that, click Add 4 Constraints.

Figure 11.5 Adding new constraints

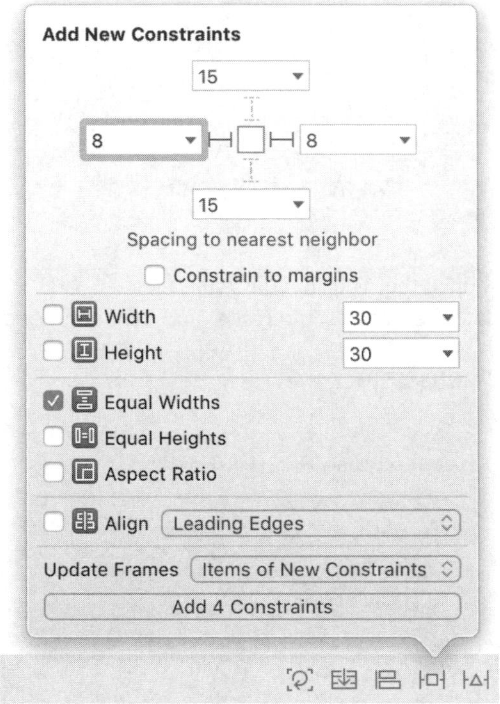

Finally, connect the actions for the two buttons as shown in Figure 11.6.

Figure 11.6 Connecting the two actions

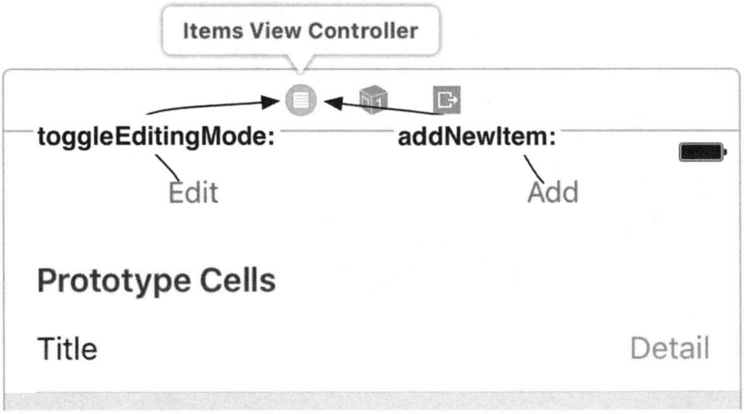

Build and run the application to see the interface.

Now let's implement the **toggleEditingMode(_:)** method. You could toggle the editing property of **UITableView** directly. However, **UIViewController** also has an editing property. A **UITableViewController** instance automatically sets the editing property of its table view to match its own editing property. By setting the editing property on the view controller itself, it can ensure that other aspects of the interface also enter and leave editing mode. You will see an example of this in Chapter 14 with **UIViewController**'s editButtonItem.

To set the isEditing property for a view controller, you call the method **setEditing(_:animated:)**. In ItemsViewController.swift, implement **toggleEditingMode(_:)**.

```
@IBAction func toggleEditingMode(_ sender: UIButton) {
    // If you are currently in editing mode...
    if isEditing {
        // Change text of button to inform user of state
        sender.setTitle("Edit", for: .normal)

        // Turn off editing mode
        setEditing(false, animated: true)
    } else {
        // Change text of button to inform user of state
        sender.setTitle("Done", for: .normal)

        // Enter editing mode
        setEditing(true, animated: true)
    }
}
```

Build and run your application. Tap the Edit button and the **UITableView** will enter editing mode (Figure 11.7).

Figure 11.7 **UITableView** in editing mode

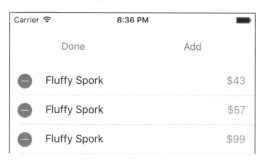

Adding Rows

There are two common interfaces for adding rows to a table view at runtime.

- *A button above the cells of the table view*: usually for adding a record for which there is a detail view. For example, in the Contacts app, you tap a button when you meet a new person and want to take down his or her information.

- *A cell with a green plus sign*: usually for adding a new field to a record, such as when you want to add a birthday to a person's record in the Contacts app. In editing mode, you tap the green plus sign next to "add birthday."

In this exercise, you will use the first option and create a New button in the header view. When this button is tapped, a new row will be added to the **UITableView**.

In ItemsViewController.swift, implement **addNewItem(_:)**.

```
@IBAction func addNewItem(_ sender: UIButton) {
    // Make a new index path for the 0th section, last row
    let lastRow = tableView.numberOfRows(inSection: 0)
    let indexPath = IndexPath(row: lastRow, section: 0)

    // Insert this new row into the table
    tableView.insertRows(at: [indexPath], with: .automatic)
}
```

Build and run the application. Tap the Add button and … the application crashes. The console tells you that the table view has an internal inconsistency exception.

Remember that, ultimately, it is the dataSource of the **UITableView** that determines the number of rows the table view should display. After inserting a new row, the table view has six rows (the original five plus the new one). When the **UITableView** asks its dataSource for the number of rows, the **ItemsViewController** consults the store and returns that there should be five rows. The **UITableView** cannot resolve this inconsistency and throws an exception.

You must make sure that the **UITableView** and its dataSource agree on the number of rows by adding a new **Item** to the **ItemStore** before inserting the new row.

In `ItemsViewController.swift`, update **addNewItem(_:)**.

```
@IBAction func addNewItem(_ sender: UIButton) {
    // Make a new index path for the 0th section, last row
    let lastRow = tableView.numberOfRows(inSection: 0)
    let indexPath = IndexPath(row: lastRow, section: 0)

    // Insert this new row into the table
    tableView.insertRows(at: [indexPath], with: .automatic)

    // Create a new item and add it to the store
    let newItem = itemStore.createItem()

    // Figure out where that item is in the array
    if let index = itemStore.allItems.index(of: newItem) {
        let indexPath = IndexPath(row: index, section: 0)

        // Insert this new row into the table
        tableView.insertRows(at: [indexPath], with: .automatic)
    }
}
```

Build and run the application. Tap the Add button, and the new row will slide into the bottom position of the table. Remember that the role of a view object is to present model objects to the user; updating views without updating the model objects is not very useful.

Now that you have the ability to add rows and items, you no longer need the code that puts five random items into the store.

Open `ItemStore.swift` and remove the initializer code.

```
init() {
    for _ in 0..<5 {
        createItem()
    }
}
```

Build and run the application. There will no longer be any rows when you first launch the application, but you can add some by tapping the Add button.

Deleting Rows

In editing mode, the red circles with the minus sign (shown in Figure 11.7) are deletion controls, and tapping one should delete that row. However, at this point, you cannot actually delete the row. (Try it and see.) Before the table view will delete a row, it calls a method on its data source about the proposed deletion and waits for confirmation.

When deleting a cell, you must do two things: remove the row from the **UITableView** and remove the **Item** associated with it from the **ItemStore**. To pull this off, the **ItemStore** must know how to remove objects from itself.

In ItemStore.swift, implement a new method to remove a specific item.

```
func removeItem(_ item: Item) {
    if let index = allItems.index(of: item) {
        allItems.remove(at: index)
    }
}
```

Now you will implement **tableView(_:commit:forRow:)**, a method from the **UITableViewDataSource** protocol. (This method is called on the **ItemsViewController**. Keep in mind that while the **ItemStore** is where the data is kept, the **ItemsViewController** is the table view's dataSource.)

When **tableView(_:commit:forRowAt:)** is called on the data source, two extra arguments are passed along with it. The first is the **UITableViewCellEditingStyle**, which, in this case, is .delete. The other argument is the **IndexPath** of the row in the table.

In ItemsViewController.swift, implement this method to have the **ItemStore** remove the right object and confirm the row deletion by calling the method **deleteRows(at:with:)** on the table view.

```
override func tableView(_ tableView: UITableView,
                        commit editingStyle: UITableViewCellEditingStyle,
                        forRowAt indexPath: IndexPath) {
    // If the table view is asking to commit a delete command...
    if editingStyle == .delete {
        let item = itemStore.allItems[indexPath.row]
        // Remove the item from the store
        itemStore.removeItem(item)

        // Also remove that row from the table view with an animation
        tableView.deleteRows(at: [indexPath], with: .automatic)
    }
}
```

Build and run your application, create some rows, and then delete a row. It will disappear. Notice that swipe-to-delete works also.

Moving Rows

To change the order of rows in a **UITableView**, you will use another method from the **UITableViewDataSource** protocol – **tableView(_:moveRowAt:to:)**.

To delete a row, you had to call the method **deleteRows(at:with:)** on the **UITableView** to confirm the deletion. Moving a row, however, does not require confirmation: The table view moves the row on its own authority and reports the move to its data source by calling the method **tableView(_:moveRowAt:to:)**. You implement this method to update your data source to match the new order.

But before you can implement this method, you need to give the **ItemStore** a method to change the order of items in its allItems array.

In ItemStore.swift, implement this new method.

```
func moveItem(from fromIndex: Int, to toIndex: Int) {
    if fromIndex == toIndex {
        return
    }

    // Get reference to object being moved so you can reinsert it
    let movedItem = allItems[fromIndex]

    // Remove item from array
    allItems.remove(at: fromIndex)

    // Insert item in array at new location
    allItems.insert(movedItem, at: toIndex)
}
```

In ItemsViewController.swift, implement **tableView(_:moveRowAt:to:)** to update the store.

```
override func tableView(_ tableView: UITableView,
                        moveRowAt sourceIndexPath: IndexPath,
                        to destinationIndexPath: IndexPath) {
    // Update the model
    itemStore.moveItem(from: sourceIndexPath.row, to: destinationIndexPath.row)
}
```

Build and run your application. Add a few items, then tap Edit and check out the new reordering controls (the three horizontal lines) on the side of each row. Touch and hold a reordering control and move the row to a new position (Figure 11.8).

Figure 11.8 Moving a row

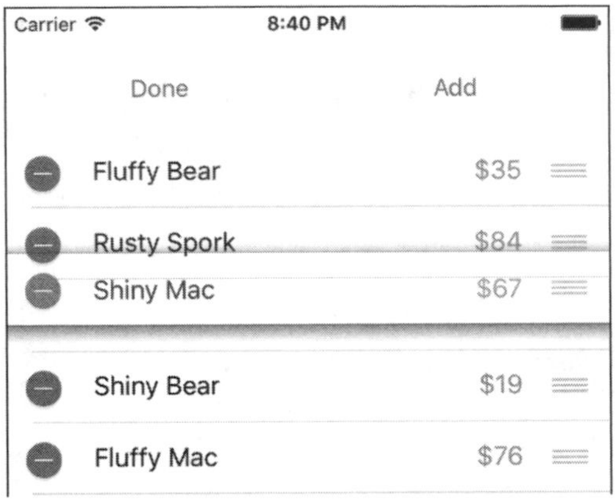

Note that simply implementing `tableView(_:moveRowAt:to:)` caused the reordering controls to appear. The **UITableView** can ask its data source at runtime whether it implements `tableView(_:moveRowAt:to:)`. If it does, then the table view adds the reordering controls whenever the table view enters editing mode.

Displaying User Alerts

In this section, you are going to learn about user alerts and the different ways of configuring and displaying them. User alerts can provide your application with a better user experience, so you will use them fairly often.

Alerts are often used to warn users that an important action is about to happen and perhaps give them the opportunity to cancel that action. When you want to display an alert, you create an instance of **UIAlertController** with a preferred style. The two available styles are **UIAlertControllerStyle.actionSheet** and **UIAlertControllerStyle.alert** (Figure 11.9).

Figure 11.9 **UIAlertController** styles

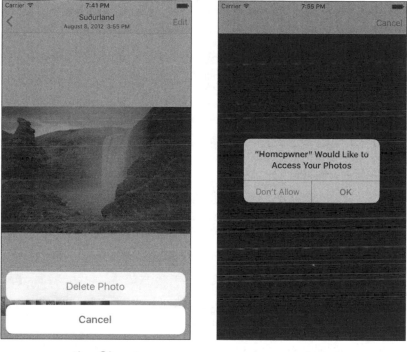

.actionSheet   .alert

The **.actionSheet** style is used to present the user with a list of actions from which to choose. The **.alert** type is used to display critical information to require the user to decide how to proceed. The distinction may seem subtle, but if the user can back out of a decision or if the action is not critical, then an **.actionSheet** is probably the best choice.

You are going to use a **UIAlertController** to confirm the deletion of items. You will use the **.actionSheet** style because the purpose of the alert is to confirm or cancel a possibly destructive action.

Open `ItemsViewController.swift` and modify **tableView(_:commit:forRowAt:)** to ask the user to confirm or cancel the deletion of an item.

```
override func tableView(_ tableView: UITableView,
                        commit editingStyle: UITableViewCellEditingStyle,
                        forRowAt indexPath: IndexPath) {
    // If the table view is asking to commit a delete command...
    if editingStyle == .delete {
        let item = itemStore.allItems[indexPath.row]

        let title = "Delete \(item.name)?"
        let message = "Are you sure you want to delete this item?"

        let ac = UIAlertController(title: title,
                                   message: message,
                                   preferredStyle: .actionSheet)

        // Remove the item from the store
        itemStore.removeItem(item)

        // Also remove that row from the table view with an animation
        tableView.deleteRows(at: [indexPath], with: .automatic)
    }
}
```

After determining that the user wants to delete an item, you create an instance of **UIAlertController** with an appropriate title and message describing what action is about to take place. Also, you specify the **.actionSheet** style for the alert.

The actions that the user can choose from when shown an alert are instances of **UIAlertAction**, and you can add multiple ones regardless of the alert's style. Actions are added to the **UIAlertController** using the **addAction(_:)** method.

Add the necessary actions to the action sheet in **tableView(_:commit:forRowAt:)**.

```
...
let ac = UIAlertController(title: title,
                           message: message,
                           preferredStyle: .actionSheet)

let cancelAction = UIAlertAction(title: "Cancel", style: .cancel, handler: nil)
ac.addAction(cancelAction)

let deleteAction = UIAlertAction(title: "Delete", style: .destructive,
                            handler: { (action) -> Void in
    // Remove the item from the store
    self.itemStore.removeItem(item)

    // Also remove that row from the table view with an animation
    self.tableView.deleteRows(at: [indexPath], with: .automatic)
})
ac.addAction(deleteAction)
...
```

The first action has a title of "Cancel" and is created using the .cancel style. The .cancel style results in text in a standard blue font. This action will allow the user to back out of deleting an **Item**. The handler parameter allows a closure to be executed when that action occurs. Because no other action is needed, nil is passed as the argument.

The second action has a title of "Delete" and is created using the .destructive style. Because destructive actions should be clearly marked and noticed, the .destructive style results in bright red text. If the user selects this action, then the item and the table view cell need to be removed. This is all done within the handler closure that is passed to the action's initializer.

Now that the actions have been added, the alert controller can be displayed to the user. Because **UIAlertController** is a subclass of **UIViewController**, you can present it to the user *modally*. A *modal view controller* takes over the entire screen until it has finished its work.

To present a view controller modally, you call **present(_:animated:completion:)** on the view controller whose view is on the screen. The view controller to be presented is passed to it, and this view controller's view takes over the screen.

```
...
let deleteAction = UIAlertAction(title: "Delete", style: .destructive,
                            handler: { (action) -> Void in
    // Remove the item from the store
    self.itemStore.removeItem(item)

    // Also remove that row from the table view with an animation
    self.tableView.deleteRows(at: [indexPath], with: .automatic)
})
ac.addAction(deleteAction)

// Present the alert controller
present(ac, animated: true, completion: nil)
...
```

Build and run the application and delete an item. An action sheet will be presented for you to confirm the deletion (Figure 11.10).

Figure 11.10 Deleting an item

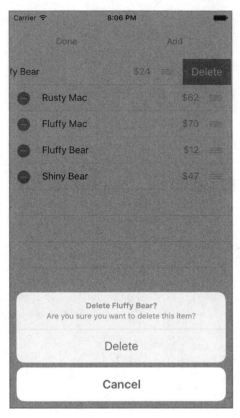

Design Patterns

A *design pattern* solves a common software engineering problem. Design patterns are not actual snippets of code, but instead are abstract ideas or approaches that you can use in your applications. Good design patterns are valuable and powerful tools for any developer.

The consistent use of design patterns throughout the development process reduces the mental overhead in solving a problem so you can create complex applications more easily and rapidly. Here are some of the design patterns that you have already used:

- *Delegation*: One object delegates certain responsibilities to another object. You used delegation with the **UITextField** to be informed when the contents of the text field change.

- *Data source*: A data source is similar to a delegate, but instead of reacting to another object, a data source is responsible for providing data to another object when requested. You used the data source pattern with table views: Each table view has a data source that is responsible for, at a minimum, telling the table view how many rows to display and which cell it should display at each index path.

- *Model-View-Controller*: Each object in your applications fulfills one of three roles. Model objects are the data. Views display the UI. Controllers provide the glue that ties the models and views together.

- *Target-action pairs*: One object calls a method on another object when a specific event occurs. The target is the object that has a method called on it, and the action is the method being called. For example, you used target-action pairs with buttons: When a touch event occurs, a method will be called on another object (often a view controller).

Apple is very consistent in its use of these design patterns, and so it is important to understand and recognize them. Keep an eye out for these patterns as you continue through this book! Recognizing them will help you learn new classes and frameworks much more easily.

Bronze Challenge: Renaming the Delete Button

When deleting a row, a confirmation button appears labeled Delete. Change the label of this button to Remove.

Silver Challenge: Preventing Reordering

Make it so the table view always shows a final row that says "No more items!" (This part of the challenge is the same as a challenge from the last chapter. If you have already done it, you can copy your code from before.) Now, make it so that the final row cannot be moved.

Gold Challenge: Really Preventing Reordering

After completing the silver challenge, you may notice that even though you cannot move the No more items! row itself, you can still drag other rows underneath it. Make it so that – no matter what – the No more items! row can never be knocked out of the last position. Finally, make it undeletable.

12

Subclassing UITableViewCell

A **UITableView** displays a list of **UITableViewCell** objects. For many applications, the basic cell with its textLabel, detailTextLabel, and imageView is sufficient. However, when you need a cell with more detail or a different layout, you subclass **UITableViewCell**.

In this chapter, you will create a subclass of **UITableViewCell** named **ItemCell** that will display **Item** instances more effectively. Each of these cells will show an **Item**'s name, its value in dollars, and its serial number (Figure 12.1).

Figure 12.1 Homepwner with subclassed table view cells

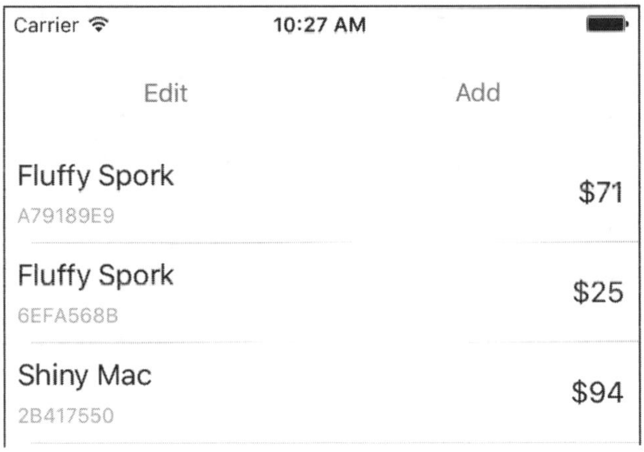

You customize the appearance of **UITableViewCell** subclasses by adding subviews to its contentView. Adding subviews to the contentView instead of directly to the cell itself is important because the cell will resize its contentView at certain times. For example, when a table view enters editing mode, the contentView resizes itself to make room for the editing controls (Figure 12.2). If you added subviews directly to the **UITableViewCell**, the editing controls would obscure the subviews. The cell cannot adjust its size when entering edit mode (it must remain the width of the table view), but the contentView can and does.

Figure 12.2 Table view cell layout in standard and editing mode

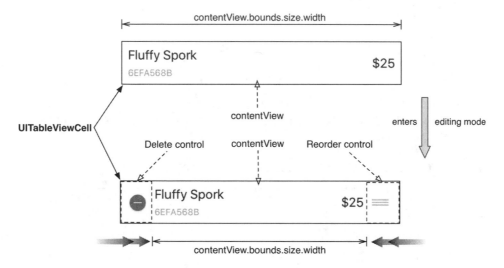

Creating ItemCell

Create a new Swift file named ItemCell. In ItemCell.swift, define **ItemCell** as a **UITableViewCell** subclass.

```
import Foundation
import UIKit

class ItemCell: UITableViewCell {

}
```

The easiest way to configure a **UITableViewCell** subclass is through a storyboard. In Chapter 10, you saw that storyboards for table view controllers have a Prototype Cells section. This is where you will lay out the content for the **ItemCell**.

Open Main.storyboard and select the UITableViewCell in the document outline. Open its attributes inspector, change the Style to Custom, and change the Identifier to ItemCell.

Now open its identity inspector (the ▦ tab). In the Class field, enter ItemCell (Figure 12.3).

Figure 12.3 Changing the cell class

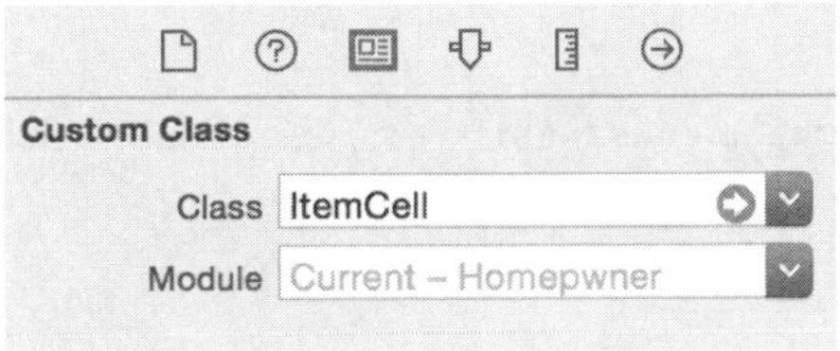

Change the height of the prototype cell to be about 65 points tall. You can change it either on the canvas or by selecting the table view cell and changing the Row Height from its size inspector.

An **ItemCell** will display three text elements, so drag three **UILabel** objects onto the cell. Configure them as shown in Figure 12.4. Make the text of the bottom label a slightly smaller font in a light shade of gray. Make sure that the labels do not overlap at all.

Figure 12.4 **ItemCell**'s layout

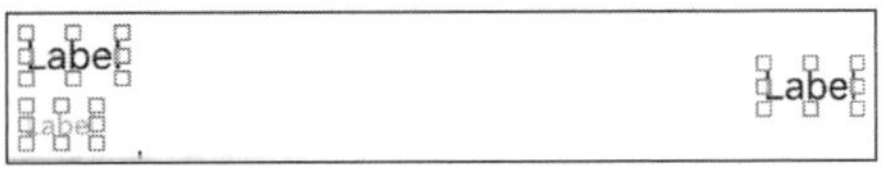

Add constraints to these three labels as follows.

1. Select the top-left label and open the Auto Layout Add New Constraints menu. Select the top and left strut and then click Add 2 Constraints.

2. You want the bottom-left label to always be aligned with the top-left label. Control-drag from the bottom-left label to the top-left label and select Leading.

3. With the bottom-left label still selected, open the Add New Constraints menu, select the bottom strut, and then click Add 1 Constraint.

4. Select the right label and Control-drag from this label to its superview on its right side. Select both Trailing Space to Container Margin and Center Vertically in Container.

5. Select the bottom-left label and open its size inspector. Find the Vertical Content Hugging Priority and lower it to 250. Lower the Vertical Content Compression Resistance Priority to 749. You will learn what these Auto Layout properties do in Chapter 13.

6. Your frames might be misplaced, so select the three labels and click the Update Frames button.

Exposing the Properties of ItemCell

For **ItemsViewController** to configure the content of an **ItemCell** in **tableView(_:cellForRowAt:)**, the cell must have properties that expose the three labels. These properties will be set through outlet connections in Main.storyboard.

The next step, then, is to create and connect outlets on **ItemCell** for each of its subviews.

Open ItemCell.swift and add three properties for the outlets.

```swift
import UIKit

class ItemCell: UITableViewCell {

    @IBOutlet var nameLabel: UILabel!
    @IBOutlet var serialNumberLabel: UILabel!
    @IBOutlet var valueLabel: UILabel!

}
```

You are going to connect the outlets for the three views to the **ItemCell**. When connecting outlets earlier in the book, you Control-dragged from view controller in the storyboard to the appropriate view. But the outlets for **ItemCell** are not outlets on a controller. They are outlets on a view: the custom **UITableViewCell** subclass.

Therefore, to connect the outlets for **ItemCell**, you will connect them to the **ItemCell**.

Open Main.storyboard. Control-click on the ItemCell in the document outline and make the three outlet connections shown in Figure 12.5.

Figure 12.5 Connecting the outlets

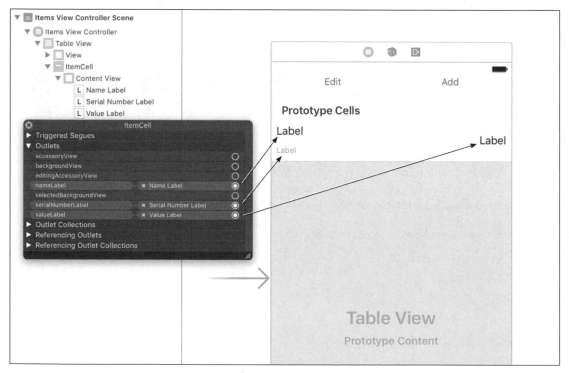

Using ItemCell

Let's get your custom cells onscreen. In **ItemsViewController**'s **tableView(_:cellForRowAt:)** method, you will dequeue an instance of **ItemCell** for every row in the table.

Now that you are using a custom **UITableViewCell** subclass, the table view needs to know how tall each row is. There are a few ways to accomplish this, but the simplest way is to set the rowHeight property of the table view to a constant value. You will see another way later in this chapter.

Open ItemsViewController.swift and update **viewDidLoad()** to set the height of the table view cells.

```
override func viewDidLoad() {
    super.viewDidLoad()

    // Get the height of the status bar
    let statusBarHeight = UIApplication.shared.statusBarFrame.height

    let insets = UIEdgeInsets(top: statusBarHeight, left: 0, bottom: 0, right: 0)
    tableView.contentInset = insets
    tableView.scrollIndicatorInsets = insets

    tableView.rowHeight = 65
}
```

Now that you have registered the **ItemCell** with the table view (using the prototype cells in the storyboard), you can ask the table view to dequeue a cell with the identifier "ItemCell."

In ItemsViewController.swift, modify **tableView(_:cellForRowAt:)**.

```
override func tableView(_ tableView: UITableView,
                        cellForRowAt indexPath: NSIndexPath) -> UITableViewCell {
    // Get a new or recycled cell
    let cell = tableView.dequeueReusableCell(withIdentifier: "UITableViewCell",
        for: indexPath)

    let cell = tableView.dequeueReusableCell(withIdentifier: "ItemCell",
        for: indexPath) as! ItemCell

    // Set the text on the cell with the description of the item
    // that is at the nth index of items, where n = row this cell
    // will appear in on the tableview
    let item = itemStore.allItems[indexPath.row]

    cell.textLabel?.text = item.name
    cell.detailTextLabel?.text = "$\(item.valueInDollars)"

    // Configure the cell with the Item
    cell.nameLabel.text = item.name
    cell.serialNumberLabel.text = item.serialNumber
    cell.valueLabel.text = "$\(item.valueInDollars)"

    return cell
}
```

First, the reuse identifier is updated to reflect your new subclass. The code at the end of this method is fairly obvious – for each label on the cell, set its text to some property from the appropriate **Item**.

Build and run the application. The new cells now load with their labels populated with the values from each **Item**.

Dynamic Cell Heights

Currently, the cells have a fixed height of 65 points. It is much better to allow the content of the cell to drive its height. That way, if the content ever changes, the table view cell's height can change automatically.

You can achieve this goal, as you have probably guessed, with Auto Layout. The **UITableViewCell** needs to have vertical constraints that will exactly determine the height of the cell. Currently, **ItemCell** does not have sufficient constraints for this. You need to add a constraint between the two left labels that fixes the vertical spacing between them.

Open Main.storyboard. Control-drag from the nameLabel to the serialNumberLabel and select Vertical Spacing.

Now open ItemsViewController.swift and update **viewDidLoad()** to tell the table view that it should compute the cell heights based on the constraints.

```
override func viewDidLoad() {
    super.viewDidLoad()

    // Get the height of the status bar
    let statusBarHeight = UIApplication.shared.statusBarFrame.height

    let insets = UIEdgeInsets(top: statusBarHeight, left: 0, bottom: 0, right: 0)
    tableView.contentInset = insets
    tableView.scrollIndicatorInsets = insets

    tableView.rowHeight = 65
    tableView.rowHeight = UITableViewAutomaticDimension
    tableView.estimatedRowHeight = 65
}
```

UITableViewAutomaticDimension is the default value for rowHeight, so while it is not necessary to add, it is useful for understanding what is going on. Setting the estimatedRowHeight property on the table view can improve performance. Instead of asking each cell for its height when the table view loads, setting this property allows some of that performance cost to be deferred until the user starts scrolling.

Build and run the application. The application will look the same as it did before. In the next section, you will learn about a technology called *Dynamic Type* that will take advantage of the automatically resizing table view cells.

Dynamic Type

Creating an interface that appeals to everyone can be daunting. Some people prefer more compact interfaces so they can see more information at once. Others might want to be able to easily see information at a glance, or perhaps they have poor eyesight. In short: People have different needs. Good developers strive to make apps that meet those needs.

Dynamic Type is a technology that helps realize this goal by providing specifically designed *text styles* that are optimized for legibility. Users can select one of seven preferred text sizes from within Apple's Settings application (plus a few additional larger sizes from within the Accessibility section), and apps that support Dynamic Type will have their fonts scaled appropriately. In this section, you will update **ItemCell** to support Dynamic Type. Figure 12.6 shows the application rendered at the smallest and largest user-selectable Dynamic Type sizes.

Figure 12.6 **ItemCell** with Dynamic Type supported

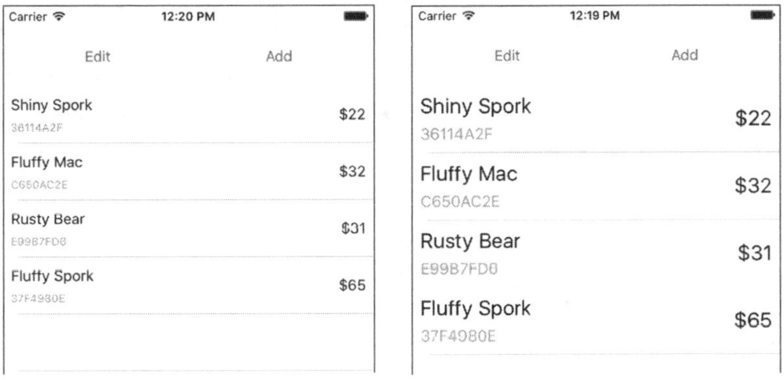

The Dynamic Type system is centered around text styles. When a font is requested for a given text style, the system will consider the user's preferred text size in association with the text style to return an appropriately configured font. Figure 12.7 shows the different text styles.

Figure 12.7 Text styles

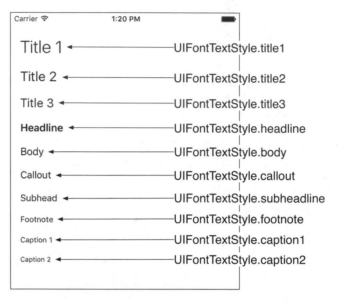

Open Main.storyboard. Let's update the labels to use the text styles instead of fixed fonts. Select the nameLabel and valueLabel and open the attributes inspector. Click on the text icon to the right of Font. For Font, choose Text Styles - Body (Figure 12.8). Repeat the same steps for the serialNumberLabel, choosing the Caption 1 text style.

Figure 12.8 Changing the text style

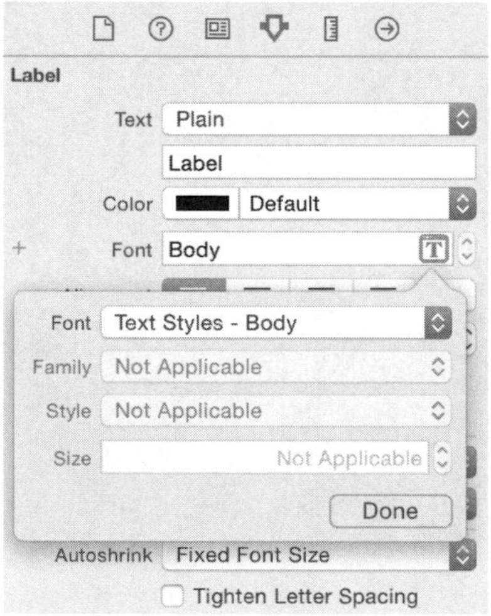

Now let's change the preferred font size. You do this through the Settings application.

Build and run the application. From the simulator's Hardware menu, select Home. Next, on the simulator's Home screen, open the Settings application. Choose General, then Accessibility, and then Larger Text. (On an actual device, this menu can also be accessed in Settings via Display & Brightness → Text Size.) Drag the slider all the way to the left to set the font size to the smallest value (Figure 12.9).

Figure 12.9 Text size settings

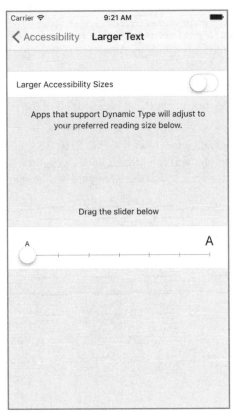

Build and run the application. (If you switch back to the application, either using the task switcher or through the Home screen, you will not see the changes. You will fix that in the next section.) Add some items to the table view and you will see the new smaller font sizes in action.

Responding to user changes

When the user changes the preferred text size and returns to the application, the table view will get reloaded. Unfortunately, the labels will not know about the new preferred text size. To fix this, you need to have the labels automatically adjust to content size changes.

Open `ItemCell.swift` and override `awakeFromNib()` to have the labels automatically adjust.

```
override func awakeFromNib() {
    super.awakeFromNib()

    nameLabel.adjustsFontForContentSizeCategory = true
    serialNumberLabel.adjustsFontForContentSizeCategory = true
    valueLabel.adjustsFontForContentSizeCategory = true
}
```

The method `awakeFromNib()` gets called on an object after it is loaded from an archive, which in this case is the storyboard file. By the time this method is called, all of the outlets have values and can be used.

Build and run the application and add a few rows. Go into Settings and change the preferred reading size to the largest size. Unlike before, you can now switch back to Homepwner, either by opening the task switcher or through the Home screen, and the table view will update to reflect the new preferred text size.

Bronze Challenge: Cell Colors

Update the **ItemCell** to display the `valueInDollars` in green if the value is less than 50 and red if the value is greater than or equal to 50.

13
Stack Views

You have been using Auto Layout throughout this book to create flexible interfaces that scale across device types and sizes. Auto Layout is a very powerful technology, but with that power comes complexity. Laying out an interface well often needs a lot of constraints, and it can be difficult to create dynamic interfaces due to the need to constantly add and remove constraints.

Often, an interface (or a subsection of the interface) can be laid out in a linear fashion. Think about the other applications you wrote: The Quiz application from Chapter 1 consisted of four subviews that were laid out vertically. The same is true for the WorldTrotter application; the `ConversionViewController` had a vertical interface consisting of a text field and a few labels.

Interfaces that have a linear layout are great candidates for using a *stack view*. A stack view is an instance of `UIStackView` that allows you to create a vertical or horizontal layout that is easy to lay out and manages most of the constraints that you would typically have to manage yourself. Perhaps best of all, you are able to nest stack views within other stack views, which allows you to create truly amazing interfaces in a fraction of the time.

In this chapter, you are going to continue working on Homepwner to create an interface for displaying the details of a specific Item. The interface that you create will consist of multiple nested stack views, both vertical and horizontal (Figure 13.1).

Figure 13.1 Homepwner with stack views

Using UIStackView

You are going to create an interface for editing the details of an **Item**. You will get the basic interface working in this chapter, and then you will finish implementing the details in Chapter 14.

At the top level, you will have a vertical stack view with four elements displaying the item's name, serial number, value, and date created (Figure 13.2).

Figure 13.2 Vertical stack view layout

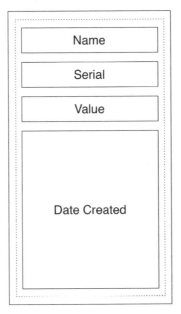

Open your Homepwner project and then open Main.storyboard. Drag a new View Controller from the object library onto the canvas. Drag a Vertical Stack View from the object library onto the view for the View Controller. Add constraints to the stack view to pin it to the leading and trailing margins, and pin the top and bottom edges to be 8 points from the top and bottom layout guides.

Now drag four instances of **UILabel** from the object library onto the stack view. From top to bottom, give these labels the text "Name," "Serial," "Value," and "Date Created" (Figure 13.3).

Figure 13.3 Labels added to the stack view

You can see a problem right away: The labels all have a red border (indicating an Auto Layout problem) and there is a warning that some views are vertically ambiguous. There are two ways you can fix this issue: by using Auto Layout, or by using a property on the stack view. Let's work through the Auto Layout solution first because it highlights an important aspect of Auto Layout.

Implicit constraints

You learned in Chapter 3 that every view has an intrinsic content size. You also learned that if you do not specify constraints that explicitly determine the width or height, the view will derive its width or height from its intrinsic content size. How does this work?

It does this using implicit constraints derived from a view's *content hugging priorities* and its *content compression resistance priorities*. A view has one of these priorities for each axis:

- horizontal content hugging priority

- vertical content hugging priority

- horizontal content compression resistance priority

- vertical content compression resistance priority

Content hugging priorities

The content hugging priority is like a rubber band that is placed around a view. The rubber band makes the view not want to be bigger than its intrinsic content size in that dimension. Each priority is associated with a value from 0 to 1000. A value of 1000 means that a view cannot get bigger than its intrinsic content size on that dimension.

Let's look at an example with just the horizontal dimension. Say you have two labels next to one another with constraints both between the two views and between each view and its superview, as shown in Figure 13.4.

Figure 13.4 Two labels side by side

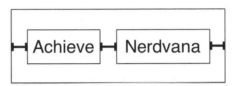

This works great until the superview becomes wider. At that point, which label should become wider? The first label, the second label, or both? As Figure 13.5 shows, the interface is currently ambiguous.

Figure 13.5 Ambiguous layout

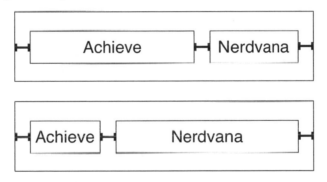

This is where the content hugging priority becomes relevant. The view with the higher content hugging priority is the one that does not stretch. You can think about the priority value as the "strength" of the rubber band. The higher the priority value, the stronger the rubber band, and the more it wants to hug to its intrinsic content size.

Content compression resistance priorities

The content compression resistance priorities determine how much a view resists getting smaller than its intrinsic content size. Consider the same two labels from Figure 13.4. What would happen if the superview's width decreased? One of the labels would need to truncate its text (Figure 13.6). But which one?

Figure 13.6 Compressed ambiguous layout

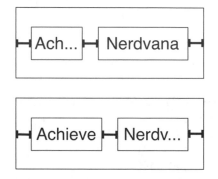

The view with the greater content compression resistance priority is the one that will resist compression and, therefore, not truncate its text.

With this knowledge, you can now fix the problem with the stack view.

Select the Date Created label and open its size inspector. Find the Vertical Content Hugging Priority and lower it to 249. Now the other three labels have a higher content hugging priority, so they will all hug to their intrinsic content height. The Date Created label will stretch to fill in the remaining space.

Stack view distribution

Let's take a look at another way of solving the problem. Stack views have a number of properties that determine how their content is laid out.

Select the stack view, either on the canvas or using the document outline. Open its attributes inspector and find the section at the top labeled Stack View. One of the properties that determines how the content is laid out is the Distribution property. Currently it is set to Fill, which lets the views lay out their content based on their intrinsic content size. Change the value to Fill Equally. This will resize the labels so that they all have the same height, ignoring the intrinsic content size (Figure 13.7). Be sure to read the documentation for the other distribution values that a stack view can have.

Figure 13.7 Stack view set to fill equally

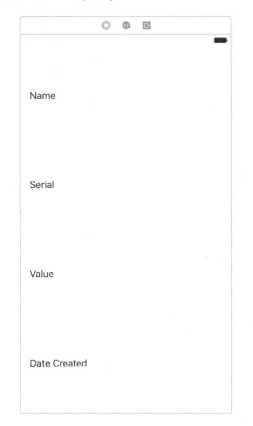

Change the Distribution of the stack view back to Fill; this is the value you will want going forward in this chapter.

Nested stack views

One of the most powerful features of stack views is that they can be nested within one another. You will use this to nest horizontal stack views within the larger vertical stack view. The top three labels will have a text field next to them that displays the corresponding value for the Item and will also allow the user to edit that value.

Select the Name label on the canvas. Click the second icon from the left in the Auto Layout constraints menu: ⊞. This will embed the selected view in a stack view.

Select the new stack view and open its attributes inspector. The stack view is currently a vertical stack view, but you want it to be a horizontal stack view. Change the Axis to Horizontal.

Now drag a Text Field from the object library to the right of the Name label. Because labels, by default, have a greater content hugging priority than text fields, the label hugs to its intrinsic content width and the text field stretches. The label and the text field currently have the same content compression resistance priorities, which would result in an ambiguous layout if the text field's text was too long. Open the size inspector for the text field and set its Horizontal Content Compression Resistance Priority to 749. This will ensure that the text field's text will be truncated if necessary, rather than the label.

Stack view spacing

The label and text field look a little squished because there is no spacing between them. Stack views allow you to customize the spacing between items.

Select the horizontal stack view and open its attributes inspector. Change the Spacing to be 8 points. Notice that the text field shrinks to accommodate the spacing, because it is less resistant to compression than the label.

Repeat these steps for the Serial and Value labels:

1. Select the label and click the ⊞ icon.

2. Change the stack view to be a horizontal stack view.

3. Drag a text field onto the horizontal stack view and change its horizontal content compression resistance priority to be 749.

4. Update the stack view to have a spacing of 8 points.

There are a couple of other tweaks you will want to make to the interface: The vertical stack view needs some spacing. The Date Created label should have a center text alignment. And the Name, Serial, and Value labels should be the same width.

Select the vertical stack view, open its attributes inspector, and update the Spacing to be 8 points. Then select the Date Created label, open its attributes inspector, and change the Alignment to be centered. That solves the first two issues.

Although stack views substantially reduce the number of constraints that you need to add to your interface, some constraints are still important. With the interface as is, the text fields do not align on their leading edge due to the difference in the widths of the labels. (The difference is not very noticeable in English, but it becomes more pronounced when localized into other languages.) To solve this, you will add leading edge constraints between the three text fields.

Control-drag from the Name text field to the Serial text field and select Leading. Then do the same for the Serial text field and the Value text field. The completed interface will look like Figure 13.8.

Figure 13.8 Final stack view interface

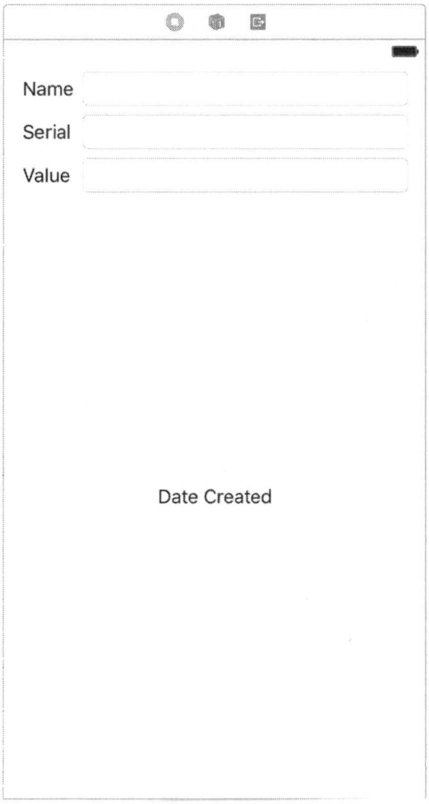

Stack views allow you to create very rich interfaces in a fraction of the time it would take to configure them manually using constraints. Constraints are still added, but they are being managed by the stack view itself instead of by you. Stack views allow you to have very dynamic interfaces at runtime. You can add and remove views from stack views by using **addArrangedSubview(_:)**, **insertArrangedSubview(_:at:)**, and **removeArrangedSubview(_:)**. You can also toggle the hidden property on a view in a stack view. The stack view will automatically lay out its content to reflect that value.

Segues

Most iOS applications have a number of view controllers that users navigate between. Storyboards allow you to set up these interactions as *segues* without having to write code.

A segue moves another view controller's view onto the screen and is represented by an instance of **UIStoryboardSegue**. Each segue has a *style*, an *action item*, and an *identifier*. The style of a segue determines how the view controller will be presented. The action item is the view object in the storyboard file that triggers the segue, like a button, a table view cell, or some other **UIControl**. The identifier is used to programmatically access the segue. This is useful when you want to trigger a segue that does not come from an action item, like a shake or some other interface element that cannot be set up in the storyboard file.

Let's start with a *show* segue. A show segue displays a view controller depending on the context in which it is displayed. The segue will be between the table view controller and the new view controller. The action items will be the table view's cells; tapping a cell will show the view controller modally.

In Main.storyboard, select the **ItemCell** prototype cell on the Items View Controller. Control-drag from the cell to the new view controller that you set up in the previous section. (Make sure you are Control-dragging from the cell and not the table view!) A black panel will appear that lists the possible styles for this segue. Select Show from the Selection Segue section (Figure 13.9).

Figure 13.9 Setting up a show segue

Notice the arrow that goes from the table view controller to the new view controller. This is a segue. The icon in the circle tells you that this segue is a show segue – each segue has a unique icon.

Build and run the application. Tap a cell and the new view controller will slide up from the bottom of the screen. (Sliding up from the bottom is the default behavior when presenting a view controller modally.)

So far, so good! But there are two problems at the moment: The view controller is not displaying the information for the **Item** that was selected, and there is no way to dismiss the view controller to return to the **ItemsViewController**. You will fix the first issue in the next section, and you will fix the second issue in Chapter 14.

Hooking Up the Content

To display the information for the selected **Item**, you will need to create a new **UIViewController** subclass.

Create a new Swift file and name it `DetailViewController`. Open `DetailViewController.swift` and declare a new **UIViewController** subclass named **DetailViewController**.

```
import Foundation
import UIKit

class DetailViewController: UIViewController {

}
```

Because you need to be able to access the subviews you created during runtime, **DetailViewController** needs outlets for them. The plan is to add four new outlets to **DetailViewController** and then make the connections. In previous exercises, you did this in two distinct steps: First, you added the outlets in the Swift file, then you made connections in the storyboard file. You can do both at once using the assistant editor.

With `DetailViewController.swift` open, Option-click on `Main.storyboard` in the project navigator. This will open the file in the assistant editor right next to `DetailViewController.swift`. (You can toggle the assistant editor by clicking the middle button from the Editor control at the top of the workspace. The shortcut to display the assistant editor is Command-Option-Return, and the shortcut to return to the standard editor is Command-Return.)

Your window has become a little cluttered. Let's make some temporary space. Hide the navigator area by clicking the left button in the View control at the top of the workspace (the shortcut for this is Command-0). Then, hide the document outline in Interface Builder by clicking the toggle button in the lower-left corner of the editor. Your workspace should now look like Figure 13.10.

Figure 13.10 Laying out the workspace

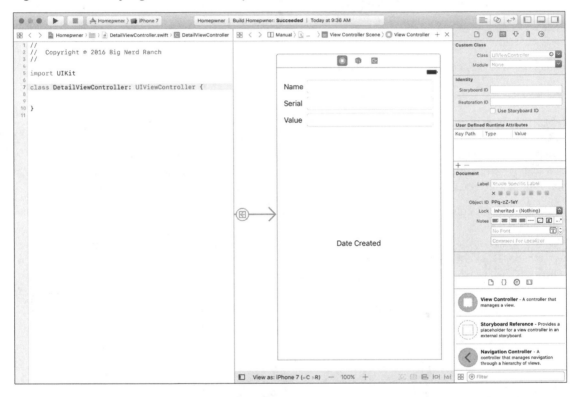

Before you connect the outlets, you need to tell the detail interface that it should be associated with the **DetailViewController**. Select the View Controller on the canvas and open its identity inspector. Change the Class to be DetailViewController (Figure 13.11).

Figure 13.11 Setting the view controller class

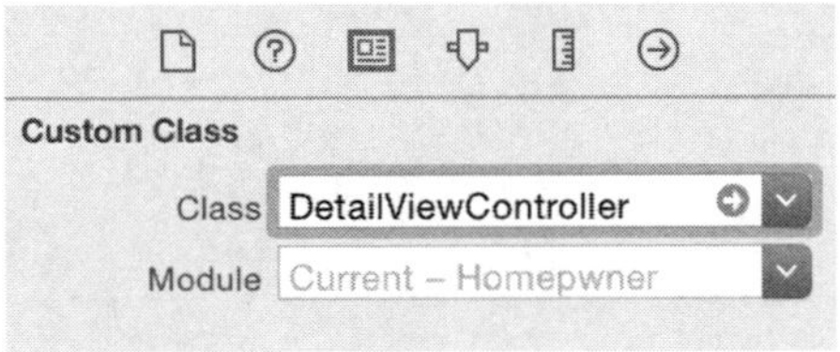

The three instances of **UITextField** and bottom instance of **UILabel** will be outlets in **DetailViewController**. Control-drag from the **UITextField** next to the Name label to the top of DetailViewController.swift, as shown in Figure 13.12.

Figure 13.12 Dragging from storyboard to source file

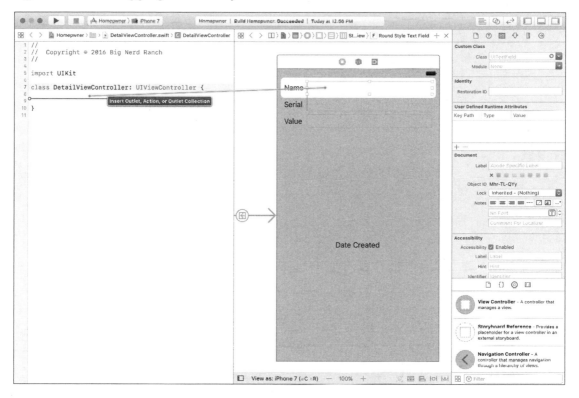

Let go and a pop-up window will appear. Enter nameField into the Name field, make sure the Storage is set to Strong, and click Connect (Figure 13.13).

Figure 13.13 Autogenerating an outlet and making a connection

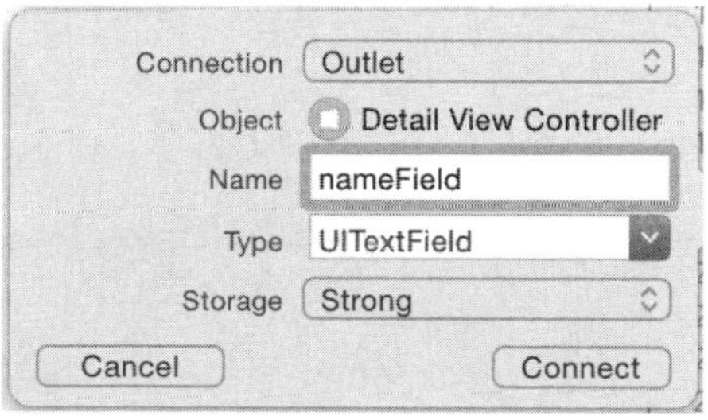

This will create an @IBOutlet property of type **UITextField** named nameField in **DetailViewController**.

In addition, this **UITextField** is already connected to the nameField outlet of the **DetailViewController**. You can verify this by Control-clicking on the Detail View Controller to see the connections. Also notice that hovering your mouse above the nameField connection in the panel that appears will reveal the **UITextField** that you connected. Two birds, one stone.

Create the other three outlets the same way and name them as shown in Figure 13.14.

Figure 13.14 Connection diagram

After you make the connections, DetailViewController.swift should look like this:

```
import UIKit

class DetailViewController: UIViewController {

    @IBOutlet var nameField: UITextField!
    @IBOutlet var serialNumberField: UITextField!
    @IBOutlet var valueField: UITextField!
    @IBOutlet var dateLabel: UILabel!

}
```

If your file looks different, then your outlets are not connected correctly. Fix any disparities between your file and the code shown above in three steps: First, go through the Control-drag process and make connections again until you have the four lines shown above in your DetailViewController.swift. Second, remove any wrong code (like non-property method declarations or properties) that got created. Finally, check for any bad connections in the storyboard file – in Main.storyboard, Control-click on the Detail View Controller. If there are yellow warning signs next to any connection, click the x icon next to those connections to disconnect them.

It is important to ensure that there are no bad connections in an interface file. A bad connection typically happens when you change the name of a property but do not update the connection in the interface file or when you completely remove a property but do not remove it from the interface file. Either way, a bad connection will cause your application to crash when the interface file is loaded.

With the connections made, you can close the assistant editor and return to viewing just DetailViewController.swift.

DetailViewController will hold on to a reference to the Item that is being displayed. When its view is loaded, you will set the text on each text field to the appropriate value from the Item instance.

In DetailViewController.swift, add a property for an Item instance and override viewWillAppear(_:) to set up the interface.

```
class DetailViewController: UIViewController {

    @IBOutlet var nameField: UITextField!
    @IBOutlet var serialNumberField: UITextField!
    @IBOutlet var valueField: UITextField!
    @IBOutlet var dateLabel: UILabel!

    var item: Item!

    override func viewWillAppear(_ animated: Bool) {
        super.viewWillAppear(animated)

        nameField.text = item.name
        serialNumberField.text = item.serialNumber
        valueField.text = "\(item.valueInDollars)"
        dateLabel.text = "\(item.dateCreated)"
    }
}
```

235

This works, but instead of using string interpolation to print out the valueInDollars and dateCreated, it would be better to use a formatter. You used an instance of **NumberFormatter** in Chapter 4. You will use another one here, as well as an instance of **DateFormatter** to format the dateCreated.

Add an instance of **NumberFormatter** and **DateFormatter** to the **DetailViewController**. Use these formatters in **viewWillAppear(_:)** to format the valueInDollars and dateCreated.

```
var item: Item!

let numberFormatter: NumberFormatter = {
    let formatter = NumberFormatter()
    formatter.numberStyle = .decimal
    formatter.minimumFractionDigits = 2
    formatter.maximumFractionDigits = 2
    return formatter
}()

let dateFormatter: DateFormatter = {
    let formatter = DateFormatter()
    formatter.dateStyle = .medium
    formatter.timeStyle = .none
    return formatter
}()

override func viewWillAppear(_ animated: Bool) {
    super.viewWillAppear(animated)

    nameField.text = item.name
    serialNumberField.text = item.serialNumber
    valueField.text = "\(item.valueInDollars)"
    dateLabel.text = "\(item.dateCreated)"
    valueField.text =
        numberFormatter.string(from: NSNumber(value: item.valueInDollars))
    dateLabel.text = dateFormatter.string(from: item.dateCreated)
}
```

Passing Data Around

When a row in the table view is tapped, you need a way of telling the **DetailViewController** which item was selected. Whenever a segue is triggered, the **prepare(for:sender:)** method is called on the view controller initiating the segue. This method has two arguments: the **UIStoryboardSegue**, which gives you information about which segue is happening, and the sender, which is the object that triggered the segue (a **UITableViewCell** or a **UIButton**, for example).

The **UIStoryboardSegue** gives you three pieces of information: the source view controller (where the segue originates), the destination view controller (where the segue ends), and the identifier of the segue. The identifier lets you differentiate segues. Let's give the segue a useful identifier.

Open Main.storyboard again. Select the show segue by clicking on the arrow between the two view controllers and open the attributes inspector. For the identifier, enter showItem (Figure 13.15).

Figure 13.15 Segue identifier

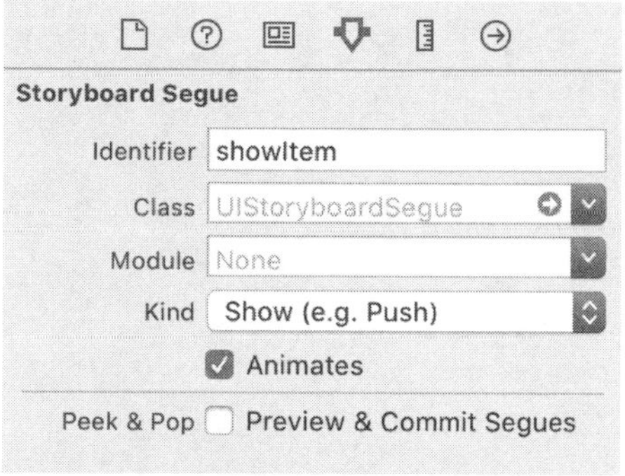

With your segue identified, you can now pass your **Item** instances around. Open ItemsViewController.swift and implement **prepare(for:sender:)**.

```
override func prepare(for segue: UIStoryboardSegue, sender: Any?) {
    // If the triggered segue is the "showItem" segue
    switch segue.identifier {
    case "showItem"?:
        // Figure out which row was just tapped
        if let row = tableView.indexPathForSelectedRow?.row {

            // Get the item associated with this row and pass it along
            let item = itemStore.allItems[row]
            let detailViewController
                    = segue.destination as! DetailViewController
            detailViewController.item = item
        }
    default:
        preconditionFailure("Unexpected segue identifier.")
    }
}
```

You learned about switch statements in Chapter 2. Here, you are using one to switch over the possible segue identifiers. Because the segue's identifier is an optional **String**, you include a ? after the case pattern (i.e., after "showItem"). The default block uses the **preconditionFailure(_:)** function to catch any unexpected segue identifiers and crash the application. This would be the case if the programmer either forgot to give a segue an identifier or if there was a typo somewhere with the segue identifiers. In either case, it is the programmer's mistake, and using **preconditionFailure(_:)** can help you identify these problems sooner.

Build and run the application. Tap on a row and the **DetailViewController** will slide onscreen, displaying the details for that item. (You will fix the inability to go back to the **ItemsViewController** in Chapter 14.)

Many programmers new to iOS struggle with how data is passed between view controllers. Having all of the data in the root view controller and passing subsets of that data to the next **UIViewController** (as you did in this chapter) is a clean and efficient way of performing this task.

Bronze Challenge: More Stack Views

Quiz and WorldTrotter are good candidates for using stack views. Update both of these applications to use **UIStackView**.

14

UINavigationController

In Chapter 5, you learned about **UITabBarController** and how it allows a user to access different screens. A tab bar controller is great for screens that are independent of each other, but what if you have screens that provide related information?

For example, the Settings application has multiple related screens of information: a list of settings (like Sounds), a detailed page for each setting, and a selection page for each detail (Figure 14.1). This type of interface is called a *drill-down interface*.

Figure 14.1 Drill-down interface in Settings

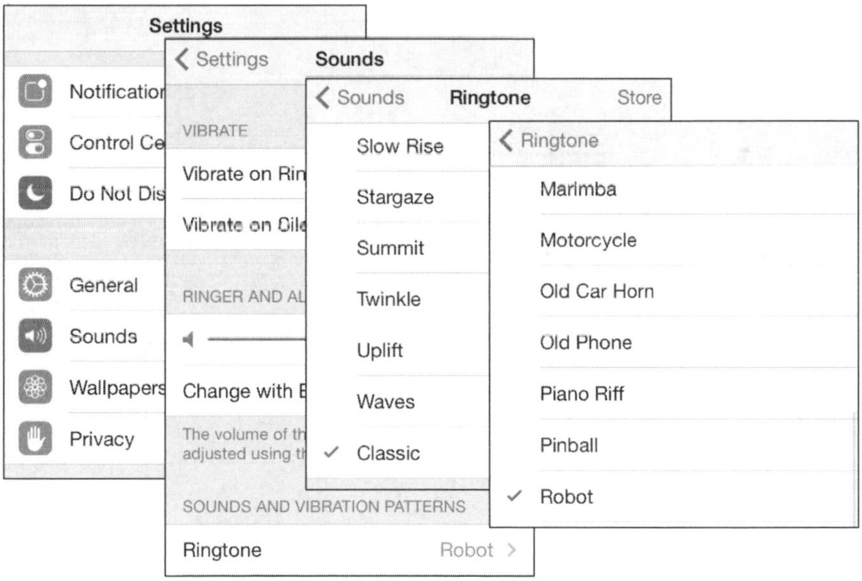

In this chapter, you will use a **UINavigationController** to add a drill-down interface to Homepwner that lets the user see and edit the details of an **Item**. These details will be presented by the **DetailViewController** that you created in Chapter 13 (Figure 14.2).

Figure 14.2 Homepwner with **UINavigationController**

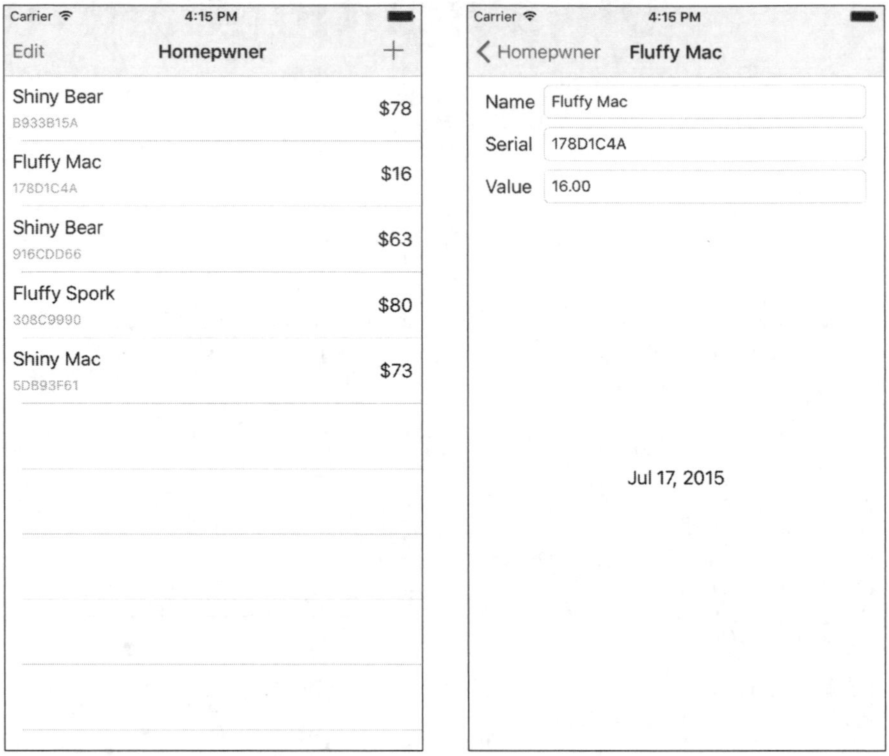

UINavigationController

A **UINavigationController** maintains an array of view controllers presenting related information in a stack. When a **UIViewController** is on top of the stack, its view is visible.

When you initialize an instance of **UINavigationController**, you give it a **UIViewController**. This **UIViewController** is added to the navigation controller's viewControllers array and becomes the navigation controller's root view controller. The root view controller is always on the bottom of the stack. (Note that while this view controller is referred to as the navigation controller's "root view controller," **UINavigationController** does not have a rootViewController property.)

More view controllers can be pushed on top of the **UINavigationController**'s stack while the application is running. These view controllers are added to the end of the viewControllers array that corresponds to the top of the stack. **UINavigationController**'s topViewController property keeps a reference to the view controller at the top of the stack.

When a view controller is pushed onto the stack, its view slides onscreen from the right. When the stack is popped (i.e., the last item is removed), the top view controller is removed from the stack and its view slides off to the right, exposing the view of the next view controller on the stack, which becomes the top view controller. Figure 14.3 shows a navigation controller with two view controllers. The view of the topViewController is what the user sees.

Figure 14.3 **UINavigationController**'s stack

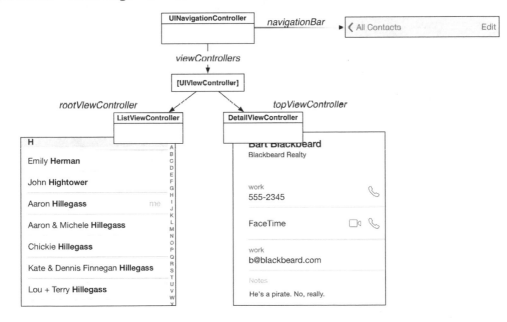

UINavigationController is a subclass of **UIViewController**, so it has a view of its own. Its view always has two subviews: a **UINavigationBar** and the view of topViewController (Figure 14.4).

Figure 14.4 A **UINavigationController**'s view

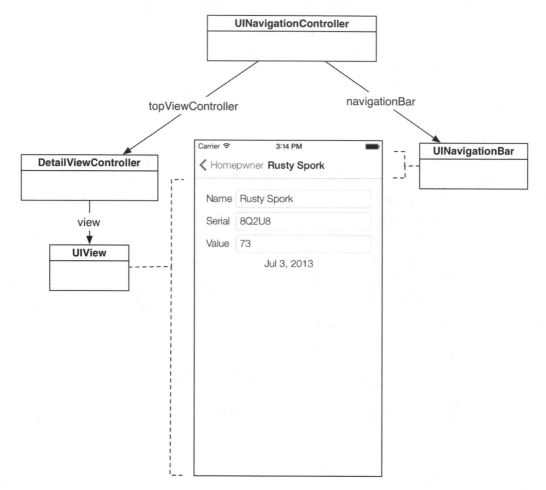

In this chapter, you will add a **UINavigationController** to the Homepwner application and make the **ItemsViewController** the **UINavigationController**'s root view controller. The **DetailViewController** will be pushed onto the **UINavigationController**'s stack when an **Item** is selected. This view controller will allow the user to view and edit the properties of an **Item** selected from the table view of **ItemsViewController**. The object diagram for the updated Homepwner application is shown in Figure 14.5.

Figure 14.5 Homepwner object diagram

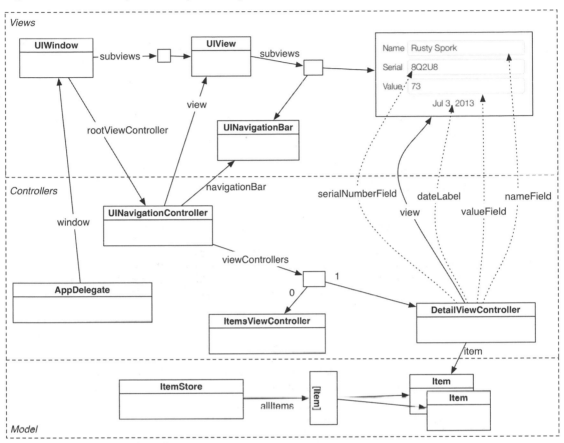

This application is getting fairly large, as you can see. Fortunately, view controllers and **UINavigationController** know how to deal with this type of complicated object diagram. When writing iOS applications, it is important to treat each **UIViewController** as its own little world. The stuff that has already been implemented in Cocoa Touch will do the heavy lifting.

Begin by giving Homepwner a navigation controller. Reopen the Homepwner project. The only requirements for using a **UINavigationController** are that you give it a root view controller and add its view to the window.

Open Main.storyboard and select the Items View Controller. Then, from the Editor menu, choose Embed In → Navigation Controller. This will set the **ItemsViewController** to be the root view controller of a **UINavigationController**. It will also update the storyboard to set the Navigation Controller as the initial view controller.

Your Detail View Controller interface may have misplaced views now that it is contained within a navigation controller. If it does, select the stack view and click the Update Frames button in the Auto Layout constraint menu.

Build and run the application and ... the application crashes. What is happening? You previously created a contract with the **AppDelegate** that an instance of **ItemsViewController** would be the rootViewController of the window:

```
let itemsController = window!.rootViewController as! ItemsViewController
```

You have now broken this contract by embedding the **ItemsViewController** in a **UINavigationController**. You need to update the contract.

Open AppDelegate.swift and update **application(_:didFinishLaunchingWithOptions:)** to reflect the new view controller hierarchy.

```
func application(_ application: UIApplication, didFinishLaunchingWithOptions
        launchOptions: [UIApplicationLaunchOptionsKey : Any]?) -> Bool {
    // Override point for customization after application launch.

    // Create an ItemStore
    let itemStore = ItemStore()

    // Access the ItemsViewController and set its item store
    let itemsController = window!.rootViewController as! ItemsViewController
    let navController = window!.rootViewController as! UINavigationController
    let itemsController = navController.topViewController as! ItemsViewController
    itemsController.itemStore = itemStore

    return true
}
```

Build and run the application again. Homepwner works again and has a very nice, if totally empty, **UINavigationBar** at the top of the screen (Figure 14.6).

Figure 14.6 Homepwner with an empty navigation bar

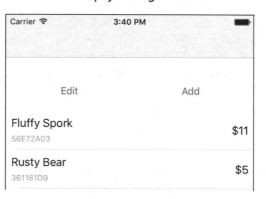

Notice how the screen adjusted to fit **ItemsViewController**'s view as well as the new navigation bar. **UINavigationController** did this for you: While the view of the **ItemsViewController** actually underlaps the navigation bar, **UINavigationController** added padding to the top so that everything fits nicely. This is because the top layout guide for the view controller is adjusted, along with any views constrained to the top layout guide – like the stack view.

Navigating with UINavigationController

With the application still running, create a new item and select that row from the **UITableView**. Not only are you taken to **DetailViewController**'s view, but you also get a free animation and a Back button in the **UINavigationBar**. Tap this button to get back to **ItemsViewController**.

Notice that you did not have to change the show segue that you created in Chapter 13 to get this behavior. As mentioned in that chapter, the show segue presents the destination view controller in a way that makes sense given the surrounding context. When a show segue is triggered from a view controller embedded within a navigation controller, the destination view controller is pushed onto the navigation controller's view controller stack.

Because the **UINavigationController**'s stack is an array, it will take ownership of any view controller added to it. Thus, the **DetailViewController** is owned only by the **UINavigationController** after the segue finishes. When the stack is popped, the **DetailViewController** is destroyed. The next time a row is tapped, a new instance of **DetailViewController** is created.

Having a view controller push the next view controller is a common pattern. The root view controller typically creates the next view controller, and the next view controller creates the one after that, and so on. Some applications may have view controllers that can push different view controllers depending on user input. For example, the Photos app pushes a video view controller or an image view controller onto the navigation stack depending on what type of media is selected.

Notice that the detail view for an item contains the information for the selected **Item**. However, while you can edit this data, the **UITableView** will not reflect those changes when you return to it. To fix this problem, you need to implement code to update the properties of the **Item** being edited. In the next section, you will see when to do this.

Appearing and Disappearing Views

Whenever a **UINavigationController** is about to swap views, it calls two methods: **viewWillDisappear(_:)** and **viewWillAppear(_:)**. The **UIViewController** that is about to be popped off the stack has **viewWillDisappear(_:)** called. The **UIViewController** that will then be on top of the stack has **viewWillAppear(_:)** called on it.

To hold on to changes in the data, when a **DetailViewController** is popped off the stack you will set the properties of its item to the contents of the text fields. When implementing these methods for views appearing and disappearing, it is important to call the superclass's implementation – it might have some work to do and needs to be given the chance to do it.

In DetailViewController.swift, implement **viewWillDisappear(_:)**.

```
override func viewWillDisappear(_ animated: Bool) {
    super.viewWillDisappear(animated)

    // "Save" changes to item
    item.name = nameField.text ?? ""
    item.serialNumber = serialNumberField.text

    if let valueText = valueField.text,
        let value = numberFormatter.number(from: valueText) {
        item.valueInDollars = value.intValue
    } else {
        item.valueInDollars = 0
    }
}
```

Now the values of the **Item** will be updated when the user taps the Back button on the **UINavigationBar**. When **ItemsViewController** appears back on the screen, the method **viewWillAppear(_:)** is called. Take this opportunity to reload the **UITableView** so the user can immediately see the changes.

In ItemsViewController.swift, override **viewWillAppear(_:)** to reload the table view.

```
override func viewWillAppear(_ animated: Bool) {
    super.viewWillAppear(animated)

    tableView.reloadData()
}
```

Build and run your application once again. Now you can move back and forth between the view controllers that you created and change the data with ease.

Dismissing the Keyboard

Run the application, add and select an item, and touch the text field with the item's name. When you touch the text field, a keyboard appears onscreen (Figure 14.7), as you saw in your WorldTrotter app in Chapter 4. (If you are using the simulator and the keyboard does not appear, remember that you can press Command-K to toggle the device keyboard.)

Figure 14.7 Keyboard appears when a text field is touched

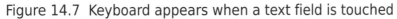

The appearance of the keyboard in response to a touch is built in to the **UITextField** class as well as **UITextView**, so you do not have to do anything extra for the keyboard to appear. However, at times you will want to make sure the keyboard behaves as you want it to.

For example, notice that the keyboard covers more than a third of the screen. Right now, it does not obscure anything, but soon you will add more details that extend to the bottom of the screen, and users will want a way to hide the keyboard when it is not needed. In this section, you are going to give the user two ways to dismiss the keyboard: pressing the keyboard's Return key, and tapping anywhere else on the detail view controller's view. But first, let's look at the combination of events that make text editing possible.

Event handling basics

When you touch a view, an event is created. This event (known as a "touch event") is tied to a specific location in the view controller's view. That location determines which view in the hierarchy the touch event is delivered to.

For example, when you tap a **UIButton** within its bounds, it will receive the touch event and respond in button-like fashion – by calling the action method on its target. It is perfectly reasonable to expect that when a view in your application is touched, that view receives a touch event, and it may choose to react to that event or ignore it. However, views in your application can also respond to events without being touched. A good example of this is a shake. If you shake the device with your application running, one of your views on the screen can respond. But which one? Another interesting case is responding to the keyboard. **DetailViewController**'s view contains three **UITextField**s. Which one will receive the text when the user types?

For both the shake and keyboard events, there is no event location within your view hierarchy to determine which view will receive the event, so another mechanism must be used. This mechanism is the *first responder* status. Many views and controls can be a first responder within your view hierarchy – but only one at a time. Think of it as a flag that can be passed among views. Whichever view holds the flag will receive the shake or keyboard event.

Instances of **UITextField** and **UITextView** have an uncommon response to touch events. When touched, a text field or a text view becomes the first responder, which in turn triggers the system to put the keyboard onscreen and send the keyboard events to the text field or view. The keyboard and the text field or view have no direct connection, but they work together through the first responder status.

This is a neat way to ensure that the keyboard input is delivered to the correct text field. The concept of a first responder is part of the broader topic of event handling in Cocoa Touch programming that includes the **UIResponder** class and the *responder chain*. You will learn more about them when you handle touch events in Chapter 18, and you can also visit Apple's *Event Handling Guide for iOS* for more information.

Dismissing by pressing the Return key

Now let's get back to allowing users to dismiss the keyboard. If you touch another text field in the application, that text field will become the first responder, and the keyboard will stay onscreen. The keyboard will only give up and go away when no text field (or text view) is the first responder. To dismiss the keyboard, then, you call **resignFirstResponder()** on the text field that is the first responder.

To have the text field resign in response to the Return key being pressed, you are going to implement the **UITextFieldDelegate** method **textFieldShouldReturn(_:)**. This method is called whenever the Return key is pressed.

First, in DetailViewController.swift, have **DetailViewController** conform to the **UITextFieldDelegate** protocol.

```
class DetailViewController: UIViewController, UITextFieldDelegate {
```

Next, implement **textFieldShouldReturn(_:)** to call **resignFirstResponder()** on the text field that is passed in.

```
func textFieldShouldReturn(_ textField: UITextField) -> Bool {
    textField.resignFirstResponder()
    return true
}
```

Finally, open Main.storyboard and connect the delegate property of each text field to the Detail View Controller (Figure 14.8). (Control-drag from each **UITextField** to the Detail View Controller and choose delegate.)

Figure 14.8 Connecting the delegate property of a text field

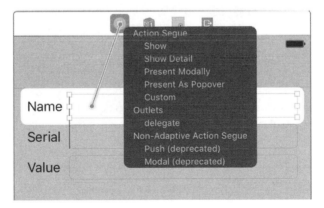

Build and run the application. Tap a text field and then press the Return key on the keyboard. The keyboard will disappear. To get the keyboard back, touch any text field.

Dismissing by tapping elsewhere

It would be stylish to also dismiss the keyboard if the user taps anywhere else on
DetailViewController's view. To do this, you are going to use a gesture recognizer when
the view is tapped, just as you did in the WorldTrotter app. In the action method, you will call
resignFirstResponder() on the text field.

Open Main.storyboard and find Tap Gesture Recognizer in the object library. Drag this object onto
the background view for the Detail View Controller. You will see a reference to this gesture recognizer
in the scene dock.

In the project navigator, Option-click DetailViewController.swift to open it in the assistant
editor. Control-drag from the tap gesture recognizer in the storyboard to the implementation of
DetailViewController.

In the pop-up that appears, select Action from the Connection menu. Name the action
backgroundTapped. For the Type, choose UITapGestureRecognizer (Figure 14.9).

Figure 14.9 Configuring a **UITapGestureRecognizer** action

Click Connect and the stub for the action method will appear in DetailViewController.swift.
Update the method to call **endEditing(_:)** on the view of **DetailViewController**.

```
@IBAction func backgroundTapped(_ sender: UITapGestureRecognizer) {
    view.endEditing(true)
}
```

Calling **endEditing(_:)** is a convenient way to dismiss the keyboard without having to know (or care)
which text field is the first responder. When the view gets this call, it checks to see if any text field in
its hierarchy is the first responder. If so, then **resignFirstResponder()** is called on that particular
view.

Build and run your application. Tap on a text field to show the keyboard. Tap on the view outside of a
text field and the keyboard will disappear.

There is one final case where you need to dismiss the keyboard. When the user taps the Back button, **viewWillDisappear(_:)** is called on the **DetailViewController** before it is popped off the stack, and the keyboard disappears instantly, with no animation. To dismiss the keyboard more smoothly, update the implementation of **viewWillDisappear(_:)** in DetailViewController.swift to call **endEditing(_:)**.

```
override func viewWillDisappear(_ animated: Bool) {
    super.viewWillDisappear(animated)

    // Clear first responder
    view.endEditing(true)

    // "Save" changes to item
    item.name = nameField.text ?? ""
    item.serialNumber = serialNumberField.text

    if let valueText = valueField.text,
        let value = numberFormatter.number(from: valueText) {
        item.valueInDollars = value.integerValue
    } else {
        item.valueInDollars = 0
    }
}
```

UINavigationBar

In this section, you are going to give the **UINavigationBar** a descriptive title for the **UIViewController** that is currently on top of the **UINavigationController**'s stack.

Every **UIViewController** has a navigationItem property of type **UINavigationItem**. However, unlike **UINavigationBar**, **UINavigationItem** is not a subclass of **UIView**, so it cannot appear on the screen. Instead, the navigation item supplies the navigation bar with the content it needs to draw. When a **UIViewController** comes to the top of a **UINavigationController**'s stack, the **UINavigationBar** uses the **UIViewController**'s navigationItem to configure itself, as shown in Figure 14.10.

Figure 14.10 **UINavigationItem**

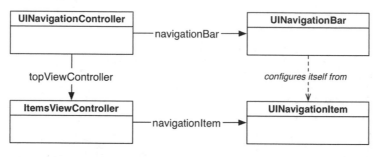

By default, a **UINavigationItem** is empty. At the most basic level, a **UINavigationItem** has a simple title string. When a **UIViewController** is moved to the top of the navigation stack and its navigationItem has a valid string for its title property, the navigation bar will display that string (Figure 14.11).

Figure 14.11 **UINavigationItem** with title

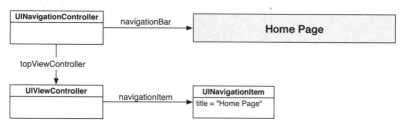

The title for the **ItemsViewController** will always remain the same, so you can set the title of its navigation item within the storyboard itself.

Open Main.storyboard. Double-click on the center of the navigation bar above the Items View Controller to edit its title. Give it a title of "Homepwner" (Figure 14.12).

Figure 14.12 Setting the title in a storyboard

Build and run the application. Notice the string Homepwner on the navigation bar. Create and tap on a row and notice that the navigation bar no longer has a title. It would be nice to have the **DetailViewController**'s navigation item title be the name of the **Item** it is displaying. Because the title will depend on the **Item** that is being displayed, you need to set the title of the navigationItem dynamically in code.

In DetailViewController.swift, add a property observer to the item property that updates the title of the navigationItem.

```
var item: Item! {
    didSet {
        navigationItem.title = item.name
    }
}
```

Build and run the application. Create and tap a row and you will see that the title of the navigation bar is the name of the **Item** you selected.

A navigation item can hold more than just a title string, as shown in Figure 14.13. There are three customizable areas for each **UINavigationItem**: a leftBarButtonItem, a rightBarButtonItem, and a titleView. The left and right bar button items are references to instances of **UIBarButtonItem**, which contain the information for a button that can only be displayed on a **UINavigationBar** or a **UIToolbar**.

Figure 14.13 **UINavigationItem** with everything

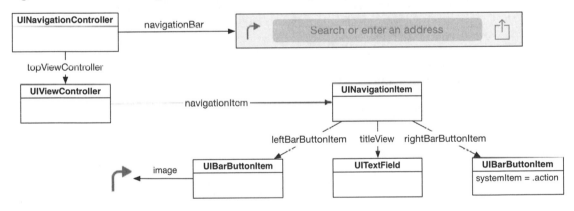

Recall that **UINavigationItem** is not a subclass of **UIView**. Instead, **UINavigationItem** encapsulates information that **UINavigationBar** uses to configure itself. Similarly, **UIBarButtonItem** is not a view, but holds the information about how a single button on the **UINavigationBar** should be displayed. (A **UIToolbar** also uses instances of **UIBarButtonItem** to configure itself.)

The third customizable area of a **UINavigationItem** is its titleView. You can either use a basic string as the title or have a subclass of **UIView** sit in the center of the navigation item. You cannot have both. If it suits the context of a specific view controller to have a custom view (like a segmented control or a text field, for example), you would set the titleView of the navigation item to that custom view. Figure 14.13 shows an example from the built-in Maps application of a **UINavigationItem** with a custom view as its titleView. Typically, however, a title string is sufficient.

Adding buttons to the navigation bar

In this section, you are going to replace the two buttons that are in the table's header view with two bar button items that will appear in the **UINavigationBar** when the **ItemsViewController** is on top of the stack. A bar button item has a target-action pair that works like **UIControl**'s target-action mechanism: When tapped, it sends the action message to the target.

First, let's work on a bar button item for adding new items. This button will sit on the right side of the navigation bar when the **ItemsViewController** is on top of the stack. When tapped, it will add a new **Item**.

Before you update the storyboard, you need to change the method signature for **addNewItem(_:)**. Currently this method is triggered by a **UIButton**. Now that you are changing the sender to a **UIBarButtonItem**, you need to update the signature.

In **ItemsViewController.swift**, update the method signature for **addNewItem(_:)**.

```
@IBAction func addNewItem(_ sender: UIButton) {
@IBAction func addNewItem(_ sender: UIBarButtonItem) {
    ...
}
```

Now open **Main.storyboard** and then open the object library. Drag a Bar Button Item to the right side of Items View Controller's navigation bar. Select this bar button item and open its attributes inspector. Change the System Item to Add (Figure 14.14).

Figure 14.14 System bar button item

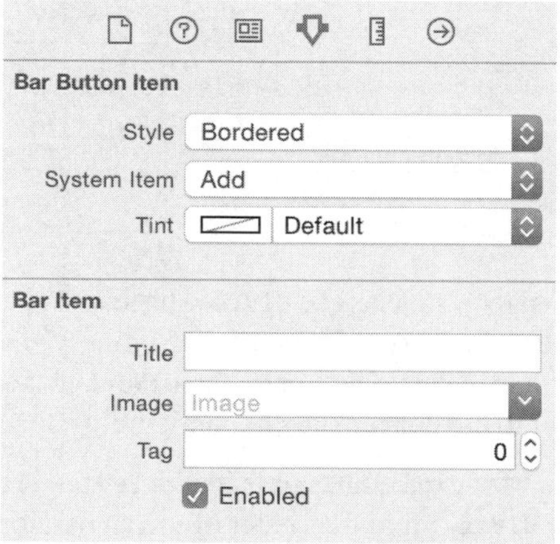

Control-drag from this bar button item to the Items View Controller and select addNewItem: (Figure 14.15).

Figure 14.15 Connecting the addNewItem: action

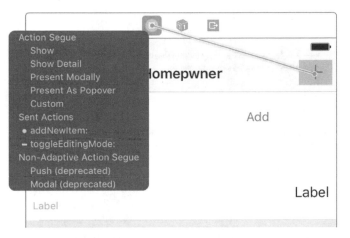

Build and run the application. Tap the + button and a new row will appear in the table.

Now let's replace the Edit button. View controllers expose a bar button item that will automatically toggle their editing mode. There is no way to access this through Interface Builder, so you will need to add this bar button item programmatically.

In ItemsViewController.swift, override the **init(coder:)** method to set the left bar button item.

```
required init?(coder aDecoder: NSCoder) {
    super.init(coder: aDecoder)

    navigationItem.leftBarButtonItem = editButtonItem
}
```

Build and run the application, add some items, and tap the Edit button. The **UITableView** enters editing mode! The editButtonItem property creates a **UIBarButtonItem** with the title Edit. Even better, this button comes with a target-action pair: It calls the method **setEditing(_:animated:)** on its **UIViewController** when tapped.

Open Main.storyboard. Now that Homepwner has a fully functional navigation bar, you can get rid of the header view and the associated code. Select the header view on the table view and press Delete.

Also, the **UINavigationController** will handle updating the insets for the table view. In ItemsViewController.swift, delete the following code.

```
override func viewDidLoad() {
    super.viewDidLoad()

    // Get the height of the status bar
    let statusBarHeight = UIApplication.shared.statusBarFrame.height

    let insets = UIEdgeInsets(top: statusBarHeight, left: 0, bottom: 0, right: 0)
    tableView.contentInset = insets
    tableView.scrollIndicatorInsets = insets

    tableView.rowHeight = UITableViewAutomaticDimension
    tableView.estimatedRowHeight = 65
}
```

Finally, remove the **toggleEditingMode(_:)** method.

```
@IBAction func toggleEditingMode(_ sender: UIButton) {
    // If you are currently in editing mode...
    if isEditing {
        // Change text of button to inform user of state
        sender.setTitle("Edit", for: .normal)

        // Turn off editing mode
        setEditing(false, animated: true)
    } else {
        // Change text of button to inform user of state
        sender.setTitle("Done", for: .normal)

        // Enter editing mode
        setEditing(true, animated: true)
    }
}
```

Build and run again. The old Edit and Add buttons are gone, leaving you with a lovely
UINavigationBar (Figure 14.16).

Figure 14.16 Homepwner with navigation bar

Bronze Challenge: Displaying a Number Pad

The keyboard for the **UITextField** that displays an **Item**'s valueInDollars is a QWERTY keyboard. It would be better if it were a number pad. Change the Keyboard Type of that **UITextField** to the Number Pad. (Hint: You can do this in the storyboard file using the attributes inspector.)

Silver Challenge: A Custom UITextField

Make a subclass of **UITextField** and override the **becomeFirstResponder()** and **resignFirstResponder()** methods (inherited from **UIResponder**) so that its border style changes when it is the first responder. You can use the **borderStyle** property of **UITextField** to accomplish this. Use your subclass for the text fields in **DetailViewController**.

Gold Challenge: Pushing More View Controllers

Currently, instances of **Item** cannot have their dateCreated property changed. Change **Item** so that they can, and then add a button underneath the dateLabel in **DetailViewController** with the title "Change Date." When this button is tapped, push another view controller instance onto the navigation stack. This view controller should have a **UIDatePicker** instance that modifies the dateCreated property of the selected **Item**.

15

Camera

In this chapter, you are going to add photos to the Homepwner application. You will present a
UIImagePickerController so that the user can take and save a picture of each item. The image will
then be associated with an **Item** instance and viewable in the item's detail view (Figure 15.1).

Figure 15.1 Homepwner with camera addition

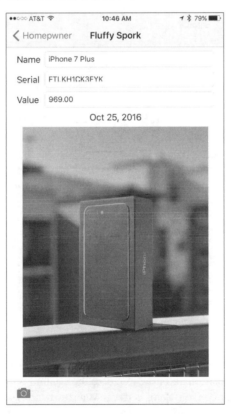

Images tend to be very large, so it is a good idea to store images separately from other data. Thus,
you are going to create a second store for images. **ImageStore** will fetch and cache images as they are
needed.

Displaying Images and UIImageView

Your first step is to have the **DetailViewController** get and display an image. An easy way to display an image is to put an instance of **UIImageView** on the screen.

Open Homepwner.xcodeproj and Main.storyboard. Then drag an instance of **UIImageView** onto the view at the bottom of the stack view. Select the image view and open its size inspector. You want the vertical content hugging and content compression resistance priorities for the image view to be lower than those of the other views. Change the Vertical Content Hugging Priority to be 248 and the Vertical Content Compression Resistance Priority to be 749. Your layout will look like Figure 15.2.

Figure 15.2 **UIImageView** on **DetailViewController**'s view

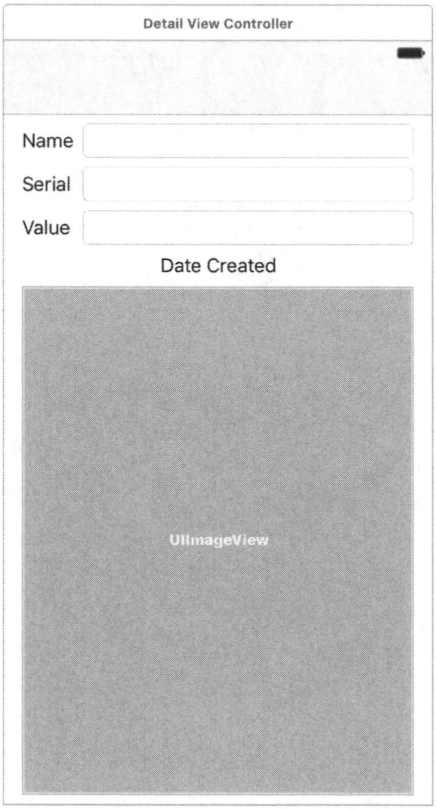

A **UIImageView** displays an image according to the image view's contentMode property. This property determines where to position and how to resize the content within the image view's frame. **UIImageView**'s default value for contentMode is UIViewContentMode.scaleToFill, which adjusts the image to exactly match the bounds of the image view. If you keep the default, an image taken by the camera will be scaled to fit into the square **UIImageView**. To maintain the image's aspect ratio, you have to update contentMode.

With the **UIImageView** selected, open the attributes inspector. Find the Content Mode attribute and change it to Aspect Fit (Figure 15.3). You will not see a change on the storyboard, but now images will be resized to fit within the bounds of the **UIImageView**.

Figure 15.3 Changing **UIImageView**'s mode to Aspect Fit

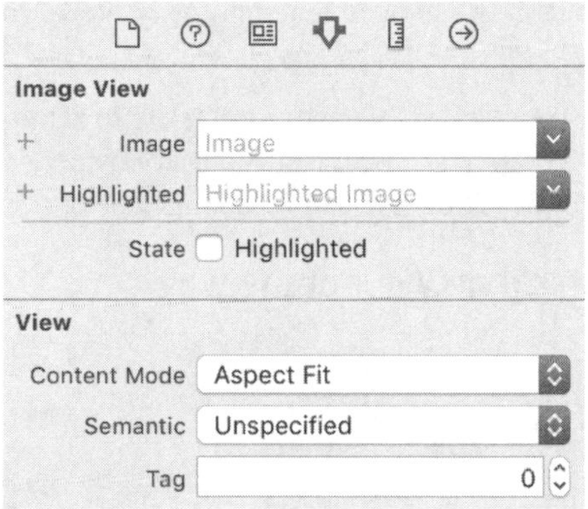

Next, Option-click DetailViewController.swift in the project navigator to open it in the assistant editor. Control-drag from the **UIImageView** to the top of DetailViewController.swift. Name the outlet imageView and make sure the storage type is Strong. Click Connect (Figure 15.4).

Figure 15.4 Creating the imageView outlet

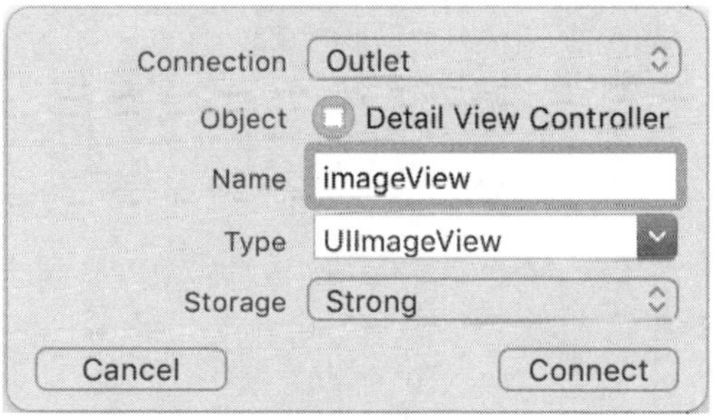

The top of DetailViewController.swift should now look like this:

```
class DetailViewController: UIViewController, UITextFieldDelegate {

    @IBOutlet var nameField: UITextField!
    @IBOutlet var serialNumberField: UITextField!
    @IBOutlet var valueField: UITextField!
    @IBOutlet var dateLabel: UILabel!
    @IBOutlet var imageView: UIImageView!
```

Adding a camera button

Now you need a button to initiate the photo-taking process. You will create an instance of **UIToolbar** and place it at the bottom of **DetailViewController**'s view.

In Main.storyboard, press Command-Return to close the assistant editor and give yourself more room to work in the storyboard. You are going to need to temporarily break your interface to add the toolbar to the interface.

Select the bottom constraint for the stack view and press Delete to remove it. You need to make room for the toolbar on the bottom. As of Xcode 8.1, it is difficult to resize the stack view. So instead, drag the stack view up a bit (Figure 15.5). The view will be misplaced for now, but you will fix this shortly.

Figure 15.5 Moving the stack view out of the way

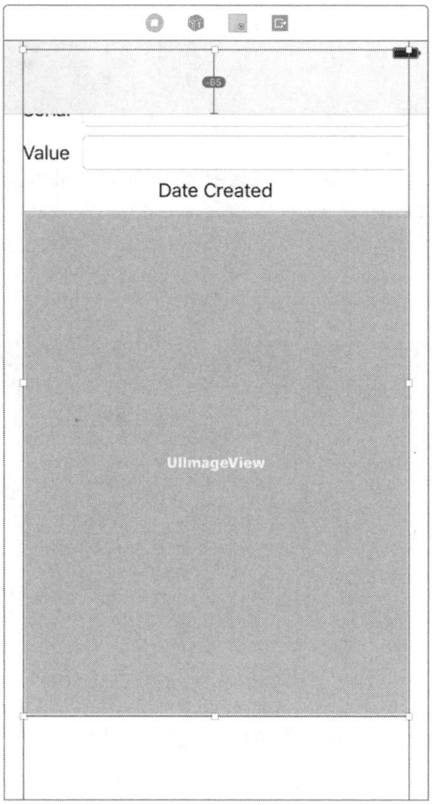

Now drag a toolbar from the object library onto the bottom of the view. Select the toolbar and open the Auto Layout Add New Constraints menu. Configure the constraints exactly as shown in Figure 15.6 and then click Add 5 Constraints. Because you chose the option to update frames, the stack view is repositioned to its correct location.

Figure 15.6 Toolbar constraints

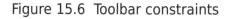

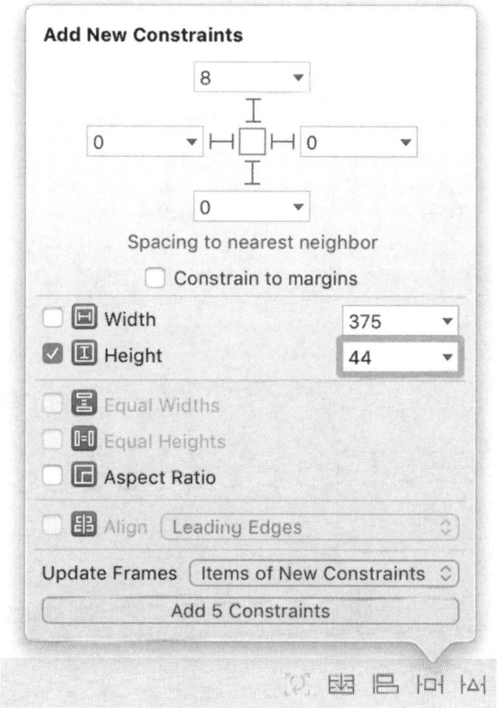

A **UIToolbar** works a lot like a **UINavigationBar** – you can add instances of **UIBarButtonItem** to it. However, where a navigation bar has two slots for bar button items, a toolbar has an array of bar button items. You can place as many bar button items in a toolbar as can fit on the screen.

By default, a new instance of **UIToolbar** that is created in an interface file comes with one **UIBarButtonItem**. Select this bar button item and open the attributes inspector. Change the System Item to Camera, and the item will show a camera icon (Figure 15.7).

Figure 15.7 **UIToolbar** with camera bar button item

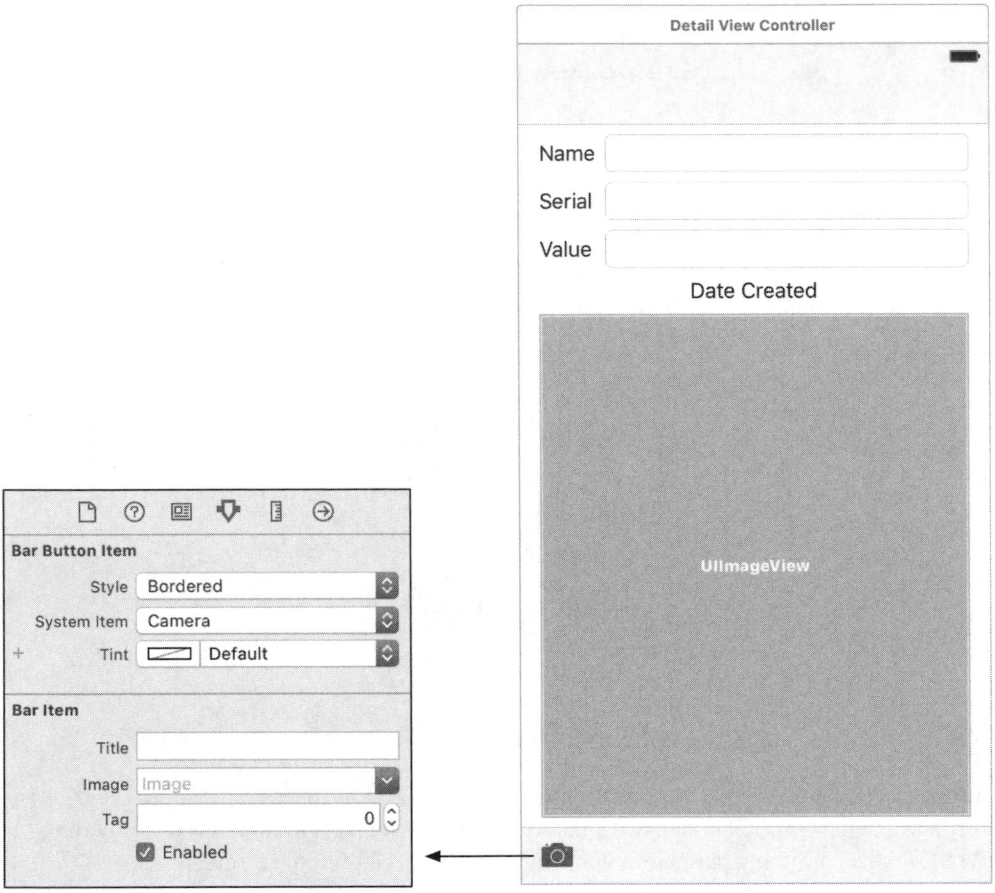

Build and run the application and navigate to an item's details to see the toolbar with its camera bar button item. You have not connected the camera button to an action yet, so tapping on it will not do anything.

The camera button needs a target and an action. With Main.storyboard still open, Option-click DetailViewController.swift in the project navigator to reopen it in the assistant editor.

In Main.storyboard, select the camera button by first clicking on the toolbar and then the button itself. Control-drag from the selected button to DetailViewController.swift.

In the Connection pop-up menu, select Action as the connection type, name it **takePicture**, select UIBarButtonItem as the type, and click Connect (Figure 15.8).

Figure 15.8 Creating an action

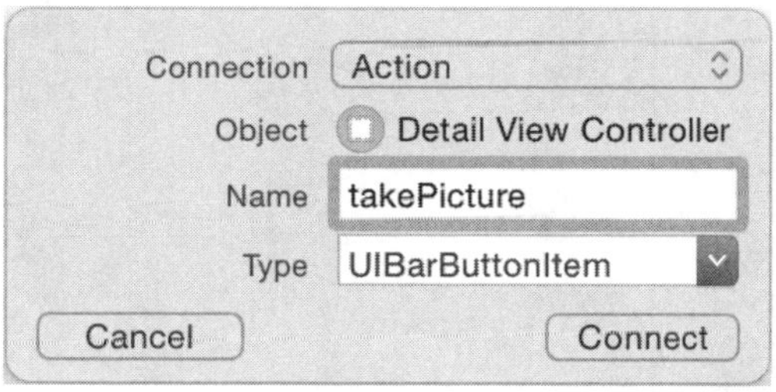

If you made any mistakes while making this connection, you will need to open Main.storyboard and disconnect any bad connections. (Look for yellow warning signs in the connections inspector.)

Taking Pictures and UIImagePickerController

In the **takePicture(_:)** method, you will instantiate a **UIImagePickerController** and present it on the screen. When creating an instance of **UIImagePickerController**, you must set its sourceType property and assign it a delegate. Because there is set-up work needed for the image picker controller, you need to create and present it programmatically instead of through the storyboard.

Setting the image picker's sourceType

The sourceType constant tells the image picker where to get images. It has three possible values:

UIImagePickerControllerSourceType.camera	Allows the user to take a new photo.
UIImagePickerControllerSourceType.photoLibrary	Prompts the user to select an album and then a photo from that album.
UIImagePickerControllerSourceType.savedPhotosAlbum	Prompts the user to choose from the most recently taken photos.

Figure 15.9 Examples of the three sourceTypes

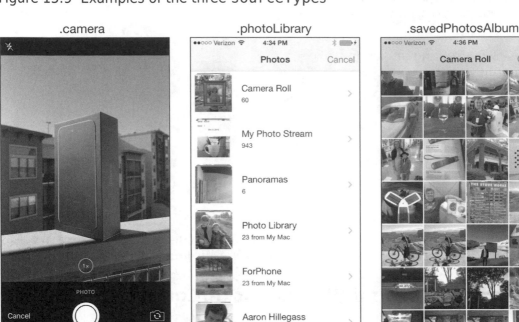

The first source type, .camera, will not work on a device that does not have a camera. So before using this type, you have to check for a camera by calling the method **isSourceTypeAvailable(_:)** on the **UIImagePickerController** class:

```
class func isSourceTypeAvailable(_ type: UIImagePickerControllerSourceType) -> Bool
```

Calling this method returns a Boolean value for whether the device supports the passed-in source type.

In DetailViewController.swift, find the stub for **takePicture(_:)**. Add the following code to create the image picker and set its sourceType.

```
@IBAction func takePicture(_ sender: UIBarButtonItem) {

    let imagePicker = UIImagePickerController()

    // If the device has a camera, take a picture; otherwise,
    // just pick from photo library
    if UIImagePickerController.isSourceTypeAvailable(.camera) {
        imagePicker.sourceType = .camera
    } else {
        imagePicker.sourceType = .photoLibrary
    }
}
```

Setting the image picker's delegate

In addition to a source type, the **UIImagePickerController** instance needs a delegate. When the user selects an image from the **UIImagePickerController**'s interface, the delegate is sent the message **imagePickerController(_:didFinishPickingMediaWithInfo:)**. (If the user taps the cancel button, then the delegate receives the message **imagePickerControllerDidCancel(_:)**.)

The image picker's delegate will be the instance of **DetailViewController**. At the top of DetailViewController.swift, declare that **DetailViewController** conforms to the **UINavigationControllerDelegate** and the **UIImagePickerControllerDelegate** protocols.

```
class DetailViewController: UIViewController, UITextFieldDelegate,
        UINavigationControllerDelegate, UIImagePickerControllerDelegate {
```

Why **UINavigationControllerDelegate**? **UIImagePickerController**'s delegate property is actually inherited from its superclass, **UINavigationController**, and while **UIImagePickerController** has its own delegate protocol, its inherited delegate property is declared to reference an object that conforms to **UINavigationControllerDelegate**.

In DetailViewController.swift, set the instance of **DetailViewController** to be the image picker's delegate in **takePicture(_:)**.

```
@IBAction func takePicture(_ sender: UIBarButtonItem) {

    let imagePicker = UIImagePickerController()

    // If the device has a camera, take a picture; otherwise,
    // just pick from photo library
    if UIImagePickerController.isSourceTypeAvailable(.camera) {
        imagePicker.sourceType = .camera
    } else {
        imagePicker.sourceType = .photoLibrary
    }

    imagePicker.delegate = self
}
```

Presenting the image picker modally

Once the **UIImagePickerController** has a source type and a delegate, you can display it by presenting the view controller modally.

In DetailViewController.swift, add code to the end of **takePicture(_:)** to present the **UIImagePickerController**.

```
    imagePicker.delegate = self

    // Place image picker on the screen
    present(imagePicker, animated: true, completion: nil)
}
```

Build and run the application. Select an **Item** to see its details and then tap the camera button on the **UIToolbar** and ... the application crashes. Take a look at the description of the crash in the console.

```
Homepwner[3575:64615] [access] This app has crashed because it attempted to
access privacy-sensitive data without a usage description.  The app's Info.plist
must contain an NSPhotoLibraryUsageDescription key with a string value explaining
to the user how the app uses this data.
```

When attempting to access private information, such as a user's photos, iOS presents a prompt to the user asking them whether they want to allow access to the application. Contained within this prompt is a description for why the application wants to access this information. Homepwner is missing this description, and therefore the application is crashing.

Permissions

There are a number of capabilities on iOS that require user approval before use. Here are a subset of those capabilities:

- Camera and photos

- Location

- Microphone

- HealthKit data

- Calendar

- Reminders

For each of these, your application must supply a *usage description* that specifies the reason that your application wants to access this information. This description will be presented to the user whenever the application accesses that capability.

In the project navigator, select the project at the top. Make sure the Homepwner target is selected and open the Info tab along the top (Figure 15.10).

Figure 15.10 Opening the project info

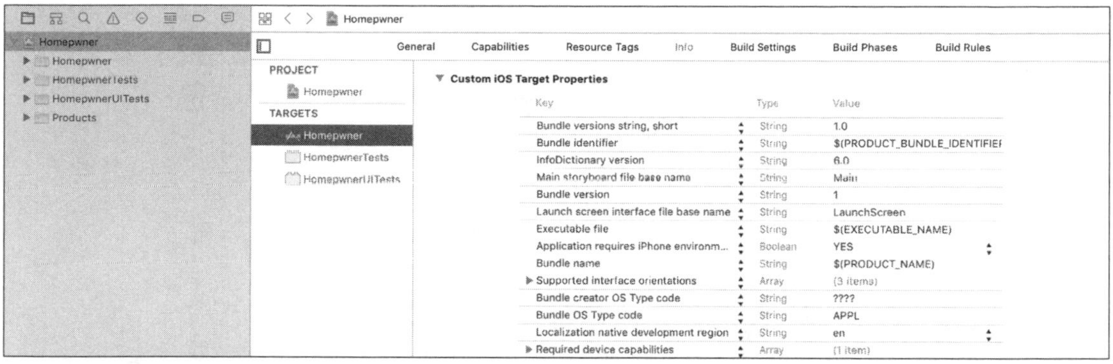

Hover over the last entry in this list of Custom iOS Target Properties and click the + button. Set the Key of this new entry to be NSCameraUsageDescription and the Type to be a String.

Double-click on the Value for this new row and enter the string “This app uses the camera to associate photos with items.” This is the string that will be presented to the user.

Now repeat the same steps above to add a usage description for the photo library. The Key will be NSPhotoLibraryUsageDescription of type String and the Value will be “This app uses the Photos library to associate photos with items.”

The Custom iOS Target Properties section will now look like Figure 15.11. (The entries in your list may be in a different order.)

Figure 15.11 Adding in the new keys

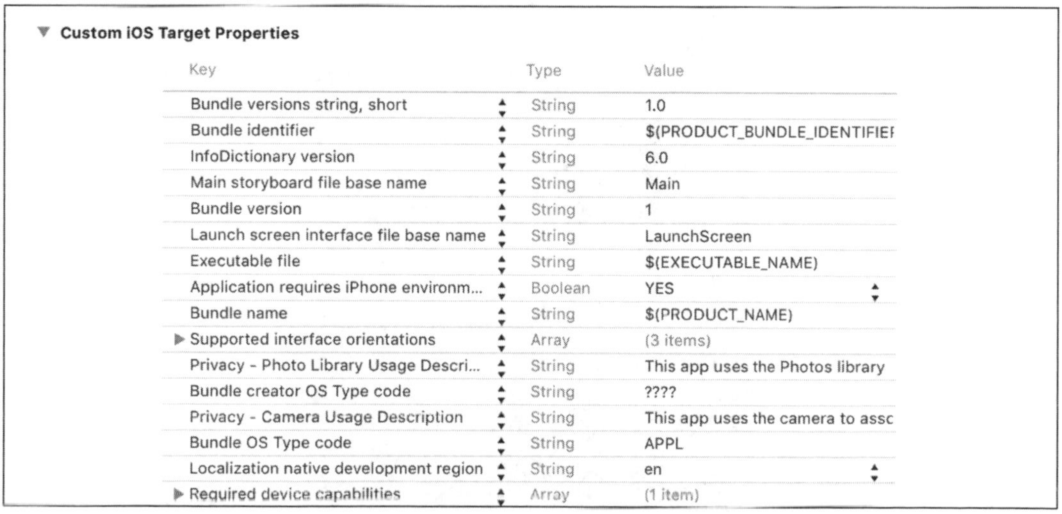

Custom iOS Target Properties

Key	Type	Value
Bundle versions string, short	String	1.0
Bundle identifier	String	$(PRODUCT_BUNDLE_IDENTIFIEI
InfoDictionary version	String	6.0
Main storyboard file base name	String	Main
Bundle version	String	1
Launch screen interface file base name	String	LaunchScreen
Executable file	String	$(EXECUTABLE_NAME)
Application requires iPhone environm...	Boolean	YES
Bundle name	String	$(PRODUCT_NAME)
▶ Supported interface orientations	Array	(3 items)
Privacy - Photo Library Usage Descri...	String	This app uses the Photos library
Bundle creator OS Type code	String	????
Privacy - Camera Usage Description	String	This app uses the camera to assc
Bundle OS Type code	String	APPL
Localization native development region	String	en
▶ Required device capabilities	Array	(1 item)

Build and run the application and navigate to an item. Tap the camera button and you will see the permission dialog presented with the usage description that you provided (Figure 15.12 shows the description for the library). After accepting, the **UIImagePickerController**'s interface will appear on the screen (Figure 15.13 shows the camera interface), and you can take a picture or choose an existing image if your device does not have a camera.

Figure 15.12 Photos library usage description

(If you are working on the simulator, there are some default images already in the photo library. If you would like to add your own, you can drag an image from your computer onto the simulator, and it will be added to the simulator's photo library. Alternatively, you can open Safari in the simulator and navigate to a page with an image. Click and hold the image and choose Save Image to save it in the simulator's photo library.)

Figure 15.13 **UIImagePickerController**'s preview interface

Saving the image

Selecting an image dismisses the **UIImagePickerController** and returns you to the detail view. However, you do not have a reference to the photo once the image picker is dismissed. To fix this, you are going to implement the delegate method **imagePickerController(_:didFinishPickingMediaWithInfo:)**. This method is called on the image picker's delegate when a photo has been selected.

In DetailViewController.swift, implement this method to put the image into the **UIImageView** and then call the method to dismiss the image picker.

```
func imagePickerController(_ picker: UIImagePickerController,
        didFinishPickingMediaWithInfo info: [String: Any]) {

    // Get picked image from info dictionary
    let image = info[UIImagePickerControllerOriginalImage] as! UIImage

    // Put that image on the screen in the image view
    imageView.image = image

    // Take image picker off the screen -
    // you must call this dismiss method
    dismiss(animated: true, completion: nil)
}
```

Build and run the application again. Take (or select) a photo. The image picker is dismissed, and you are returned to the **DetailViewController**'s view, where you will see the selected photo.

Homepwner's users could have hundreds of items to catalog, and each one could have a large image associated with it. Keeping hundreds of instances of **Item** in memory is not a big deal. Keeping hundreds of images in memory would be bad: First, you will get a low memory warning. Then, if your app's memory footprint continues to grow, the OS will terminate it. The solution, which you are going to implement in the next section, is to store images to disk and only fetch them into RAM when they are needed. This fetching will be done by a new class, **ImageStore**. When the application receives a low-memory notification, the **ImageStore**'s cache will be flushed to free the memory that the fetched images were occupying.

Creating ImageStore

In Chapter 16, you will have instances of **Item** write out their properties to a file, which will then be read in when the application starts. However, because images tend to be very large, it is a good idea to keep them separate from other data. You are going to store the pictures the user takes in an instance of a class named **ImageStore**. The image store will fetch and cache the images as they are needed. It will also be able to flush the cache if the device runs low on memory.

Create a new Swift file named ImageStore. In ImageStore.swift, define the **ImageStore** class and add a property that is an instance of **NSCache**.

```
import Foundation
import UIKit

class ImageStore {

    let cache = NSCache<NSString,UIImage>()

}
```

The cache works very much like a dictionary (which you saw in Chapter 2). You are able to add, remove, and update values associated with a given key. Unlike a dictionary, the cache will automatically remove objects if the system gets low on memory. While this could be a problem in this chapter (because images will only exist within the cache), you will fix the problem in Chapter 16 when you will also write the images to the filesystem.

Note that the cache is associating an instance of **NSString** with **UIImage**. **NSString** is Objective-C's version of **String**. Due to the way **NSCache** is implemented (it is an Objective-C class, like most of Apple's classes that you have been working with), it requires you to use **NSString** instead of **String**.

Now implement three methods for adding, retrieving, and deleting an image from the dictionary.

```
class ImageStore {

    let cache = NSCache<NSString,UIImage>()

    func setImage(_ image: UIImage, forKey key: String) {
        cache.setObject(image, forKey: key as NSString)
    }

    func image(forKey key: String) -> UIImage? {
        return cache.object(forKey: key as NSString)
    }

    func deleteImage(forKey key: String) {
        cache.removeObject(forKey: key as NSString)
    }

}
```

These three methods all take in a key of type **String** so that the rest of your codebase does not have to think about the underlying implementation of **NSCache**. You then cast each **String** to an **NSString** when passing it to the cache.

Giving View Controllers Access to the Image Store

The **DetailViewController** needs an instance of **ImageStore** to fetch and store images. You will inject this dependency into the **DetailViewController**'s designated initializer, just as you did for **ItemsViewController** and **ItemStore** in Chapter 10.

In DetailViewController.swift, add a property for an **ImageStore**.

```
var item: Item! {
    didSet {
        navigationItem.title = item.name
    }
}
var imageStore: ImageStore!
```

Now do the same in ItemsViewController.swift.

```
var itemStore: ItemStore!
var imageStore: ImageStore!
```

Next, still in ItemsViewController.swift, update **prepare(for:sender:)** to set the imageStore property on **DetailViewController**.

```
override func prepare(for segue: UIStoryboardSegue, sender: Any?) {
    // If the triggered segue is the "showItem" segue"
    switch segue.identifier {
    case "showItem"?:
        // Figure out which row was just tapped
        if let row = tableView.indexPathForSelectedRow?.row {

            // Get the item associated with this row and pass it along
            let item = itemStore.allItems[row]
            let detailViewController
                    = segue.destination as! DetailViewController
            detailViewController.item = item
            detailViewController.imageStore = imageStore
        }
    default:
        preconditionFailure("Unexpected segue identifier.")
    }
}
```

Finally, update AppDelegate.swift to create and inject the **ImageStore**.

```
func application(_ application: UIApplication, didFinishLaunchingWithOptions
        launchOptions: [UIApplicationLaunchOptionsKey: Any]?) -> Bool {
    // Override point for customization after application launch.

    // Create an ItemStore
    let itemStore = ItemStore()

    // Create an ImageStore
    let imageStore = ImageStore()

    // Access the ItemsViewController and set its item store and image store
    let navController = window!.rootViewController as! UINavigationController
    let itemsController = navController.topViewController as! ItemsViewController
    itemsController.itemStore = itemStore
    itemsController.imageStore = imageStore
```

Creating and Using Keys

When an image is added to the store, it will be put into the cache under a unique key, and the associated **Item** object will be given that key. When the **DetailViewController** wants an image from the store, it will ask its item for the key and search the cache for the image.

Add a property to Item.swift to store the key.

```
let dateCreated: Date
let itemKey: String
```

The image keys need to be unique for your cache to work. While there are many ways to hack together a unique string, you are going to use the Cocoa Touch mechanism for creating universally unique identifiers (UUIDs), also known as globally unique identifiers (GUIDs). Objects of type **NSUUID** represent a UUID and are generated using the time, a counter, and a hardware identifier, which is usually the MAC address of the Wi-Fi card. When represented as a string, UUIDs look something like this:

```
4A73B5D2-A6F4-4B40-9F82-EA1E34C1DC04
```

In Item.swift, generate a UUID and set it as the itemKey.

```
init(name: String, serialNumber: String?, valueInDollars: Int) {
    self.name = name
    self.valueInDollars = valueInDollars
    self.serialNumber = serialNumber
    self.dateCreated = Date()
    self.itemKey = UUID().uuidString

    super.init()
}
```

Then, in DetailViewController.swift, update **imagePickerController(_:didFinishPickingMediaWithInfo:)** to store the image in the **ImageStore**.

```
func imagePickerController(_ picker: UIImagePickerController,
        didFinishPickingMediaWithInfo info: [String : Any]) {

    // Get picked image from info dictionary
    let image = info[UIImagePickerControllerOriginalImage] as! UIImage

    // Store the image in the ImageStore for the item's key
    imageStore.setImage(image, forKey: item.itemKey)

    // Put that image on the screen in the image view
    imageView.image = image

    // Take image picker off the screen -
    // you must call this dismiss method
    dismiss(animated: true, completion: nil)
}
```

Each time an image is captured, it will be added to the store. Both the **ImageStore** and the **Item** will know the key for the image, so both will be able to access it as needed (Figure 15.14).

Figure 15.14 Accessing images from the cache

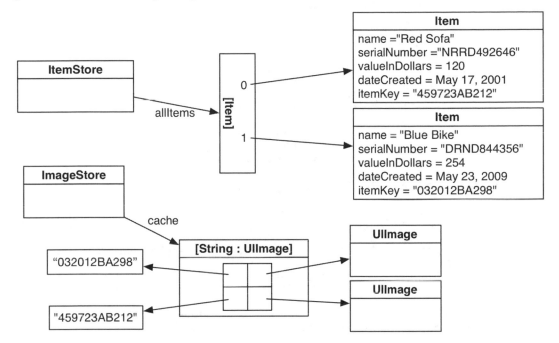

Similarly, when an item is deleted, you need to delete its image from the image store. In
ItemsViewController.swift, update **tableView(_:commit:forRowAt:)** to remove the item's image
from the image store.

```
override func tableView(_ tableView: UITableView,
                        commit editingStyle: UITableViewCellEditingStyle,
                        forRowAt indexPath: IndexPath) {
    // If the table view is asking to commit a delete command...
    if editingStyle == .delete {
        let item = itemStore.allItems[indexPath.row]

        let title = "Delete \(item.name)?"
        let message = "Are you sure you want to delete this item?"

        let ac = UIAlertController(title: title,
                                   message: message,
                                   preferredStyle: .actionSheet)

        let cancelAction = UIAlertAction(title: "Cancel",
                                         style: .cancel,
                                         handler: nil)
        ac.addAction(cancelAction)

        let deleteAction = UIAlertAction(title: "Delete", style: .destructive,
                              handler: { (action) -> Void in
            // Remove the item from the store
            self.itemStore.removeItem(item)

            // Remove the item's image from the image store
            self.imageStore.deleteImage(forKey: item.itemKey)

            // Also remove that row from the table view with an animation
            self.tableView.deleteRows(at: [indexPath], with: .automatic)
        })
        ac.addAction(deleteAction)

        // Present the alert controller
        present(ac, animated: true, completion: nil)
    }
}
```

Wrapping Up ImageStore

Now that the **ImageStore** can store images and instances of **Item** have a key to get an image (Figure 15.14), you need to teach **DetailViewController** how to grab the image for the selected **Item** and place it in its imageView.

The **DetailViewController**'s view will appear when the user taps a row in **ItemsViewController** and when the **UIImagePickerController** is dismissed. In both of these situations, the imageView should be populated with the image of the **Item** being displayed. Currently, it is only happening when the **UIImagePickerController** is dismissed.

In DetailViewController.swift, make this happen in **viewWillAppear(_:)**.

```
override func viewWillAppear(_ animated: Bool) {
    super.viewWillAppear(animated)

    nameField.text = item.name
    serialNumberField.text = item.serialNumber
    valueField.text =
        numberFormatter.string(from: NSNumber(value: item.valueInDollars))
    dateLabel.text = dateFormatter.string(from: item.dateCreated)

    // Get the item key
    let key = item.itemKey

    // If there is an associated image with the item
    // display it on the image view
    let imageToDisplay = imageStore.image(forKey: key)
    imageView.image = imageToDisplay
}
```

Build and run the application. Create an item and select it from the table view. Then, tap the camera button and take a picture. The image will appear as it should. Pop out from the item's details to the list of items. Unlike before, if you tap and drill down to see the details of the item you added a picture to, you will see the image.

Bronze Challenge: Editing an Image

UIImagePickerController has a built-in interface for editing an image once it has been selected. Allow the user to edit the image and use the edited image instead of the original image in **DetailViewController**.

Silver Challenge: Removing an Image

Add a button that clears the image for an item.

Gold Challenge: Camera Overlay

UIImagePickerController has a cameraOverlayView property. Make it so that presenting the **UIImagePickerController** shows a crosshair in the middle of the image capture area.

For the More Curious: Navigating Implementation Files

Both of your view controllers have quite a few methods in their implementation files. To be an effective iOS developer, you must be able to go to the code you are looking for quickly and easily. The source editor jump bar in Xcode is one tool at your disposal (Figure 15.15).

Figure 15.15 Source editor jump bar

Source editor jump bar

The jump bar shows you where exactly you are within the project (and also where the cursor is within a given file). Figure 15.16 breaks down the jump bar details.

Figure 15.16 Jump bar details

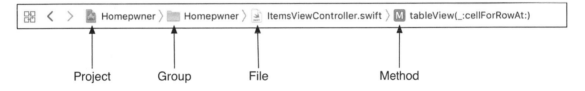

Project   Group   File   Method

The breadcrumb trail navigation of the jump bar mirrors the project navigation hierarchy. If you click on any of the sections, you will be presented with a popover of that section in the project hierarchy. From there, you can easily navigate to other parts of the project.

Figure 15.17 shows the file popover for the Homepwner folder.

Figure 15.17 File popover

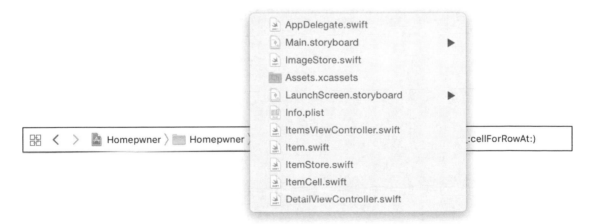

Perhaps most useful is the ability to navigate easily within an implementation file. If you click on the last element in the breadcrumb trail, you will get a popover with the contents of the file, including all of the methods implemented within that file.

While the popover is visible, you can type to filter the items in the list. At any point, you can use the up and down arrow keys and then press the Return key to jump to that method in the code. Figure 15.18 shows what you get when you search for "tableview" in `ItemsViewController.swift`.

Figure 15.18 File popover with "tableview" search

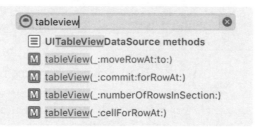

// **MARK:**

As your classes get longer, it can get more difficult to find a method buried in a long list of methods. A good way to organize your methods is to use // MARK: comments.

Two useful // MARK: comments are the divider and the label:

```
// This is a divider
// MARK: -

// This is a label
// MARK: My Awesome Methods
```

The divider and label can be combined:

```
// MARK: - View life cycle
override func viewDidLoad() { ... }
override func viewWillAppear(_ animated: Bool) { ... }

// MARK: - Actions
func addNewItem(_ sender: UIBarButtonItem) {...}
```

Adding // MARK: comments to your code does not change the code itself; it just tells Xcode how to visually organize your methods. You can see the results by opening the current file item in the jump bar. Figure 15.19 presents a well-organized ItemsViewController.swift.

Figure 15.19 File popover with // MARK:s

If you make a habit of using // MARK: comments, you will force yourself to organize your code. If done thoughtfully, this will make your code more readable and easier to work with.

16

Saving, Loading, and Application States

There are many ways to save and load data in an iOS application. This chapter will take you through some of the most common mechanisms as well as the concepts you need for writing to or reading from the filesystem in iOS. Along the way, you will be updating Homepwner so that its data persists between runs (Figure 16.1).

Figure 16.1 Homepwner in the task switcher

Archiving

Most iOS applications are, at base, doing the same thing: providing an interface for the user to manipulate data. Every object in an application has a role in this process. Model objects are responsible for holding on to the data that the user manipulates. View objects reflect that data, and controllers are responsible for keeping the views and the model objects in sync. Therefore, saving and loading "data" almost always means saving and loading model objects.

In Homepwner, the model objects that a user manipulates are instances of **Item**. For Homepwner to be a useful application, instances of **Item** must persist between runs of the application. You will be using *archiving* to save and load **Item** objects.

Archiving is one of the most common ways of persisting model objects in iOS. Archiving an object involves recording all of its properties and saving them to the filesystem. *Unarchiving* re-creates the object from that data.

Classes whose instances need to be archived and unarchived must conform to the **NSCoding** protocol and implement its two required methods, **encode(with:)** and **init(coder:)**.

```
protocol NSCoding {
    func encode(with aCoder: NSCoder)
    init?(coder aDecoder: NSCoder)
}
```

When objects are added to an interface file, such as a storyboard file, they are archived. At runtime, the objects are loaded into memory by being unarchived from the interface file. **UIView** and **UIViewController** both conform to the **NSCoding** protocol, so both can be archived and unarchived without any extra effort from you.

Your **Item** class, on the other hand, does not currently conform to **NSCoding**. Open Homepwner.xcodeproj and add this protocol declaration in Item.swift.

```
class Item: NSObject, NSCoding {
```

The next step is to implement the required methods. Let's start with **encode(with:)**. When an **Item** is sent the message **encode(with:)**, it will encode all of its properties into the **NSCoder** object that is passed as an argument. While saving, you will use **NSCoder** to write out a stream of data. That stream will be organized as key-value pairs and stored on the filesystem.

In Item.swift, implement **encode(with:)** to add the names and values of the item's properties to the stream.

```
func encode(with aCoder: NSCoder) {
    aCoder.encode(name, forKey: "name")
    aCoder.encode(dateCreated, forKey: "dateCreated")
    aCoder.encode(itemKey, forKey: "itemKey")
    aCoder.encode(serialNumber, forKey: "serialNumber")

    aCoder.encode(valueInDollars, forKey: "valueInDollars")
}
```

To find out which encoding methods to use for other Swift types, you can check the documentation for **NSCoder**. Regardless of the type of the encoded value, there is always a key, which is a string that identifies which property is being encoded. By convention, this key is the name of the property being encoded.

Encoding is a recursive process. When an instance is encoded (that is, when it is the first argument in **encode(_:forKey:)**), that instance is sent **encode(with:)**. During the execution of its **encode(with:)** method, it encodes its properties using **encode(_:forKey:)** (Figure 16.2). Thus, each instance encodes any properties that it references, which encode any properties that they reference, and so on.

Figure 16.2 Encoding an object

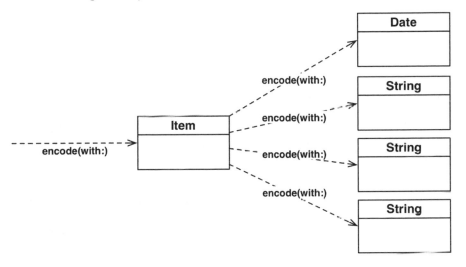

The purpose of the key is to retrieve the encoded value when this **Item** is loaded from the filesystem later. Objects being loaded from an archive are sent the message **init(coder:)**. This method should grab all of the objects that were encoded in **encode(with:)** and assign them to the appropriate property.

In Item.swift, implement **init(coder:)**.

```
required init(coder aDecoder: NSCoder) {
    name = aDecoder.decodeObject(forKey: "name") as! String
    dateCreated = aDecoder.decodeObject(forKey: "dateCreated") as! Date
    itemKey = aDecoder.decodeObject(forKey: "itemKey") as! String
    serialNumber = aDecoder.decodeObject(forKey: "serialNumber") as! String?

    valueInDollars = aDecoder.decodeInteger(forKey: "valueInDollars")

    super.init()
}
```

Notice that this method has an **NSCoder** argument, too. In **init(coder:)**, the **NSCoder** is full of data to be consumed by the **Item** being initialized. Also notice that you call **decodeObject(forKey:)** on the container to get objects and **decodeInteger(forKey:)** to get the valueInDollars.

In Chapter 10, we talked about the initializer chain and designated initializers. The **init(coder:)** method is not part of this design pattern. You will keep **Item**'s designated initializer the same, and **init(coder:)** will not call it.

Instances of **Item** are now **NSCoding** compliant and can be saved to and loaded from the filesystem using archiving. You can build the application now to make sure there are no syntax errors, but you do not yet have a way to kick off the saving and loading. You also need a place on the filesystem to store the saved items.

Application Sandbox

Every iOS application has its own *application sandbox*. An application sandbox is a directory on the filesystem that is barricaded from the rest of the filesystem. Your application must stay in its sandbox, and no other application can access its sandbox. Figure 16.3 shows the application sandbox for iTunes/iCloud.

Figure 16.3 Application sandbox

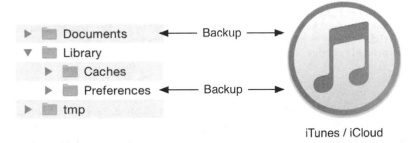

The application sandbox contains a number of directories:

Documents/   This directory is where you write data that the application generates during runtime and that you want to persist between runs of the application. It is backed up when the device is synchronized with iTunes or iCloud. If something goes wrong with the device, files in this directory can be restored from iTunes or iCloud. In Homepwner, the file that holds the data for all your items will be stored here.

Library/Caches/   This directory is where you write data that the application generates during runtime and that you want to persist between runs of the application. However, unlike the Documents directory, it does not get backed up when the device is synchronized with iTunes or iCloud. A major reason for not backing up cached data is that the data can be very large and extend the time it takes to synchronize your device. Data stored somewhere else – like a web server – can be placed in this directory. If the user needs to restore the device, this data can be downloaded from the web server again. If the device is very low on disk space, the system may delete the contents of this directory.

Library/Preferences/   This directory is where any preferences are stored and where the Settings application looks for application preferences. Library/Preferences is handled automatically by the class **NSUserDefaults** and is backed up when the device is synchronized with iTunes or iCloud.

tmp/   This directory is where you write data that you will use temporarily during an application's runtime. The OS may purge files in this directory when your application is not running. However, to be tidy you should explicitly remove files from this directory when you no longer need them. This directory does not get backed up when the device is synchronized with iTunes or iCloud.

Constructing a file URL

The instances of **Item** from Homepwner will be saved to a single file in the Documents directory. The **ItemStore** will handle writing to and reading from that file. To do this, the **ItemStore** needs to construct a URL to this file.

Implement a new property in ItemStore.swift to store this URL.

```
var allItems = [Item]()
let itemArchiveURL: URL = {
    let documentsDirectories =
        FileManager.default.urls(for: .documentDirectory, in: .userDomainMask)
    let documentDirectory = documentsDirectories.first!
    return documentDirectory.appendingPathComponent("items.archive")
}()
```

Instead of assigning a value to the property directly, the value is being set using a closure. You may recall that you did this with the numberFormatter property in Chapter 4. Notice that the closure here has a signature of () -> URL, meaning it does not take in any arguments and it returns an instance of **URL**. When the **ItemStore** class is instantiated, this closure will be run and the return value will be assigned to the itemArchiveURL property. Using a closure like this allows you to set the value for a variable or constant that requires multiple lines of code, which can be very useful when configuring objects. This makes your code more maintainable because it keeps the property and the code needed to generate the property together.

The method **urls(for:in:)** searches the filesystem for a URL that meets the criteria given by the arguments. (Double-check that your first argument is .documentDirectory and not .documentationDirectory. Autocomplete's first suggestion is .documentationDirectory, so it is easy to introduce this error and end up with the wrong URL.)

In iOS, the last argument is always the same. (This method is borrowed from macOS, where there are significantly more options.) The first argument is a **SearchPathDirectory** enumeration that specifies the directory in the sandbox you want the URL for. For example, searching for .cachesDirectory will return the Caches directory in the application's sandbox.

You can search the documentation for SearchPathDirectory to locate the other options. Remember that these enumeration values are shared by iOS and macOS, so not all of them will work on iOS.

The return value of **urls(for:in:)** is an array of URLs. It is an array because in macOS there may be multiple URLs that meet the search criteria. In iOS, however, there will only be one (if the directory you searched for is an appropriate sandbox directory). Therefore, the name of the archive file is appended to the first and only URL in the array. This will be where the archive of **Item** instances will live.

NSKeyedArchiver and NSKeyedUnarchiver

You now have a place to save data on the filesystem and a model object that can be saved to the filesystem. The final two questions are: How do you kick off the saving and loading processes, and when do you do it? To save instances of **Item**, you will use the class **NSKeyedArchiver** when the application "exits."

In ItemStore.swift, implement a new method that calls **archiveRootObject(_:toFile:)** on the **NSKeyedArchiver** class.

```
func saveChanges() -> Bool {
    print("Saving items to: \(itemArchiveURL.path)")
    return NSKeyedArchiver.archiveRootObject(allItems, toFile: itemArchiveURL.path)
}
```

The **archiveRootObject(_:toFile:)** method takes care of saving every single **Item** in allItems to the **itemArchiveURL**. Yes, it is that simple. Here is how **archiveRootObject(_:toFile:)** works:

- The method begins by creating an instance of **NSKeyedArchiver**. (**NSKeyedArchiver** is a concrete subclass of the abstract class **NSCoder**.)

- The method **encode(with:)** is called on allItems and is passed the instance of **NSKeyedArchiver** as an argument.

- The allItems array then calls **encode(with:)** to all of the objects it contains, passing the same **NSKeyedArchiver**. Thus, all your instances of **Item** encode their instance variables into the very same **NSKeyedArchiver** (Figure 16.4).

- The **NSKeyedArchiver** writes the data it collected to the path.

Figure 16.4 Archiving the allItems array

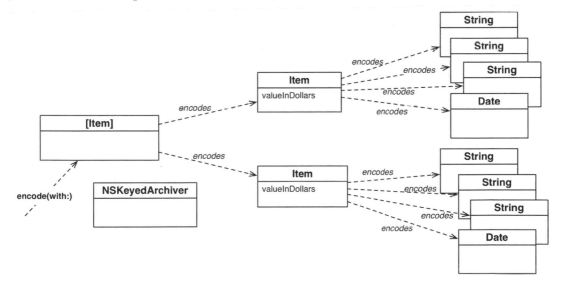

When the user presses the Home button on the device, the message
applicationDidEnterBackground(_:) is sent to the **AppDelegate**. That is when you want to send
saveChanges to the **ItemStore**.

Open AppDelegate.swift and add a property to the class to store the **ItemStore** instance. You will
need a property to reference the instance in **applicationDidEnterBackground(_:)**.

```
class AppDelegate: UIResponder, UIApplicationDelegate {

    var window: UIWindow?
    let itemStore = ItemStore()
```

Then update **application(_:didFinishLaunchingWithOptions:)** to use this property instead of the
local constant.

```
func application(_ application: UIApplication, didFinishLaunchingWithOptions
        launchOptions: [UIApplicationLaunchOptionsKey : Any]?) -> Bool {
    // Override point for customization after application launch.

    // Create an ItemStore
    let itemStore = ItemStore()

    // Create an ImageStore
    let imageStore = ImageStore()

    // Access the ItemsViewController and set its item store and image store
    let navController = window!.rootViewController as! UINavigationController
    let itemsController = navController.topViewController as! ItemsViewController
    itemsController.itemStore = itemStore
    itemsController.imageStore = imageStore

    return true
}
```

Because the property and the local constant were named the same, you only needed to remove the code
that created the local constant.

Now, still in AppDelegate.swift, implement **applicationDidEnterBackground(_:)** to kick off
saving the **Item** instances. (This method may have already been implemented by the template. If so,
make sure to add this code to the existing method instead of writing a new one.)

```
func applicationDidEnterBackground(_ application: UIApplication) {
    let success = itemStore.saveChanges()
    if (success) {
        print("Saved all of the Items")
    } else {
        print("Could not save any of the Items")
    }
}
```

Build and run the application on the simulator. Create a few instances of **Item**, then press the Home button to leave the application. Check the console and you should see a log statement indicating that the items were saved.

While you cannot yet load these instances of **Item** back into the application, you can still verify that *something* was saved.

In the console's log statements, find one that logs out the itemArchiveURL location and another that indicates whether saving was successful. If saving was not successful, confirm that your itemArchiveURL is being created correctly. If the items were saved successfully, copy the path that is printed to the console.

Open Finder and press Command-Shift-G. Paste the file path that you copied from the console and press Return. You will be taken to the directory that contains the items.archive file. Press Command-Up to navigate to the parent directory of items.archive. This is the application's sandbox directory. Here, you can see the Documents, Library, and tmp directories alongside the application itself (Figure 16.5).

Figure 16.5 Homepwner's sandbox

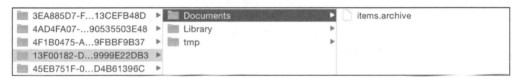

The location of the sandbox directory can change between runs of the application; however, the contents of the sandbox will remain unchanged. Due to this, you may need to copy and paste the directory into Finder frequently while working on an application.

Loading files

Now let's turn to loading these files. To load instances of **Item** when the application launches, you will use the class **NSKeyedUnarchiver** when the **ItemStore** is created.

In ItemStore.swift, override **init()** to add the following code.

```
init() {
    if let archivedItems =
        NSKeyedUnarchiver.unarchiveObject(withFile: itemArchiveURL.path) as? [Item] {
        allItems = archivedItems
    }
}
```

The **unarchiveObject(withFile:)** method will create an instance of **NSKeyedUnarchiver** and load the archive located at the itemArchiveURL into that instance. The **NSKeyedUnarchiver** will then inspect the type of the root object in the archive and create an instance of that type. In this case, the type will be an array of **Item**s because you created this archive with a root object of type **[Item]**. (If the root object were an instance of **Item** instead, then **unarchiveObject(withFile:)** would return an **Item**.)

The newly created array is then sent **init(coder:)** and, as you may have guessed, the **NSKeyedUnarchiver** is passed as the argument. The array starts decoding its contents (instances of **Item**) from the **NSKeyedUnarchiver** and sends each of these objects the message **init(coder:)**, passing the same **NSKeyedUnarchiver**.

Build and run the application. Your items will be available until you explicitly delete them. One thing to note about testing your saving and loading code: If you kill Homepwner from Xcode, the method **applicationDidEnterBackground(_:)** will not get a chance to be called and the item array will not be saved. You must press the Home button first and *then* kill it from Xcode by clicking the Stop button.

Application States and Transitions

In Homepwner, the items are archived when the application enters the *background state*. It is useful to understand the states an application can be in, what causes applications to transition between states, and how your code can be notified of these transitions. This information is summarized in Figure 16.6.

Figure 16.6 States of a typical application

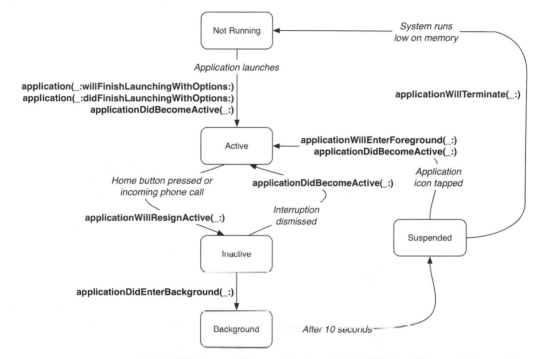

When an application is not running, it is in the *not running state* and it does not execute any code or have any memory reserved in RAM.

After the user launches an application, it enters the *active state*. When in the active state, an application's interface is on the screen, it is accepting events, and its code is handling those events.

While in the active state, an application can be temporarily interrupted by a system event like an SMS message, push notification, phone call, or alarm. An overlay will appear on top of your application to handle this event, and the application enters the *inactive state*. In the inactive state, an application is visible behind the overlay and is executing code, but it is not receiving events. Applications typically spend very little time in the inactive state. You can force an active application into the inactive state by pressing the Lock button at the top of the device. The application will stay inactive until the device is unlocked.

When the user presses the Home button or switches to another application in some other way, the application enters the *background state*. (Actually, it spends a brief moment in the inactive state before transitioning to the background state.) In the background state, an application's interface is not visible or receiving events, but it can still execute code. By default, an application that enters the background state has about 10 seconds before it enters the *suspended state*. Your application should not rely on this number; instead, it should save user data and release any shared resources as quickly as possible.

An application in the suspended state cannot execute code. You cannot see its interface, and any resources it does not need while suspended are destroyed. A suspended application is essentially flash-frozen and can be quickly thawed when the user relaunches it. Table 16.1 summarizes the characteristics of the different application states.

Table 16.1 Application states

State	Visible	Receives Events	Executes Code
Not Running	no	no	no
Active	yes	yes	yes
Inactive	mostly	no	yes
Background	no	no	yes
Suspended	no	no	no

You can see what applications are in the background or suspended by double-tapping the Home button to get to the task switcher (Figure 16.7). You can do this in the simulator by pressing Command-Shift-H twice. (Recently run applications that have been terminated may also appear in this display.)

Figure 16.7 Background and suspended applications in the task switcher

An application in the suspended state will remain in that state as long as there is adequate system memory. When the OS decides memory is getting low, it will terminate suspended applications as needed. A suspended application gets no indication that it is about to be terminated. It is simply removed from memory. (An application may remain in the task switcher after it has been terminated, but it will have to relaunch when tapped.)

When an application changes its state, a method is called on the application delegate. Here are some of the methods from the **UIApplicationDelegate** protocol that announce application state transitions. (These are also shown in Figure 16.6.)

```
optional func application(_ application: UIApplication, didFinishLaunchingWithOptions
        launchOptions: [UIApplicationLaunchOptionsKey : Any]?) -> Bool
optional func applicationDidBecomeActive(_ application: UIApplication)
optional func applicationWillResignActive(_ application: UIApplication)
optional func applicationDidEnterBackground(_ application: UIApplication)
optional func applicationWillEnterForeground(_ application: UIApplication)
```

You can implement these methods to take the appropriate actions for your application. Transitioning to the background state is a good place to save any outstanding changes because it is the last time your application can execute code before it enters the suspended state. Once in the suspended state, an application can be terminated at the whim of the OS.

Writing to the Filesystem with Data

Your archiving in Homepwner saves and loads the itemKey for each **Item**, but what about the images? At the moment, they are lost when the app enters the background state. In this section, you will extend the image store to save images as they are added and fetch them as they are needed.

The images for **Item** instances should also be stored in the Documents directory. You can use the image key generated when the user takes a picture to name the image in the filesystem.

Implement a new method in ImageStore.swift named **imageURL(forKey:)** to create a URL in the documents directory using a given key.

```
func imageURL(forKey key: String) -> URL {

    let documentsDirectories =
        FileManager.default.urls(for: .documentDirectory, in: .userDomainMask)
    let documentDirectory = documentsDirectories.first!

    return documentDirectory.appendingPathComponent(key)
}
```

To save and load an image, you are going to copy the JPEG representation of the image into a buffer in memory. Instead of just creating a buffer, Swift programmers have a handy class to create, maintain, and destroy these sorts of buffers – **Data**. A **Data** instance holds some number of bytes of binary data, and you will use **Data** to store image data.

In `ImageStore.swift`, modify **setImage(_:forKey:)** to get a URL and save the image.

```
func setImage(_ image: UIImage, forKey key: String) {
    cache.setObject(image, forKey: key as NSString)

    // Create full URL for image
    let url = imageURL(forKey: key)

    // Turn image into JPEG data
    if let data = UIImageJPEGRepresentation(image, 0.5) {
        // Write it to full URL
        let _ = try? data.write(to: url, options: [.atomic])
    }
}
```

Let's examine this code more closely. The function **UIImageJPEGRepresentation** takes two parameters: a **UIImage** and a compression quality. The compression quality is a **Float** from 0 to 1, where 1 is the highest quality (least compression). The function returns an instance of **Data** if the compression succeeds and nil if it does not.

This **Data** instance can be written to the filesystem by calling **write(to:options:)**. The bytes held in the **Data** are then written to the URL specified by the first parameter. The second parameter allows for some options to be passed into the method. If the .atomic option is present, the file is written to a temporary place on the filesystem, and, once the writing operation is complete, that file is renamed to the URL of the first parameter, replacing any previously existing file. Writing atomically prevents data corruption should your application crash during the write procedure.

It is worth noting that this way of writing data to the filesystem is *not* archiving. While **Data** instances can be archived, using the method **write(to:options:)** copies the bytes in the **Data** directly to the filesystem.

Now that the image is stored in the filesystem, the **ImageStore** will need to load that image when it is requested. The initializer **init(contentsOfFile:)** of **UIImage** will read in an image from a file, given a URL.

In `ImageStore.swift`, update the method **image(forKey:)** so that the **ImageStore** will load the image from the filesystem if it does not already have it.

```
func image(forKey key: String) -> UIImage? {
    return cache.object(forKey: key as NSString)

    if let existingImage = cache.object(forKey: key as NSString) {
        return existingImage
    }

    let url = imageURL(forKey: key)
    guard let imageFromDisk = UIImage(contentsOfFile: url.path) else {
        return nil
    }

    cache.setObject(imageFromDisk, forKey: key as NSString)
    return imageFromDisk
}
```

What is that `guard` statement? `guard` is a conditional statement, like an `if` statement. The compiler will only continue past the `guard` statement if the condition within the `guard` is `true`. Here, the condition is whether the **UIImage** initialization is successful. If the initialization fails, the `else` block is executed, which allows you to have an early return. If the initialization succeeds, any variables or constants bound in the `guard` statement (here, `imageFromDisk`) are usable after the `guard` statement.

The code above is functionally equivalent to the following code:

```
if let imageFromDisk = UIImage(contentsOfFile: url.path) {
    cache.setObject(imageFromDisk, forKey: key)
    return imageFromDisk
}

return nil
```

While you could do this, `guard` provides both a cleaner – and, more importantly, a safer – way to ensure that you exit if you do not have what you need. Using `guard` also forces the failure case to be directly tied to the condition being checked. This makes the code more readable and easier to reason about.

You are able to save an image to disk and retrieve an image from disk, so the last thing you need to do is add functionality to remove an image from disk.

In `ImageStore.swift`, make sure that when an image is deleted from the store, it is also deleted from the filesystem. (You will see an error when you type in this code, which we will discuss next.)

```
func deleteImage(forKey key: String) {
    cache.removeObject(forKey: key as NSString)

    let url = imageURL(forKey: key)
    FileManager.default.removeItem(at: url)
}
```

Let's take a look at the error message that this code generated, shown in Figure 16.8.

Figure 16.8 Error when removing the image from disk

```
func deleteImage(forKey key: String) {
    cache.removeObject(forKey: key as NSString)

    let url = imageURL(forKey: key)
    FileManager.default.removeItem(at: url)    ● Call can throw, but it is not marked with 'try' and the error is not handled
}
```

This error message is letting you know that the method **removeItem(at:)** can fail, but you are not handling the error. Let's fix this.

Error Handling

It is often useful to have a way of representing the possibility of failure when creating methods. You have seen one way of representing failure throughout this book with the use of optionals. Optionals provide a simple way to represent failure when you do not care about the reason for failure. Consider the creation of an **Int** from a **String**.

```
let theMeaningOfLife = "42"
let numberFromString = Int(theMeaningOfLife)
```

This initializer on **Int** takes a **String** parameter and returns an optional **Int** (an **Int?**). This is because the string may not be able to be represented as an **Int**. The code above will successfully create an **Int**, but the following code will not:

```
let pi = "Apple Pie"
let numberFromString = Int(pi)
```

The string "Apple Pie" cannot be represented as an **Int**, so numberFromString will contain nil. An optional works well for representing failure here because you do not care *why* it failed. You just want to know whether it was successful.

When you need to know why something failed, an optional will not provide enough information. Think about removing the image from the filesystem – why might that fail? Perhaps there is no file at the specified URL, or the URL is malformed, or you do not have permission to remove that file. There are a number of reasons this method could fail, and you might want to handle each case differently.

Swift provides a rich error handling system with compiler support to ensure that you recognize when something bad could happen. You already saw this when the Swift compiler told you that you were not handling a possible error when removing the file from disk.

If a method could generate an error, its method signature needs to indicate this using the throws keyword. Here is the method definition for **removeItem(at:)**:

```
func removeItem(at URL: URL) throws
```

The throws keyword indicates that this method could *throw* an error. (If you are familiar with throwing exception in other languages, Swift's error handling is *not* the same as throwing exception.) By using this keyword, the compiler ensures that anyone who uses this method knows that this method can throw an error – and, more importantly, that the caller also handles any potential errors. This is how the compiler was able to let you know that you are not handling errors when attempting to remove a file from disk.

To call a method that can throw, you use a do-catch statement. Within the do block, you annotate any methods that might throw an error using the try keyword to reinforce the idea that the call might fail.

In ImageStore.swift, update **deleteImage(forKey:)** to call **removeItem(at:)** using a do-catch statement.

```
func deleteImage(forKey key: String) {
    cache.removeObject(forKey: key as NSString)

    let url = imageURL(forKey: key)
    FileManager.default.removeItem(at: url)
    do {
        try FileManager.default.removeItem(at: url)
    } catch {

    }
}
```

If a method does throw an error, then the program immediately exits the do block; no further code in the do block is executed. At that point, the error is passed to the catch block for it to be handled in some way.

Now, update **deleteImage(forKey:)** to print out the error to the console.

```
func deleteImage(forKey key: String) {
    cache.removeObject(forKey: key as NSString)

    let url = imageURL(forKey: key)
    do {
        try FileManager.default.removeItem(at: url)
    } catch {
        print("Error removing the image from disk: \(error)")
    }
}
```

Within the catch block, there is an implicit error constant that contains information describing the error. You can optionally give this constant an explicit name.

Update **deleteImage(forKey:)** again to use an explicit name for the error being caught.

```
func deleteImage(forKey key: String) {
    cache.removeObject(forKey: key as NSString)

    let url = imageURL(forKey: key)
    do {
        try FileManager.default.removeItem(at: url)
    } catch let deleteError {
        print("Error removing the image from disk: \(errordeleteError)")
    }
}
```

There is a lot more that you can do with error handling, but this is the basic knowledge that you need for now. We will cover more details as you progress through this book.

Build and run the application now that the **ImageStore** is complete. Take a photo for an item and exit the application to the Home screen (on the simulator, select Hardware → Home or press Shift-Command-H; on a hardware device simply press the Home button). Launch the application again. Selecting that same item will show all its saved details – including the photo you just took.

Notice that the images are saved immediately after being taken, while the instances of **Item** are saved only when the application enters the background. You save the images right away because they are just too big to keep in memory for long.

Bronze Challenge: PNG

Instead of saving each image as a JPEG, save it as a PNG.

For the More Curious: Application State Transitions

Let's write some quick code to get a better understanding of the different application state transitions.

In AppDelegate.swift, implement the application state transition delegate methods so that they print out the name of the method. You will need to add four more methods. (Check to make sure the template has not already created these methods before writing brand new ones.) Rather than hardcoding the name of the method in the call to **print()**, use the #function expression. At compile time, the #function expression will evaluate to a **String** representing the name of the method.

```
func applicationWillResignActive(_ application: UIApplication) {
    print(#function)
}

func applicationDidEnterBackground(_ application: UIApplication) {
    print(#function)
    let success = itemStore.saveChanges()
    if success {
        print("Saved all of the Items")
    } else {
        print("Could not save any of the Items")
    }
}

func applicationWillEnterForeground(_ application: UIApplication) {
    print(#function)
}

func applicationDidBecomeActive(_ application: UIApplication) {
    print(#function)
}

func applicationWillTerminate(_ application: UIApplication) {
    print(#function)
}
```

Finally, add the same **print()** statement to the top of **application(_:didFinishLaunchingWithOptions:)**.

```
func application(_ application: UIApplication, didFinishLaunchingWithOptions
        launchOptions: [UIApplicationLaunchOptionsKey : Any]?) -> Bool {
    print(#function)
    ...
}
```

Build and run the application. You will see that the application gets sent **application(_:didFinishLaunchingWithOptions:)** and then **applicationDidBecomeActive(_:)**. Play around to see what actions cause what transitions.

Press the Home button and the console will report that the application briefly inactivated and then went into the background state. Relaunch the application by tapping its icon on the Home screen or in the task switcher. The console will report that the application entered the foreground and then became active.

Press the Home button to exit the application again. Then, double-press the Home button to open the task switcher. Swipe the Homepwner application up and off this display to quit the application. Note that no method is called on your application delegate at this point – it is simply terminated.

For the More Curious: Reading and Writing to the Filesystem

In addition to archiving and **Data**'s binary read and write methods, there are a few more methods for transferring data to and from the filesystem. One of them, Core Data, is coming up in Chapter 22. A couple others are worth mentioning here.

Using **Data** works well for binary data. For text data, **String** has two instance methods: **write(to:atomically:encoding:)** and **init(contentsOf:encoding:)**. They are used as follows:

```
// Save someString to the filesystem
do {
    try someString.write(to: someURL,
        atomically: true,
        encoding: .utf8)
} catch {
    print("Error writing to URL: \(error)")
}

// Load someString from the filesystem
do {
    let myEssay = try String(contentsOf: someURL, encoding: .utf8)
    print(myEssay)
} catch {
    print("Error reading from URL: \(error)")
}
```

Note that in many languages, anything unexpected results in an exception being thrown. In Swift, exceptions are nearly always used to indicate programmer error. When an exception *is* thrown, the information about what went wrong is in an **NSException** object. That information is usually just a hint to the programmer, like, "You tried to access the seventh object in this array, but there are only two." The symbols for the call stack (as it appeared when the exception was thrown) are also in the **NSException**.

When do you use exceptions, and when do you use error handling? If you are writing a method that should only be called with an odd number as an argument, throw an exception if it is called with an even number – the caller is making an error and you want to help that programmer find the error. If you are writing a method that wants to read the contents of a particular directory but does not have the necessary privileges, use Swift's error handling and throw an error to the caller to indicate why you were unable to fulfill this very reasonable request.

Property list serializable types can also be written to the filesystem. The only types that are property list serializable are **String**, **NSNumber** (including primitives like **Int**, **Double**, and **Bool**), **Date**, **Data**, **Array<Element>**, and **Dictionary<Key: Hashable,Value>**. When an **Array<Element>** or **Dictionary<Key,Value>** is written to the filesystem with these methods, an *XML property list* is created. An XML property list is a collection of tagged values, like:

```xml
<?xml version="1.0" encoding="UTF-8"?>
<!DOCTYPE plist PUBLIC "-//Apple//DTD PLIST 1.0//EN"
        "http://www.apple.com/DTDs/PropertyList-1.0.dtd">
<plist version="1.0">
<array>
    <dict>
        <key>firstName</key>
        <string>Christian</string>
        <key>lastName</key>
        <string>Keur</string>
    </dict>
    <dict>
        <key>firstName</key>
        <string>Aaron</string>
        <key>lastName</key>
        <string>Hillegass</string>
    </dict>
</array>
</plist>
```

XML property lists are a convenient way to store data because they can be read on nearly any system. Many web service applications use property lists as input and output. The code for writing and reading a property list looks like this:

```swift
let authors = [
    ["firstName":"Christian", "lastName":"Keur"],
    ["firstName":"Aaron", "lastName":"Hillegass"]
]

// Write array to disk
if PropertyListSerialization.propertyList(authors,
    isValidFor: .xml) {
        do {
            let data = try PropertyListSerialization.data(with: authors,
                format: .xml,
                options: [])
            data.write(to: url, options: [.atomic])
        } catch {
            print("Error writing plist: \(error)")
        }
}

// Read array from disk
do {
    let data = try Data(contentsOf: url, options: [])
    let authors = try NSPropertyListSerialization.propertyList(from: data,
        options: [],
        format: nil)
    print("Read in authors: \(authors)")
} catch {
    print("Error reading plist: \(error)")
}
```

For the More Curious: The Application Bundle

When you build an iOS application project in Xcode, you create an *application bundle*. The application bundle contains the application executable and any resources you have bundled with your application. Resources are things like storyboard files, images, and audio files – any files that will be used at runtime. When you add a resource file to a project, Xcode is smart enough to realize that it should be bundled with your application.

How can you tell which files are being bundled with your application? Select the Homepwner project from the project navigator. Check out the Build Phases pane in the Homepwner target. Everything under Copy Bundle Resources will be added to the application bundle when it is built.

Each item in the Homepwner target group is one of the phases that occurs when you build a project. The Copy Bundle Resources phase is where all of the resources in your project get copied into the application bundle.

You can check out what an application bundle looks like on the filesystem after you install an application on the simulator. Print the application bundle path to the console and then navigate to that directory.

```
print(Bundle.main.bundlePath)
```

Control-click the application bundle and choose Show Package Contents from the contextual menu (Figure 16.9).

Figure 16.9 Viewing an application bundle

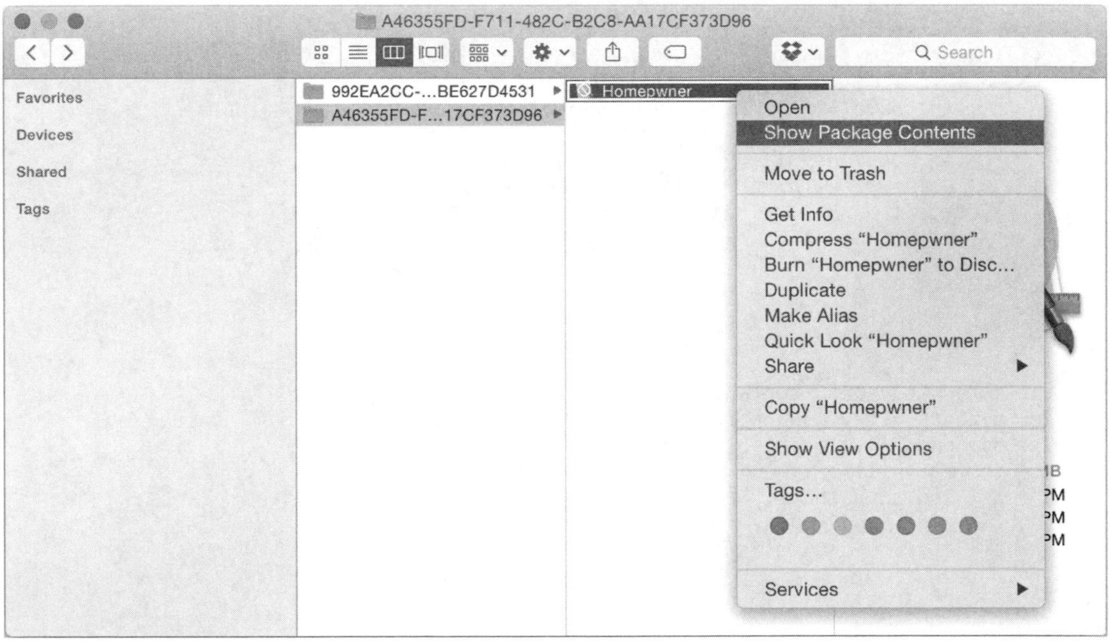

A Finder window will appear showing you the contents of the application bundle (Figure 16.10). When users download your application from the App Store, these files are copied to their devices.

Figure 16.10 The application bundle

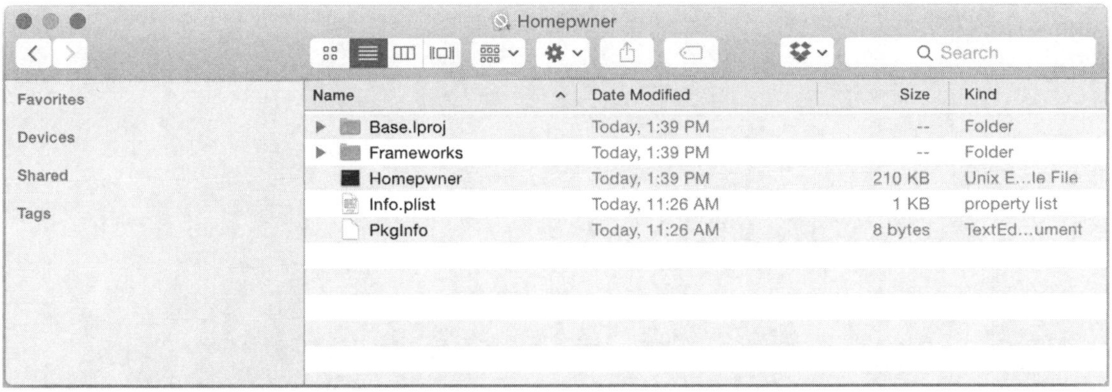

You can load files from the application's bundle at runtime. To get the full URL for files in the application bundle, you need to get a reference to the application bundle and then ask it for the URL of a resource.

```
// Get a reference to the application bundle
let applicationBundle = Bundle.main

// Ask for the URL to a resource named myImage.png in the bundle
if let url = applicationBundle.url(forResource: "myImage", ofType: "png") {
    // Do something with URL
}
```

If you ask for the URL to a file that is not in the application's bundle, this method will return nil. If the file does exist, then the full URL is returned, and you can use this URL to load the file with the appropriate class.

Bear in mind that files within the application bundle are read-only. You cannot modify them, nor can you dynamically add files to the application bundle at runtime. Files in the application bundle are typically things like button images, interface sound effects, or the initial state of a database you ship with your application. You will use this method in later chapters to load these types of resources at runtime.

17

Size Classes

Often, you want an application's interface to have a different layout depending on the dimensions and orientation of the screen. In this chapter, you will modify the interface for **DetailViewController** in Homepwner so that when it appears on a screen that has a relatively small height, the set of text fields and the image view are side by side instead of stacked on top of one another (Figure 17.1).

Figure 17.1 Two layouts for Homepwner's **DetailViewController**

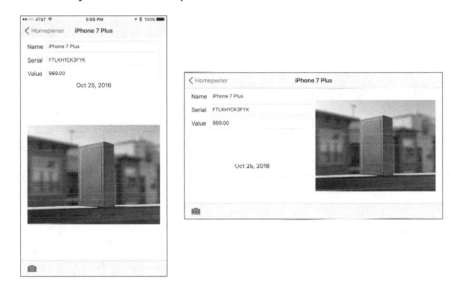

The relative sizes of screens are defined in *size classes*. A size class represents a relative amount of screen space in a given dimension. Each dimension (width and height) can either be compact or regular, so there are four possible combinations of size classes:

Compact Width | Compact Height	iPhones with 3.5, 4, or 4.7-inch screens in landscape orientation
Compact Width | Regular Height	iPhones of all sizes in portrait orientation
Regular Width | Compact Height	iPhones with 5.5-inch screens in landscape orientation
Regular Width | Regular Height	iPads of all sizes in all orientations

Notice that the size classes cover both screen sizes and orientations. Instead of thinking about interfaces in terms of orientation or device, it is better to think in terms of size classes.

Modifying Traits for a Specific Size Class

When editing the interface for a specific size class combination, you are able to change:

- properties for many views

- whether a specific subview is installed

- whether a specific constraint is installed

- the constant of a constraint

- the font for subviews that display text

In Homepwner, you are going to focus on the first item in that list – adjusting view properties depending on the size class configuration. The goal is to have the image view be on the right side of the labels and text fields in a compact height environment. In a regular height environment, the image view will be below the labels and text fields (as it currently is). Stack views will make this remarkably easy.

To begin, you are going to embed the existing vertical stack view within another stack view. This will make it easy to add an image view to the right side of the labels and text fields.

Open `Homepwner.xcodeproj` and `Main.storyboard`. Select the vertical stack view and click the ⊞ icon to embed this stack view within another stack view. With this new stack view selected, open the Auto Layout Add New Constraints menu, configure it as shown in Figure 17.2, and add the constraints.

Figure 17.2 Stack view constraints

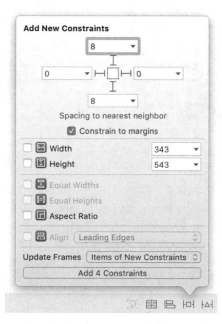

Next, open the new stack view's attributes inspector. Increase the Spacing to be 8.

Now you are going to move the image view from the inner stack view to the outer stack view that you just created. This is how you will be able to have the image view on the right side of the rest of the interface: In a compact height environment, the stack view will be set to be horizontal and the image view will take up the right side of the interface.

Moving the image view from one stack view to the other can be a little tricky, so you are going to do it in a few steps.

Open the document outline and expand the section for the Detail View Controller Scene. Expand the outer two stack views as shown in Figure 17.3.

Figure 17.3 Expanding the document outline

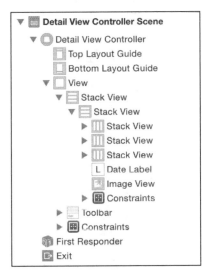

Drag the Image View right above the stack view that it is currently contained within (Figure 17.4). This will move it from the inner stack view to the outer stack view.

Figure 17.4 Moving the image view to the outer stack view

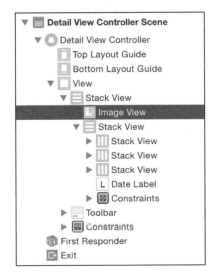

Finally, collapse the inner stack view and drag the Image View to be below it in the stack (Figure 17.5). Make sure the Image View is indented at the same level as the inner stack view. You may need to update frames at this point to get rid of any warnings.

Figure 17.5 Moving the image view below the inner stack view

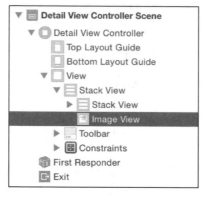

Build and run the application. Confirm that the behavior of the stack view is unchanged.

At this point, you have updated everything that is common to all size classes. Next you will modify specific size classes to change the layout of the content.

At the bottom of Interface Builder, click on the text View as: iPhone 7 (wC hR) to expand the view options. Then select the landscape Orientation (Figure 17.6). Leave the Device as iPhone 7.

Figure 17.6 **DetailViewController** viewed as iPhone 7 landscape

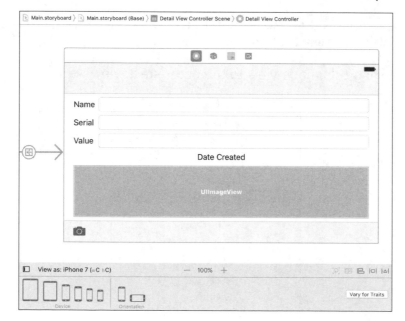

Next, you will update the properties for the outer stack view so that the image view is on the right side.

Select the outer stack view and open its attributes inspector. Under the Stack View heading, find the Axis property and click the + button on its left side. From the pop-up menu, choose Any for the Width variation and Compact for the Height variation (Figure 17.7). Click Add Variation. This will allow you to customize the axis property for all iPhones in landscape.

Figure 17.7 Adding a size-class-specific option

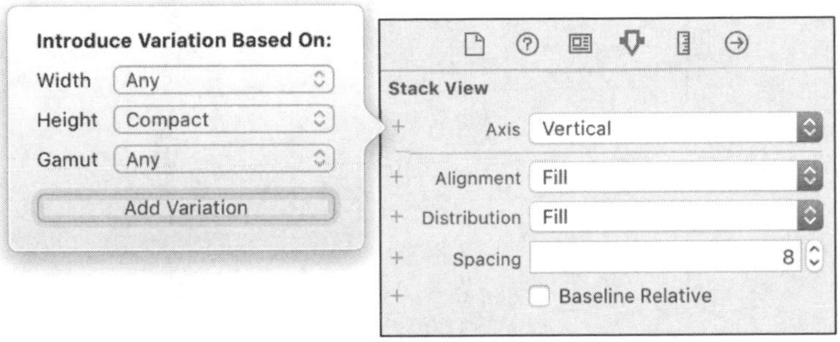

For the new option (hC), choose Horizontal (Figure 17.8). Now, whenever the interface has a compact height, the outer stack view will have a horizontal configuration. When the interface has a regular height, the outer stack view will have a vertical configuration.

Figure 17.8 Customizing the axis

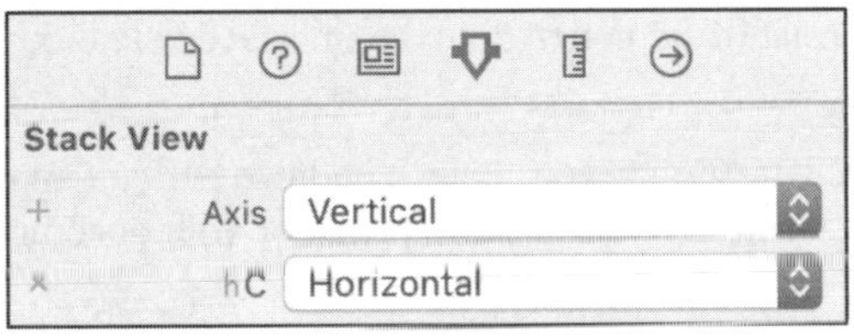

The last change you want to make is for the inner stack view and the image view to fill the outer stack view equally. To do this, you will customize the outer stack view's distribution.

With the attributes inspector still open for the outer stack view, click on the + next to Distribution and once again select Any for the Width variation and Compact for the Height variation from the pop-up menu. Change the distribution for this size class to be Fill Equally (Figure 17.9).

Figure 17.9 Customizing the distribution

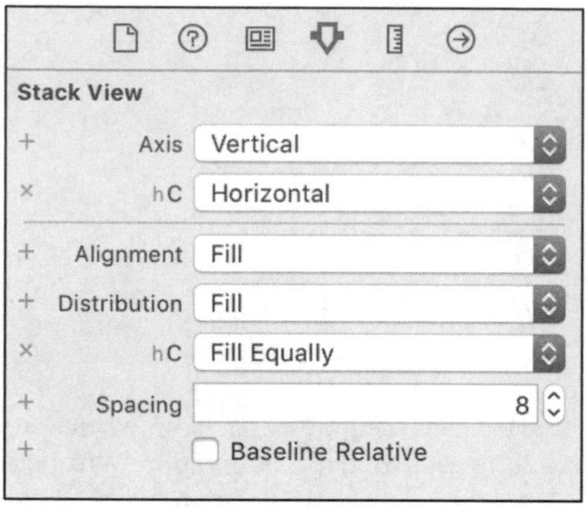

Build and run the application. Select an item and drill down to its details to add a photo, if it does not already have one. Rotate between portrait and landscape (on the simulator, you can use Command plus the left or right arrow key to rotate) and notice how the interface is laid out as you specified for both regular and compact height.

With that, your Homepwner application is complete. You have built an app with a flexible interface that can take photos and store data, and we hope you are proud of your accomplishment! Take some time to celebrate.

Bronze Challenge: Stacked Text Field and Labels

In a compact height environment, make it so the text fields and labels are stacked vertically instead of horizontally (Figure 17.10).

Figure 17.10 Text fields and labels stacked

18

Touch Events and UIResponder

In the next two chapters, you will create TouchTracker, an app that lets the user draw by touching the screen. In this chapter, you will create a view that draws lines in response to the user dragging across it (Figure 18.1). Using multitouch, the user will be able to draw more than one line at a time.

Figure 18.1 TouchTracker

Touch Events

As a subclass of **UIResponder**, a **UIView** can override four methods to handle the four distinct touch events:

- one or more fingers touch the screen

  ```
  func touchesBegan(_ touches: Set<UITouch>, with event: UIEvent?)
  ```

- one or more fingers move across the screen (this message is sent repeatedly as a finger moves)

  ```
  func touchesMoved(_ touches: Set<UITouch>, with event: UIEvent?)
  ```

- one or more fingers are removed from the screen

  ```
  func touchesEnded(_ touches: Set<UITouch>, with event: UIEvent?)
  ```

- a system event, like an incoming phone call, interrupts a touch before it ends

  ```
  func touchesCancelled(_ touches: Set<UITouch>, with event: UIEvent?)
  ```

Let's walk through the typical lifecycle of a touch. When the user's finger touches the screen, an instance of **UITouch** is created. The **touchesBegan(_:with:)** method is called on the **UIView** that the finger touched, and the **UITouch** is passed in through the **Set** of touches.

As the finger moves around the screen, the touch object is updated to contain the current location of the finger on the screen. Then, the same **UIView** that the touch began on is sent the message **touchesMoved(_:with:)**. The **Set** that is passed as an argument to this method contains the same **UITouch** that originally was created when the finger it represents touched the screen.

When the finger is removed from the screen, the touch object is updated one last time to contain the final location of the finger, and the view that the touch began on is sent the message **touchesEnded(_:with:)**. After that method finishes executing, the **UITouch** object is destroyed.

From this information, you can draw a few conclusions about how touch objects work:

- One **UITouch** corresponds to one finger on the screen. This touch object lives as long as the finger is on the screen and always contains the current position of the finger on the screen.

- The view that the finger started on will receive every touch event message for that finger. Even if the finger moves beyond the frame of the **UIView** that the touch began on, the **touchesMoved(_:with:)** and **touchesEnded(_:with:)** methods will still be called on that view. Thus, if a touch begins on a view, then that view owns the touch for the life of the touch.

- You do not have to – nor should you ever – keep a reference to a **UITouch** object. The application will give you access to a touch object via the **UIResponder** methods called at the distinct points in the touch's lifecycle.

Every time a touch does something – like begins, moves, or ends – a *touch event* is added to a queue of events that the **UIApplication** object manages. In practice, the queue rarely fills up, and events are delivered immediately. The delivery of these touch events involves sending one of the **UIResponder** messages to the view that owns the touch.

What about multiple touches? If multiple fingers do the same thing at the exact same time to the same view, all of these touch events are delivered at once. Each touch object – one for each finger – is included in the **Set** passed as an argument in the **UIResponder** messages. However, the window of opportunity for the "exact same time" is fairly short. So, instead of one responder message with all of the touches, there are usually multiple responder messages with one or more of the touches. You will see how to handle multiple touches later in this chapter.

Creating the TouchTracker Application

Now let's get started with your application. In Xcode, create a new single view universal project and name it TouchTracker (Figure 18.2).

Figure 18.2 Creating TouchTracker

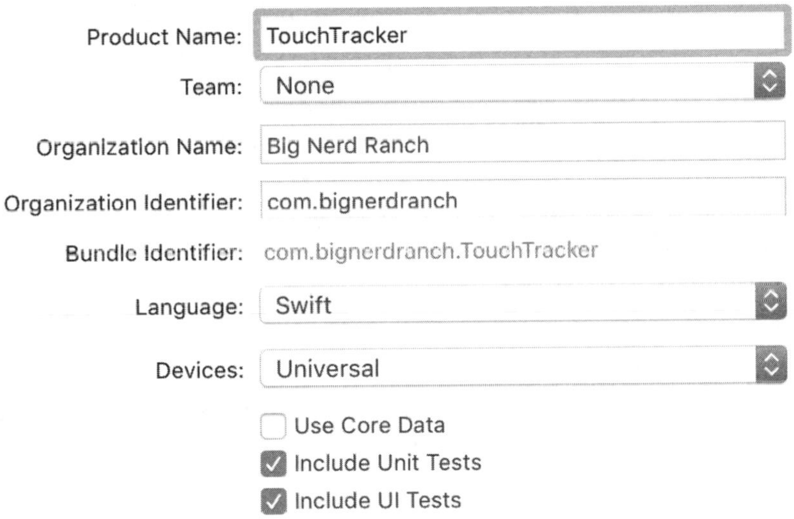

Product Name:	TouchTracker
Team:	None
Organization Name:	Big Nerd Ranch
Organization Identifier:	com.bignerdranch
Bundle Identifier:	com.bignerdranch.TouchTracker
Language:	Swift
Devices:	Universal
	☐ Use Core Data
	☑ Include Unit Tests
	☑ Include UI Tests

In building TouchTracker, you are going to use the default view controller and the storyboard that the template created. For its view and model layers, you are going to create a custom view class and a custom structure. Figure 18.3 shows the major pieces of TouchTracker.

Figure 18.3 Object diagram for TouchTracker

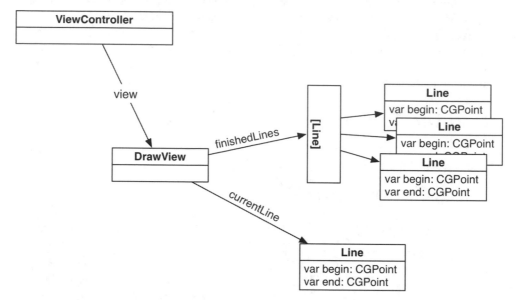

Let's begin with your custom struct.

Creating the Line Struct

You are going to create the custom **Line** type. So far, all of the types that you have created have been classes. In fact, they have been Cocoa Touch subclasses; for example, you have created subclasses of **NSObject**, **UIViewController**, and **UIView**.

Line will be a *struct*. You have used structs throughout this book – **CGRect**, **CGSize**, and **CGPoint** are all structs. So too are **String**, **Int**, **Array**, and **Dictionary**. Now you are going to create one of your own.

Create a new Swift file named Line.

In Line.swift, import CoreGraphics and declare the **Line** struct. Declare two **CGPoint** properties that will determine the beginning and ending point for the line.

```
import Foundation
import CoreGraphics

struct Line {
    var begin = CGPoint.zero
    var end = CGPoint.zero
}
```

Structs

Structs differ from classes in a number of ways:

- Structs do not support inheritance.

- Structs get a *member-wise initializer* if no other initializers are declared. The member-wise initializer takes in an argument for each property within the type. The **Line** struct, for example, has the member-wise initializer **init(begin: CGPoint, end: CGPoint)**.

- If all properties have default values and no other initializers are declared, structs also gain an empty initializer (**init()**) that creates an instance and sets all of the properties to their default value.

- Perhaps most importantly, structs (and enums) are *value types* – as opposed to classes, which are *reference types*.

Value types vs reference types

Value types are types whose values are copied when they are assigned to another instance or passed in the argument of a function. This means that assigning an instance of a value type to another actually assigns a copy of the first instance to the second instance. Value types play an important role in Swift. For example, arrays and dictionaries are both value types. All enums and structs you write are value types as well.

Reference types are not copied when they are assigned to an instance or passed into an argument of a function. Instead, a reference to the same instance is passed. Classes and closures are reference types.

So which do you choose? In general, we suggest starting out with a value type (such as a struct) unless you absolutely know you need the benefits of a reference type. Value types are easier to reason about because you do not need to worry about what happens to an instance when you change values on a copy. If you would like a deeper discussion on this topic, check out *Swift Programming: The Big Nerd Ranch Guide*.

Creating DrawView

In addition to a custom struct, TouchTracker needs a custom view.

Create a new Swift file named DrawView. In DrawView.swift, define the **DrawView** class. Add two properties: an optional **Line** to keep track of a line that is possibly being drawn and an array of **Line**s to keep track of lines that have been drawn.

```
import Foundation
import UIKit

class DrawView: UIView {

    var currentLine: Line?
    var finishedLines = [Line]()

}
```

An instance of **DrawView** will be the view of the application's rootViewController, the default **ViewController** included in the project. The view controller needs to know that its view will be an instance of **DrawView**.

Open Main.storyboard. Select the View and open the identity inspector (Command-Option-3). Under Custom Class, change the Class to DrawView (Figure 18.4).

Figure 18.4 Changing the view class

Drawing with DrawView

An instance of **DrawView** needs to be able draw lines. You are going to write a method that uses **UIBezierPath** to create and stroke a path based on the properties of a given **Line**. Then you will override **draw(_:)** to draw the lines in the array of finished lines as well as the current line, if any.

In DrawView.swift, implement the method for stroking lines and override **draw(_:)**.

```swift
var currentLine: Line?
var finishedLines = [Line]()

func stroke(_ line: Line) {
    let path = UIBezierPath()
    path.lineWidth = 10
    path.lineCapStyle = .round

    path.move(to: line.begin)
    path.addLine(to: line.end)
    path.stroke()
}

override func draw(_ rect: CGRect) {
    // Draw finished lines in black
    UIColor.black.setStroke()
    for line in finishedLines {
        stroke(line)
    }

    if let line = currentLine {
        // If there is a line currently being drawn, do it in red
        UIColor.red.setStroke()
        stroke(line)
    }
}
```

Turning Touches into Lines

A line is defined by two points. Your **Line** stores these points as properties named begin and end. When a touch begins, you will create a **Line** and set both of its properties to the point where the touch began. When the touch moves, you will update the **Line**'s end. When the touch ends, you will have your complete **Line**.

In DrawView.swift, implement **touchesBegan(_:with:)** to create a new line.

```
override func touchesBegan(_ touches: Set<UITouch>, with event: UIEvent?) {
    let touch = touches.first!

    // Get location of the touch in view's coordinate system
    let location = touch.location(in: self)

    currentLine = Line(begin: location, end: location)

    setNeedsDisplay()
}
```

This code first figures out the location of the touch within the view's coordinate system. Then it calls **setNeedsDisplay()**, which flags the view to be redrawn at the end of the run loop.

Next, also in DrawView.swift, implement **touchesMoved(_:with:)** so that it updates the end of the currentLine.

```
override func touchesMoved(_ touches: Set<UITouch>, with event: UIEvent?) {
    let touch = touches.first!
    let location = touch.location(in: self)

    currentLine?.end = location

    setNeedsDisplay()
}
```

Finally, still in DrawView.swift, update the end location of the currentLine and add it to the finishedLines array when the touch ends.

```
override func touchesEnded(_ touches: Set<UITouch>, with event: UIEvent?) {
    if var line = currentLine {
        let touch = touches.first!
        let location = touch.location(in: self)
        line.end = location

        finishedLines.append(line)
    }
    currentLine = nil

    setNeedsDisplay()
}
```

Build and run the application and draw some lines on the screen. While you are drawing, the lines will appear in red. Once finished, they will appear in black.

Handling multiple touches

When drawing lines, you may have noticed that having more than one finger on the screen does not do anything – that is, you can only draw one line at a time. Let's update **DrawView** so that you can draw as many lines as you can fit fingers on the screen.

By default, a view will only accept one touch at a time. If one finger has already triggered **touchesBegan(_:with:)** but has not finished – and therefore has not triggered **touchesEnded(_:with:)** – subsequent touches are ignored. In this context, "ignored" means that neither **touchesBegan(_:with:)** nor any other **UIResponder** method related to the extra touches will be called on the **DrawView**.

In Main.storyboard, select the Draw View and open the attributes inspector. Check the box labeled Multiple Touch (Figure 18.5), which will set the **DrawView** instance's multipleTouchesEnabled property to true.

Figure 18.5 Multiple Touch enabled

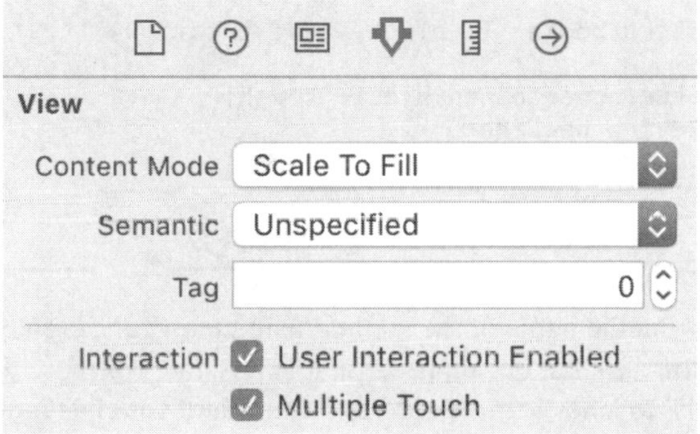

Now that **DrawView** will accept multiple touches, each time a finger touches the screen, moves, or is removed from the screen, the appropriate **UIResponder** will be called on the view. However, you now have a problem: Your **UIResponder** code assumes there will only be one touch active and one line being drawn at a time.

For example, each touch-handling method asks for the first element in the set of touches it receives. In a single-touch view, there will only ever be one object in the set, so asking for any object always returns the touch that triggered the event. In a multiple-touch view, the set can contain more than one touch. Also, **DrawView** has only one property (currentLine) that hangs on to a line in progress. Obviously, you will need to hold as many lines as there are touches currently on the screen. While you could create a few more properties, like currentLine1 and currentLine2, it would be a hassle to manage which property corresponds to which touch.

Instead of adding more properties, you are going to replace the single **Line** with a dictionary containing instances of **Line**. In DrawView.swift, add a new property to replace currentLine.

```
class DrawView: UIView {

    var currentLine: Line?
    var currentLines = [NSValue:Line]()
```

The key to store the line in the dictionary will be derived from the **UITouch** object that the line corresponds to. As more touch events occur, you can use the same algorithm to derive the key from the **UITouch** that triggered the event and use it to look up the appropriate **Line** in the dictionary.

Now you need to update the **UIResponder** methods to add lines that are currently being drawn to this dictionary. In DrawView.swift, update the code in **touchesBegan(_:with:)**.

```
override func touchesBegan(_ touches: Set<UITouch>, with event: UIEvent?) {
    let touch = touches.first!

    // Get location of the touch in view's coordinate system
    let location = touch.location(in: self)

    currentLine = Line(begin: location, end: location)

    // Log statement to see the order of events
    print(#function)

    for touch in touches {
        let location = touch.location(in: self)

        let newLine = Line(begin: location, end: location)

        let key = NSValue(nonretainedObject: touch)
        currentLines[key] = newLine
    }

    setNeedsDisplay()
}
```

In this code, you first print out the name of the method using the #function expression. Second, you enumerate over all of the touches that began, because it is possible for more than one touch to begin at the same time. (Typically, touches begin at different times and **touchesBegan(_:with:)** gets called multiple times on the **DrawView** for each touch. But you have to prepare for the improbable, if not the impossible.)

Next, notice the use of `NSValue(nonretainedObject:)` to derive the key to store the **Line**. This method creates an **NSValue** instance that holds on to the address of the **UITouch** object that will be associated with this line. Because a **UITouch** is created when a touch begins, updated throughout its lifetime, and destroyed when the touch ends, the address of that object will be constant through each touch-event-handling method. Figure 18.6 shows the new state of affairs.

Figure 18.6 Object diagram for multitouch TouchTracker

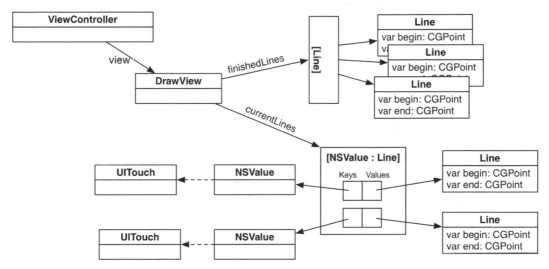

You may be wondering: Why not use the **UITouch** itself as the key? Why go through the hoop of creating an **NSValue**? The documentation for **UITouch** says that you should never keep a strong reference to a **UITouch** object. The details of memory management are outside the scope of this book, but to avoid creating a strong reference to a touch object, you wrap the memory address of the **UITouch** in an instance of **NSValue** using its `init(nonretainedObject:)` initializer. The documentation for this method states: "This method is useful if you want to add an object to a collection but don't want the collection to create a strong reference to it," which is exactly what you want. Because the same **UITouch** object is reused for the entirety of that touch's lifecycle (and therefore has the same memory address), you can re-create the same **NSValue** using the same **UITouch**.

Next, update `touchesMoved(_:with:)` in DrawView.swift so that it can look up the right **Line**.

```
override func touchesMoved(_ touches: Set<UITouch>, with event: UIEvent?) {
    let touch = touches.first!
    let location = touch.location(in: self)

    currentLine?.end = location

    // Log statement to see the order of events
    print(#function)

    for touch in touches {
        let key = NSValue(nonretainedObject: touch)
        currentLines[key]?.end = touch.location(in: self)
    }

    setNeedsDisplay()
}
```

Now, update **touchesEnded(_:with:)** to move any finished lines into the finishedLines array.

```
override func touchesEnded(_ touches: Set<UITouch>, with event: UIEvent?) {
    if var line = currentLine {
        let touch = touches.first!
        let location = touch.location(in: self)
        line.end = location

        finishedLines.append(line)
    }
    currentLine = nil

    // Log statement to see the order of events
    print(#function)

    for touch in touches {
        let key = NSValue(nonretainedObject: touch)
        if var line = currentLines[key] {
            line.end = touch.location(in: self)

            finishedLines.append(line)
            currentLines.removeValue(forKey: key)
        }
    }

    setNeedsDisplay()
}
```

Finally, update **draw(_:)** to draw each line in currentLines.

```
override func draw(_ rect: CGRect) {
    // Draw finished lines in black
    UIColor.black.setStroke()
    for line in finishedLines {
        stroke(line)
    }

    if let line = currentLine {
        // If there is a line currently being drawn, do it in red
        UIColor.red.setStroke()
        stroke(line)
    }

    // Draw current lines in red
    UIColor.red.setStroke()
    for (_, line) in currentLines {
        stroke(line)
    }
}
```

Build and run the application and start drawing lines with multiple fingers. (On the simulator, hold down the Option key while you drag to simulate multiple fingers.) Notice the ordering of the log messages in the console.

You should know that when a **UIResponder** method like **touchesMoved(_:with:)** is called on a view, only the touches that have moved will be in the set of touches. Thus, it is possible for three touches to be on a view, but only one touch to be in the set of touches passed into one of these methods. Additionally, once a **UITouch** begins on a view, all touch event methods are called on that same view over the touch's lifetime, even if that touch moves off of the view it began on.

The last thing left for the basics of TouchTracker is to handle what happens when a touch is canceled. A touch can be canceled when the application is interrupted by the OS (for example, when a phone call comes in) while a touch is currently on the screen. When a touch is canceled, any state it set up should be reverted. In this case, you should remove any lines in progress.

In DrawView.swift, implement **touchesCancelled(_:with:)**.

```swift
override func touchesCancelled(_ touches: Set<UITouch>, with event: UIEvent?) {
    // Log statement to see the order of events
    print(#function)

    currentLines.removeAll()

    setNeedsDisplay()
}
```

@IBInspectable

When working in Interface Builder, you are able to modify attributes for the views that you add to the canvas. For example, you can set the background color on a view, the text on a label, and the current progress on a slider. You can add this same behavior to your own custom **UIView** subclasses for certain types. Let's add in the ability for the **DrawView**'s current line color, finished line color, and line thickness to be customized through Interface Builder.

In DrawView.swift, declare three properties to reference these values. Give them default values and have the view flag itself for redrawing whenever these properties change.

```
var currentLines = [NSValue:Line]()
var finishedLines = [Line]()

@IBInspectable var finishedLineColor: UIColor = UIColor.black {
    didSet {
        setNeedsDisplay()
    }
}

@IBInspectable var currentLineColor: UIColor = UIColor.red {
    didSet {
        setNeedsDisplay()
    }
}

@IBInspectable var lineThickness: CGFloat = 10 {
    didSet {
        setNeedsDisplay()
    }
}
```

The @IBInspectable keyword lets Interface Builder know that this is a property that you want to customize through the attributes inspector. Many of the common types are supported by @IBInspectable: Booleans, strings, numbers, **CGPoint**, **CGSize**, **CGRect**, **UIColor**, **UIImage**, and a few more are all candidates.

Now update **stroke(_:)** and **drawView(_:)** to use these new properties.

```
func stroke(_ line: Line) {
    let path = UIBezierPath()
    path.lineWidth = 10
    path.lineWidth = lineThickness
    path.lineCapStyle = .round

    path.move(to: line.begin)
    path.addLine(to: line.end)
    path.stroke()
}

override func draw(_ rect: CGRect) {
    // Draw finished lines in black
    UIColor.black.setStroke()
    finishedLineColor.setStroke()
    for line in finishedLines {
        stroke(line)
    }

    // Draw current lines in red
    UIColor.red.setStroke()
    currentLineColor.setStroke()
    for (_, line) in currentLines {
        stroke(line)
    }
}
```

Now, when you add a **DrawView** to the canvas in Interface Builder, you can customize these three properties in the attributes inspector to be different for different instances (Figure 18.7).

Figure 18.7 Customizing DrawView

329

Silver Challenge: Colors

Make it so that the angle at which a line is drawn dictates its color once it has been added to currentLines.

Gold Challenge: Circles

Use two fingers to draw circles. Try having each finger represent one corner of the bounding box around the circle. Recall that you can simulate two fingers on the simulator by holding down the Option key. (Hint: This is much easier if you track touches that are working on a circle in a separate dictionary.)

For the More Curious: The Responder Chain

In Chapter 14, we talked briefly about the first responder. A **UIResponder** can be a first responder and receive touch events. **UIView** is one example of a **UIResponder** subclass, but there are many others, including **UIViewController**, **UIApplication**, and **UIWindow**. You are probably thinking, "But you can't touch a **UIViewController**. It's not an onscreen object." You are right – you cannot send a touch event *directly* to a **UIViewController**, but view controllers can receive events through the *responder chain*.

Every **UIResponder** can reference another **UIResponder** through its next property, and together these objects make up the responder chain (Figure 18.8). A touch event starts at the view that was touched. The next responder of a view is typically its **UIViewController** (if it has one) or its superview (if it does not). The next responder of a view controller is typically its view's superview. The top-most superview is the window. The window's next responder is the singleton instance of **UIApplication**.

Figure 18.8 Responder chain

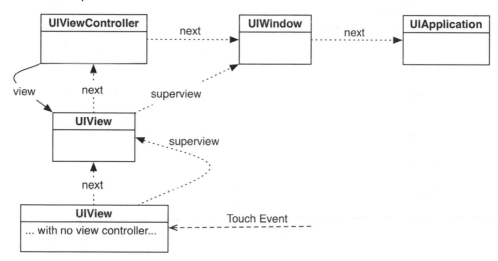

How does a **UIResponder** *not* handle an event? It calls the same method on its next responder. That is what the default implementation of methods like **touchesBegan(_:with:)** does. So if a method is not overridden, its next responder will attempt to handle the touch event. If the application (the last object in the responder chain) does not handle the event, then it is discarded.

You can explicitly call a method on a next responder, too. Let's say there is a view that tracks touches, but if a double-tap occurs, its next responder should handle it. The code would look like this:

```
override func touchesBegan(_ touches: Set<UITouch>, with event: UIEvent?) {
    let touch = touches.first!
    if touch.tapCount == 2 {
        next?.touchesBegan(touches, with: event)
    } else {
        // Go on to handle touches that are not double-taps
    }
}
```

For the More Curious: UIControl

The class **UIControl** is the superclass for several classes in Cocoa Touch, including **UIButton** and **UISlider**. You have seen how to set the targets and actions for these controls. Now we can take a closer look at how **UIControl** overrides the same **UIResponder** methods you implemented in this chapter.

In **UIControl**, each possible *control event* is associated with a constant. Buttons, for example, typically send action messages on the UIControlEvents.touchUpInside control event. A target registered for this control event will only receive its action message if the user touches the control and then lifts the finger off the screen inside the frame of the control.

For a button, however, you can have actions on other event types. For example, you might trigger a method if the user removes the finger *inside or outside* the frame. Assigning the target and action programmatically would look like this:

```
button.addTarget(self,
    action: #selector(Thermostat.resetTemperature(_:)),
    for: [.touchUpInside, .touchUpOutside])
```

Now consider how **UIControl** handles UIControlEvents.touchUpInside.

```
// Not the exact code. There is a bit more going on!
override func touchesEnded(_ touches: Set<UITouch>, with event: UIEvent?) {

    // Reference to the touch that is ending
    let touch = touches.first!

    // Location of that point in this control's coordinate system
    let touchLocation = touch.location(in: self)

    // Is that point still in my viewing bounds?
    if bounds.contains(touchLocation) {
        // Send out action messages to all targets registered for this event!
        sendActions(for: .touchUpInside)
    }
    else {
        // The touch ended outside the bounds: different control event
        sendActions(for: .touchUpOutside)
    }
}
```

So how do these actions get sent to the right target? At the end of the **UIResponder** method implementations, the control calls the method **sendActions(for:)** on itself. This method looks at all of the target-action pairs the control has. If any of them are registered for the control event passed as the argument, the corresponding action method is called on those targets.

However, a control never calls a method directly on its targets. Instead, it routes these method calls through the **UIApplication** object. Why not have controls call the action methods directly on the targets? Controls can also have nil-targeted actions. If a **UIControl**'s target is nil, the **UIApplication** finds the first responder of its **UIWindow** and calls the action method on it.

19

UIGestureRecognizer and UIMenuController

In Chapter 18, you handled raw touches by implementing methods from **UIResponder**. Sometimes you want to detect a specific pattern of touches that make a gesture, like a pinch or a swipe. Instead of writing code to detect common gestures yourself, you can use instances of **UIGestureRecognizer**.

A **UIGestureRecognizer** intercepts touches that are on their way to being handled by a view. When it recognizes a particular gesture, it calls a method on the object of your choice. There are several types of gesture recognizers built into the SDK. In this chapter, you will use three of them to allow TouchTracker users to select, move, and delete lines (Figure 19.1). You will also see how to use another interesting iOS class, **UIMenuController**.

Figure 19.1 TouchTracker by the end of the chapter

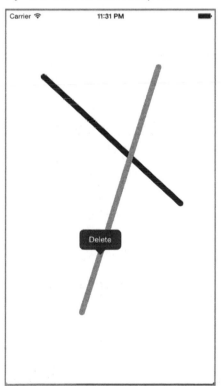

UIGestureRecognizer Subclasses

You do not instantiate **UIGestureRecognizer** itself. Instead, there are a number of subclasses of **UIGestureRecognizer**, and each one is responsible for recognizing a particular gesture.

To use an instance of a **UIGestureRecognizer** subclass, you give it a target-action pair and attach it to a view. Whenever the gesture recognizer recognizes its gesture on the view, it will send the action message to its target. All **UIGestureRecognizer** action messages have the same form:

```
func action(_ gestureRecognizer: UIGestureRecognizer) { }
```

When recognizing a gesture, the gesture recognizer intercepts the touches destined for the view (Figure 19.2). Thus, the typical **UIResponder** methods like **touchesBegan(_:with:)** may not be called on a view with gesture recognizers.

Figure 19.2 Gesture recognizers intercept touches

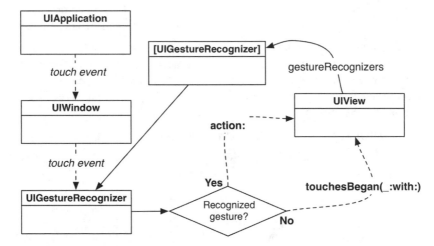

Detecting Taps with UITapGestureRecognizer

The first **UIGestureRecognizer** subclass you will use is **UITapGestureRecognizer**. When the user taps the screen twice, all of the lines on the screen will be cleared.

Open TouchTracker.xcodeproj and DrawView.swift. Add an **init?(coder:)** method and instantiate a **UITapGestureRecognizer** that requires two taps to fire and calls the action method on its target.

```
required init?(coder aDecoder: NSCoder) {
    super.init(coder: aDecoder)

    let doubleTapRecognizer = UITapGestureRecognizer(target: self,
        action: #selector(DrawView.doubleTap(_:)))
    doubleTapRecognizer.numberOfTapsRequired = 2
    addGestureRecognizer(doubleTapRecognizer)
}
```

Now when a double-tap occurs on an instance of **DrawView**, the method **doubleTap(_:)** will be called on that instance. Implement this method in DrawView.swift.

```
func doubleTap(_ gestureRecognizer: UIGestureRecognizer) {
    print("Recognized a double tap")

    currentLines.removeAll()
    finishedLines.removeAll()
    setNeedsDisplay()
}
```

Notice that the argument to the action method for a gesture recognizer is the instance of
UIGestureRecognizer that called the method. In the case of a double-tap, you do not need any
information from the recognizer, but you will need information from the other recognizers you install
later in the chapter.

Build and run the application, draw a few lines, and double-tap the screen to clear them.

You may have noticed (especially on the simulator) that the first tap of a double-tap results in a small
red dot being drawn. This dot appears because **touchesBegan(_:with:)** is called on the **DrawView** on
the first tap, creating a very short line. Check the console and you will see the following sequence of
events:

```
touchesBegan(_:with:)
Recognized a double tap
touchesCancelled(_:with:)
```

Gesture recognizers work by inspecting touch events to determine whether their particular gesture has
occurred. Before a gesture is recognized, the gesture recognizer intercepts all the **UIResponder** method
calls. If it has not recognized its gesture, each call is forwarded on to the view.

Recognizing a tap requires that a touch begin and end. This means that the **UITapGestureRecognizer**
cannot know whether the touch is a tap when **touchesBegan(_:with:)** is originally called, so the
method is called on the view as well. When the touch ends, the tap is recognized and the gesture
recognizer claims the touch for itself. It does so by calling **touchesCancelled(_:with:)** on the view.
After that, no more **UIResponder** methods will be called on the view for that particular touch.

To prevent this red dot from appearing temporarily, you must prevent **touchesBegan(_:with:)**
from being called on the view. You can tell a **UIGestureRecognizer** to delay calling
touchesBegan(_:with:) on its view if it is still possible that its gesture might be recognized for that
touch.

In DrawView.swift, modify **init?(coder:)** to do just this.

```
required init?(coder aDecoder: NSCoder) {
    super.init(coder: aDecoder)

    let doubleTapRecognizer = UITapGestureRecognizer(target: self,
        action: #selector(DrawView.doubleTap(_:)))
    doubleTapRecognizer.numberOfTapsRequired = 2
    doubleTapRecognizer.delaysTouchesBegan = true
    addGestureRecognizer(doubleTapRecognizer)
}
```

Build and run the application, draw some lines, and then double-tap to clear them. You will no longer
see the red dot while double-tapping.

Multiple Gesture Recognizers

The next step is to add another gesture recognizer that allows the user to select a line. (Later, a user will be able to delete the selected line.) You will install another **UITapGestureRecognizer** on the **DrawView** that only requires one tap.

In DrawView.swift, modify **init?(coder:)** to add this gesture recognizer.

```
required init?(coder aDecoder: NSCoder) {
    super.init(coder: aDecoder)

    let doubleTapRecognizer = UITapGestureRecognizer(target: self,
        action: #selector(DrawView.doubleTap(_:)))
    doubleTapRecognizer.numberOfTapsRequired = 2
    doubleTapRecognizer.delaysTouchesBegan = true
    addGestureRecognizer(doubleTapRecognizer)

    let tapRecognizer =
        UITapGestureRecognizer(target: self, action: #selector(DrawView.tap(_:)))
    tapRecognizer.delaysTouchesBegan = true
    addGestureRecognizer(tapRecognizer)
}
```

Now, implement **tap(_:)** in DrawView.swift to log the tap to the console.

```
func tap(_ gestureRecognizer: UIGestureRecognizer) {
    print("Recognized a tap")
}
```

Build and run the application. Try tapping and double-tapping. Tapping once logs the appropriate message to the console. Double-tapping, however, triggers both **tap(_:)** and **doubleTap(_:)**.

In situations where you have multiple gesture recognizers, it is not uncommon to have one gesture recognizer fire and claim a touch when you really wanted another gesture recognizer to handle it. In these cases, you set up dependencies between recognizers that say, "Wait a moment before you fire, because this touch might be mine!"

In **init?(coder:)**, make it so the tapRecognizer waits until the doubleTapRecognizer fails to recognize a double-tap before claiming the single tap for itself.

```
required init?(coder aDecoder: NSCoder) {
    super.init(coder: aDecoder)

    let doubleTapRecognizer = UITapGestureRecognizer(target: self,
        action: #selector(DrawView.doubleTap(_:)))
    doubleTapRecognizer.numberOfTapsRequired = 2
    doubleTapRecognizer.delaysTouchesBegan = true
    addGestureRecognizer(doubleTapRecognizer)

    let tapRecognizer =
        UITapGestureRecognizer(target: self, action: #selector(DrawView.tap(_:)))
    tapRecognizer.delaysTouchesBegan = true
    tapRecognizer.require(toFail: doubleTapRecognizer)
    addGestureRecognizer(tapRecognizer)
}
```

Build and run the application again and try out some taps. A single tap now takes a small amount of time to fire after the tap occurs, but double-tapping no longer triggers the **tap(_:)** message.

Next, let's build on the **DrawView** so that the user can select a line when it is tapped. First, add a property at the top of DrawView.swift to hold on to the index of a selected line.

```
class DrawView: UIView {

    var currentLines = [NSValue:Line]()
    var finishedLines = [Line]()
    var selectedLineIndex: Int?
```

Now modify **draw(_:)** to draw the selected line in green.

```
override func draw(_ rect: CGRect) {
    finishedLineColor.setStroke()
    for line in finishedLines {
        stroke(line)
    }

    currentLineColor.setStroke()
    for (_,line) in currentLines {
        stroke(line)
    }

    if let index = selectedLineIndex {
        UIColor.green.setStroke()
        let selectedLine = finishedLines[index]
        stroke(selectedLine)
    }
}
```

Still in DrawView.swift, add an **indexOfLine(at:)** method that returns the index of the **Line** closest to a given point.

```
func indexOfLine(at point: CGPoint) -> Int? {
    // Find a line close to point
    for (index, line) in finishedLines.enumerated() {
        let begin = line.begin
        let end = line.end

        // Check a few points on the line
        for t in stride(from: CGFloat(0), to: 1.0, by: 0.05) {
            let x = begin.x + ((end.x - begin.x) * t)
            let y = begin.y + ((end.y - begin.y) * t)

            // If the tapped point is within 20 points, let's return this line
            if hypot(x - point.x, y - point.y) < 20.0 {
                return index
            }
        }
    }

    // If nothing is close enough to the tapped point, then we did not select a line
    return nil
}
```

The **stride(from:to:by:)** method will allow t to start at the from value and go up to (but not reach) the to value, incrementing the value of t by the by value.

There are other, better ways to determine the closest line to a point, but this simple implementation will work for your purposes.

The point to be passed in is the point where the tap occurred. You can easily get this information. Every **UIGestureRecognizer** has a **location(in:)** method. Calling this method on the gesture recognizer will give you the coordinate where the gesture occurred in the coordinate system of the view that is passed as the argument.

In DrawView.swift, update **tap(_:)** to call **location(in:)** on the gesture recognizer, pass the result to **indexOfLine(at:)**, and make the returned index the selectedLineIndex.

```
func tap(_ gestureRecognizer: UIGestureRecognizer) {
    print("Recognized a tap")

    let point = gestureRecognizer.location(in: self)
    selectedLineIndex = indexOfLine(at: point)

    setNeedsDisplay()
}
```

If the user double-taps to clear all lines while a line is selected, the application will trap. To address this, update **doubleTap(_:)** to set the selectedLineIndex to nil.

```
func doubleTap(_ gestureRecognizer: UIGestureRecognizer) {
    print("Recognized a double tap")

    selectedLineIndex = nil
    currentLines.removeAll()
    finishedLines.removeAll()
    setNeedsDisplay()
}
```

Build and run the application. Draw a few lines and then tap one. The tapped line should appear in green (remember that it takes a moment before the tap is known not to be a double-tap).

UIMenuController

Next you are going to make it so that when the user selects a line, a menu with the option to delete that line appears where the user tapped. There is a built-in class for providing this sort of menu called **UIMenuController** (Figure 19.3). A menu controller has a list of **UIMenuItem** objects and is presented in an existing view. Each item has a title (what shows up in the menu) and an action (the message it sends the first responder of the window).

Figure 19.3 A **UIMenuController**

There is only one **UIMenuController** per application. When you wish to present this instance, you fill it with menu items, give it a rectangle to present from, and set it to be visible.

Do this in DrawView.swift's **tap(_:)** method if the user has tapped on a line. If the user tapped somewhere that is not near a line, the currently selected line will be deselected and the menu controller will hide.

```
func tap(_ gestureRecognizer: UIGestureRecognizer) {
    print("Recognized a tap")

    let point = gestureRecognizer.location(in: self)
    selectedLineIndex = indexOfLine(at: point)

    // Grab the menu controller
    let menu = UIMenuController.shared

    if selectedLineIndex != nil {

        // Make DrawView the target of menu item action messages
        becomeFirstResponder()

        // Create a new "Delete" UIMenuItem
        let deleteItem = UIMenuItem(title: "Delete",
                                    action: #selector(DrawView.deleteLine(_:)))
        menu.menuItems = [deleteItem]

        // Tell the menu where it should come from and show it
        let targetRect = CGRect(x: point.x, y: point.y, width: 2, height: 2)
        menu.setTargetRect(targetRect, in: self)
        menu.setMenuVisible(true, animated: true)
    } else {
        // Hide the menu if no line is selected
        menu.setMenuVisible(false, animated: true)
    }

    setNeedsDisplay()
}
```

For a menu controller to appear, a view that responds to at least one action message in the **UIMenuController**'s menu items must be the first responder of the window – this is why you called the method **becomeFirstResponder()** on the **DrawView** before setting up the menu controller.

If you have a custom view class that needs to become the first responder, you must also override canBecomeFirstResponder. In DrawView.swift, override this property to return true.

```
override var canBecomeFirstResponder: Bool {
    return true
}
```

Finally, implement **deleteLine(_:)** in DrawView.swift.

```
func deleteLine(_ sender: UIMenuController) {
    // Remove the selected line from the list of finishedLines
    if let index = selectedLineIndex {
        finishedLines.remove(at: index)
        selectedLineIndex = nil

        // Redraw everything
        setNeedsDisplay()
    }
}
```

When being presented, the menu controller goes through each menu item and asks the first responder if it implements the action method for that item. If the first responder does not implement that method, then the menu controller will not show the associated menu item. If no menu items have their action methods implemented by the first responder, the menu is not shown at all.

Build and run the application. Draw a line, tap on it, and then select Delete from the menu item.

If you select a line and then double-tap to clear all lines, the menu controller will still be visible. If the selectedLineIndex ever becomes nil, the menu controller should not be visible.

Add a property observer to selectedLineIndex in DrawView.swift that sets the menu controller to be not visible if the index is set to nil.

```
var selectedLineIndex: Int? {
    didSet {
        if selectedLineIndex == nil {
            let menu = UIMenuController.shared
            menu.setMenuVisible(false, animated: true)
        }
    }
}
```

Build and run the application. Draw a line, select it, and then double-tap the background. The line and the menu controller will no longer be visible.

More Gesture Recognizers

In this section, you are going to add the ability for a user to select a line by pressing and holding (a long press) and then move the selected line by dragging the finger (a pan). This will require two more subclasses of **UIGestureRecognizer**: **UILongPressGestureRecognizer** and **UIPanGestureRecognizer**.

UILongPressGestureRecognizer

In DrawView.swift, instantiate a **UILongPressGestureRecognizer** in **init?(coder:)** and add it to the **DrawView**.

```
    ...
    addGestureRecognizer(tapRecognizer)

    let longPressRecognizer = UILongPressGestureRecognizer(target: self,
            action: #selector(DrawView.longPress(_:)))
    addGestureRecognizer(longPressRecognizer)
}
```

Now when the user holds down on the **DrawView**, the method **longPress(_:)** will be called on it. By default, a touch must be held 0.5 seconds to become a long press, but you can change the minimumPressDuration of the gesture recognizer if you like.

So far, you have worked with tap gestures. A tap is a *discrete* gesture. By the time it is recognized, the gesture is over, and the action message has been delivered. A long press, on the other hand, is a *continuous* gesture. Continuous gestures occur over time. To keep track of what is going on with a continuous gesture, you can check a recognizer's state property.

For example, consider a typical long press:

- When the user touches a view, the long-press recognizer notices a *possible* long press, but it must wait to see whether the touch is held long enough to become a long-press gesture. The recognizer's state is UIGestureRecognizerState.possible.

- Once the user holds the touch long enough, the long press is recognized and the gesture has *begun*. The recognizer's state is UIGestureRecognizerState.began.

- When the user removes the finger, the gesture has *ended*. The recognizer's state is UIGestureRecognizerState.ended.

When the long-press gesture recognizer transitions from possible to began and from began to ended, it sends its action message to its target. To determine which transition triggered the action, you check the gesture recognizer's state.

Remember that the long press is part of a larger feature. In the next section, you will enable the user to move the selected line by dragging it with the same finger that began the long press. So here is the plan for implementing the **longPress(_:)** action method: When the recognizer is in the began state, you will select the closest line to where the gesture occurred. When the recognizer is in the ended state, you will deselect the line.

In `DrawView.swift`, implement **longPress(_:)**.

```
func longPress(_ gestureRecognizer: UIGestureRecognizer) {
    print("Recognized a long press")

    if gestureRecognizer.state == .began {
        let point = gestureRecognizer.location(in: self)
        selectedLineIndex = indexOfLine(at: point)

        if selectedLineIndex != nil {
            currentLines.removeAll()
        }
    } else if gestureRecognizer.state == .ended {
        selectedLineIndex = nil
    }

    setNeedsDisplay()
}
```

Build and run the application. Draw a line and then press and hold it; the line will turn green and become the selected line. When you let go, the line will revert to its former color and will no longer be the selected line.

UIPanGestureRecognizer and simultaneous recognizers

In `DrawView.swift`, declare a **UIPanGestureRecognizer** as a property so that you have access to it in all of your methods.

```
class DrawView: UIView {

    var currentLines = [NSValue:Line]()
    var finishedLines = [Line]()
    var selectedLineIndex: Int? {
        ...
    }
    var moveRecognizer: UIPanGestureRecognizer!
```

Next, in `DrawView.swift`, add code to **init?(coder:)** to instantiate a **UIPanGestureRecognizer**, set one of its properties, and add it to the **DrawView**.

```
    let longPressRecognizer = UILongPressGestureRecognizer(target: self,
            action: #selector(DrawView.longPress(_:)))
    addGestureRecognizer(longPressRecognizer)

    moveRecognizer = UIPanGestureRecognizer(target: self,
                                    action: #selector(DrawView.moveLine(_:)))
    moveRecognizer.cancelsTouchesInView = false
    addGestureRecognizer(moveRecognizer)
}
```

What is `cancelsTouchesInView`? Every **UIGestureRecognizer** has this property, which defaults to true. When `cancelsTouchesInView` is `true`, the gesture recognizer will "eat" any touch it recognizes, and the view will not get a chance to handle the touch via the traditional **UIResponder** methods, like **touchesBegan(_:with:)**.

Usually, this is what you want, but not always. In this case, if the pan gesture recognizer were to eat its touches, then users would not be able to draw lines. When you set cancelsTouchesInView to false, you ensure that any touch recognized by the gesture recognizer will also be delivered to the view via the **UIResponder** methods.

In DrawView.swift, add a simple implementation for the action method:

```swift
func moveLine(_ gestureRecognizer: UIPanGestureRecognizer) {
    print("Recognized a pan")
}
```

Build and run the app and draw some lines. Because cancelsTouchesInView is false, the pan gesture is recognized, but lines can still be drawn. You can comment out the line that sets cancelsTouchesInView and run again to see the difference.

Soon, you will update **moveLine(_:)** to redraw the selected line as the user's finger moves across the screen. But first you need two gesture recognizers to be able to handle the same touch. Normally, when a gesture recognizer recognizes its gesture, it eats it and no other recognizer gets a chance to handle that touch. Try it: Run the app, draw a line, press and hold to select the line, and then move your finger around. The console reports the long press but not the pan.

In this case, the default behavior is problematic: Your users will press and hold to select a line and then pan to move the line – without lifting the finger in between. Thus, the two gestures will occur simultaneously, and the pan gesture recognizer must be allowed to recognize a pan even though the long-press gesture has already recognized a long press.

To allow a gesture recognizer to recognize its gesture simultaneously with another gesture recognizer, you implement a method from the **UIGestureRecognizerDelegate** protocol:

```swift
optional func gestureRecognizer(_ gestureRecognizer: UIGestureRecognizer,
    shouldRecognizeSimultaneouslyWith
    otherGestureRecognizer: UIGestureRecognizer) -> Bool
```

The first parameter is the gesture recognizer that is asking for guidance. It says to its delegate, "So there's me and this other recognizer, and one of us just recognized a gesture. Should the one who did *not* recognize it stay in the possible state and continue to track this touch?"

Note that the call itself does not tell you which of the two recognizers has recognized its gesture – and, thus, which of them will potentially be deprived of the chance to recognize its gesture.

By default, the method returns false, and the gesture recognizer still in the possible state leaves the touch in the hands of the gesture already in the recognized state. You can implement the method to return true to allow both recognizers to recognize their gestures in the same touch. (If you need to determine which of the two recognizers has recognized its gesture, you can check the recognizers' state properties.)

To enable panning while long pressing, you are going to give the pan gesture recognizer a delegate (the **DrawView**). Then, when the long-press recognizer recognizes its gesture, the pan gesture recognizer will call the simultaneous recognition method on its delegate. You will implement this method in **DrawView** to return true. This will allow the pan gesture recognizer to recognize any panning that occurs while a long press is in progress.

First, in `DrawView.swift`, declare that **DrawView** conforms to the **UIGestureRecognizerDelegate** protocol.

```
class DrawView: UIView, UIGestureRecognizerDelegate {

    var currentLines = [NSValue:Line]()
    var finishedLines = [Line]()
    var selectedLineIndex: Int? {
        ...
    }
    var moveRecognizer: UIPanGestureRecognizer!
```

Next, in **init?(coder:)**, set the **DrawView** to be the delegate of the **UIPanGestureRecognizer**.

```
    let longPressRecognizer = UILongPressGestureRecognizer(target: self,
            action: #selector(DrawView.longPress(_:)))
    addGestureRecognizer(longPressRecognizer)

    moveRecognizer = UIPanGestureRecognizer(target: self,
                                            action: #selector(DrawView.moveLine(_:)))
    moveRecognizer.delegate = self
    moveRecognizer.cancelsTouchesInView = false
    addGestureRecognizer(moveRecognizer)
}
```

Finally, in `DrawView.swift`, implement the delegate method to return `true`.

```
func gestureRecognizer(_ gestureRecognizer: UIGestureRecognizer,
        shouldRecognizeSimultaneouslyWith
        otherGestureRecognizer: UIGestureRecognizer) -> Bool {
    return true
}
```

For this situation, where only your pan gesture recognizer has a delegate, there is no need to do more than return `true`. In more complicated scenarios, you would use the passed-in gesture recognizers to more carefully control simultaneous recognition.

Now, when a long press begins, the **UIPanGestureRecognizer** will continue to keep track of the touch, and if the user's finger begins to move, the pan recognizer will recognize the pan. To see the difference, run the app, draw a line, select it, and then pan. The console will report both gestures.

(The **UIGestureRecognizerDelegate** protocol includes other methods to help you tweak the behavior of your gesture recognizers. Visit the protocol reference page for more information.)

In addition to the states you have already seen, a pan gesture recognizer supports the *changed* state. When a finger starts to move, the pan recognizer enters the began state and calls a method on its target. While the finger moves around the screen, the recognizer transitions to the changed state and calls the action method on its target repeatedly. When the finger leaves the screen, the recognizer's state is set to ended, and the method is called on the target for the final time.

The next step is to implement the **moveLine(_:)** method that the pan recognizer calls on its target. In this implementation, you will call the method **translationInView(_:)** on the pan recognizer. This **UIPanGestureRecognizer** method returns how far the pan has moved as a **CGPoint** in the coordinate system of the view passed as the argument. When the pan gesture begins, this property is set to the zero point (where x and y are 0). As the pan moves, this value is updated – if the pan goes far to the right, it has a high x value; if the pan returns to where it began, its translation goes back to the zero point.

In DrawView.swift, implement **moveLine(_:)**. Notice that because you will send the gesture recognizer a method from the **UIPanGestureRecognizer** class, the parameter of this method must be a reference to an instance of **UIPanGestureRecognizer** rather than **UIGestureRecognizer**.

```
func moveLine(_ gestureRecognizer: UIPanGestureRecognizer) {
    print("Recognized a pan")

    // If a line is selected...
    if let index = selectedLineIndex {
        // When the pan recognizer changes its position...
        if gestureRecognizer.state == .changed {
            // How far has the pan moved?
            let translation = gestureRecognizer.translation(in: self)

            // Add the translation to the current beginning and end points of the line
            // Make sure there are no copy and paste typos!
            finishedLines[index].begin.x += translation.x
            finishedLines[index].begin.y += translation.y
            finishedLines[index].end.x += translation.x
            finishedLines[index].end.y += translation.y

            // Redraw the screen
            setNeedsDisplay()
        }
    } else {
        // If no line is selected, do not do anything
        return
    }
}
```

Build and run the application. Touch and hold on a line and begin dragging – and you will immediately notice that the line and your finger are way out of sync. What is going on?

You are adding the current translation over and over again to the line's original end points. You really need the gesture recognizer to report the change in translation since the last time this method was called instead. Fortunately, you can do this. You can set the translation of a pan gesture recognizer back to the zero point every time it reports a change. Then, the next time it reports a change, it will have the translation since the last event.

Near the bottom of **moveLine(_:)** in DrawView.swift, add the following line of code.

```
finishedLines[index].end.x += translation.x
finishedLines[index].end.y += translation.y

gestureRecognizer.setTranslation(CGPoint.zero, in: self)

// Redraw the screen
setNeedsDisplay()
```

Build and run the application and move a line around. Works great!

More on UIGestureRecognizer

You have only scratched the surface of **UIGestureRecognizer**. There are more subclasses, more properties, and more delegate methods – and you can even create recognizers of your own. This section will give you an idea of what **UIGestureRecognizer** is capable of. You can study the documentation to learn even more.

When a gesture recognizer is on a view, it is really handling all of the **UIResponder** methods, like **touchesBegan(_:with:)**, for you. Gesture recognizers are pretty greedy, so they typically do not let a view receive touch events, or they at least delay the delivery of those events. You can set properties on the recognizer, like delaysTouchesBegan, delaysTouchesEnded, and cancelsTouchesInView, to change this behavior. If you need finer control than this all-or-nothing approach, you can implement delegate methods for the recognizer.

At times, you may have two gesture recognizers looking for very similar gestures. You can chain recognizers together so that one is required to fail for the next one to start using the method **require(toFail:)**. You used this method in **init?(coder:)** to make the tap recognizer wait for the double-tap recognizer to fail.

One thing you must understand to master gesture recognizers is how they interpret their state. Overall, there are seven states a recognizer can enter:

- UIGestureRecognizerState.possible
- UIGestureRecognizerState.failed
- UIGestureRecognizerState.began
- UIGestureRecognizerState.cancelled
- UIGestureRecognizerState.changed
- UIGestureRecognizerState.recognized
- UIGestureRecognizerState.ended

The possible state is where recognizers spend most of their time. When a gesture transitions to any state other than the possible state or the failed state, the action message of the recognizer is sent and its state property can be checked to see why.

The failed state is used by recognizers watching for a multitouch gesture. At some point, the user's fingers may achieve a position from which they can no longer make that recognizer's gesture. At that point, the gesture recognizer fails. A recognizer enters the canceled state when it is interrupted, such as by an incoming phone call.

If a gesture is continuous, like a pan, the gesture recognizer will enter the began state and then go into the changed state until the gesture ends. When the gesture ends (or is canceled), the recognizer enters the ended (or canceled) state and sends its action message a final time before returning to the possible state.

For gesture recognizers that pick up on a discrete gesture like a tap, you will only see the recognized state (which has the same value as the ended state).

The four built-in recognizers that you did not implement in this chapter are **UIPinchGestureRecognizer**, **UISwipeGestureRecognizer**, **UIScreenEdgePanGestureRecognizer**, and **UIRotationGestureRecognizer**. Each has properties that allow you to fine-tune its behavior. The documentation will show you how.

Finally, if there is a gesture that you want to recognize that is not implemented by the built-in subclasses of **UIGestureRecognizer**, you can subclass **UIGestureRecognizer** yourself. This is an intense undertaking and outside the scope of this book. You can read the *Methods for Subclassing* section of the **UIGestureRecognizer** documentation to learn what is required.

Silver Challenge: Mysterious Lines

There is a bug in the application. If you tap on a line and then start drawing a new one while the menu is visible, you will drag the selected line *and* draw a new line at the same time. Fix this bug.

Gold Challenge: Speed and Size

Piggy-back off of the pan gesture recognizer to record the velocity of the pan when you are drawing a line. Adjust the thickness of the line being drawn based on this speed. Make no assumptions about how small or large the velocity value of the pan recognizer can be. (In other words, log a variety of velocities to the console first.)

Platinum Challenge: Colors

Have a three-finger swipe upward bring up a panel that shows colors. Selecting one of those colors should make any lines you draw afterward appear in that color. No extra lines should be drawn by putting up that panel – or any lines drawn should be immediately deleted when the application realizes that it is dealing with a three-finger swipe.

For the More Curious: UIMenuController and UIResponderStandardEditActions

The **UIMenuController** is typically responsible for showing the user an "edit" menu when it is displayed. (Think of a text field or text view when you press and hold.) Therefore, an unmodified menu controller (one that you do not set the menu items for) already has default menu items that it presents, like Cut, Copy, and other familiar options. Each item has an action message wired up. For example, **cut:** is sent to the view presenting the menu controller when the Cut menu item is tapped.

All instances of **UIResponder** implement these methods, but, by default, these methods do not do anything. Subclasses like **UITextField** override these methods to do something appropriate for their context, like cut the currently selected text. The methods are all declared in the **UIResponderStandardEditActions** protocol.

If you override a method from **UIResponderStandardEditActions** in a view, its menu item will automatically appear in any menu you show for that view. This works because the menu controller calls the method **canPerformAction(_:withSender:)** on its view, which returns true or false depending on whether the view implements this method.

If you want to implement one of these methods but *do not* want it to appear in the menu, you can override **canPerformAction(_:withSender:)** to return false:

```
override func canPerformAction(_ action: Selector,
        withSender sender: Any?) -> Bool {

    if action == #selector(copy(_:)) {
        return false
    } else {
        // Else return the default behavior
        return super.canPerformAction(action, withSender: sender)
    }
}
```

20
Web Services

In the next four chapters, you will create an application named Photorama that reads in a list of interesting photos from Flickr. This chapter will lay the foundation and focus on implementing the web service requests responsible for fetching the metadata for interesting photos as well as downloading the image data for a specific photo. In Chapter 21, you will display all of the interesting photos in a grid layout. Figure 20.1 shows Photorama at the end of this chapter.

Figure 20.1 Photorama

Your web browser uses HTTP to communicate with a web server. In the simplest interaction, the browser sends a request to the server specifying a URL. The server responds by sending back the requested page (typically HTML and images), which the browser formats and displays.

In more complex interactions, browser requests include other parameters, such as form data. The server processes these parameters and returns a customized, or dynamic, web page.

Web browsers are widely used and have been around for a long time, so the technologies surrounding HTTP are stable and well developed: HTTP traffic passes neatly through most firewalls, web servers are very secure and have great performance, and web application development tools have become easy to use.

You can write a client application for iOS that leverages the HTTP infrastructure to talk to a web-enabled server. The server side of this application is a *web service*. Your client application and the web service can exchange requests and responses via HTTP.

Because HTTP does not care what data it transports, these exchanges can contain complex data. This data is typically in JSON (JavaScript Object Notation) or XML format. If you control the web server as well as the client, you can use any format you like. If not, you have to build your application to use whatever the server supports.

Photorama will make a web service request to get interesting photos from Flickr. The web service is hosted at `https://api.flickr.com/services/rest`. The data that is returned will be JSON that describes the photos.

Starting the Photorama Application

Create a new Single View Application for the Universal device family. Name this application Photorama, as shown in Figure 20.2.

Figure 20.2 Creating a single view application

Product Name:	Photorama
Team:	None
Organization Name:	Big Nerd Ranch
Organization Identifier:	com.bignerdranch
Bundle Identifier:	com.bignerdranch.Photorama
Language:	Swift
Devices:	Universal

☐ Use Core Data
☑ Include Unit Tests
☑ Include UI Tests

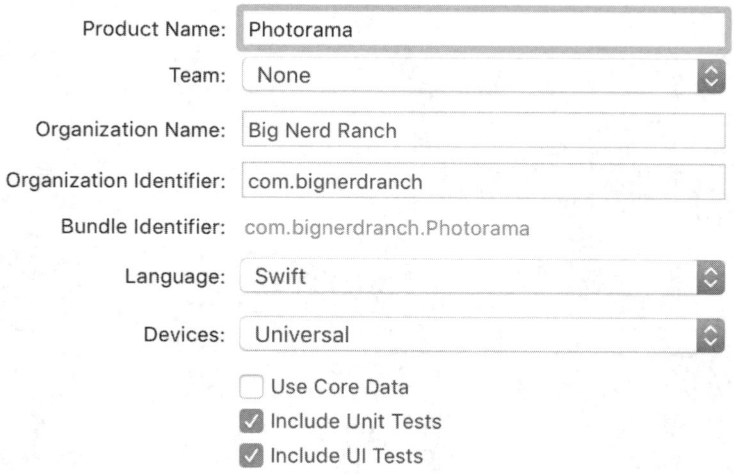

Let's knock out the basic UI before focusing on web services. Create a new Swift file named PhotosViewController. In PhotosViewController.swift, define the **PhotosViewController** class and give it an imageView property.

```swift
import Foundation
import UIKit

class PhotosViewController: UIViewController {

    @IBOutlet var imageView: UIImageView!

}
```

In the project navigator, delete the existing ViewController.swift.

Open Main.storyboard and select the View Controller. Open its identity inspector and change the Class to PhotosViewController. With the Photos View Controller still selected, select the Editor menu and choose Embed In → Navigation Controller.

Select the Navigation Controller and open its attributes inspector. Under the View Controller heading, make sure the box for Is Initial View Controller is checked.

Drag an Image View onto the canvas for **PhotosViewController** and add constraints to pin it to all edges of the superview. Connect the image view to the imageView outlet on **PhotosViewController**. Open the attributes inspector for the image view and change the Content Mode to Aspect Fill.

Finally, double-click on the center of the navigation bar for the Photos View Controller and give it a title of "Photorama." Your interface will look like Figure 20.3.

Figure 20.3 Initial Photorama interface

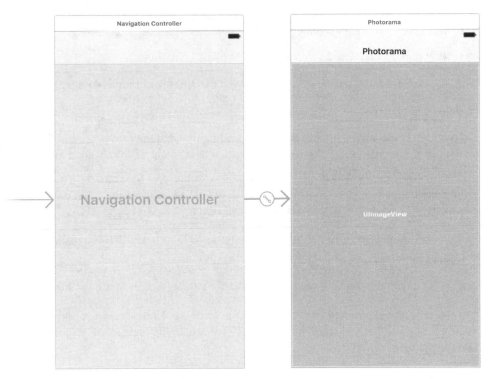

Build and run the application to make sure there are no errors.

Building the URL

Communication with servers is done via *requests*. A request encapsulates information about the interaction between the application and the server, and its most important piece of information is the destination URL.

In this section, you will build up the URL for retrieving interesting photos from the Flickr web service. The architecture of the application will reflect best practices. For example, each type that you create will encapsulate a single responsibility. This will make your types robust and flexible and your application easier to reason about. To be a good iOS developer, you not only need to get the job done, but you also need to get it done thoughtfully and with foresight.

Formatting URLs and requests

The format of a web service request varies depending on the server that the request is reaching out to. There are no set-in-stone rules when it comes to web services. You will need to find the documentation for the web service to know how to format a request. As long as a client application sends the server what it wants, you have a working exchange.

Flickr's interesting photos web service wants a URL that looks like this:

```
https://api.flickr.com/services/rest/?method=flickr.interestingness.getList
&api_key=a6d819499131071f158fd740860a5a88&extras=url_h,date_taken
&format=json&nojsoncallback=1
```

Web service requests come in all sorts of formats, depending on what the creator of that web service is trying to accomplish. The interesting photos web service, where pieces of information are broken up into key-value pairs, is pretty common.

The key-value pairs that are supplied as part of the URL are called *query items*. Each of the query items for the interesting photos request is defined by and is unique to the Flickr API.

- The `method` determines which endpoint you want to hit on the Flickr API. For the interesting photos, this is the string `"flickr.interestingness.getList"`.

- The `api_key` is a key that Flickr generates to authorize an application to use the Flickr API.

- The `extras` are attributes passed in to customize the response. Here, the `url_h,date_taken` value tells the Flickr server that you want the photo URLs to also come back in the response along with the date the photo was taken.

- The `format` item specifies that you want the payload coming back to be JSON.

- The `nojsoncallback` item specifies that you want JSON back in its raw format.

URLComponents

You will create two types to deal with all of the web service information. The **FlickrAPI** struct will be responsible for knowing and handling all Flickr-related information. This includes knowing how to generate the URLs that the Flickr API expects as well as knowing the format of the incoming JSON and how to parse that JSON into the relevant model objects. The **PhotoStore** class will handle the actual web service calls. Let's start by creating the **FlickrAPI** struct.

Create a new Swift file named FlickrAPI and declare the **FlickrAPI** struct, which will contain all of the knowledge that is specific to the Flickr API.

```
import Foundation

struct FlickrAPI {

}
```

You are going to use an enumeration to specify which endpoint on the Flickr server to hit. For this application, you will only be working with the endpoint to get interesting photos. However, Flickr supports many additional APIs, such as searching for images based on a string. Using an enum now will make it easier to add endpoints in the future.

In FlickrAPI.swift, create the **Method** enumeration. Each case of **Method** has a raw value that matches the corresponding Flickr endpoint.

```
import Foundation

enum Method: String {
    case interestingPhotos = "flickr.interestingness.getList"
}

struct FlickrAPI {

}
```

In Chapter 2, you learned that enumerations can have raw values associated with them. Although the raw values are often **Int**s, you can see here a great use of **String** as the raw value for the **Method** enumeration.

Now declare a type-level property to reference the base URL string for the web service requests.

```
enum Method: String {
    case interestingPhotos = "flickr.interestingness.getList"
}

struct FlickrAPI {

    static let baseURLString = "https://api.flickr.com/services/rest"
}
```

A type-level property (or method) is one that is accessed on the type itself – in this case, the **FlickrAPI** type. For structs, type properties and methods are declared with the `static` keyword; classes use the `class` keyword. You used a type method on the **UIView** class in Chapter 8 when you called the **animate(withDuration:animations:)** method. You also used a type method on **UIImagePickerController** in Chapter 15 when you called the **isSourceTypeAvailable(_:)** method. Here, you are declaring a type-level property on **FlickrAPI**.

The `baseURLString` is an implementation detail of the **FlickrAPI** type, and no other type needs to know about it. Instead, they will ask for a completed URL from **FlickrAPI**. To keep other files from being able to access `baseURLString`, mark the property as `private`.

```
struct FlickrAPI {

    private static let baseURLString = "https://api.flickr.com/services/rest"
}
```

This is called *access control*. You can control what can access the properties and methods on your own types. There are five levels of access control that can be applied to types, properties, and methods:

- open – This is used only for classes, and mostly by framework or third-party library authors. Anything can access this class, property, or method. Additionally, classes marked as open can be subclassed and methods can be overridden outside of the module.

- public – This is very similar to open; however, classes can only be subclassed and methods can only be overridden inside (not outside of) the module.

- internal – This is the default. Anything in the current module can access this type, property, or method. For an app, only files within your project can access these. If you write a third-party library, then only files within that third-party library can access them – apps that use your third-party library cannot.

- fileprivate – Anything in the same source file can see this type, property, or method.

- private – Anything within the enclosing scope can access this type, property, or method.

Now you are going to create a type method that builds up the Flickr URL for a specific endpoint. This method will accept two arguments. The first will specify which endpoint to hit using the **Method** enumeration, and the second will be an optional dictionary of query item parameters associated with the request.

Implement this method in your **FlickrAPI** struct in FlickrAPI.swift. For now, this method will return an empty URL.

```
private static func flickrURL(method: Method,
                             parameters: [String:String]?) -> URL {

    return URL(string: "")!
}
```

Notice that the **flickrURL(method:parameters:)** method is private. It is an implementation detail of the **FlickrAPI** struct. An internal type method will be exposed to the rest of the project for each of the specific endpoint URLs (currently, just the interesting photos endpoint). These internal type methods will call through to the **flickrURL(method:parameters:)** method.

In FlickrAPI.swift, define and implement the interestingPhotosURL computed property.

```
static var interestingPhotosURL: URL {
    return flickrURL(method: .interestingPhotos,
                    parameters: ["extras": "url_h,date_taken"])
}
```

Time to construct the full URL. You have the base URL defined as a constant, and the query items are being passed into the **flickrURL(method:parameters:)** method via the parameters argument. You will build up the URL using the **URLComponents** class, which is designed to take in these various components and construct a **URL** from them.

Update the **flickrURL(method:parameters:)** method to construct an instance of **URLComponents** from the base URL. Then, loop over the incoming parameters and create the associated **URLQueryItem** instances.

```
private static func flickrURL(method: Method,
                             parameters: [String:String]?) -> URL {

    return URL(string: "")!

    var components = URLComponents(string: baseURLString)!

    var queryItems = [URLQueryItem]()

    if let additionalParams = parameters {
        for (key, value) in additionalParams {
            let item = URLQueryItem(name: key, value: value)
            queryItems.append(item)
        }
    }
    components.queryItems = queryItems

    return components.url!
}
```

The last step in setting up the URL is to pass in the parameters that are common to all requests: method, api_key, format, and nojsoncallback.

The API key is a token generated by Flickr to identify your application and authenticate it with the web service. We have generated an API key for this application by creating a Flickr account and registering this application. (If you would like your own API key, you will need to register an application at www.flickr.com/services/apps/create.)

In FlickrAPI.swift, create a constant that references this token.

```
struct FlickrAPI {

    private static let baseURLString = "https://api.flickr.com/services/rest"
    private static let apiKey = "a6d819499131071f158fd740860a5a88"
```

Double-check to make sure you have typed in the API key exactly as presented here. It has to match or the server will reject your requests. If your API key is not working or if you have any problems with the requests, check out the forums at forums.bignerdranch.com for help.

Finish implementing **flickrURL(method:parameters:)** to add the common query items to the **URLComponents**.

```
private static func flickrURL(method: Method,
                             parameters: [String:String]?) -> URL {

    var components = URLComponents(string: baseURLString)!

    var queryItems = [URLQueryItem]()

    let baseParams = [
        "method": method.rawValue,
        "format": "json",
        "nojsoncallback": "1",
        "api_key": apiKey
    ]

    for (key, value) in baseParams {
        let item = URLQueryItem(name: key, value: value)
        queryItems.append(item)
    }

    if let additionalParams = parameters {
        for (key, value) in additionalParams {
            let item = URLQueryItem(name: key, value: value)
            queryItems.append(item)
        }
    }
    components.queryItems = queryItems

    return components.url!
}
```

Sending the Request

A *URL request* encapsulates information about the communication from the application to the server. Most importantly, it specifies the URL of the server for the request, but it also has a timeout interval, a cache policy, and other metadata about the request. A request is represented by the **URLRequest** class. Check out the For the More Curious section at the end of this chapter for more information.

The **URLSession** API is a collection of classes that use a request to communicate with a server in a number of ways. The **URLSessionTask** class is responsible for communicating with a server. The **URLSession** class is responsible for creating tasks that match a given configuration.

In Photorama, a new class, **PhotoStore**, will be responsible for initiating the web service requests. It will use the **URLSession** API and the **FlickrAPI** struct to fetch a list of interesting photos and download the image data for each photo.

Create a new Swift file named PhotoStore and declare the **PhotoStore** class.

```
import Foundation

class PhotoStore {

}
```

URLSession

Let's look at a few of the properties on **URLRequest**:

- allHTTPHeaderFields – a dictionary of metadata about the HTTP transaction, including character encoding and how the server should handle caching

- allowsCellularAccess – a Boolean that represents whether a request is allowed to use cellular data

- cachePolicy – the property that determines whether and how the local cache should be used

- httpMethod – the request method; the default is GET, and other values are POST, PUT, and DELETE

- timeoutInterval – the maximum duration a connection to the server will be attempted for

The class that communicates with the web service is an instance of **URLSessionTask**. There are three kinds of tasks: data tasks, download tasks, and upload tasks. **URLSessionDataTask** retrieves data from the server and returns it as **Data** in memory. **URLSessionDownloadTask** retrieves data from the server and returns it as a file saved to the filesystem. **URLSessionUploadTask** sends data to the server.

Often, you will have a group of requests that have many properties in common. For example, maybe some downloads should never happen over cellular data, or maybe certain requests should be cached differently than others. It can become tedious to configure related requests the same way.

This is where **URLSession** comes in handy. **URLSession** acts as a factory for **URLSessionTask** instances. The session is created with a configuration that specifies properties that are common across all of the tasks that it creates. Although many applications might only need to use a single instance of **URLSession**, having the power and flexibility of multiple sessions is a great tool to have at your disposal.

In PhotoStore.swift, add a property to hold on to an instance of **URLSession**.

```
class PhotoStore {

    private let session: URLSession = {
        let config = URLSessionConfiguration.default
        return URLSession(configuration: config)
    }()

}
```

In PhotoStore.swift, implement the **fetchInterestingPhotos()** method to create a **URLRequest** that connects to api.flickr.com and asks for the list of interesting photos. Then, use the **URLSession** to create a **URLSessionDataTask** that transfers this request to the server.

```
func fetchInterestingPhotos() {

    let url = FlickrAPI.interestingPhotosURL
    let request = URLRequest(url: url)
    let task = session.dataTask(with: request) {
        (data, response, error) -> Void in

        if let jsonData = data {
            if let jsonString = String(data: jsonData,
                                       encoding: .utf8) {
                print(jsonString)
            }
        } else if let requestError = error {
            print("Error fetching interesting photos: \(requestError)")
        } else {
            print("Unexpected error with the request")
        }
    }
    task.resume()
}
```

Creating the **URLRequest** is fairly straightforward: You create a **URL** instance using the **FlickrAPI** struct and instantiate a request object with it.

By giving the session a request and a completion closure to call when the request finishes, the session will return an instance of **URLSessionTask**. Because Photorama is requesting data from a web service, the type of task will be an instance of **URLSessionDataTask**. Tasks are always created in the suspended state, so calling **resume()** on the task will start the web service request. For now, the completion block will just print out the JSON data returned from the request.

To make a request, **PhotosViewController** will call the appropriate methods on **PhotoStore**. To do this, **PhotosViewController** needs a reference to an instance of **PhotoStore**.

At the top of PhotosViewController.swift, add a property to hang on to an instance of **PhotoStore**.

```
class PhotosViewController: UIViewController {

    @IBOutlet var imageView: UIImageView!
    var store: PhotoStore!
```

The store is a dependency of the **PhotosViewController**. You will use property injection to give the **PhotosViewController** its store dependency, just as you did with the view controllers in Homepwner.

Open AppDelegate.swift and use property injection to give the **PhotosViewController** an instance of **PhotoStore**.

```
func application(_ application: UIApplication, didFinishLaunchingWithOptions
        launchOptions: [UIApplicationLaunchOptionsKey : Any]?) -> Bool {
    // Override point for customization after application launch.

    let rootViewController = window!.rootViewController as! UINavigationController
    let photosViewController =
        rootViewController.topViewController as! PhotosViewController
    photosViewController.store = PhotoStore()

    return true
}
```

Now that the **PhotosViewController** can interact with the **PhotoStore**, kick off the web service exchange when the view controller is coming onscreen for the first time.

In PhotosViewController.swift, override **viewDidLoad()** and fetch the interesting photos.

```
override func viewDidLoad() {
    super.viewDidLoad()

    store.fetchInterestingPhotos()
}
```

Build and run the application. A string representation of the JSON data coming back from the web service will print to the console. (If you do not see anything print to the console, make sure you typed the URL and API key correctly.)

The response will look something like Figure 20.4.

Figure 20.4 Web service console output

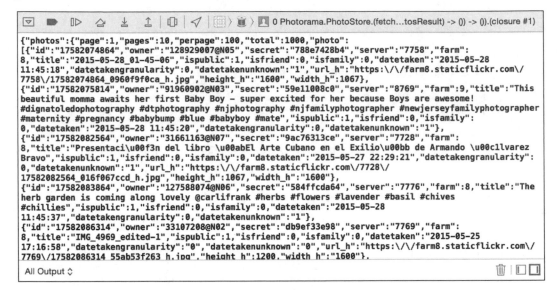

Modeling the Photo

Next, you will create a **Photo** class to represent each photo that is returned from the web service request. The relevant pieces of information that you will need for this application are the id, the title, the url_h, and the datetaken.

Create a new Swift file called Photo and declare the **Photo** class with properties for the photoID, the title, and the remoteURL. Finally, add a designated initializer that sets up the instance.

```
import Foundation

class Photo {

    let title: String
    let remoteURL: URL
    let photoID: String
    let dateTaken: Date

    init(title: String, photoID: String, remoteURL: URL, dateTaken: Date) {
        self.title = title
        self.photoID = photoID
        self.remoteURL = remoteURL
        self.dateTaken = dateTaken
    }
}
```

You will use this class shortly once you are parsing the JSON data.

JSON Data

JSON data, especially when it is condensed like it is in your console, may seem daunting. However, it is actually a very simple syntax. JSON can contain the most basic types used to represent model objects: arrays, dictionaries, strings, and numbers. A JSON dictionary contains one or more key-value pairs, where the key is a string and the value can be another dictionary or a string, number, or array. An array can consist of strings, numbers, dictionaries, and other arrays. Thus, a JSON document is a nested set of these types of values.

Here is an example of some really simple JSON:

```
{
    "name" : "Christian",
    "friends" : ["Stacy", "Mikey"],
    "job" : {
        "company" : "Big Nerd Ranch",
        "title" : "Senior Nerd"
    }
}
```

This JSON document begins and ends with curly braces ({ and }), which in JSON delimit a dictionary. Within the curly braces are the key-value pairs that belong to the dictionary. This dictionary contains three key-value pairs (name, friends, and job).

A string is represented by text within quotation marks. Strings are used as the keys within a dictionary and can be used as values, too. Thus, the value associated with the name key in the top-level dictionary is the string Christian.

Arrays are represented with square brackets ([and]). An array can contain any other JSON information. In this case, the friends key holds an array of strings (Stacy and Mikey).

A dictionary can contain other dictionaries, and the final key in the top-level dictionary, job, is associated with a dictionary that has two key-value pairs (company and title).

Photorama will parse out the useful information from the JSON data and store it in a **Photo** instance.

JSONSerialization

Apple has a built-in class for parsing JSON data, **JSONSerialization**. You can hand this class a bunch of JSON data, and it will create a dictionary for every JSON dictionary (the JSON specification calls these "objects"), an array for every JSON array, a **String** for every JSON string, and an **NSNumber** for every JSON number. Let's see how this class helps you.

Open PhotoStore.swift and update **fetchInterestingPhotos()** to print the JSON object to the console.

```
func fetchInterestingPhotos() {

    let url = FlickrAPI.interestingPhotosURL
    let request = URLRequest(url: url)
    let task = session.dataTask(with: request) {
        (data, response, error) -> Void in

        if let jsonData = data {
            if let jsonString = String(data: jsonData,
                                       encoding: .utf8) {
                print(jsonString)
            }
            do {
                let jsonObject = try JSONSerialization.jsonObject(with: jsonData,
                                                              options: [])
                print(jsonObject)
            } catch let error {
                print("Error creating JSON object: \(error)")
            }
        } else if let requestError = error {
            print("Error fetching interesting photos: \(requestError)")
        } else {
            print("Unexpected error with the request")
        }
    }
    task.resume()
}
```

Build and run the application, then check the console. You will see the JSON data again, but now it will be formatted differently because **print()** does a good job formatting dictionaries and arrays.

The format of the JSON data is dictated by the API, so you will add the code to parse the JSON to the **FlickrAPI** struct.

Parsing the data that comes back from the server could go wrong in a number of ways: The data might not contain JSON. The data could be corrupt. The data might contain JSON but not match the format that you expect. To manage the possibility of failure, you will use an enumeration with *associated values* to represent the success or failure of the parsing.

Enumerations and associated values

You learned about the basics of enumerations in Chapter 2, and you have been using them throughout this book – including the **Method** enum used earlier in this chapter. Associated values are a useful feature of enumerations. Let's take a moment to look at a simple example before you use this feature in Photorama.

Enumerations are a convenient way of defining and restricting the possible values for a variable. For example, let's say you are working on a home automation app. You could define an enumeration to specify the oven state, like this:

```
enum OvenState {
    case on
    case off
}
```

If the oven is on, you also need to know what temperature it is set to. Associated values are a perfect solution to this situation.

```
enum OvenState {
    case on(Double)
    case off
}

var ovenState = OvenState.on(450)
```

Each case of an enumeration can have data of any type associated with it. For **OvenState**, its .on case has an associated **Double** that represents the oven's temperature. Notice that not all cases need to have associated values.

Retrieving the associated value from an **enum** is often done using a switch statement.

```
switch ovenState {
case let .on(temperature):
    print("The oven is on and set to \(temperature) degrees.")
case .off:
    print("The oven is off.")
}
```

Note that the .on case uses a let keyword to store the associated value in the temperature constant, which can be used within the case clause. (You can use the var keyword instead if temperature needs to be a variable.) Considering the value given to ovenState, the switch statement above would result in the line The oven is on and set to 450 degrees. printed to the console.

In the next section, you will use an enumeration with associated values to tie the result status of a request to the Flickr web service with data. A successful result status will be tied to the data containing interesting photos; a failure result status will be tied with error information.

Parsing JSON data

In PhotoStore.swift, add an enumeration named **PhotosResult** to the top of the file that has a case for both success and failure.

```
import Foundation

enum PhotosResult {
    case success([Photo])
    case failure(Error)
}

class PhotoStore {
```

If the data is valid JSON and contains an array of photos, those photos will be associated with the success case. If there are any errors during the parsing process, the relevant **Error** will be passed along with the failure case.

Error is a protocol that all errors conform to. **NSError** is the error that many iOS frameworks throw, and it conforms to **Error**. You will create your own **Error** shortly.

In FlickrAPI.swift, implement a method that takes in an instance of **Data** and uses the **JSONSerialization** class to convert the data into the basic foundation objects.

```
static func photos(fromJSON data: Data) -> PhotosResult {
    do {
        let jsonObject = try JSONSerialization.jsonObject(with: data,
                                                          options: [])

        var finalPhotos = [Photo]()
        return .success(finalPhotos)
    } catch let error {
        return .failure(error)
    }
}
```

(This code will generate some warnings. You will resolve them shortly.)

If the incoming data is valid JSON data, then the jsonObject instance will reference the appropriate model object. If not, then there was a problem with the data and you pass along the error. You now need to get the photo information out of the JSON object and into instances of **Photo**.

When the **URLSessionDataTask** finishes, you will use **JSONSerialization** to convert the JSON data into a dictionary. Figure 20.5 shows how the data will be structured.

Figure 20.5 JSON objects

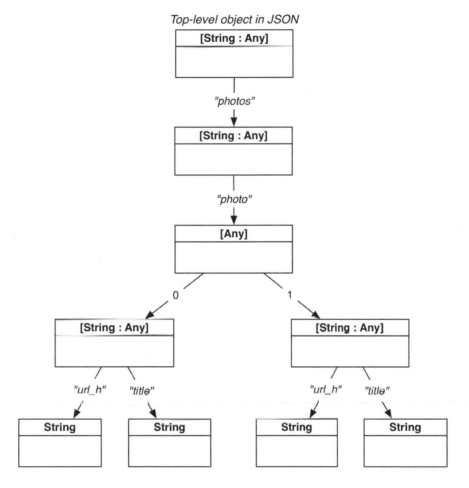

At the top level of the incoming JSON data is a dictionary. The value associated with the "photos" key contains the important information, and the most important is the array of dictionaries.

As you can see, you have to dig pretty deep to get the information that you need.

If the structure of the JSON data does not match your expectations, you will return a custom error.

At the top of FlickrAPI.swift, declare a custom enum to represent possible errors for the Flickr API.

```
enum FlickrError: Error {
    case invalidJSONData
}

enum Method: String {
    case interestingPhotos = "flickr.interestingness.getList"
}
```

Now, in **photos(fromJSON:)**, dig down through the JSON data to get to the array of dictionaries representing the individual photos.

```
static func photos(fromJSON data: Data) -> PhotosResult {
    do {
        let jsonObject = try JSONSerialization.jsonObject(with: data,
                                                    options: [])

        guard
            let jsonDictionary = jsonObject as? [AnyHashable:Any],
            let photos = jsonDictionary["photos"] as? [String:Any],
            let photosArray = photos["photo"] as? [[String:Any]] else {

                // The JSON structure doesn't match our expectations
                return .failure(FlickrError.invalidJSONData)
        }

        var finalPhotos = [Photo]()
        return .success(finalPhotos)
    } catch let error {
        return .failure(error)
    }
}
```

The next step is to get the photo information out of the dictionary and into **Photo** model objects.

You will need an instance of **DateFormatter** to convert the datetaken string into an instance of **Date**.

In FlickrAPI.swift, add a constant instance of **DateFormatter**.

```
private static let baseURLString = "https://api.flickr.com/services/rest"
private static let apiKey = "a6d819499131071f158fd740860a5a88"

private static let dateFormatter: DateFormatter = {
    let formatter = DateFormatter()
    formatter.dateFormat = "yyyy-MM-dd HH:mm:ss"
    return formatter
}()
```

Still in FlickrAPI.swift, write a new method to parse a JSON dictionary into a **Photo** instance.

```
private static func photo(fromJSON json: [String : Any]) -> Photo? {
    guard
        let photoID = json["id"] as? String,
        let title = json["title"] as? String,
        let dateString = json["datetaken"] as? String,
        let photoURLString = json["url_h"] as? String,
        let url = URL(string: photoURLString),
        let dateTaken = dateFormatter.date(from: dateString) else {

            // Don't have enough information to construct a Photo
            return nil
    }

    return Photo(title: title, photoID: photoID, remoteURL: url, dateTaken: dateTaken)
}
```

Now update **photos(fromJSON:)** to parse the dictionaries into **Photo** instances and then return these as part of the success enumerator. Also handle the possibility that the JSON format has changed, so no photos were able to be found.

```
static func photos(fromJSON data: Data) -> PhotosResult {
    do {
        let jsonObject = try JSONSerialization.jsonObject(with: data,
                                                    options: [])

        guard
            let jsonDictionary = jsonObject as? [AnyHashable:Any],
            let photos = jsonDictionary["photos"] as? [String:Any],
            let photosArray = photos["photo"] as? [[String:Any]] else {

                // The JSON structure doesn't match our expectations
                return .failure(FlickrError.invalidJSONData)
        }

        var finalPhotos = [Photo]()
        for photoJSON in photosArray {
            if let photo = photo(fromJSON: photoJSON) {
                finalPhotos.append(photo)
            }
        }

        if finalPhotos.isEmpty && !photosArray.isEmpty {
            // We weren't able to parse any of the photos
            // Maybe the JSON format for photos has changed
            return .failure(FlickrError.invalidJSONData)
        }
        return .success(finalPhotos)
    } catch let error {
        return .failure(error)
    }
}
```

Next, in `PhotoStore.swift`, write a new method that will process the JSON data that is returned from the web service request.

```
private func processPhotosRequest(data: Data?, error: Error?) -> PhotosResult {
    guard let jsonData = data else {
        return .failure(error!)
    }

    return FlickrAPI.photos(fromJSON: jsonData)
}
```

Now, update **fetchInterestingPhotos()** to use the method you just created.

```
func fetchInterestingPhotos() {

    let url = FlickrAPI.interestingPhotosURL
    let request = URLRequest(url: url)
    let task = session.dataTask(with: request) {
        (data, response, error) -> Void in

        if let jsonData = data {
            do {
                let jsonObject = try JSONSerialization.jsonObject(with: jsonData,
                                                                  options: [])
                print(jsonObject)
            } catch let error {
                print("Error creating JSON object: \(error)")
            }
        } else if let requestError = error {
            print("Error fetching interesting photos: \(requestError)")
        } else {
            print("Unexpected error with the request")
        }

        let result = self.processPhotosRequest(data: data, error: error)
    }
    task.resume()
}
```

Finally, update the method signature for **fetchInterestingPhotos()** to take in a completion closure that will be called once the web service request is completed.

```
func fetchInterestingPhotos(completion: @escaping (PhotosResult) -> Void) {

    let url = FlickrAPI.interestingPhotosURL
    let request = URLRequest(url: url)
    let task = session.dataTask(with: request) {
        (data, response, error) -> Void in

        let result = self.processPhotosRequest(data: data, error: error)
        completion(result)
    }
    task.resume()
}
```

Fetching data from a web service is an *asynchronous* process: Once the request starts, it may take a nontrivial amount of time for a response to come back from the server. Because of this, the **fetchInterestingPhotos(completion:)** method cannot directly return an instance of **PhotosResult**. Instead, the caller of this method will supply a completion closure for the **PhotoStore** to call once the request is complete.

This follows the same pattern that **URLSessionTask** uses with its completion handler: The task is created with a closure for it to call once the web service request completes. Figure 20.6 describes the flow of data with the web service request.

Figure 20.6 Web service request data flow

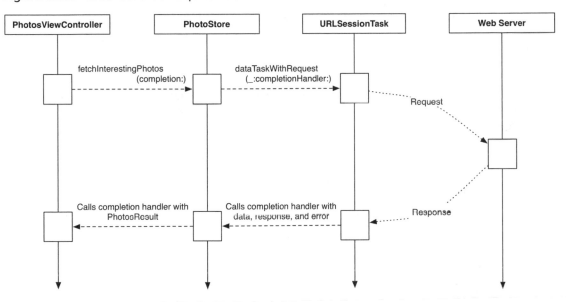

The closure is marked with the @escaping annotation. This annotation lets the compiler know that the closure might not get called immediately within the method. In this case, the closure is getting passed to the **URLSessionDataTask**, which will call it when the web service request completes.

In PhotosViewController.swift, update the implementation of the **viewDidLoad()** using the trailing closure syntax to print out the result of the web service request.

```
override func viewDidLoad() {
    super.viewDidLoad()

    store.fetchInterestingPhotos() {
        (photosResult) -> Void in

        switch photosResult {
        case let .success(photos):
            print("Successfully found \(photos.count) photos.")
        case let .failure(error):
            print("Error fetching interesting photos: \(error)")
        }

    }
}
```

Build and run the application. Once the web service request completes, you should see the number of photos found printed to the console.

Downloading and Displaying the Image Data

You have done a lot already in this chapter: You have successfully interacted with the Flickr API via a web service request, and you have parsed the incoming JSON data into **Photo** model objects. Unfortunately, you have nothing to show for it except some log messages in the console.

In this section, you will use the URL returned from the web service request to download the image data. Then you will create an instance of **UIImage** from that data, and, finally, you will display the first image returned from the request in a **UIImageView**. (In the next chapter, you will display all of the images that are returned in a grid layout driven by a **UICollectionView**.)

The first step is downloading the image data. This process will be very similar to the web service request to download the photos' JSON data.

Open PhotoStore.swift, import UIKit, and add an enumeration to the top of the file that represents the result of downloading the image. This enumeration will follow the same pattern as the **PhotosResult** enumeration, taking advantage of associated values. You will also create an **Error** to represent photo errors.

```
import Foundation
import UIKit

enum ImageResult {
    case success(UIImage)
    case failure(Error)
}

enum PhotoError: Error {
    case imageCreationError
}

enum PhotosResult {
    case success([Photo])
    case failure(Error)
}
```

If the download is successful, the success case will have the **UIImage** associated with it. If there is an error, the failure case will have the **Error** associated with it.

Now, in the same file, implement a method to download the image data. Like the fetchInterestingPhotos(completion:) method, this new method will take in a completion closure that will return an instance of **ImageResult**.

```
func fetchImage(for photo: Photo, completion: @escaping (ImageResult) -> Void) {

    let photoURL = photo.remoteURL
    let request = URLRequest(url: photoURL)

    let task = session.dataTask(with: request) {
        (data, response, error) -> Void in

    }
    task.resume()
}
```

Now implement a method that processes the data from the web service request into an image, if possible.

```
private func processImageRequest(data: Data?, error: Error?) -> ImageResult {
    guard
        let imageData = data,
        let image = UIImage(data: imageData) else {

            // Couldn't create an image
            if data == nil {
                return .failure(error!)
            } else {
                return .failure(PhotoError.imageCreationError)
            }
    }

    return .success(image)
}
```

Still in PhotoStore.swift, update **fetchImage(for:completion:)** to use this new method.

```
func fetchImage(for photo: Photo, completion: @escaping (ImageResult) -> Void) {

    let photoURL = photo.remoteURL
    let request = URLRequest(url: photoURL)

    let task = session.dataTask(with: request) {
        (data, response, error) -> Void in

        let result = self.processImageRequest(data: data, error: error)
        completion(result)
    }
    task.resume()
}
```

To test this code, you will download the image data for the first photo that is returned from the interesting photos request and display it on the image view.

Open PhotosViewController.swift and add a new method that will fetch the image and display it on the image view.

```
func updateImageView(for photo: Photo) {
    store.fetchImage(for: photo) {
        (imageResult) -> Void in

        switch imageResult {
        case let .success(image):
            self.imageView.image = image
        case let .failure(error):
            print("Error downloading image: \(error)")
        }
    }
}
```

Now update **viewDidLoad()** to use this new method.

```
override func viewDidLoad() {
    super.viewDidLoad()

    store.fetchInterestingPhotos {
        (photosResult) -> Void in

        switch photosResult {
        case let .success(photos):
            print("Successfully found \(photos.count) photos.")
            if let firstPhoto = photos.first {
                self.updateImageView(for: firstPhoto)
            }
        case let .failure(error):
            print("Error fetching interesting photos: \(error)")
        }
    }
}
```

Although you could build and run the application at this point, the image may or may not appear in the image view when the web service request finishes. Why? The code that updates the image view is not being run on the main thread.

The Main Thread

Modern iOS devices have multicore processors that enable them to run multiple chunks of code simultaneously. These computations proceed in parallel, so this is referred to as *parallel computing*. When different computations are in flight at the same time, this is known as *concurrency*, and the computations are said to be happening *concurrently*. A common way to express this is by representing each computation with a different *thread* of control.

So far in this book, all of your code has been running on the *main thread*. The main thread is sometimes referred to as the UI thread, because any code that modifies the UI must run on the main thread.

When the web service completes, you want it to update the image view. But by default, **URLSessionDataTask** runs the completion handler on a background thread. You need a way to force code to run on the main thread to update the image view. You can do that easily using the **OperationQueue** class.

You will update the asynchronous **PhotoStore** methods to call their completion handlers on the main thread.

In PhotoStore.swift, update **fetchInterestingPhotos(completion:)** to call the completion closure on the main thread.

```
func fetchInterestingPhotos(completion: @escaping (PhotosResult) -> Void) {

    let url = FlickrAPI.interestingPhotosURL
    let request = URLRequest(url: url)
    let task = session.dataTask(with: request) {
        (data, response, error) -> Void in

        let result = self.processPhotosRequest(data: data, error: error)
        OperationQueue.main.addOperation {
            completion(result)
        }
    }
    task.resume()
}
```

Do the same for **fetchImage(for:completion:)**.

```
func fetchImage(for photo: Photo, completion: @escaping (ImageResult) -> Void) {

    let photoURL = photo.remoteURL
    let request = URLRequest(url: photoURL)

    let task = session.dataTask(with: request) {
        (data, response, error) -> Void in

        let result = self.processImageRequest(data: data, error: error)
        OperationQueue.main.addOperation {
            completion(result)
        }
    }
    task.resume()
}
```

Build and run the application. Now that the image view is being updated on the main thread, you will have something to show for all your hard work: An image will appear when the web service request finishes. (It might take a little time to show the image if the web service request takes a while to finish.)

Bronze Challenge: Printing the Response Information

The completion handler for **dataTask(with:completionHandler:)** provides an instance of **URLResponse**. When making HTTP requests, this response is of type **HTTPURLResponse** (a subclass of **URLResponse**). Print the statusCode and headerFields to the console. These properties are very useful when debugging web service calls.

Silver Challenge: Fetch Recent Photos from Flickr

In this chapter, you fetched the interesting photos from Flickr using the flickr.interestingness.getList endpoint. Add a new case to your **Method** enumeration for recent photos. The endpoint for this is flickr.photos.getRecent. Extend the application so you are able to switch between interesting photos and recent photos. (Hint: The JSON format for both endpoints is the same, so your existing parsing code will still work.)

For the More Curious: HTTP

When **URLSessionTask** interacts with a web server, it does so according to the rules outlined in the HTTP specification. The specification is very clear about the exact format of the request/response exchange between the client and the server. An example of a simple HTTP request is shown in Figure 20.7.

Figure 20.7 HTTP request format

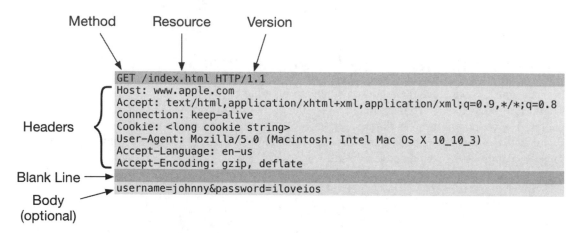

An HTTP request has three parts: a request line, request headers, and an optional request body. The request line is the first line of the request and tells the server what the client is trying to do. In this request, the client is trying to GET the resource at /index.html. (It also specifies the HTTP version that the request will be conforming to.)

The word GET is an HTTP method. While there are a number of supported HTTP methods, you will see GET and POST most often. The default of **URLRequest**, GET, indicates that the client wants a resource *from* the server. The resource requested might be an actual file on the web server's filesystem, or it could be generated dynamically at the moment the request is received. As a client, you should not care about this detail, but more than likely the JSON resources you requested in this chapter were created dynamically.

In addition to getting things from a server, you can send it information. For example, many web servers allow you to upload photos. A client application would pass the image data to the server through an HTTP request. In this situation, you would use the HTTP method POST, and you would include a request body. The body of a request is the payload you are sending to the server – typically JSON, XML, or binary data.

When the request has a body, it must also have the Content-Length header. Handily, **URLRequest** will compute the size of the body and add this header for you.

Here is an example of how to POST an image to an imaginary site using a **URLRequest**.

```
if let someURL = URL(string: "http://www.photos.example.com/upload") {
    let image = profileImage()
    let data = UIImagePNGRepresentation(image)

    var req = URLRequest(url: someURL)

    // This adds the HTTP body data and automatically sets the content-length header
    req.httpBody = data

    // This changes the HTTP method in the request line
    req.httpMethod = "POST"

    // If you wanted to set a request header, such as the Accept header
    req.setValue("text/json", forHTTPHeaderField: "Accept")
}
```

Figure 20.8 shows what a simple HTTP response might look like. While you will not be modifying the corresponding **HTTPURLResponse** instance, it is nice to understand what it is modeling.

Figure 20.8 HTTP response format

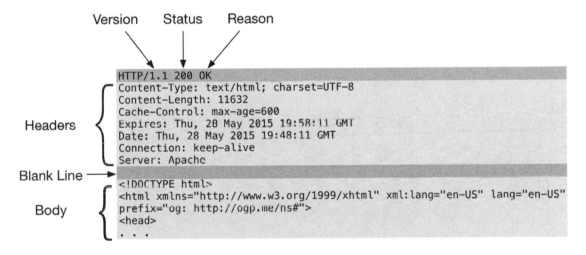

As you can see, the format of the response is not too different from the request. It includes a status line, response headers, and, of course, the response body. Yes, this is where that pesky 404 Not Found comes from!

21

Collection Views

In this chapter, you will continue working on the Photorama application by displaying the interesting Flickr photos in a grid using the **UICollectionView** class. This chapter will also reinforce the data source design pattern that you used in previous chapters. Figure 21.1 shows you what the application will look like at the end of this chapter.

Figure 21.1 Photorama with a collection view

In Chapter 10, you worked with **UITableView**. Table views are a great way to display and edit a column of information in a hierarchical list. Like a table view, a *collection view* also displays an ordered collection of items, but instead of displaying the information in a hierarchical list, the collection view has a *layout* object that drives the display of information. You will use a built-in layout object, the **UICollectionViewFlowLayout**, to present the interesting photos in a scrollable grid.

Displaying the Grid

Let's tackle the interface first. You are going to change the UI for **PhotosViewController** to display a collection view instead of displaying the image view.

Open Main.storyboard and locate the Photorama image view. Delete the image view from the canvas and drag a Collection View onto the canvas. Select both the collection view and its superview. (The easiest way to do this is using the document outline.) Open the Auto Layout Align menu, configure it like Figure 21.2, and click Add 4 Constraints.

Figure 21.2 Collection view constraints

Because you used the Align menu to pin the edges, the collection view will be pinned to the top of the entire view instead of to the top layout guide. This is useful for scroll views (and their subclasses, like **UITableView** and **UICollectionView**) so that the content will scroll underneath the navigation bar. The scroll view will automatically update its insets to make the content visible, as you saw in Chapter 10. The canvas will now look like Figure 21.3.

Figure 21.3 Storyboard canvas

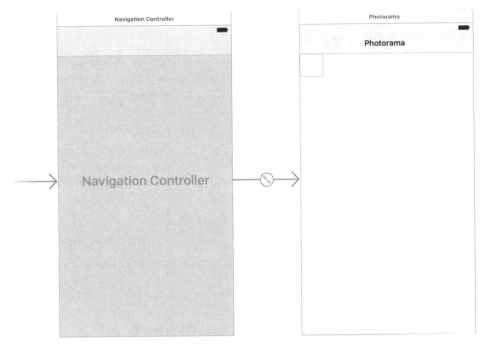

Currently, the collection view cells have a clear background color. Select the collection view cell – the small rectangle in the upper-left corner of the collection view – and give it a black background color.

Select the black collection view cell and open its attributes inspector. Set the Identifier to UICollectionViewCell (Figure 21.4).

Figure 21.4 Setting the reuse identifier

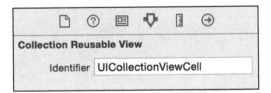

The collection view is now on the canvas, but you need a way to populate the cells with data. To do this, you will create a new class to act as the data source of the collection view.

Collection View Data Source

Applications are constantly changing, so part of being a good iOS developer is building applications in a way that allows them to adapt to changing requirements.

The Photorama application will display a single collection view of photos. You could do something similar to what you did in Homepwner and make the **PhotosViewController** be the data source of the collection view. The view controller would implement the required data source methods, and everything would work just fine.

At least, it would work for now. What if, sometime in the future, you decided to have a different screen that also displayed a collection view of photos? Maybe instead of displaying the interesting photos, it would use a different web service to display all the photos matching a search term. In this case, you would need to reimplement the same data source methods within the new view controller with essentially the same code. That would not be ideal.

Instead, you will abstract out the collection view data source code into a new class. This class will be responsible for responding to data source questions – and it will be reusable as necessary.

Create a new Swift file named PhotoDataSource and declare the **PhotoDataSource** class.

```
import Foundation
import UIKit

class PhotoDataSource: NSObject, UICollectionViewDataSource {

    var photos = [Photo]()

}
```

To conform to the **UICollectionViewDataSource** protocol, a type also needs to conform to the **NSObjectProtocol**. The easiest and most common way to conform to this protocol is to subclass from **NSObject**, as you did above.

The **UICollectionViewDataSource** protocol declares two required methods to implement:

```
func collectionView(_ collectionView: UICollectionView,
                    numberOfItemsInSection section: Int) -> Int
func collectionView(_ collectionView: UICollectionView,
                    cellForItemAt indexPath: IndexPath) -> UICollectionViewCell
```

You might notice that these two methods look very similar to the two required methods of
UITableViewDataSource that you saw in Chapter 10. The first data source callback asks how many
cells to display, and the second asks for the **UICollectionViewCell** to display for a given index path.

Implement these two methods in PhotoDataSource.swift.

```
class PhotoDataSource: NSObject, UICollectionViewDataSource {

    var photos = [Photo]()

    func collectionView(_ collectionView: UICollectionView,
                        numberOfItemsInSection section: Int) -> Int {
        return photos.count
    }

    func collectionView(_ collectionView: UICollectionView,
                        cellForItemAt indexPath: IndexPath) -> UICollectionViewCell {

        let identifier = "UICollectionViewCell"
        let cell =
            collectionView.dequeueReusableCell(withReuseIdentifier: identifier,
                                               for: indexPath)

        return cell
    }
}
```

Next, the collection view needs to know that an instance of **PhotoDataSource** is the data source object.

In PhotosViewController.swift, add a property to reference an instance of **PhotoDataSource** and an
outlet for a **UICollectionView** instance. Also, you will not need the imageView anymore, so delete it.

```
class PhotosViewController: UIViewController {

    @IBOutlet var imageView: UIImageView!
    @IBOutlet var collectionView: UICollectionView!

    var store: PhotoStore!
    let photoDataSource = PhotoDataSource()
```

Without the imageView property, you will not need the method **updateImageView(for:)** anymore. Go
ahead and remove it.

```
func updateImageView(for photo: Photo) {
    store.fetchImage(for: photo) {
        (imageResult) -> Void in

        switch imageResult {
        case let .success(image):
            self.imageView.image = image
        case let .failure(error):
            print("Error downloading image: \(error)")
        }
    }
}
```

Update **viewDidLoad()** to set the data source on the collection view.

```
override func viewDidLoad() {
    super.viewDidLoad()

    collectionView.dataSource = photoDataSource
```

Finally, update the photoDataSource object with the result of the web service request and reload the collection view.

```
override func viewDidLoad()
    super.viewDidLoad()

    collectionView.dataSource = photoDataSource

    store.fetchInterestingPhotos {
        (photosResult) -> Void in

        switch photosResult {
        case let .success(photos):
            print("Successfully found \(photos.count) photos.")
            if let firstPhoto = photos.first {
                self.updateImageView(for: firstPhoto)
            }
            self.photoDataSource.photos = photos
        case let .failure(error):
            print("Error fetching interesting photos: \(error)")
            self.photoDataSource.photos.removeAll()
        }
        self.collectionView.reloadSections(IndexSet(integer: 0))
    }
}
```

The last thing you need to do is make the collectionView outlet connection.

Open Main.storyboard and navigate to the collection view. Control-drag from the Photorama view controller to the collection view and connect it to the collectionView outlet.

Build and run the application. After the web service request completes, check the console to confirm that photos were found. On the iOS device, there will be a grid of black squares corresponding to the number of photos found (Figure 21.5). These cells are arranged in a *flow layout*. A flow layout fits as many cells on a row as possible before flowing down to the next row. If you rotate the iOS device, you will see the cells fill the given area.

Figure 21.5 Initial flow layout

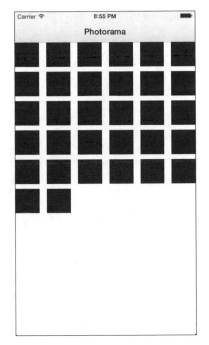

Customizing the Layout

The display of cells is not driven by the collection view itself but by the collection view's *layout*. The layout object is responsible for the placement of cells onscreen. Layouts, in turn, are driven by a subclass of **UICollectionViewLayout**.

The flow layout that Photorama is currently using is **UICollectionViewFlowLayout**, which is the only concrete **UICollectionViewLayout** subclass provided by the UIKit framework.

Some of the properties you can customize on **UICollectionViewFlowLayout** are:

- **scrollDirection** – Do you want to scroll vertically or horizontally?

- **minimumLineSpacing** – What is the minimum spacing between lines?

- **minimumInteritemSpacing** – What is the minimum spacing between items in a row (or column, if scrolling horizontally)?

- **itemSize** – What is the size of each item?

- **sectionInset** – What are the margins used to lay out content for each section?

Figure 21.6 shows how these properties affect the presentation of cells using
UICollectionViewFlowLayout.

Figure 21.6 **UICollectionViewFlowLayout** properties

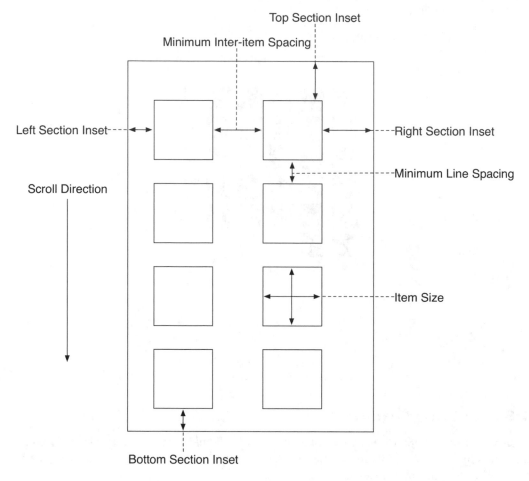

Open `Main.storyboard` and select the collection view. Open the size inspector and configure the Cell Size, Min Spacing, and Section Insets as shown in Figure 21.7.

Figure 21.7 Collection view size inspector

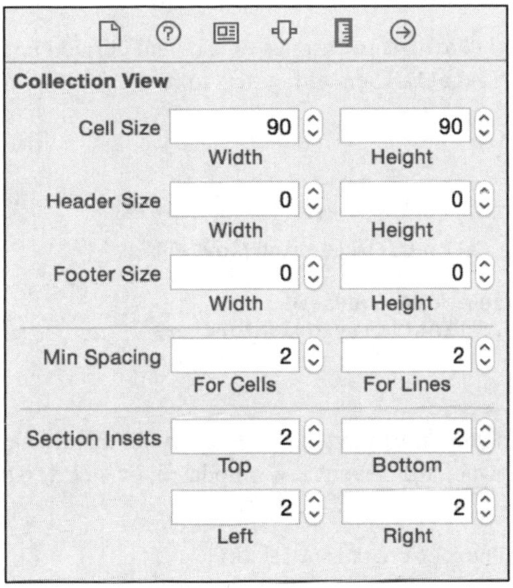

Build and run the application to see how the layout has changed.

Creating a Custom UICollectionViewCell

Next you are going to create a custom **UICollectionViewCell** subclass to display the photos. While the image data is downloading, the collection view cell will display a spinning activity indicator using the **UIActivityIndicatorView** class.

Create a new Swift file named `PhotoCollectionViewCell` and define **PhotoCollectionViewCell** as a subclass of **UICollectionViewCell**. Then add outlets to reference the image view and the activity indicator view.

```swift
import Foundation
import UIKit

class PhotoCollectionViewCell: UICollectionViewCell {

    @IBOutlet var imageView: UIImageView!
    @IBOutlet var spinner: UIActivityIndicatorView!

}
```

The activity indicator view should only spin when the cell is not displaying an image. Instead of always updating the `spinner` when the `imageView` is updated, or vice versa, you will write a helper method to take care of it for you.

Create this helper method in `PhotoCollectionViewCell.swift`.

```swift
func update(with image: UIImage?) {
    if let imageToDisplay = image {
        spinner.stopAnimating()
        imageView.image = imageToDisplay
    } else {
        spinner.startAnimating()
        imageView.image = nil
    }
}
```

It would be nice to reset each cell to the spinning state both when the cell is first created and when the cell is getting reused. The method **awakeFromNib()** will be used for the former, and the method **prepareForReuse()** will be used for the latter. Recall that you used **awakeFromNib()** in Chapter 12. The method **prepareForReuse()** is called when a cell is about to be reused.

Implement these two methods in `PhotoCollectionViewCell.swift` to reset the cell back to the spinning state.

```swift
override func awakeFromNib() {
    super.awakeFromNib()

    update(with: nil)
}

override func prepareForReuse() {
    super.prepareForReuse()

    update(with: nil)
}
```

You will use a prototype cell to set up the interface for the collection view cell in the storyboard, just as you did in Chapter 12 for `ItemCell`. If you recall, each prototype cell corresponds to a visually unique cell with a unique reuse identifier. Most of the time, the prototype cells will be associated with different **UICollectionViewCell** subclasses to provide behavior specific to that kind of cell.

In the collection view's attributes inspector, you can adjust the number of Items that the collection view displays, and each item corresponds to a prototype cell in the canvas. For Photorama, you only need one kind of cell: the **PhotoCollectionViewCell** that displays a photo.

Open `Main.storyboard` and select the collection view cell. In the identity inspector, change the Class to PhotoCollectionViewCell (Figure 21.8) and, in the attributes inspector, change the Identifier to PhotoCollectionViewCell.

Figure 21.8 Changing the cell class

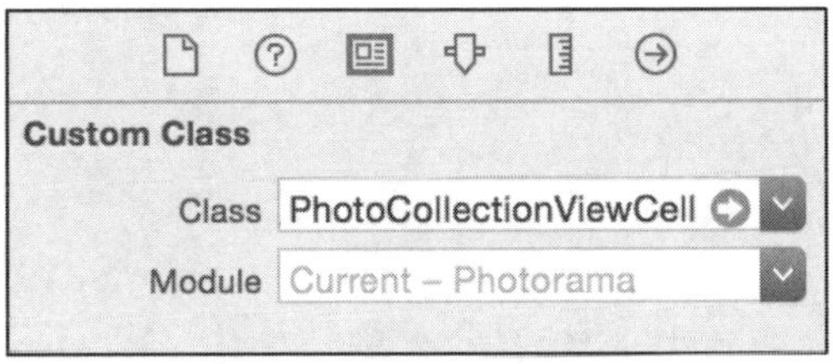

Drag an image view onto the UICollectionViewCell. Add constraints to pin the image view to the edges of the cell. Open the attributes inspector for the image view and set the Content Mode to Aspect Fill. This will cut off parts of the photos, but it will allow the photos to completely fill in the collection view cell.

Next, drag an activity indicator view on top of the image view. Add constraints to center the activity indicator view both horizontally and vertically with the image view. Open its attributes inspector and select Hides When Stopped (Figure 21.9).

Figure 21.9 Configuring the activity indicator

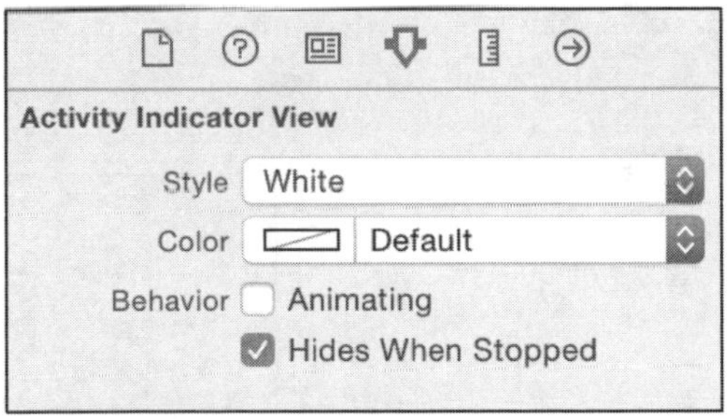

Select the collection view cell again. This can be a bit tricky to do on the canvas because the newly added subviews completely cover the cell itself. A helpful Interface Builder tip is to hold Control and Shift together and then click on top of the view you want to select. You will be presented with a list of all of the views and controllers under the point you clicked (Figure 21.10).

Figure 21.10 Selecting the cell on the canvas

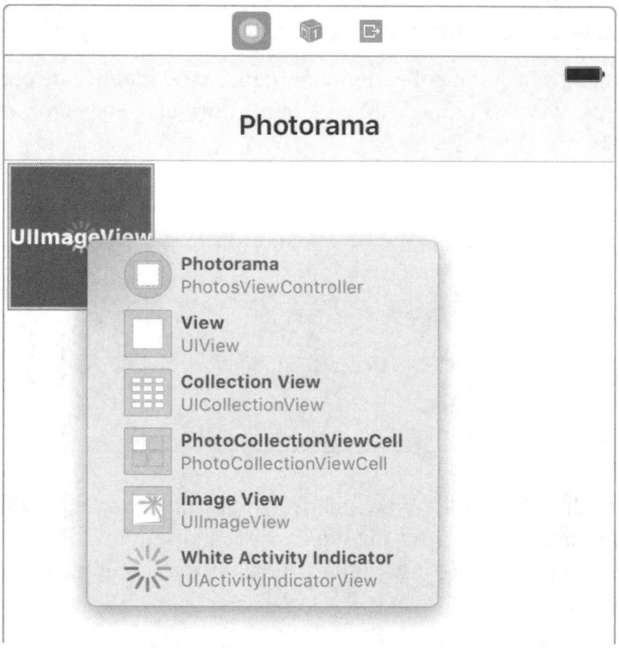

With the cell selected, open the connections inspector and connect the imageView and spinner properties to the image view and activity indicator view on the canvas (Figure 21.11).

Figure 21.11 Connecting **PhotoCollectionViewCell** outlets

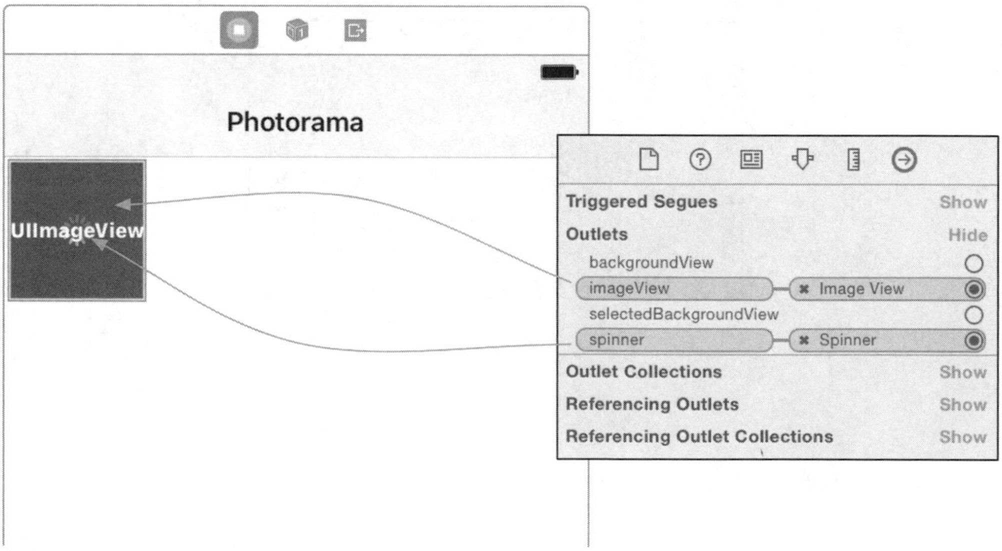

Next, open PhotoDataSource.swift and update the data source method to use the
PhotoCollectionViewCell.

```
func collectionView(_ collectionView: UICollectionView,
                    cellForItemAt indexPath: IndexPath) -> UICollectionViewCell {

    let identifier = "UICollectionViewCell" "PhotoCollectionViewCell"
    let cell =
        collectionView.dequeueReusableCell(withReuseIdentifier: identifier,
                                           for: indexPath) as! PhotoCollectionViewCell

    return cell
}
```

Build and run the application. When the interesting photos request completes, you will see the activity
indicator views all spinning (Figure 21.12).

Figure 21.12 Custom collection view subclass

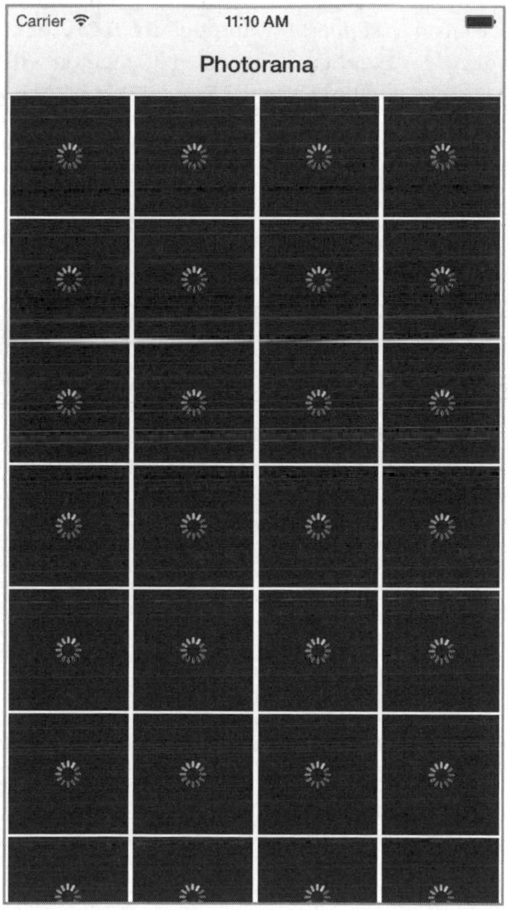

Downloading the Image Data

Now all that is left is downloading the image data for the photos that come back in the request. This task is not very difficult, but it requires some thought. Images are large files, and downloading them could eat up your users' cellular data allowance. As a considerate iOS developer, you want to make sure your app's data usage is only what it needs to be.

Consider your options. You could download the image data in **viewDidLoad()** when the **fetchInterestingPhotos(completion:)** method calls its completion closure. At that point, you already assign the incoming photos to the photos property, so you could iterate over all of those photos and download their image data then.

Although this would work, it would be very costly. There could be a large number of photos coming back in the initial request, and the user may never even scroll down in the application far enough to see some of them. On top of that, if you initialize too many requests simultaneously, some of the requests may time out while waiting for other requests to finish. So this is probably not the best solution.

Instead, it makes sense to download the image data for only the cells that the user is attempting to view. **UICollectionView** has a mechanism to support this through its **UICollectionViewDelegate** method **collectionView(_:willDisplay:forItemAt:)**. This delegate method will be called every time a cell is getting displayed onscreen and is a great opportunity to download the image data.

Recall that the data for the collection view is driven by an instance of **PhotoDataSource**, a reusable class with the single responsibility of displaying photos in a collection view. Collection views also have a delegate, which is responsible for handling user interaction with the collection view. This includes tasks such as managing cell selection and tracking cells coming into and out of view. This responsibility is more tightly coupled with the view controller itself, so whereas the data source is an instance of **PhotoDataSource**, the collection view's delegate will be the **PhotosViewController**.

In PhotosViewController.swift, have the class conform to the **UICollectionViewDelegate** protocol.

```
class PhotosViewController: UIViewController, UICollectionViewDelegate {
```

(Because the **UICollectionViewDelegate** protocol only defines optional methods, Xcode does not report any errors when you add this declaration.)

Update **viewDidLoad()** to set the **PhotosViewController** as the delegate of the collection view.

```
override func viewDidLoad() {
    super.viewDidLoad()

    collectionView.dataSource = photoDataSource
    collectionView.delegate = self
```

Finally, implement the delegate method in PhotosViewController.swift.

```swift
func collectionView(_ collectionView: UICollectionView,
                    willDisplay cell: UICollectionViewCell,
                    forItemAt indexPath: IndexPath) {

    let photo = photoDataSource.photos[indexPath.row]

    // Download the image data, which could take some time
    store.fetchImage(for: photo) { (result) -> Void in

        // The index path for the photo might have changed between the
        // time the request started and finished, so find the most
        // recent index path

        // (Note: You will have an error on the next line; you will fix it soon)
        guard let photoIndex = self.photoDataSource.photos.index(of: photo),
            case let .success(image) = result else {
                return
        }
        let photoIndexPath = IndexPath(item: photoIndex, section: 0)

        // When the request finishes, only update the cell if it's still visible
        if let cell = self.collectionView.cellForItem(at: photoIndexPath)
                                                as? PhotoCollectionViewCell {
            cell.update(with: image)
        }
    }
}
```

You are using a new form of pattern matching in the above code. The result that is returned from **fetchImage(for:completion:)** is an enumeration with two cases: **.success** and **.failure**. Because you only need to handle the **.success** case, you use a case statement to check whether result has a value of **.success**. Compare the following code to see how you could use pattern matching in an if statement versus a switch statement.

This code:

```swift
if case let .success(image) = result {
    photo.image = image
}
```

behaves just like this code:

```swift
switch result {
case let .success(image):
    photo.image = image
case .failure:
    break
}
```

Let's fix the error you saw when finding the index of photo in the photos array. The **index(of:)** method works by comparing the item that you are looking for to each of the items in the collection. It does this using the == operator. Types that conform to the **Equatable** protocol must implement this operator, and **Photo** does not yet conform to **Equatable**.

In Photo.swift, declare that **Photo** conforms to the **Equatable** protocol and implement the required overloading of the == operator.

```
class Photo: Equatable {
    ...
    static func == (lhs: Photo, rhs: Photo) -> Bool {
        // Two Photos are the same if they have the same photoID
        return lhs.photoID == rhs.photoID
    }
}
```

In Swift, it is common to group related chunks of functionality into an *extension*. Let's take a short detour to learn about extensions and then use this knowledge to see how conforming to the **Equatable** protocol is often done in practice.

Extensions

Extensions serve a couple of purposes: They allow you to group chunks of functionality into a logical unit, and they also allow you to add functionality to your own types as well as types provided by the system or other frameworks. Being able to add functionality to a type whose source code you do not have access to is a very powerful and flexible tool. Extensions can be added to classes, structs, and enums. Let's take a look at an example.

Say you wanted to add functionality to the **Int** type to provide a doubled value of that **Int**. For example:

```
let fourteen = 7.doubled // The value of fourteen is '14'
```

You can add this functionality by extending the **Int** type:

```
extension Int {
    var doubled: Int {
        return self * 2
    }
}
```

With extensions, you can add computed properties, add methods, and conform to protocols. However, you cannot add stored properties to an extension.

Extensions provide a great mechanism for grouping related pieces of functionality. They can make the code more readable and help with long-term maintainability of your code base. One common chunk of functionality that is often grouped into an extension is conformance to a protocol along with the methods of that protocol.

Update Photo.swift to use an extension to conform to the **Equatable** protocol.

```
class Photo: Equatable {
    ...
    static func == (lhs: Photo, rhs: Photo) -> Bool {
        // Two Photos are the same if they have the same photoID
        return lhs.photoID == rhs.photoID
    }
}

extension Photo: Equatable {
    static func == (lhs: Photo, rhs: Photo) -> Bool {
        // Two Photos are the same if they have the same photoID
        return lhs.photoID == rhs.photoID
    }
}
```

This is a simplified example, but extensions are very powerful for both extending existing types and grouping related functionality. In fact, the Swift standard library makes extensive use of extensions – and you will, too.

Build and run the application. The image data will download for the cells visible onscreen (Figure 21.13). Scroll down to make more cells visible. At first, you will see the activity indicator views spinning, but soon the image data for those cells will load.

Figure 21.13 Image downloads in progress

If you scroll back up, you will see a delay in loading the image data for the previously visible cells. This is because whenever a cell comes onscreen, the image data is redownloaded. To fix this, you will implement image caching, similar to what you did in the Homepwner application.

Image caching

For the image data, you will use the same approach that you used in your Homepwner application. In fact, you will use the same **ImageStore** class that you wrote for that project.

Open Homepwner.xcodeproj and drag the ImageStore.swift file from the Homepwner application to the Photorama application. Make sure to choose Copy items if needed. Once the ImageStore.swift file has been added to Photorama, you can close the Homepwner project.

Back in Photorama, open PhotoStore.swift and give it a property for an **ImageStore**.

```
class PhotoStore {

    let imageStore = ImageStore()
```

Then update **fetchImage(for:completion:)** to save the images using the imageStore.

```
func fetchImage(for photo: Photo, completion: @escaping (ImageResult) -> Void) {

    let photoKey = photo.photoID
    if let image = imageStore.image(forKey: photoKey) {
        OperationQueue.main.addOperation {
            completion(.success(image))
        }
        return
    }

    let photoURL = photo.remoteURL
    let request = URLRequest(url: photoURL)

    let task = session.dataTask(with: request) {
        (data, response, error) -> Void in

        let result = self.processImageRequest(data: data, error: error)

        if case let .success(image) = result {
            self.imageStore.setImage(image, forKey: photoKey)
        }

        OperationQueue.main.addOperation {
            completion(result)
        }
    }
    task.resume()
}
```

Build and run the application. Now when the image data is downloaded, it will be saved to the filesystem. The next time that photo is requested, it will be loaded from the filesystem if it is not currently in memory.

Navigating to a Photo

In this section, you are going to add functionality to allow a user to navigate to and display a single photo.

Create a new Swift file named PhotoInfoViewController, declare the **PhotoInfoViewController** class, and add an imageView outlet.

```
import Foundation
import UIKit

class PhotoInfoViewController: UIViewController {

    @IBOutlet var imageView: UIImageView!
}
```

Now set up the interface for this view controller. Open Main.storyboard and drag a new View Controller onto the canvas from the object library. With this view controller selected, open its identity inspector and change the Class to PhotoInfoViewController.

When the user taps on one of the collection view cells, the application will navigate to this new view controller. Control-drag from the PhotoCollectionViewCell to the Photo Info View Controller and select the Show segue. With the new segue selected, open its attributes inspector and give the segue an Identifier of showPhoto (Figure 21.14).

Figure 21.14 Navigation to a photo

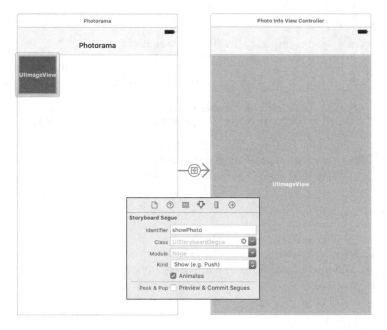

Add an image view to the Photo Info View Controller's view. Set up its Auto Layout constraints to pin the image view to all four sides. Open the attributes inspector for the image view and set its Content Mode to Aspect Fit.

Finally, connect the image view to the imageView outlet.

When the user taps a cell, the showPhoto segue will be triggered. At this point, the
PhotosViewController will need to pass both the Photo and the PhotoStore to the
PhotoInfoViewController.

Open PhotoInfoViewController.swift and add two properties.

```
class PhotoInfoViewController: UIViewController {

    @IBOutlet var imageView: UIImageView!

    var photo: Photo! {
        didSet {
            navigationItem.title = photo.title
        }
    }
    var store: PhotoStore!
}
```

When photo is set on this view controller, the navigation item will be updated to display the name of
the photo.

Now override **viewDidLoad()** to set the image on the imageView when the view is loaded.

```
override func viewDidLoad() {
    super.viewDidLoad()

    store.fetchImage(for: photo) { (result) -> Void in
        switch result {
        case let .success(image):
            self.imageView.image = image
        case let .failure(error):
            print("Error fetching image for photo: \(error)")
        }
    }
}
```

In PhotosViewController.swift, implement **prepare(for:sender:)** to pass along the photo and the
store.

```
override func prepare(for segue: UIStoryboardSegue, sender: Any?) {
    switch segue.identifier {
    case "showPhoto"?:
        if let selectedIndexPath =
                collectionView.indexPathsForSelectedItems?.first {

            let photo = photoDataSource.photos[selectedIndexPath.row]

            let destinationVC = segue.destination as! PhotoInfoViewController
            destinationVC.photo = photo
            destinationVC.store = store
        }
    default:
        preconditionFailure("Unexpected segue identifier.")
    }
}
```

Build and run the application. After the web service request has finished, tap on one of the photos to see it in the new view controller (Figure 21.15).

Figure 21.15 Displaying a photo

Collection views are a powerful way to display data using a flexible layout. You have just barely tapped into the power of collection views in this chapter.

Silver Challenge: Updated Item Sizes

Have the collection view always display four items per row, taking up as much as the screen width as possible. This should work in both portrait and landscape orientations.

Gold Challenge: Creating a Custom Layout

Create a custom layout that displays the photos in a flipbook. You will need to use the `transform` property on the cell layer to get an appropriate 3-D effect. You can subclass **UICollectionViewLayout** for this challenge, but also consider subclassing **UICollectionViewFlowLayout**. Check out the class reference for **UICollectionViewLayout** for more information.

22

Core Data

When deciding between approaches to saving and loading for iOS applications, the first question is "Local or remote?" If you want to save data to a remote server, you will likely use a web service. If you want to store data locally, you have to ask another question: "Archiving or Core Data?"

Your Homepwner application used keyed archiving to save item data to the filesystem. The biggest drawback to archiving is its all-or-nothing nature: To access anything in the archive, you must unarchive the entire file, and to save any changes, you must rewrite the entire file. Core Data, on the other hand, can fetch a subset of the stored objects. And if you change any of those objects, you can update just that part of the file. This incremental fetching, updating, deleting, and inserting can radically improve the performance of your application when you have a lot of model objects being shuttled between the filesystem and RAM.

Object Graphs

Core Data is a framework that lets you express what your model objects are and how they are related to one another. It then takes control of the lifetimes of these objects, making sure the relationships are kept up to date. When you save and load the objects, Core Data makes sure everything is consistent. This collection of model objects is often called an *object graph*, as the objects can be thought of as nodes and the relationships as vertices in a mathematical graph.

Often you will have Core Data save your object graph to a SQLite database. Developers who are used to other SQL technologies might expect to treat Core Data like an object-relational mapping system, but this mindset will lead to confusion. Unlike an ORM, Core Data takes complete control of the storage, which just happens to be a relational database. You do not have to describe things like the database schema and foreign keys – Core Data does that. You just tell Core Data *what* needs storing and let it work out *how* to store it.

Core Data gives you the ability to fetch and store data in a relational database without having to know the details of the underlying storage mechanism. This chapter will give you an understanding of Core Data as you add persistence to the Photorama application.

Entities

A relational database has something called a *table*. A table represents a type: You can have a table of people, a table of a credit card purchases, or a table of real estate listings. Each table has a number of columns to hold pieces of information about the type. A table that represents people might have columns for last name, date of birth, and height. Every row in the table represents an example of the type – e.g., a single person.

This organization translates well to Swift. Every table is like a Swift type. Every column is one of the type's properties. Every row is an instance of that type. Thus, Core Data's job is to move data to and from these two representations (Figure 22.1).

Figure 22.1 Role of Core Data

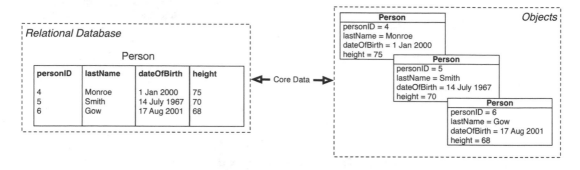

Core Data uses different terminology to describe these ideas: A table/type is called an *entity*, and the columns/properties are called *attributes*. A Core Data model file is the description of every entity along with its attributes in your application. In Photorama, you are going to describe a **Photo** entity in a model file and give it attributes like `title`, `remoteURL`, and `dateTaken`.

Modeling entities

Open `Photorama.xcodeproj`. Create a new file, but do not make it a Swift file like the ones you have created before. Instead, select iOS at the top and scroll down to the Core Data section. Create a new Data Model (Figure 22.2). Name it `Photorama`.

Figure 22.2 Creating the model file

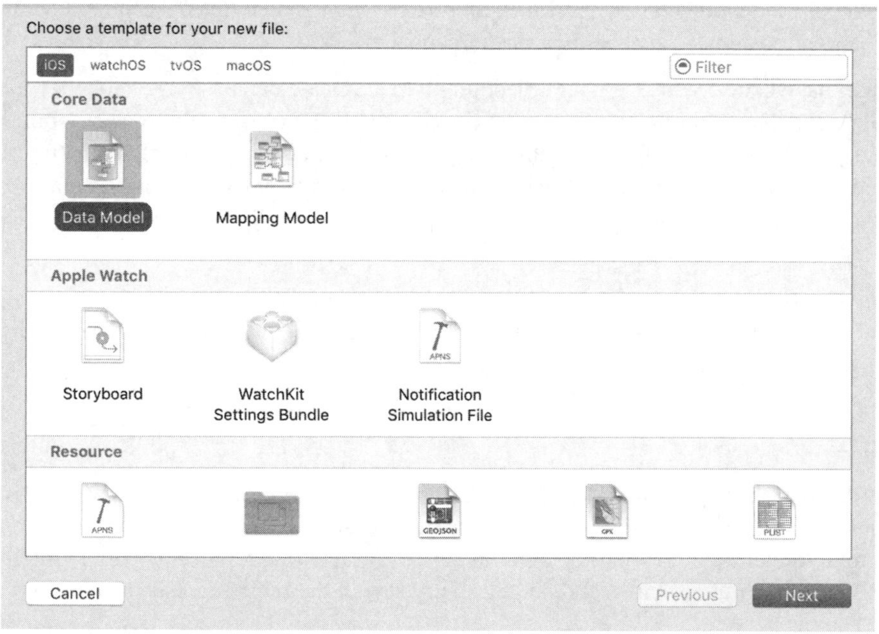

This will create the `Photorama.xcdatamodeld` file and add it to your project. Select this file from the project navigator and the editor area will reveal the UI for manipulating a Core Data model file.

Find the Add Entity button at the bottom left of the window and click it. A new entity will appear in the list of entities in the lefthand table. Double-click this entity and change its name to **Photo** (Figure 22.3).

Figure 22.3 Creating the **Photo** entity

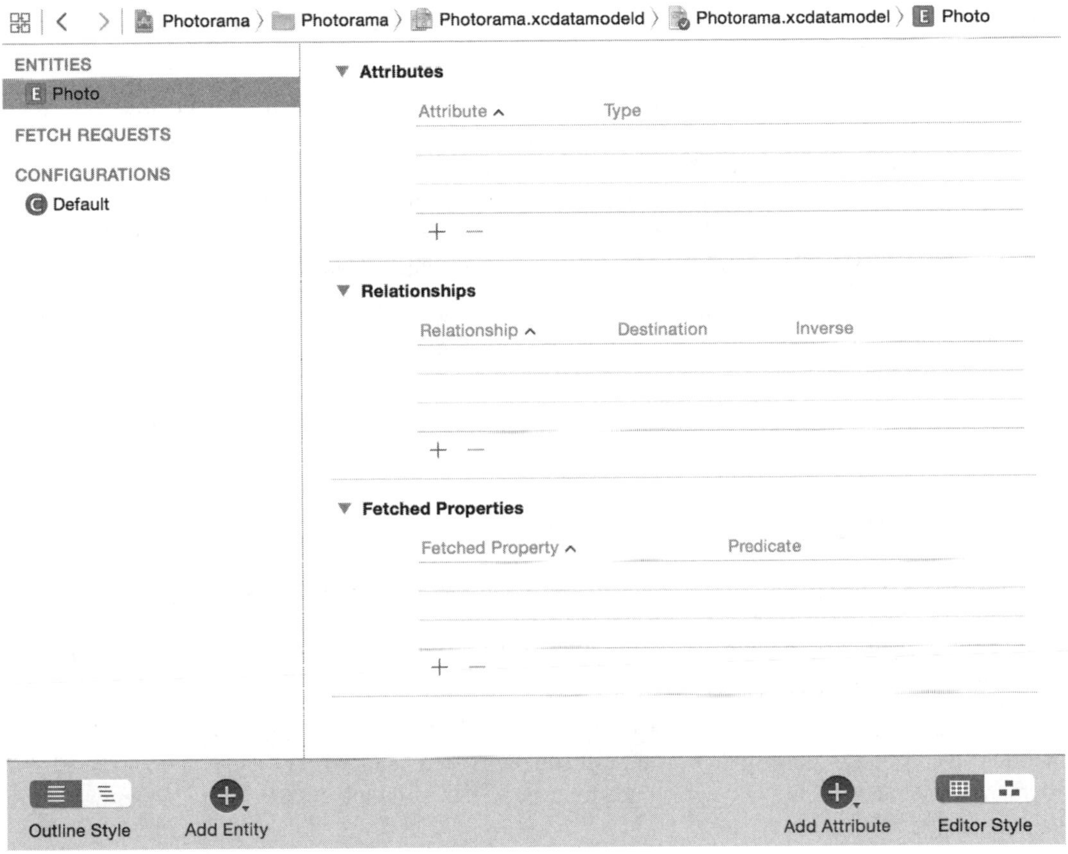

Now your **Photo** entity needs attributes. Remember that these will be the properties of the **Photo** class. The necessary attributes are listed below. For each attribute, click the + button in the Attributes section and edit the Attribute and Type values.

- `photoID` is a String.

- `title` is a String.

- `dateTaken` is a Date.

- `remoteURL` is a Transformable. (It is a **URL**, but that is not one of the possibilities. We will discuss "transformable" next.)

405

Transformable attributes

Core Data is only able to store certain data types in its store. **URL** is not one of these types, so you declared the remoteURL attribute as *transformable*. With a transformable attribute, Core Data will convert the object into a type that it can store when saving and then convert it back to the original object when loading from the filesystem.

Core Data works with classes under the hood because it is an Objective-C framework. So instead of working with an instance of **URL** (which is a struct), you will work with an instance of **NSURL** (which is a class) when dealing with Core Data. Swift provides a mechanism for converting a **URL** to an **NSURL** and vice versa, which you will see later on in this chapter.

A transformable attribute requires a **ValueTransformer** subclass to handle the conversions between types. If you do not specify a custom subclass, the system will use the transformer named **NSKeyedUnarchiveFromDataTransformer**. This transformer uses archiving to convert the object to and from **Data**. Because **NSURL** conforms to **NSCoding**, the default **NSKeyedUnarchiveFromDataTransformer** will be sufficient. If the type you wanted to transform did not conform to **NSCoding**, you would need to write your own custom **ValueTransformer** subclass.

With Photorama.xcdatamodeld still open, select the remoteURL attribute and open its Data Model inspector on the righthand side. Under the Attribute section, enter NSURL as the Custom Class. This will allow Core Data to do the transformation for you.

At this point, your model file is sufficient to save and load photos. In the next section, you will create a custom subclass for the **Photo** entity.

NSManagedObject and subclasses

When an object is fetched with Core Data, its class, by default, is **NSManagedObject**. **NSManagedObject** is a subclass of **NSObject** that knows how to cooperate with the rest of Core Data. An **NSManagedObject** works a bit like a dictionary: It holds a key-value pair for every property (attribute or relationship) in the entity.

An **NSManagedObject** is little more than a data container. If you need your model objects to *do* something in addition to holding data, you must subclass **NSManagedObject**. Then, in your model file, you specify that this entity is represented by instances of your subclass, not the standard **NSManagedObject**.

Xcode can generate **NSManagedObject** subclasses for you based on what you have defined in your Core Data model file.

In the project navigator, select the Photo.swift file and delete it. When prompted, move it to the trash to make sure it does not still exist in the project directory.

Open Photorama.xcdatamodeld. Select the Photo entity and open the Data Model inspector. Locate the Codegen option and select Manual/None.

With the Photo entity still selected, open the Editor menu and select Create NSManagedObject Subclass.... On the next screen, check the box for Photorama and click Next. Check the box for the Photo entity and click Next again. Finally, click Create. There will be a few errors in the project. You will fix those shortly.

The template will create two files for you: Photo+CoreDataClass.swift and Photo
+CoreDataProperties.swift. The template places all of the attributes that you defined in the model
file into Photo+CoreDataProperties.swift. If you ever change your entity in the model file, you
can simply delete Photo+CoreDataProperties.swift and regenerate the **NSManagedObject** subclass.
Xcode will recognize that you already have Photo+CoreDataClass.swift and will only re-create
Photo+CoreDataProperties.swift.

Open Photo+CoreDataProperties.swift and take a look at what the template created for you.

All of the properties are marked with the @NSManaged keyword. This keyword, which is specific to
Core Data, lets the compiler know that the storage and implementation of these properties will be
provided at runtime. Because Core Data will create the **NSManagedObject** instances, you can no longer
use a custom initializer, so the properties are declared as variables instead of constants. Any custom
properties or code that you want to add should be added to Photo+CoreDataClass.swift.

Let's fix some of the errors that are in the project.

Open PhotoStore.swift and find **fetchImage(for:completion:)**. This method expects the
photoID and the remoteURL to be non-optional; however, Core Data models its attributes as optionals.
Additionally, the **URLRequest** initializer expects a **URL** instance as its argument instead of an **NSURL**
instance. Update the method to address these issues.

```
func fetchImage(for photo: Photo, completion: @escaping (ImageResult) -> Void) {

        guard let photoKey = photo.photoID else {
            preconditionFailure("Photo expected to have a photoID.")
        }
        if let image = imageStore.image(forKey: photoKey) {
            OperationQueue.main.addOperation {
                completion(.success(image))
            }
            return
        }

        guard let photoURL = photo.remoteURL else {
            preconditionFailure("Photo expected to have a remote URL.")
        }
        let request = URLRequest(url: photoURL as URL)
```

To address the first issue, you are using a guard statement to unwrap the optional **NSURL**. To address
the second issue, you bridge the **NSURL** instance to a **URL** instance using an as cast. The compiler knows
that **NSURL** and **URL** are related, so it handles the bridging conversion.

You have created your model graph and defined your **Photo** entity. The next step is to set up the
persistent container, which will manage the interactions between the application and Core Data. There
are still some errors in the project; you will fix them after you have added a Core Data persistent
container instance.

NSPersistentContainer

Core Data is represented by a collection of classes often referred to as the *Core Data stack*. This collection of classes is abstracted away from you via the **NSPersistentContainer** class. You will learn more about the Core Data stack classes in the For the More Curious section at the end of this chapter.

To use Core Data, you will need to import the Core Data framework in the files that need it.

Open PhotoStore.swift and import Core Data at the top of the file.

```
import UIKit
import CoreData
```

Also in PhotoStore.swift, add a property to hold on to an instance of **NSPersistentContainer**.

```
class PhotoStore {

    let imageStore = ImageStore()

    let persistentContainer: NSPersistentContainer = {
        let container = NSPersistentContainer(name: "Photorama")
        container.loadPersistentStores { (description, error) in
            if let error = error {
                print("Error setting up Core Data (\(error)).")
            }
        }
        return container
    }()
```

You instantiate an **NSPersistentContainer** with a name. This name must match the name of the data model file that describes your entities. After creating the container, it needs to load its persistent stores. The store is where the data is actually stored on disk. By default, this is going to be a SQLite database. Due to the possibility of this operation taking some time, loading the persistent stores is an asynchronous operation that calls a completion handler when complete.

Updating Items

With the persistent container set up, you can now interact with Core Data. Primarily, you will do this through its viewContext. This is how you will both create new entities and save changes.

The viewContext is an instance of **NSManagedObjectContext**. This is the portal through which you interact with your entities. You can think of the managed object context as an intelligent scratch pad. When you ask the context to fetch some entities, the context will work with its persistent store coordinator to bring temporary copies of the entities and object graph into memory. Unless you ask the context to save its changes, the persisted data remains the same.

Inserting into the context

When an entity is created, it should be inserted into a managed object context.

Open FlickrAPI.swift and import CoreData.

```
import Foundation
import CoreData
```

Next, update the **photo(fromJSON:)** method to take in an additional argument of type **NSManagedObjectContext** and use this context to insert new **Photo** instances.

```
private static func photo(fromJSON json: [String : Any],
                        into context: NSManagedObjectContext) -> Photo? {
    guard
        let photoID = json["id"] as? String,
        let title = json["title"] as? String,
        let dateString = json["datetaken"] as? String,
        let photoURLString = json["url_h"] as? String,
        let url = URL(string: photoURLString),
        let dateTaken = dateFormatter.date(from: dateString) else {

            // Don't have enough information to construct a Photo
            return nil
    }

    return Photo(title: title, photoID: photoID, remoteURL: url, dateTaken: dateTaken)

    var photo: Photo!
    context.performAndWait {
        photo = Photo(context: context)
        photo.title = title
        photo.photoID = photoID
        photo.remoteURL = url as NSURL
        photo.dateTaken = dateTaken as NSDate
    }

    return photo
}
```

Each **NSManagedObjectContext** is associated with a specific concurrency queue, and the viewContext is associated with the main, or UI, queue. You have to interact with a context on the queue that it is associated with. **NSManagedObjectContext** has two methods that ensure this happens: **perform(_:)** and **performAndWait(_:)**. The difference between them is that **perform(_:)** is asynchronous and **performAndWait(_:)** is synchronous. Because you are returning the result of the insert operation from the **photo(fromJSON:into:)** method, you use the synchronous method.

The **photo(fromJSON:into:)** method is called from the method **photos(fromJSON:)**. Update this method to take in a context and pass it to the **photo(fromJSON:into:)** method.

```
static func photos(fromJSON data: Data,
                   into context: NSManagedObjectContext) -> PhotosResult {
    do {
        ...
        var finalPhotos = [Photo]()
        for photoJSON in photosArray {
            if let photo = photo(fromJSON: photoJSON, into: context) {
                finalPhotos.append(photo)
            }
        }
    }
```

Finally, you need to pass the viewContext to the **FlickrAPI** struct once the web service request successfully completes.

Open PhotoStore.swift and update **processPhotosRequest(data:error:)**.

```
private func processPhotosRequest(data: Data?, error: Error?) -> PhotosResult {
    guard let jsonData = data else {
        return .failure(error!)
    }

    return FlickrAPI.photos(fromJSON: jsonData,
                            into: persistentContainer.viewContext)
}
```

Build and run the application now that all errors have been addressed. Although the behavior remains unchanged, the application is now backed by Core Data. In the next section, you will implement saving for both the photos and their associated image data.

Saving changes

Recall that **NSManagedObject** changes do not persist until you tell the context to save these changes.

Open PhotoStore.swift and update **fetchInterestingPhotos(completion:)** to save the changes to the context after **Photo** entities have been inserted into the context.

```
func fetchInterestingPhotos(completion: @escaping (PhotosResult) -> Void) {

    let url = FlickrAPI.interestingPhotosURL
    let request = URLRequest(url: url)
    let task = session.dataTask(with: request) {
        (data, response, error) -> Void in

        let var result = self.processPhotosRequest(data: data, error: error)

        if case .success = result {
            do {
                try self.persistentContainer.viewContext.save()
            } catch let error {
                result = .failure(error)
            }
        }

        OperationQueue.main.addOperation {
            completion(result)
        }
    }
    task.resume()
}
```

Updating the Data Source

One problem with the app at the moment is that `fetchInterestingPhotos(completion:)` only returns the newly inserted photos. Now that the application supports saving, it should return all of the photos – the previously saved photos as well as the newly inserted ones. You need to ask Core Data for all of the **Photo** entities, and you will accomplish this using a *fetch request*.

Fetch requests and predicates

To get objects back from the **NSManagedObjectContext**, you must prepare and execute an **NSFetchRequest**. After a fetch request is executed, you will get an array of all the objects that match the parameters of that request.

A fetch request needs an entity description that defines which entity you want to get objects from. To fetch **Photo** instances, you specify the **Photo** entity. You can also set the request's *sort descriptors* to specify the order of the objects in the array. A sort descriptor has a key that maps to an attribute of the entity and a **Bool** that indicates whether the order should be ascending or descending.

The `sortDescriptors` property on **NSFetchRequest** is an array of **NSSortDescriptor** instances. Why an array? The array is useful if you think there might be collisions when sorting. For example, say you are sorting an array of people by their last names. It is entirely possible that multiple people have the same last name, so you can specify that people with the same last name should be sorted by their first names. This would be implemented by an array of two **NSSortDescriptor** instances. The first sort descriptor would have a key that maps to the person's last name, and the second sort descriptor would have a key that maps to the person's first name.

A *predicate* is represented by the **NSPredicate** class and contains a condition that can be true or false. If you wanted to find all photos with a given identifier, you would create a predicate and add it to the fetch request like this:

```
let predicate = NSPredicate(format: "#keyPath(Photo.photoID) == \(someIdentifier)")
request.predicate = predicate
```

The format string for a predicate can be very long and complex. Apple's *Predicate Programming Guide* is a complete discussion of what is possible.

You want to sort the returned instances of **Photo** by `dateTaken` in descending order. To do this, you will instantiate an **NSFetchRequest** for requesting "Photo" entities. Then you will give the fetch request an array of **NSSortDescriptor** instances. For Photorama, this array will contain a single sort descriptor that sorts photos by their `dateTaken` properties. Finally, you will ask the managed object context to execute this fetch request.

In `PhotoStore.swift`, implement a method that will fetch the **Photo** instances from the view context.

```
func fetchAllPhotos(completion: @escaping (PhotosResult) -> Void) {
    let fetchRequest: NSFetchRequest<Photo> = Photo.fetchRequest()
    let sortByDateTaken = NSSortDescriptor(key: #keyPath(Photo.dateTaken),
                                           ascending: true)
    fetchRequest.sortDescriptors = [sortByDateTaken]

    let viewContext = persistentContainer.viewContext
    viewContext.perform {
        do {
            let allPhotos = try viewContext.fetch(fetchRequest)
            completion(.success(allPhotos))
        } catch {
            completion(.failure(error))
        }
    }
}
```

Next, open `PhotosViewController.swift` and add a new method that will update the data source with all of the photos.

```
private func updateDataSource() {
    store.fetchAllPhotos {
        (photosResult) in

        switch photosResult {
        case let .success(photos):
            self.photoDataSource.photos = photos
        case .failure:
            self.photoDataSource.photos.removeAll()
        }
        self.collectionView.reloadSections(IndexSet(integer: 0))
    }
}
```

Now update **viewDidLoad()** to call this method to fetch and display all of the photos saved to Core Data.

```
override func viewDidLoad() {
    super.viewDidLoad()

    collectionView.dataSource = photoDataSource
    collectionView.delegate = self

    store.fetchInterestingPhotos {
        (photosResult) -> Void in

        switch photosResult {
        case let .success(photos):
            print("Successfully found \(photos.count) photos.")
            self.photoDataSource.photos = photos
        case let .failure(error):
            print("Error fetching interesting photos: \(error)")
            self.photoDataSource.photos.removeAll()
        }
        self.collectionView.reloadSections(IndexSet(integer: 0))

        self.updateDataSource()
    }
}
```

Previously saved photos will now be returned when the web service request finishes. But there is still one problem: If the application is run multiple times and the same photo is returned from the web service request, it will be inserted into the context multiple times. This is not good – you do not want duplicate photos. Luckily there is a unique identifier for each photo. When the interesting photos web service request finishes, the identifier for each photo in the incoming JSON data can be compared to the photos stored in Core Data. If one is found with the same identifier, that photo will be returned. Otherwise, a new photo will be inserted into the context.

To do this, you need a way to tell the fetch request that it should not return all photos but instead only the photos that match some specific criteria. In this case, the specific criteria is "only photos that have this specific identifier," of which there should either be zero or one photo. In Core Data, this is done with a predicate.

In FlickrAPI.swift, update **photo(fromJSON:into:)** to check whether there is an existing photo with a given ID before inserting a new one.

```
private static func photo(fromJSON json: [String : Any],
                          into context: NSManagedObjectContext) -> Photo? {
    guard
        let photoID = json["id"] as? String,
        let title = json["title"] as? String,
        let dateString = json["datetaken"] as? String,
        let photoURLString = json["url_h"] as? String,
        let url = URL(string: photoURLString),
        let dateTaken = dateFormatter.date(from: dateString) else {

            // Don't have enough information to construct a Photo
            return nil
    }

    let fetchRequest: NSFetchRequest<Photo> = Photo.fetchRequest()
    let predicate = NSPredicate(format: "\(#keyPath(Photo.photoID)) == \(photoID)")
    fetchRequest.predicate = predicate

    var fetchedPhotos: [Photo]?
    context.performAndWait {
        fetchedPhotos = try? fetchRequest.execute()
    }
    if let existingPhoto = fetchedPhotos?.first {
        return existingPhoto
    }

    var photo: Photo!
    context.performAndWait {
        photo = Photo(context: context)
        photo.title = title
        photo.photoID = photoID
        photo.remoteURL = url as NSURL
        photo.dateTaken = dateTaken as NSDate
    }

    return photo

}
```

Duplicate photos will no longer be inserted into Core Data.

Build and run the application. The photos will appear just as they did before introducing Core Data. As you did in Chapter 16, close the application using the Home button (or Shift-Command-H in the simulator). Launch the application again and you will see the photos that Core Data saved in the collection view.

There is one last small problem to address: The user will not see any photos appear in the collection view unless the web service request completes. If the user has slow network access, it might take up to 60 seconds (which is the default timeout interval for the request) to see any photos. It would be best to see the previously saved photos immediately on launch and then refresh the collection view once new photos are fetched from Flickr.

Go ahead and do this. In `PhotosViewController.swift`, update the data source as soon as the view is loaded.

```
override func viewDidLoad() {
    super.viewDidLoad()

    collectionView.dataSource = photoDataSource
    collectionView.delegate = self

    updateDataSource()

    store.fetchInterestingPhotos {
        (photosResult) -> Void in

        self.updateDataSource()
    }
}
```

The Photorama application is now persisting its data between runs. The photo metadata is being persisted using Core Data, and the image data is being persisted directly to the filesystem. As you have seen, there is no one-size-fits-all approach to data persistence. Instead, each persistence mechanism has its own set of benefits and drawbacks. In this chapter, you have explored one of those, Core Data, but you have only seen the tip of the iceberg. In Chapter 23, you will explore the Core Data framework further to learn about relationships and performance.

Bronze Challenge: Photo View Count

Add an attribute to the **Photo** entity that tracks how many times a photo is viewed. Display this number somewhere on the **PhotoInfoViewController** interface.

For the More Curious: The Core Data Stack

NSManagedObjectModel

You worked with the model file earlier in the chapter. The model file is where you define the entities for your application along with their properties. The model file is an instance of **NSManagedObjectModel**.

NSPersistentStoreCoordinator

Core Data can persist data in several formats:

SQLite	Data is saved to disk using a SQLite database. This is the most commonly used store type.
Atomic	Data is saved to disk using a binary format.
XML	Data is saved to disk using an XML format. This store type is not available on iOS.
In-Memory	Data is not saved to disk, but instead is stored in memory.

The mapping between an object graph and the persistent store is accomplished using an instance of **NSPersistentStoreCoordinator**. The persistent store coordinator needs to know two things: "What are my entities?" and, "Where am I saving to and loading data from?" To answer these questions, you instantiate an **NSPersistentStoreCoordinator** with the **NSManagedObjectModel**. Then you add a persistent store, representing one of the persistence formats above, to the coordinator.

After the coordinator is created, you attempt to add a specific store to the coordinator. At a minimum, this store needs to know its type and where it should persist the data.

NSManagedObjectContext

The portal through which you interact with your entities is the **NSManagedObjectContext**. The managed object context is associated with a specific persistent store coordinator. You can think of the managed object context as an intelligent scratch pad. When you ask the context to fetch some entities, the context will work with its persistent store coordinator to bring temporary copies of the entities and object graph into memory. Unless you ask the context to save its changes, the persisted data remains the same.

23

Core Data Relationships

Core Data is not that exciting with just one entity. Much of the power behind Core Data comes to light when there are multiple entities that are related to one another, because Core Data manages *relationships* between entities.

In this chapter, you are going to add tags to the photos in Photorama with labels such as "Nature," "Electronics," or "Selfies." Users will be able to add one or more tags to photos and also create their own custom tags (Figure 23.1).

Figure 23.1 Final Photorama application

Relationships

One of the benefits of using Core Data is that entities can be related to one another in a way that allows you to describe complex models. Relationships between entities are represented by references between objects. There are two kinds of relationships: *to-one* and *to-many*.

When an entity has a to-one relationship, each instance of that entity will have a reference to an instance in the entity it has a relationship to.

When an entity has a to-many relationship, each instance of that entity has a reference to a **Set**. This set contains the instances of the entity that it has a relationship with. To see this in action, you are going to add a new entity to the model file.

Reopen the Photorama application. In `Photorama.xcdatamodeld`, add another entity called **Tag**. Give it an attribute called `name` of type **String**. **Tag** will allow users to tag photos.

Unlike with the **Photo** entity in Chapter 22, you will not generate an **NSManagedObject** subclass for the **Tag** entity. Instead, you will let Xcode autogenerate a subclass for you through a feature called *code generation*. If you do not need any custom behavior for your Core Data entity, letting Xcode generate your subclass for you is quite helpful.

The **NSManagedObject** subclass for the **Tag** entity is already being generated for you. To see the setting that determines this, select the **Tag** entity and open its data model inspector. In the Class section, notice the setting for Codegen: It is currently set to Class Definition. This setting means that an entire class definition will be generated for you. The other code generation settings are Category/Extension (which allows you to define an **NSManagedObject** subclass with custom behavior while still allowing Xcode to generate the extension that defines the attributes and relationships) and Manual/None (which tells Xcode not to generate any code for the entity).

A photo might have multiple tags that describe it, and a tag might be associated with multiple photos. For example, a picture of an iPhone might be tagged "Electronics" and "Apple," and a picture of a Betamax player might be tagged "Electronics" and "Rare." The **Tag** entity will have a to-many relationship to the **Photo** entity because many instances of **Photo** can have the same **Tag**. And the **Photo** entity will have a to-many relationship to the **Tag** entity because a photo can be associated with many **Tag**s.

As Figure 23.2 shows, a **Photo** will have a reference to a set of **Tag**s, and a **Tag** will have a reference to a set of **Photo**s.

Figure 23.2 Entities in Photorama

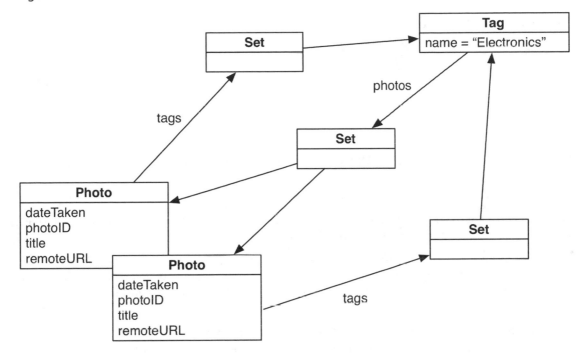

When these relationships are set up, you will be able to ask a **Photo** object for the set of **Tag** objects that it is associated with and ask a **Tag** object for the set of **Photo** objects that it is associated with.

To add these two relationships to the model file, first select the Tag entity and click the + button in the Relationships section. Click in the Relationship column and enter photos. In the Destination column, select Photo. In the data model inspector, change the Type dropdown from To One to To Many (Figure 23.3).

Figure 23.3 Creating the photos relationship

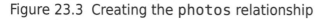

Next, select the **Photo** entity. Add a relationship named tags and pick Tag as its destination. In the data model inspector, change the Type dropdown to To Many and uncheck its Optional checkbox.

Now that you have two unidirectional relationships, you can make them into an *inverse relationship*. An inverse relationship is a bidirectional relationship between two entities. With an inverse relationship set up between **Photo** and **Tag**, Core Data can ensure that your object graph remains in a consistent state when any changes are made.

To create the inverse relationship, click the dropdown next to Inverse in the data model inspector and change it from No Inverse Relationship to photos (Figure 23.4). (You can also make this change in the Relationships section in the editor area by clicking No Inverse in the Inverse column and selecting photos.)

If you return to the **Tag** entity, you will see that the photos relationship now shows tags as its inverse.

Figure 23.4 Creating the tags relationship

Now that the model has changed for the **Photo** entity, you will need to regenerate the Photo +CoreDataProperties.swift file.

From the project navigator, select and delete the `Photo+CoreDataProperties.swift` file. Make sure to select Move to Trash when prompted. Open `Photorama.xcdatamodeld` and select the **Photo** entity. From the Editor menu, select Create NSManagedObject Subclass.... On the next screen, check the box for Photorama and click Next. Check the box for the Photo entity and click Next. Make sure you are creating the file in the same directory as the `Photo+CoreDataClass.swift` file; this will ensure that Xcode will only create the necessary `Photo+CoreDataProperties.swift` file. Once you have confirmed this, click Create.

Adding Tags to the Interface

When users navigate to a specific photo, they currently see only the title of the photo and the image itself. Let's update the interface to include a photo's associated tags.

Open `Main.storyboard` and navigate to the interface for Photo Info View Controller. Add a toolbar to the bottom of the view. Update the Auto Layout constraints so that the toolbar is anchored to the bottom, just as it was in Homepwner. The bottom constraint for the `imageView` should be anchored to the top of the toolbar instead of the bottom of the superview. Add a **UIBarButtonItem** to the toolbar, if one is not already present, and give it a title of Tags. Your interface will look like Figure 23.5.

Figure 23.5 Photo Info View Controller interface

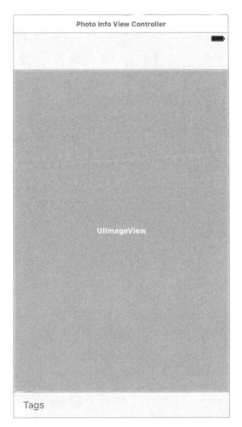

Create a new Swift file named TagsViewController. Open this file and declare the
TagsViewController class as a subclass of **UITableViewController**. Import UIKit and CoreData in
this file.

```
import Foundation
import UIKit
import CoreData

class TagsViewController: UITableViewController {

}
```

The **TagsViewController** will display a list of all the tags. The user will see and be able to select
the tags that are associated with a specific photo. The user will also be able to add new tags from this
screen. The completed interface will look like Figure 23.6.

Figure 23.6 **TagsViewController**

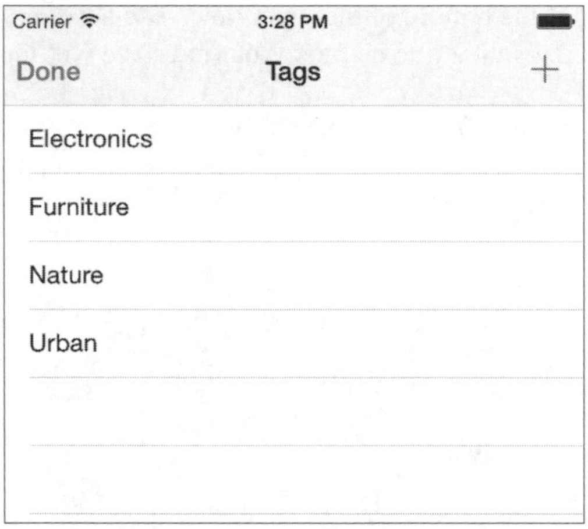

Give the **TagsViewController** class a property to reference the **PhotoStore** as well as a specific
Photo. You will also need a property to keep track of the currently selected tags, which you will track
using an array of **IndexPath** instances.

```
class TagsViewController: UITableViewController {

    var store: PhotoStore!
    var photo: Photo!

    var selectedIndexPaths = [IndexPath]()
}
```

The data source for the table view will be a separate class. As we discussed when you created
PhotoDataSource in Chapter 21, an application whose types have a single responsibility is easier to
adapt to future changes. This class will be responsible for displaying the list of tags in the table view.

Create a new Swift file named TagDataSource.swift. Declare the **TagDataSource** class and implement the table view data source methods. You will need to import UIKit and CoreData.

```
import Foundation
import UIKit
import CoreData

class TagDataSource: NSObject, UITableViewDataSource {

    var tags: [Tag] = []

    func tableView(_ tableView: UITableView,
                   numberOfRowsInSection section: Int) -> Int {
        return tags.count
    }

    func tableView(_ tableView: UITableView,
                   cellForRowAt indexPath: IndexPath) -> UITableViewCell {

        let cell = tableView.dequeueReusableCell(withIdentifier: "UITableViewCell",
                                                 for: indexPath)

        let tag = tags[indexPath.row]
        cell.textLabel?.text = tag.name

        return cell
    }

}
```

Open PhotoStore.swift and define a new result type at the top for use when fetching tags.

```
enum PhotosResult {
    case success([Photo])
    case failure(Error)
}

enum TagsResult {
    case success([Tag])
    case failure(Error)
}

class PhotoStore {
```

Now define a new method that fetches all the tags from the view context.

```
func fetchAllTags(completion: @escaping (TagsResult) -> Void) {
    let fetchRequest: NSFetchRequest<Tag> = Tag.fetchRequest()
    let sortByName = NSSortDescriptor(key: #keyPath(Tag.name), ascending: true)
    fetchRequest.sortDescriptors = [sortByName]

    let viewContext = persistentContainer.viewContext
    viewContext.perform {
        do {
            let allTags = try fetchRequest.execute()
            completion(.success(allTags))
        } catch {
            completion(.failure(error))
        }
    }
}
```

423

Open `TagsViewController.swift` and set the `dataSource` for the table view to be an instance of
TagDataSource.

```
class TagsViewController: UITableViewController {

    var store: PhotoStore!
    var photo: Photo!

    var selectedIndexPaths = [IndexPath]()

    let tagDataSource = TagDataSource()

    override func viewDidLoad() {
        super.viewDidLoad()

        tableView.dataSource = tagDataSource
    }
}
```

Now fetch the tags and associate them with the `tags` property on the data source.

```
override func viewDidLoad() {
    super.viewDidLoad()

    tableView.dataSource = tagDataSource

    updateTags()
}

func updateTags() {
    store.fetchAllTags {
        (tagsResult) in

        switch tagsResult {
        case let .success(tags):
            self.tagDataSource.tags = tags
        case let .failure(error):
            print("Error fetching tags: \(error).")
        }

        self.tableView.reloadSections(IndexSet(integer: 0),
                                        with: .automatic)
    }
}
```

The **TagsViewController** needs to manage the selection of tags and update the **Photo** instance when the user selects or deselects a tag.

In TagsViewController.swift, add the appropriate index paths to the selectedIndexPaths array.

```swift
override func viewDidLoad() {
    super.viewDidLoad()

    tableView.dataSource = tagDataSource
    tableView.delegate = self

    updateTags()
}

func updateTags() {
    store.fetchAllTags {
        (tagsResult) in

        switch tagsResult {
        case let .success(tags):
            self.tagDataSource.tags = tags

            guard let photoTags = self.photo.tags as? Set<Tag> else {
                return
            }

            for tag in photoTags {
                if let index = self.tagDataSource.tags.index(of: tag) {
                    let indexPath = IndexPath(row: index, section: 0)
                    self.selectedIndexPaths.append(indexPath)
                }
            }
        case let .failure(error):
            print("Error fetching tags: \(error).")
        }

        self.tableView.reloadSections(IndexSet(integer: 0),
                                      with: .automatic)
    }
}
```

Now add the appropriate **UITableViewDelegate** methods to handle selecting and displaying the checkmarks.

```swift
override func tableView(_ tableView: UITableView,
                        didSelectRowAt indexPath: IndexPath) {

    let tag = tagDataSource.tags[indexPath.row]

    if let index = selectedIndexPaths.index(of: indexPath) {
        selectedIndexPaths.remove(at: index)
        photo.removeFromTags(tag)
    } else {
        selectedIndexPaths.append(indexPath)
        photo.addToTags(tag)
    }

    do {
        try store.persistentContainer.viewContext.save()
    } catch {
        print("Core Data save failed: \(error).")
    }

    tableView.reloadRows(at: [indexPath], with: .automatic)
}

override func tableView(_ tableView: UITableView,
                        willDisplay cell: UITableViewCell,
                        forRowAt indexPath: IndexPath) {

    if selectedIndexPaths.index(of: indexPath) != nil {
        cell.accessoryType = .checkmark
    } else {
        cell.accessoryType = .none
    }
}
```

Let's set up **TagsViewController** to be presented modally when the user taps the Tags bar button item on the **PhotoInfoViewController**.

Open Main.storyboard and drag a Navigation Controller onto the canvas. This should give you a **UINavigationController** with a root view controller that is a **UITableViewController**. If the root view controller is not a **UITableViewController**, delete the root view controller, drag a Table View Controller onto the canvas, and make it the root view controller of the Navigation Controller.

Control-drag from the Tags item on Photo Info View Controller to the new Navigation Controller and select the Present Modally segue type (Figure 23.7). Open the attributes inspector for the segue and give it an Identifier named showTags.

Figure 23.7 Adding the tags view controller

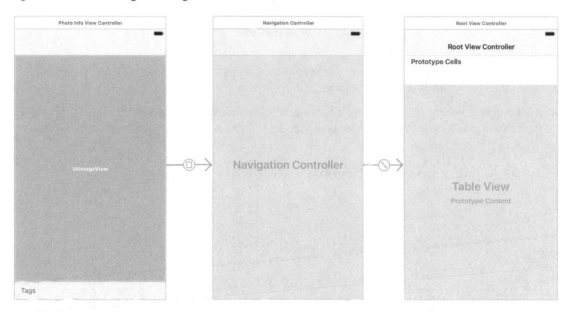

Select the Root View Controller that you just added to the canvas and open its identity inspector. Change its Class to TagsViewController. This new view controller does not have a navigation item associated with it, so find Navigation Item in the object library and drag it onto the view controller. Double-click the new navigation item's Title label and change it to Tags.

Next, the **UITableViewCell** on the Tags View Controller interface needs to match what the **TagDataSource** expects. It needs to use the correct style and have the correct reuse identifier.

Select the UITableViewCell. (It might be easier to select in the document outline.) Open its attributes inspector. Change the Style to Basic and set the Identifier to UITableViewCell (Figure 23.8).

Figure 23.8 Configuring the UITableViewCell

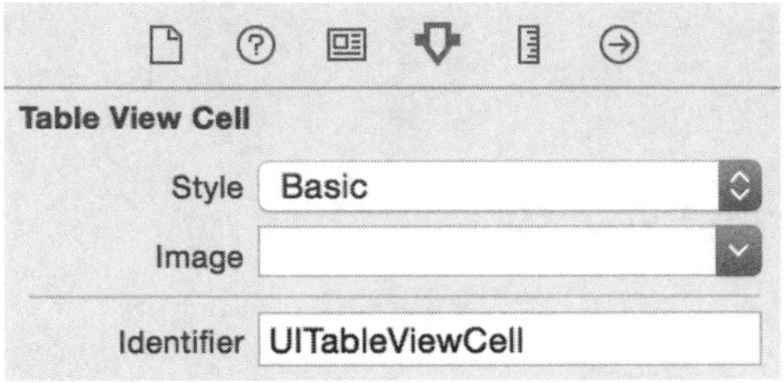

Now, the Tags View Controller needs two bar button items on its navigation bar: a Done button that dismisses the view controller and a + button that allows the user to add a new tag.

Drag a bar button item to the left and right bar button item slots for the Tags View Controller. Set the left item to use the Done style and system item. Set the right item to use the Bordered style and Add system item (Figure 23.9).

Figure 23.9 Bar button item attributes

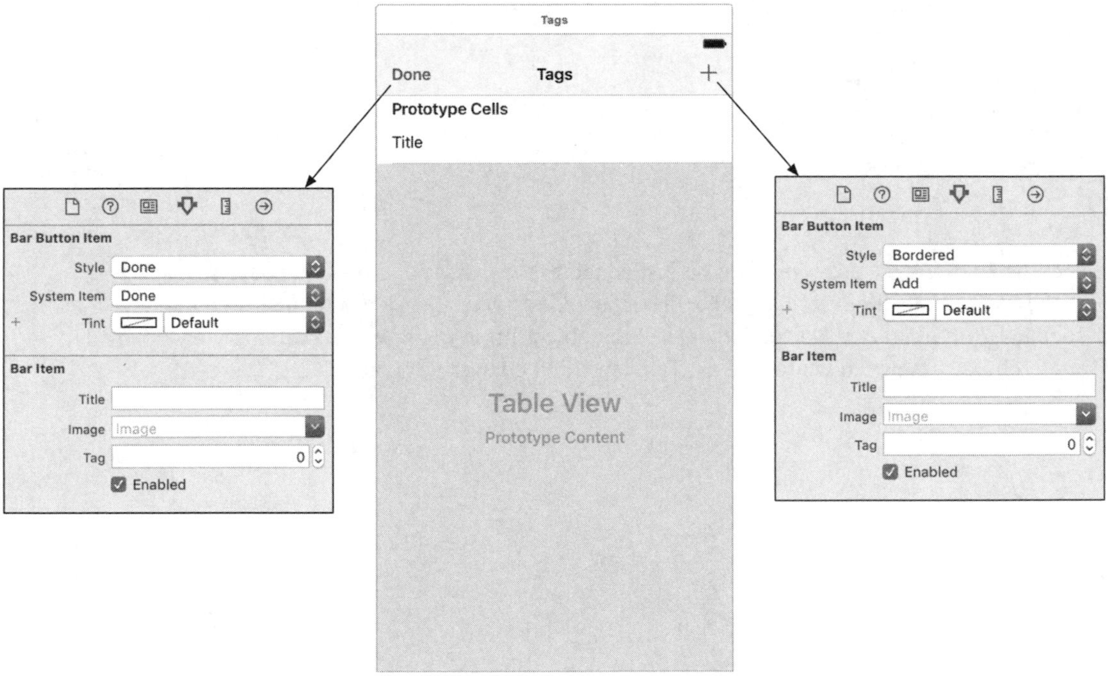

Create and connect an action for each of these items to the **TagsViewController**. The Done item should be connected to a method named **done(_:)**, and the + item should be connected to a method named **addNewTag(:)**. The two methods in TagsViewController.swift will be:

```
@IBAction func done(_ sender: UIBarButtonItem) {

}

@IBAction func addNewTag(_ sender: UIBarButtonItem) {

}
```

The implementation of **done(_:)** is simple: The view controller just needs to be dismissed. Implement this functionality in **done(_:)**.

```
@IBAction func done(_ sender: UIBarButtonItem) {
    presentingViewController?.dismiss(animated: true,
                                      completion: nil)
}
```

When the user taps the + item, an alert will be presented that will allow the user to type in the name for a new tag.

Figure 23.10 Adding a new tag

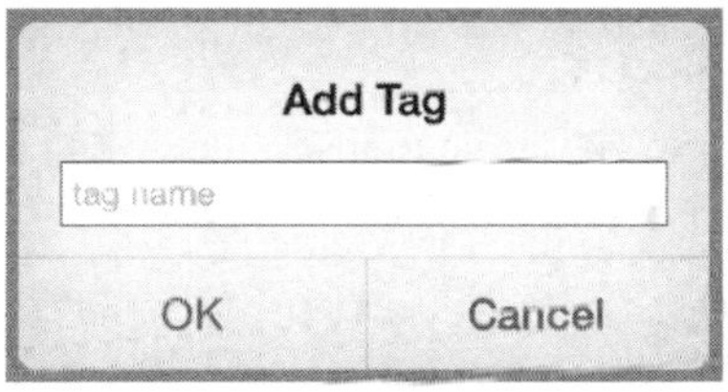

Set up and present an instance of **UIAlertController** in **addNewTag(_:)**.

```
@IBAction func addNewTag(_ sender: UIBarButtonItem) {
    let alertController = UIAlertController(title: "Add Tag",
                                           message: nil,
                                           preferredStyle: .alert)

    alertController.addTextField {
        (textField) -> Void in
        textField.placeholder = "tag name"
        textField.autocapitalizationType = .words
    }

    let okAction = UIAlertAction(title: "OK", style: .default) {
        (action) -> Void in

    }
    alertController.addAction(okAction)

    let cancelAction = UIAlertAction(title: "Cancel",
                                     style: .cancel,
                                     handler: nil)
    alertController.addAction(cancelAction)

    present(alertController,
            animated: true,
            completion: nil)
}
```

Update the completion handler for the okAction to insert a new **Tag** into the context. Then save the context, update the list of tags, and reload the table view section.

```
let okAction = UIAlertAction(title: "OK", style: .default) {
    (action) -> Void in

    if let tagName = alertController.textFields?.first?.text {
        let context = self.store.persistentContainer.viewContext
        let newTag = NSEntityDescription.insertNewObject(forEntityName: "Tag",
                                                         into: context)
        newTag.setValue(tagName, forKey: "name")

        do {
            try self.store.persistentContainer.viewContext.save()
        } catch let error {
            print("Core Data save failed: \(error)")
        }
        self.updateTags()
    }
}
alertController.addAction(okAction)
```

Finally, when the Tags bar button item on **PhotoInfoViewController** is tapped, the
PhotoInfoViewController needs to pass along its store and photo to the **TagsViewController**.

Open PhotoInfoViewController.swift and implement **prepare(for:)**.

```
override func prepare(for segue: UIStoryboardSegue, sender: Any?) {
    switch segue.identifier {
    case "showTags"?:
        let navController = segue.destination as! UINavigationController
        let tagController = navController.topViewController as! TagsViewController

        tagController.store = store
        tagController.photo = photo
    default:
        preconditionFailure("Unexpected segue identifier.")
    }
}
```

Build and run the application. Navigate to a photo and tap the Tags item on the toolbar at the bottom.
The **TagsViewController** will be presented modally. Tap the + item, enter a new tag, and select the
new tag to associate it with the photo.

Background Tasks

The `viewContext` of **NSPersistentContainer** is associated with the main queue. Because of this, any operations that take a long time will block the main queue, which can lead to an unresponsive application. To address this, it is often a good idea to do expensive operations on a background task. The insertion of photos from the web service is a good candidate for a background task.

You are going to update **processPhotosRequest(data:error:)** to use a background task. Background tasks are an asynchronous operation, so you will need to update the method signature to use a completion handler.

Open `PhotoStore.swift` and update **processPhotosRequest(data:error:)** to take in a completion handler. You will have some errors in the code due to the signature change; you will fix these shortly.

```
private func processPhotosRequest(data: Data?, error: Error?) -> PhotosResult {
private func processPhotosRequest(data: Data?,
                                  error: Error?,
                                  completion: @escaping (PhotosResult) -> Void) {
    guard let jsonData = data else {
        return .failure(error!)
    }

    return FlickrAPI.photos(fromJSON: jsonData,
                            into: persistentContainer.viewContext)
}
```

If there is no data, you will need to call the completion handler, passing in the failure error instead of directly returning. Update the `guard` statement to pass along the failure.

```
private func processPhotosRequest(data: Data?,
                                  error: Error?,
                                  completion: @escaping (PhotosResult) -> Void) {
    guard let jsonData = data else {
        return .failure(error!)
        completion(.failure(error!))
        return
    }

    return FlickrAPI.photos(fromJSON: jsonData,
                            into: persistentContainer.viewContext)
}
```

Notice the use of `return` within the `guard` statement. Recall that with a `guard` statement, you must exit scope. The scope of the `guard` statement is the function itself, so you must exit the scope of the function somehow. This is a fantastic benefit to using a `guard` statement. The compiler will enforce this requirement, so you can be certain that no code below the `guard` statement will be executed.

Now you can add in the code for the background task. **NSPersistentContainer** has a method to perform a background task. This method takes in a closure to call and this closure vends a new **NSManagedObjectContext** to use.

Update **processPhotosRequest(data:error:completion:)** to kick off a new background task.

```
private func processPhotosRequest(data: Data?,
                                  error: Error?,
                                  completion: @escaping (PhotosResult) -> Void) {
    guard let jsonData = data else {
        completion(.failure(error!))
        return
    }

    return FlickrAPI.photos(fromJSON: jsonData,
                       into: persistentContainer.viewContext)

    persistentContainer.performBackgroundTask {
        (context) in

    }
}
```

Within the background task, you will do essentially the same thing you did before. The **FlickrAPI** struct will ingest the JSON data and convert it to **Photo** instances. Then you will save the context so that the insertions persist.

Update the background task in **processPhotosRequest(data:error:completion:)** to do this.

```
persistentContainer.performBackgroundTask {
    (context) in

    let result = FlickrAPI.photos(fromJSON: jsonData, into: context)

    do {
        try context.save()
    } catch {
        print("Error saving to Core Data: \(error).")
        completion(.failure(error))
        return
    }
}
```

Here is where things change a bit. An **NSManagedObject** should only be accessed from the queue that it is associated with. After the expensive operation of inserting the **Photo** instances and saving the context, you will want to fetch the same photos, but only those that are associated with the viewContext (i.e., the photos associated with the main queue).

Each **NSManagedObject** has an objectID that is the same across different contexts. You will use this objectID to fetch the corresponding **Photo** instances associated with the viewContext.

Update **processPhotosRequest(data:error:completion:)** to get the **Photo** instances associated with the viewContext and pass them back to the caller via the completion handler.

```
persistentContainer.performBackgroundTask {
    (context) in

    let result = FlickrAPI.photos(fromJSON: jsonData, into: context)

    do {
        try context.save()
    } catch {
        print("Error saving to Core Data: \(error).")
        completion(.failure(error))
        return
    }

    switch result {
    case let .success(photos):
        let photoIDs = photos.map { return $0.objectID }
        let viewContext = self.persistentContainer.viewContext
        let viewContextPhotos =
            photoIDs.map { return viewContext.object(with: $0) } as! [Photo]
        completion(.success(viewContextPhotos))
    case .failure:
        completion(result)
    }
}
```

Here you are using the **map** method on **Array** to transform one array into another array. This code:

```
let photoIDs = photos.map { return $0.objectID }
```

has the same result as this code:

```
var photoIDs = [String]()
for photo in photos {
    photoIDs.append(photo.objectID)
}
```

The $0 in the closure is a shorthand way of accessing the arguments of the closure. If there are two parameters, for example, their arguments can be accessed by $0 and $1. So this code:

```
let photosIDs = photos.map { return $0.objectID }
```

also has the same result as this code:

```
let photoIDs = photos.map {
    (photo: Photo) in
    return photo.objectID
}
```

Let's take a look at the code being using in the background task again.

```
let photoIDs = photos.map { return $0.objectID }
let viewContext - self.persistentContainer.viewContext
let viewContextPhotos =
    photoIDs.map { return viewContext.object(with: $0) } as! [Photo]
```

The first thing that you are doing is getting an array of all of the objectIDs associated with the **Photo** instances. This will be an array of **String** instances. Within the closure, $0 is of type **Photo**.

Then you create a local variable to reference the viewContext. Finally, you **map** over the photoIDs. Within the closure, $0 is of type **String**. You use this string to ask the viewContext for the object associated with a specific object identifier. The method **object(with:)** returns an **NSManagedObject**, so the result of the entire **map** operation will be an array of **NSManagedObject** instances. You know that the instances being returned will be of type **Photo**, so you downcast the array of **NSManagedObject** instances into an array of **Photo** instances.

The **map** method is a useful abstraction for the common operation of converting one array into another array.

The final change you need to make is to update **fetchInterestingPhotos(completion:)** to use the updated **processPhotosRequest(data:error:completion:)** method.

```
func fetchInterestingPhotos(completion: @escaping (PhotosResult) -> Void) {

    let url = FlickrAPI.interestingPhotosURL
    let request = URLRequest(url: url)
    let task = session.dataTask(with: request) {
        (data, response, error) -> Void in

        var result = self.processPhotosRequest(data: data, error: error)

        if case .success = result {
            do {
                try self.persistentContainer.viewContext.save()
            } catch let error {
                result = .failure(error)
            }
        }

        OperationQueue.main.addOperation {
            completion(result)
        }

        self.processPhotosRequest(data: data, error: error) {
            (result) in

            OperationQueue.main.addOperation {
                completion(result)
            }
        }
    }
    task.resume()
}
```

Build and run the application. Although the behavior has not changed, the application is no longer in danger of becoming unresponsive while new photos are being added. As the scale of your applications increases, handling Core Data entities somewhere other than the main queue as you have done here can result in huge performance wins.

Congratulations! Over the past four chapters, you have worked on a rather complex app. Photorama is able to make multiple web service calls, display photos in a grid, cache image data to the filesystem, and persist photo data using Core Data. To accomplish this, you used knowledge that you have gained throughout this book, and you applied that knowledge to create an awesome app that is also robust and maintainable. It was hard work, and you should be proud of yourself.

Silver Challenge: Favorites

Allow the user to favorite photos. Be creative in how you present the favorite photos to the user. Two possibilities include viewing them using a **UITabBarController** or adding a **UISegmentedControl** to the **PhotosViewController** that switches between all photos and favorite photos. (Hint: You will need to add a new attribute to the **Photo** entity.)

24

Accessibility

iOS is the most accessible mobile platform in the world. Whether a user needs support for vision, hearing, motor skills, or learning challenges, iOS provides ways to help. Most accessibility features are built into the system, so you, the developer, do not need to do anything. Some allow the developer to provide an even richer experience for the user, often with very little work on the developer's part. Let's take a look at some of the accessibility options that iOS provides.

VoiceOver

VoiceOver is an accessibility feature that helps users with visual impairments navigate your application's interface. Apple provides hooks into the system that allow you to describe aspects of your interface to the user. Most UIKit views and controls automatically provide useful information to the user, but it is often beneficial to provide additional information that cannot be inferred. And you will always need to provide the information yourself for custom views or controls you create.

These hints to the user are largely provided through the `UIAccessibility` protocol. Let's take a look at this protocol and the information that it provides.

The `UIAccessibility` protocol is an informal protocol that is implemented on all of the standard UIKit views and controls. An *informal protocol* is a looser "contract" than the formal protocols that you have been introduced to before. A formal protocol is declared using the `protocol` keyword and declares a list of methods and properties that must be implemented by something that conforms to that protocol. An informal protocol is implemented as an extension on `NSObject`; therefore, all subclasses of `NSObject` implicitly conform to the protocol.

You might be wondering why `UIAccessibility` is not a regular, formal protocol like the others you have seen throughout this book. Informal protocols are a legacy of the days when Objective-C did not have optional methods in formal protocols. Informal protocols were a workaround to solve this issue. Essentially, they required every `NSObject` to declare a method with no corresponding implementation. Then, subclasses could implement the methods that they were interested in. At runtime, an object would be asked if it had an implementation for those methods.

Some of the useful properties provided by the **UIAccessibility** protocol are:

accessibilityLabel	A short description of an element. For views with text, this is often the text that the view is displaying.
accessibilityHint	A short description of the result of interacting with the associated element. For example, the accessibility hint for a button that stops video recording might be "Stop recording."
accessibilityFrame	The frame of the accessibility element. For **UIView** objects, this is equal to the frame of the view.
accessibilityTraits	Descriptions of the characteristics of the element. There are a lot of traits, and multiple traits can be used to describe the element. To see a list of all of the possible traits, look at the documentation for **UIAccessibilityTraits**.
accessibilityValue	A description of the value of an element, independent of its label description. For example, a **UITextField** will have an accessibility value that is the contents of the text field, and a **UISlider** will have an accessibility value that is the percentage that the slider has been set to.

Let's take a look at how to implement accessibility via the Photorama application.

Reopen Photorama.xcodeproj. You are going to implement VoiceOver accessibility features. Currently, Photorama is not very accessible at all. Let's start by considering how the application would look to someone with visual impairments.

Testing VoiceOver

The best way to test VoiceOver is with an actual device, so we strongly recommend using a device if you have one available.

If you do not have a device available, you can use the simulator. Begin by clicking on the Xcode menu and choosing Open Developer Tool → Accessibility Inspector. Build and run the application; once the simulator is running the app, switch to the Accessibility Inspector and select the simulator from the target dropdown list (Figure 24.1).

Figure 24.1 Changing targets in the Accessibility Inspector

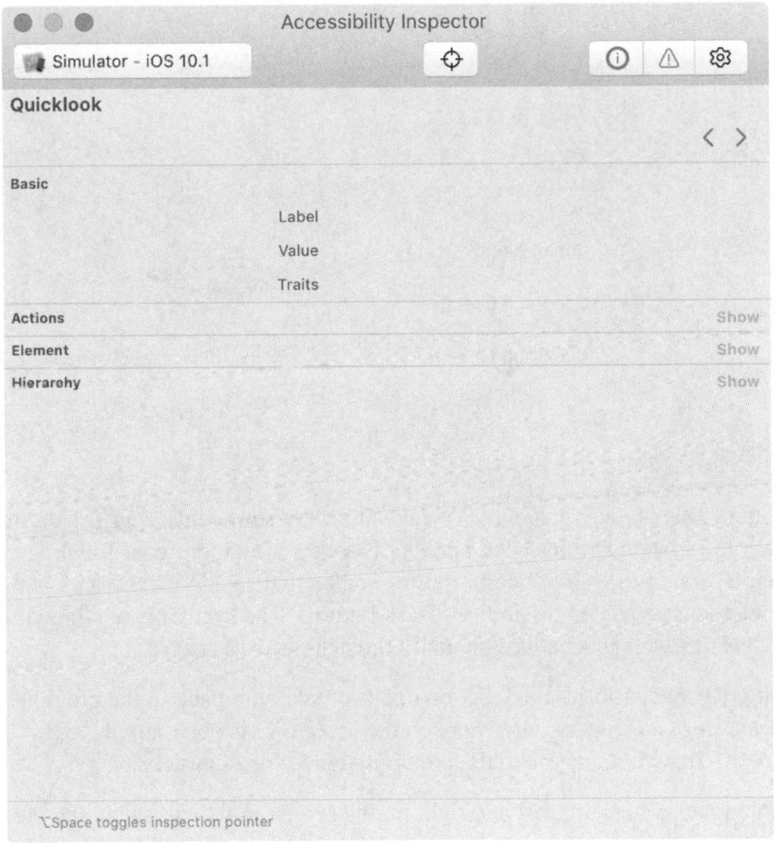

Once the target has been set to the simulator, click the Start inspection follows point button on the Accessibility Inspector's toolbar. As you mouse over and navigate in the simulator, the Accessibility Inspector will provide information about whatever element has focus on the simulator's screen. VoiceOver is not included on the simulator, but the information shown in the Accessibility Inspector is similar.

If you have a device, open Settings, choose General → Accessibility → VoiceOver, and finally turn on VoiceOver (Figure 24.2).

Figure 24.2 Enabling VoiceOver

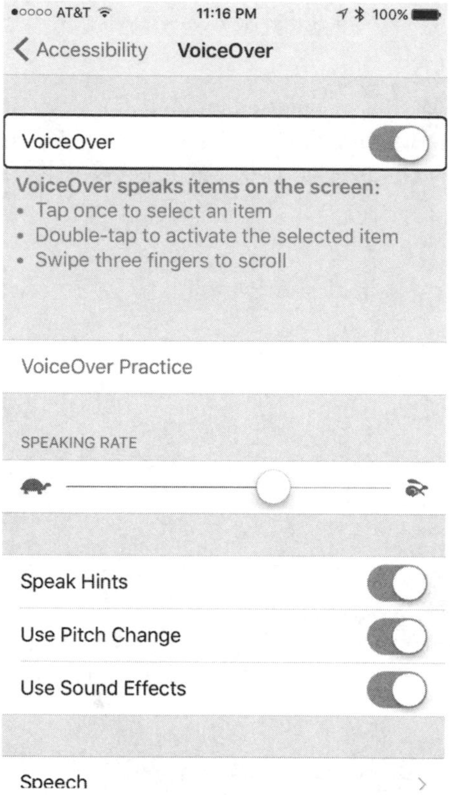

There are a couple of ways to navigate with VoiceOver on. To start, slide your finger around the screen. Notice that the system speaks a description of whatever element your finger is currently over. Now tap the Back button in the top left corner of the screen that says Accessibility. The system will tell you that this element is the "Accessibility - Back button." The system is reading you both the accessibilityLabel as well as what is essentially the accessibilityTraits.

Notice that tapping the Accessibility Back button does not take you back to the previous screen. To activate the selected item, double-tap anywhere on the screen. This corresponds to a single-tap with VoiceOver disabled. This will take you to the previous screen for Accessibility.

Another way to navigate is to swipe left and right on the screen. This will select the previous and next accessible elements on the screen, respectively. The VoiceOver row should be selected. Play around with swiping left and right to move the focus around the screen.

Swipe with three fingers to scroll. Note that to scroll, the scroll view or one of its subviews must be the currently focused element. Play around with single- and double-taps to select and activate items as well as using three fingers to scroll. This is how you will navigate with VoiceOver enabled.

One final useful gesture to know is how to enable Screen Curtain. Using three fingers, triple-tap anywhere on the screen. The entire screen will go black, allowing you to truly test and experience how your app will feel to someone with a visual impairment. Three-finger triple-tap anywhere again to turn Screen Curtain off.

Accessibility in Photorama

With VoiceOver still enabled, build and run Photorama on your device to test its accessibility. Once the application is running, drag your finger around the screen. Notice that the system is playing a dulled beeping sound as you drag over the photos. This is the system's way of informing you that it is not able to find an accessibility element under your finger.

Currently, the **PhotoCollectionViewCell**s are not accessibility elements. This is easy to fix.

Open PhotoCollectionViewCell.swift and override the isAccessibilityElement property to let the system know that each cell is accessible.

```
override var isAccessibilityElement: Bool {
    get {
        return true
    }
    set {
        super.isAccessibilityElement = newValue
    }
}
```

Now build and run the application. As you drag your finger across the photos, you will hear a more affirming beep and see each cell outlined with the focus rectangle (Figure 24.3). No description is spoken, but you are making progress.

Figure 24.3 Accessible cells

Go back to `PhotoCollectionViewCell.swift`. You are going to add an accessibility label for VoiceOver to read when an item is selected. Currently, a cell knows nothing about the **Photo** that it is displaying, so add a new property to hold on to this information.

```
class PhotoCollectionViewCell: UICollectionViewCell {

    @IBOutlet var imageView: UIImageView!
    @IBOutlet var spinner: UIActivityIndicatorView!

    var photoDescription: String?
```

In the same file, override the `accessibilityLabel` to return this string.

```
override var accessibilityLabel: String? {
    get {
        return photoDescription
    }
    set {
        // Ignore attempts to set
    }
}
```

Open `PhotoDataSource.swift` and update **collectionView(_:cellForItemAt:)** to set the `photoDescription` on the cell.

```
func collectionView(_ collectionView: UICollectionView,
                    cellForItemAt indexPath: IndexPath) -> UICollectionViewCell {

    let identifier = "PhotoCollectionViewCell"
    let cell =
        collectionView.dequeueReusableCell(withReuseIdentifier: identifier,
                                           for: indexPath) as! PhotoCollectionViewCell

    let photo = photos[indexPath.row]
    cell.photoDescription = photo.title

    return cell
}
```

Build and run the application. Drag your finger over the screen and you will hear the titles for each photo.

Currently there is no indication to users that they can double-tap to drill down to a specific photo. This is because the cells do not have any accessibility traits set.

In `PhotoCollectionViewCell.swift`, override the `accessibilityTraits` property to let the system know that a cell holds an image.

```
override var accessibilityTraits: UIAccessibilityTraits {
    get {
        return super.accessibilityTraits | UIAccessibilityTraitImage
    }
    set {
        // Ignore attempts to set
    }
}
```

You are combining any traits inherited from the superclass with the UIAccessibilityTraitImage. This is done using the | (or) operator to combine the two. Like many other things related to accessibility, this is a legacy of the past. In current, idiomatic Swift, this would be done using an optionSet by passing the options as an array. But **UIAccessibility** does not support this syntax, so instead you are using | to group the options, which is how this is done in C and Objective-C.

Build and run the application. Notice that the new trait you added is spoken when you select a cell.

The remaining parts of the application are mostly accessible because they use standard views and controls. The only thing you need to update is the image view when drilling down to a specific **Photo**. You can customize many views' accessibility information from within storyboards, and you will be able to do that for the image view.

Open Main.storyboard and navigate to the scene associated with the **PhotoInfoViewController**. Select the image view and open its identity inspector. Scroll to the bottom to the section labeled Accessibility. Check the box at the top of this section to enable accessibility for this image view and uncheck the box next to User Interaction Enabled (Figure 24.4).

Figure 24.4 Updating the accessibility options

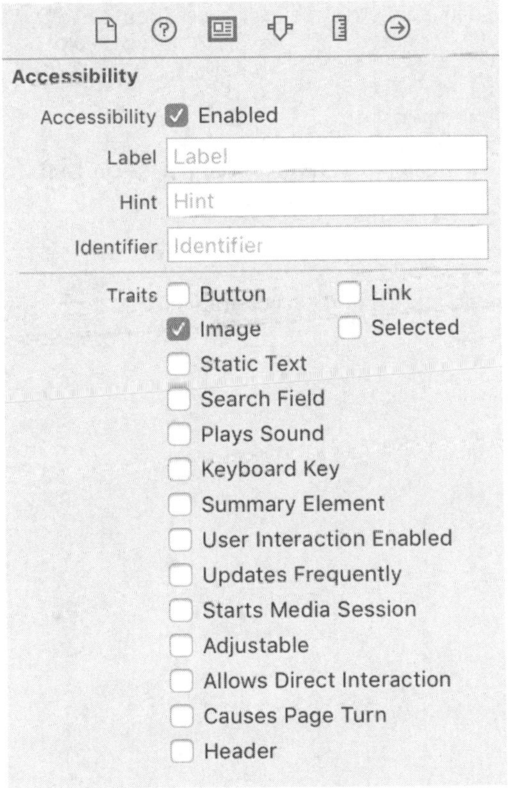

Open `PhotoInfoViewController.swift` and update **viewDidLoad()** to give the image view a more meaningful accessibility label.

```
override func viewDidLoad() {
    super.viewDidLoad()

    imageView.accessibilityLabel = photo.title
```

Build and run the application and navigate to a specific photo. You will notice that with this small addition, this entire screen is accessible. Finally, let's turn our attention to the **TagsViewController**.

While still running the application, drill down to the **TagsViewController**. Add a tag to the table view if one is not already present. Select a row in the table and notice that VoiceOver reads the name of this tag; however, there is no indication to users that they can toggle the checkmark for each row, nor is the presence or absence of that checkmark communicated.

Open `TagDataSource.swift` and update the cell's accessibility hint in **tableView(_:cellForRowAt:)**.

```
func tableView(_ tableView: UITableView,
               cellForRowAt indexPath: IndexPath) -> UITableViewCell {

    let cell = tableView.dequeueReusableCell(withIdentifier: "UITableViewCell",
                                             for: indexPath)

    let tag = tags[indexPath.row]
    cell.textLabel?.text = tag.name

    cell.accessibilityHint = "Double tap to toggle selected"

    return cell
}
```

Build and run the application and marvel at its accessibility.

25
Afterword

Welcome to the end of the book! You should be very proud of all your work and all that you have learned. Now there is good news and bad news:

- *The good news:* The stuff that leaves programmers befuddled when they come to the iOS platform is behind you now. You are an iOS developer.

- *The bad news:* You are probably not a very good iOS developer.

What to Do Next

It is now time to make some mistakes, read some really tedious documentation, and be humbled by the heartless experts who will ridicule your questions. Here is what we recommend:

Write apps now. If you do not immediately use what you have learned, it will fade. Exercise and extend your knowledge. Now.

Go deep. This book has consistently favored breadth over depth; any chapter could have been expanded into an entire book. Find a topic that you find interesting and really wallow in it – do some experiments, read Apple's docs on the topic, and read postings on blogs and StackOverflow.

Connect. There are iOS Developer Meetups in most cities, and the talks are surprisingly good. There are CocoaHeads chapters around the world. There are discussion groups online. If you are doing a project, find people to help you: designers, testers (AKA guinea pigs), and other developers.

Make mistakes and fix them. You will learn a lot on the days when you say, "This application has become a ball of crap! I'm going to throw it away and write it again with an architecture that makes sense." Polite programmers call this *refactoring*.

Give back. Share the knowledge. Answer a dumb question with grace. Give away some code.

Shameless Plugs

You can find us on Twitter, where we keep you informed about programming and entertained about life: @cbkeur and @aaronhillegass.

Keep an eye out for other guides from Big Nerd Ranch. We also offer week-long courses for developers. And if you just need some code written, we do contract programming. For more information, visit our website at www.bignerdranch.com.

You, dear reader, make our lives of writing, coding, and teaching possible. So thank you for buying our book.

At Big Nerd Ranch, we create elegant, authentically useful solutions through best-in-class development and training.

CLIENT SOLUTIONS

Big Nerd Ranch designs, develops and deploys applications for clients of all sizes—from small start-ups to large corporations. Our in-house engineering and design teams possess expertise in iOS, Android and full-stack web application development.

TEAM TRAINING

For companies with capable engineering teams, Big Nerd Ranch can provide on-site corporate training in iOS, Android, Front-End Web, Back-End Web, macOS and Design.

Of the top 25 apps in the U.S., 19 are built by companies that brought in Big Nerd Ranch to train their developers.

CODING BOOTCAMPS

Big Nerd Ranch offers intensive app development and design retreats for individuals. Lodging, food and course materials are included, and we'll even pick you up at the airport!

These courses are not for the faint of heart. You will learn new skills in iOS, Android, Front-End Web, Back-End Web, macOS or Design in days—not weeks.

www.bignerdranch.com

Index

Symbols

#column expression, 164
#file expression, 164
#function expression, 164, 301
#line expression, 164
$0, $1... (shorthand argument names), 434
.xcassets (Asset Catalog), 26
.xcdatamodeld (data model file), 404
// MARK:, 281
@discardableResult, 184
@escaping annotation, 369
@IBAction, 19
@IBInspectable, 328
@IBOutlet, 17, 233-235
@NSManaged keyword, 407

A

access control, 354
accessibility
    accessibility elements, 441
    adding accessibility hints, 444
    adding accessibility labels, 442
    setting accessibility information in
    storyboards, 443
    setting accessibility traits, 442
    UIAccessibility protocol, 437
    VoiceOver, 437, 439
Accessibility Inspector, 439
accessory view (**UITableViewCell**), 187
action methods
    about, 19
    implementing, 23
    UIControl class and, 332
active state, 293
addSubview(_:) method, 50
alerts, displaying, 205-208
alignment rectangle, 60, 61
anchors, 109
animate(withDuration:animations:) method,
144-146
animations
    basic, 144-146
    for constraints, 149-154
    marking completion of, 149
    spring, 156
    timing functions, 154, 155
anti-aliasing, 102
append(_:) method, 37
application bundle
    about, 304, 305
    internationalization and, 125, 140
application sandbox, 287, 288, 304
application states, 293-295, 301
applicationDidBecomeActive(_:) method, 295,
301
applicationDidEnterBackground(_:) method,
290, 295
applications
    (see also application bundle, debugging,
    projects)
    building, 13, 135
    cleaning, 135
    data storage, 287, 288
    directories in, 287, 288
    icons for, 25-27
    launch images for, 28
    multiple threads in, 374
    running on simulator, 13
applicationWillEnterForeground(_:) method,
295, 301
applicationWillResignActive(_:) method,
295, 301
archiveRootObject(_:toFile:) method, 289
archiving
    about, 284
    Core Data vs, 403
    implementing, 284-286
    with **NSKeyedArchiver**, 289-292
    unarchiving, 292
arrays
    about, 34, 35
    count property, 37
    literal, 35
    subscripting, 35
Asset Catalog (Xcode), 26
assistant editor, 231
attributes (Core Data), 404
Auto Layout
    (see also constraints (Auto Layout), views)
    about, 14-16
    alignment rectangle, 60, 61
    autoresizing masks and, 117, 118

W

X